D0941169

SINGERS OF AUSTRALIA

Dame Nellie Melba

SINGERS OF AUSTRALIA
from Melba to Sutherland

BARBARA MACKENZIE
and
FINDLAY MACKENZIE

LANSDOWNE PRESS

Frontispiece:
portrait of Melba in 1895 by
Adolfo Muller-Ury. Reproduced by permission
from the original in the collection
of Miss Jessica Dragonette. Photo: Peter Juley, New York.

First published 1967

This book was planned in Australia by
Lansdowne Press Pty. Ltd., 380 Bourke Street
Melbourne, C.1, and designed by Genevieve Melrose
The type was set by Dover's Pty. Ltd., Drewery Lane
Melbourne, and the book was printed and
bound by Lee Fung Printing Company
78 Marble Road, North Point
Hong Kong

Text set in Garamond 12 on 13

To our mothers from whom we learned to love music
and to value achievements of the human spirit.

Contents

Notes on the text will be found at the end of each section.

ERRATA*

Singers of Australia by Barbara & Findlay MacKenzie

p. 7, par. 3: reference to Armes Beaumont is incorrect. See 3rd paragraph p. 267. He was born in Norwich, England on December 15, 1940, and arrived in Australia at the age of 8.

p. 22, par. 4: Miss Mansfield's first name is *Veronica.*

p. 37, line 1: David Mitchell died on March 25, *1916.*

p. 42, par. 2: the names of the gentlemen referred to were Brinsmead and Randegger.

p. 46, par. 4: Edouard de Reszke was a basso.

p. 57, par. 2: delete *Lucia* and *Ophelie* from the list of roles Melba sang in Australia in 1911.

p. 62, last line: the recording referred to was made by M.M.V., not Mapleson.

p. 101, par. 2: Alda died in Venice in 1952.

p. 105, par. 3: Selma *Kurz* is the singer referred to.

p. 114, footnote 2 under Amy Castles: Pauline Bindley sang the role of *Norina* in Don Pasquale, not *Norma.*

p. 135, par. 2: *Oakbank,* not Outbank, is the name of the town in South Australia.

p. 190, line 1: the name of the role is Don Alvaro.

p. 209, par. 4: review by Alexander Fried.

p. 232, par. 4: Amelia is, of course, the "Leading", not the title role, in the Masked Ball.

p. 267, par. 2: Lucy Chambers made her Australian debut during the 1870 season.

p. 280, par. 2: the date of Nellie Stewart's birth is November 20, 1858.

p. 287, appendix 4: Elsasser is the name of the musican, in whose honour the concert was given.

* No attempt has been made to correct occasional mistakes in the spelling of the names of roles or of operas.

ERRATA*

Foreword

By Harold Rosenthal, editor of Opera, *London*

ONE EVENING RECENTLY at Sadler's Wells, a large audience was present for the revival of *Fidelio*. Sitting behind me was Ronald Dowd, who is generally heard on the stage as Florestan. He was at this performance to hear his fellow-countryman, Gregory Dempsey, who was singing the part of Jacquino. Dowd, of course, is one of the finest dramatic tenors of the day and should long ago have been singing regularly at Covent Garden — but that's another story.

The evening's Leonore was Elizabeth Fretwell, a soprano whose glorious voice, warm human stage presence and personality have combined, over the last decade, to give London memorable performances of Leonore, Ariadne, Minnie in *The Girl of the Golden West* and many other parts. (A few weeks later she sang one of the Norns in *Gotterdammerung* at the Royal Opera House, Covent Garden.) The evening's Jacquino appeared not long after in San Francisco in the United States premiere of Janacek's *The Makropulos Case* opposite another Australian artist, Marie Collier, who repeated a Sadler's Wells success as Emily Marty. Miss Collier, an ornament of Covent Garden over the last ten years (Tosca, Gutrune, Elisabeth de Valois, Musetta, Liu, Santuzza, Marie in *Wozzeck*, Lisa in *The Queen of Spades*, Cressida, Katerina Ismailova, Giorgetta, Chrysothemis) has also appeared at Sadler's Wells in several modern works, in Buenos Aires, San Francisco and at the new Metropolitan in New York; as well as in Monaco, Rome and Vienna.

The same *Fidelio* performance introduced, as Marcellina, a young soprano from Tasmania, Cynthia Johnston, well-known during the last few years as a member of the Elizabethan Opera Company.

A score of three out of seven principal roles in *Fidelio* at Sadler's Wells is not so bad; and so I began looking at the casts for the first few weeks of the London season at Sadler's Wells to see how many more singers of Australian birth were included there. The result was most impressive — Sylvia Fisher and John Cameron were announced for the important revival of

Britten's *Gloriana,* Ronald Dowd and Robert Bickerstaff for the revival of *Samson and Delilah,* Jenifer Eddy and Jon Andrew for *Die Fledermaus,* John Fryatt in several operas; and the company also includes Maurine London, Neil Easton and Donald Smith.

The Covent Garden picture was not quite the same — but even in Wagner's *Ring* we had John Shaw as Gunther, John Lanigan as Mime, and Margreta Elkins and Maureen Guy among the Valkyries. Later in the season, Shaw was again to sing the title-role of *Simon Boccanegra* (sharing the part with the one and only Tito Gobbi); Marie Collier returned to sing Tosca with Gobbi as Scarpia; Miss Minton was heard in the important role of Ascanio in a new production of Berlioz's rarely performed *Benvenuto Cellini;* Shaw sang Ford in *Falstaff* opposite Fischer-Dieskau; and of course Joan Sutherland returned to repeat her *La Fille du Regiment.*

All this leads me to the conclusion that not only London, but most of the leading opera houses of the world would, if not actually forced to close their doors, be very hard put to perform certain operas if it were not for the existence of Australian singers. And not only singers, for there are also fine conductors like Charles Mackerras, and distinguished composers, among them Malcolm Williamson, whose new opera, *The Violins of Saint-Jacques* had its world premiere at Sadler's Wells in November, 1966.

In this book readers will be able to learn about the many fine singers from Australia who have enriched the operatic world from the time of Melba. In her day, she stood virtually alone; in the 1960's the number of Australian singers is legion — large enough to establish more than one permanent company in Australia itself. Should this happen, Europe and America would be the poorer for the time being, but the world of opera would be the richer, for eventually there would be an even larger talent for the opera houses of the world to draw upon. The future for Australian artists in opera is truly an exciting one.

H.D.R.
London, 1966

Preface

THIS BOOK GREW out of a long-standing interest of my husband, Findlay MacKenzie, who is Australian-born, in the fact that for over seventy-five years Australia has been represented in the great opera houses and concert halls of the world by outstanding singers whose country of origin has often been lost sight of. Critics who wrote enthusiastic reviews of a singer's performance sometimes knew little of his professional reputation or background. This was the case when Elsa Stralia appeared at Carnegie Hall on March 24, 1922, with the New York Symphony Society conducted by Walter Damrosch. After praising her singing a well-known critic of the day said he did not know who she was or where she came from.

Other critics reviewing performances of Australian singers spoke of the characteristic brightness of their voices which brought to mind the sunshine of their native land.

In 1924, for instance, Henry Tate of Melbourne wrote of Melba: "Her sunlit tones are debonair with echoes of the wide and gracious skies of Australia", adding:

> She infused the virility and sunlight of Australia into the dwindling tissues of the sentimental . . . 'il bel canto' art of perfect vocalization. The art of other Australians may be greater in type, but as an individual the prima donna towers . . . In each case the sacred portals have opened to strongly distinctive work. The drive of a conscious or unconscious Australianism has been potent in every instance.[1]

My husband heard Melba and other famous artists who came to Sydney during his student days, and when he went on to Columbia University he began to attend the many concerts and opera performances that were available in New York City. In addition, he managed to secure walk-on parts at the Metropolitan Opera House in order to hear many of the operas. In this way he was on stage when Frances Alda and Evelyn Scotney sang, and for Caruso's last performance at this opera house.

As more and more Australian singers won international recognition he became increasingly interested in learning about their early interests and musical development. On periodic trips back home before the Second World War he visited the communities in which artists had grown up and talked with some of their relations and friends; in New York and London he interviewed many of the artists themselves. For years the information gleaned from these conversations was stored away.

In 1960 it was possible for both of us to go to Australia and combine my husband's long-time interest in the singers with mine in the country where he and they had been raised. Being well aware that talent does not develop in a vacuum I was interested in trying to discover whether any particular aspects of life in Australia had contributed to the development of so many fine voices. At the end of a year it was necessary for us to return to the United States but I came back to Australia three times for a total of another twelve months and meanwhile corresponded with Australian artists in all parts of the world.

It was necessary to secure much of our information by means of interviews with several hundred musicians and others active in the musical life of the Commonwealth, because libraries contain few accounts of past musical events and very few records of the sort usually to be found in archives — probably because a young country is dependent on "doers" for its early development and the focus of attention is on the future. Individuals who had had personal collections of programmes, newspaper cuttings, diaries and scrapbooks tended to burn them when they moved or when a famous relative died, instead of recognizing their possible historical value. Fortunately, however, the scrapbooks of some of the artists as well as old announcements of the conservatoria and student magazines were discovered and yielded information not available elsewhere.

Additional interviews with knowledgeable persons in the several Australian states provided "clues" to further sources of information; many were very advanced in years but had a rich background of musical experience and acquaintance which they could recall; others were aware that they could no longer do this but had preserved a few numbers of old journals for which they had written articles twenty-five or more years before. When these were located they tended to be invaluable, not only for the particular articles concerned but also for the acquaintance they provided with periodicals now defunct. These interviews provided much more than information, *per se;* they conveyed a sense of the atmosphere in which many artists had lived and worked. They were a source of special gratification when it became apparent that much of the data secured in this way would now be preserved and not lost when the persons providing them died. In order to add perspective to our account we asked Mr Ronald Campbell, a journalist, to write the story of early visiting opera companies and singers and the effect they had on the musical life of Australia. His account will be found in the appendixes.

The biographies which comprise most of the book reveal how distinctly Australian were the lives of many of the artists. One reads of the Outback, of experiences characteristic of life in a developing country, of long distances from one major settlement to another, of life on sheep stations, of concerts in remote areas, of family groups making music for their own pleasure, of visits by itinerant opera companies and the influence of teachers who came from abroad and settled in centres of population. Together, we believe, these helped to produce a kind of national character that is quite distinctive and has been important in the development of "God-given voices" into disciplined artistry.

BARBARA MACKENZIE,
Croton-on-Hudson
September, 1966

NOTES.

[1]Tate, H., *Australian Musical Possibilities.* Melbourne, E. A. Vidler, 1924.

Acknowledgements

THE AUTHORS HAVE had the co-operation of so many individuals and groups that it is impossible to single out everyone worthy of mention. There are certain persons, however, without whose help it would not have been possible to carry out a project involving so large a number of individuals residing in widely separated areas. P. T. W. Black of Sydney provided the necessary Australian headquarters through which all kinds of information could be cleared and his secretary, Doris Peters, gave generously of her time and talents. Elisabeth Callander of Melbourne made consistent contributions over the entire period and her help was essential in bringing the manuscript to completion.

John Brownlee in New York and his sister Jessie in Melbourne helped in innumerable ways during two decades. Others in New York, London and the several Australian states provided wise counsel and made valuable suggestions in the early stages of this undertaking. Among these were Geraldine Farrar, Edwin McArthur, Alfred J. Mapleson, Percy Grainger, Clive Carey, Dudley Glass, Veronica Mansfield, Louise Hanson-Dyer and Dr Hanson, Margaret Mead, Barbara Ward (Lady Jackson) and the late Lieutenant-General Edward K. Smart, Australian Consul General in New York; Ernest Briggs, Percy Brier, Ethel Osborne Gilmour, and Basil Jones in Brisbane; Sir Bernard Heinze, Herbert Cannon, Joseph Post, Roland Foster, Dorothy Helmrich, Franz Holford, Freda Barrymore, Clement Hosking, Catherine Mackerras, the late Vinia de Loitte, Kitty Archer-Burton and Cyril and Varney Monk in Sydney; Margaret Sutherland, Dr A. E. Floyd, J. Sutton Crow, Dr Percy Jones, A. J. and Spencer Brodney, Richard Hindle Fowler, Marie Bremner Chapple, Mr and Mrs Eric Clapham, Basil Hart, Claude Kingston and Mr Arthur Mayer, Mrs D'Hage's son-in-law, in Melbourne; Mrs Fritz Hart in Honolulu; the late Professor John Bishop, Professor John Horner in Adelaide; and Professors Frank Callaway and Hugh Roberts of Western Australia; Donald Wilson of Tasmania and John M. Thomson of New Zealand who supplied valuable family documents; also John J. Thompson, Roger Covell and John Antill.

Acknowledgements

For their critical judgment at later stages we acknowledge our indebtedness to Roland Gelatt and Winthrop Sargeant of New York.

Miss G. E. Morris of Hobart contributed the fruits of months of research in Tasmania and Victoria. Clement Hosking did preliminary sketches of many singers of the early period and thanks to his former association with the Sydney *Bulletin,* under the pseudonym of 'Maitri', was able to fill in many gaps in information on others. During the Second World War Margaret Schofield Cochrane collected data from newspapers and periodicals which later proved invaluable. Rodney Marriott, an American graduate student, rendered valuable assistance in helping to determine the early format of the book and Ellen Migdal, Louise Crisp and Lois Bolton helped to give it further form.

In addition to the artists themselves, members of their families, neighbours and friends provided information and pictures not otherwise procurable. We are especially indebted to Melba's niece, Helen Lempriere and her husband Keith Wood; to Mme Wiedermann's daughters Elizabeth Finley and Louise Hutchins; Marie Narelle's daughter, Mrs H. Newton Quinn of London; Kate Rooney's niece Jeanette; Clara Serena's husband Roy Mellish; Dolly Castles' daughter Patty Finn; Margherita Grandi's sister Mrs Humble; Agnes and Frank Caspers, Cyril Lawrence, Mrs Ada Boddington and Emma and Steve Smith of Dean's Marsh; Beatrice Miranda's daughter Lalla Miranda Currie of Buffalo, New York; Frederic Collier's daughter Mrs Hickey; Mrs Horace Stevens, Mrs Peter Dawson; Mrs Malcolm McEachern of London; Mrs A. J. Bonynge, Ann Brightley and Lolita Marriot; also John Brasier, Henry Portnoj, Glenda Raymond, Fritz Homburg, Lindley Evans, Hilda Gill and Vera Bradford.

For their help in providing information about Amy Sherwin we are also grateful to Mrs Ann Fysh of Launceston, and other members of the Sherwin family; Miss Allison McMullen of Inlet Farm, Huonville; the staff of the Archivist of the State Library of Tasmania; Miss Doreen Helmrich of Sydney who interrupted her travels to secure data from the public library of Cincinnati, Ohio (U.S.A.), and the Central Music Library in London, and librarians at the Music Library of Lincoln Center, New York City, who supplied accounts and critiques on micro film of Mme Sherwin's appearances in New York and Boston. Grateful acknowledgement is also made to Mr and Mrs E. R. Howroyd of Hobart who furnished transportation to Inlet Farm and to Mr Basil Rait of the Office of the Secretary of Tourism, who arranged for interviews.

For valuable information cheerfully given we cite Betty Bateman of the Australian Elizabethan Theatre Trust, Lois Keep and Bonnie McCallum of the Australian Broadcasting Commission, Miss M. Gunn of the City of Sydney Eisteddfod, Dot Jones and Mr E. R. Weston of the Melbourne *Herald,* Denise Dyson of Sadler's Wells, Allan Giles of the British Broadcasting Corporation,

London writer Don White, Miss Sybil Hewitt of the British Music Society of Melbourne; Betty Chisholm, the late Harold Elvins and the late Herbert Davis of the Melba Conservatorium, Paull Fiddian of the University Conservatorium, L. J. Keegan of the New South Wales Conservatorium, S. W. Keough of the Sydney *Bulletin,* R. M. Younger of the Australian National Travel Association, Doreen Green of Norfolk, George Baker of London, John Tainsh of Edinburgh; K. L. Lawson, Ruth Llewellyn, Regina Ridge, William Freeman, James O'Neil and Ethel Walker of Sydney; Dorothy Briggs of Queensland and Mr J. R. McEwen of the Royal Historical Society of Victoria.

Librarians whose assistance was essential include Philip Miller and Sirvart Poladian of the Music Library, Lincoln Center; Mollie Thompson, Margaret Cameron, Margaret Gale, Dulcie Penfold and Laurel Dowling of the Australian Consulate in New York, Louis Rachow of the Players Club, members of the Staffs of the Public Library of Cincinnati and Hamilton County, Ohio; the Music Library in London; the Fisher Library in Sydney; the La Trobe Library in Melbourne; the Public Library in Adelaide and the Archives of Tasmania.

We are grateful to our friends and colleagues Gertrude Stewart, Josef Alexander, Margaret Bryant, Benjamin Grosbayne, Jacob Loft, Margaret and Roderick Marshall, and Edward B. Wisely for critical evaluations.

To the officers and members and to the staff of the Lyceum Club, Melbourne, the authors owe a special debt of gratitude for providing one of them not only with "a home away from home" but also with delightful companionship and moral support. Toward this end Mrs Emmerson, Lady Lindsay, the Misses I. J. Anderson, Margaret Sutherland, Margareta Webber and Mrs Stanton, made unique contributions as did Kathy Dunn and Jean Pasco.

We acknowledge our indebtedness to the following publishers for permission to quote passages identified throughout the text and in footnotes: Chatto and Windus, Victor Gollancz, Hansom Books, publishers of *Music and Musicians,* Macdonald & Company, *Opera Magazine,* The Society of Authors, *The Sunday Times* and *The Times,* all of London; Appleton Century, Coleman-Ross, Curtis Brown, Farrar Straus and Giroux, F.M. Music Program Guide, *New York Post,* Robert Speller and Sons, *Saturday Review,* Simon and Schuster, The Dial Press, *The New Yorker, The New York Times, The New York Times Book Review, The Village Voice, World Journal Tribune* and *World Telegram and Sun,* all of New York; and the Australian Broadcasting Commission, Australian Consolidated Press, *Australian Letters, Australian Musical News,* Australian National Travel Association, publishers of *Walkabout* magazine, Brisbane *Courier Mail,* F. W. Cheshire, Lansdowne Press, The Melbourne *Herald,* Melba Memorial Conservatorium Past and Present Students' Association, *Rockhampton Morning Bulletin, The Sydney Morning Herald, Woman's Day* and *Women's Weekly.*

1

Factors fostering talent

FOR SEVENTY-FIVE years Australia has been contributing a large number of singers of high quality to the opera houses and concert platforms of the world and has been exporting, in large numbers, talented instrumentalists who have achieved international reputations. In 1961, alone, besides Joan Sutherland, fifteen Australian singers were important members of the Royal Opera Company of Covent Garden and eleven others were singing principal roles at Sadler's Wells. Sir William McKie was organist and master of choristers at Westminster Abbey, Geoffrey Parsons was one of the most sought-after accompanists in England and Barry Tuckwell was proving himself a worthy successor to the great English horn player, Dennis Brain. In addition, nine of the ten most distinguished orchestras in the British Isles had at least two Australian members. Young instrumentalists, too, were winning international awards and appearing as soloists at the Edinburgh Festival and in London.

Nor was this kind of international recognition new for Australians. As early as 1880 Amy Sherwin, "The Tasmanian Nightingale", had sung at concerts and festivals in the United States, always in distinguished company and under the direction of world-famous conductors. Many of her compatriots sang major roles in opera and oratorio in England and on the Continent: Frances Alda, Florence Austral, John Brownlee, Marjorie Lawrence and Elsa Stralia were so well-known to audiences in Paris, Milan and many cities of the United States that the country of their origin was lost sight of.

It is noteworthy that a country with a relatively small population separated by thousands of miles and, until comparatively recently, by several weeks in time, from its sources of cultural origin, should have nurtured so much musical talent. Are there any discernible aspects of Australian culture that may have contributed to this development? There appear to be several. There is strong evidence that the traditions the colonists brought with them had an effect on the development of interest in music. The British choral tradition, for instance, found immediate expression in church choirs and out of these

1

grew oratorio societies.[1] Vocal groups of all kinds appeared wherever there was a settlement of any size and children accustomed to hearing their parents sing while doing chores about the house were stimulated to do the same.[2]

Wherever Welsh or Cornish people settled — often in mining communities where there was gold, as in Ballarat, Victoria, or coal, as in Newcastle, New South Wales — eisteddfodau were organized and young people were encouraged to take part in music and other competitions. Brass bands flourished in British, Scottish and German settlements and like the choirs, many of them travelled thousands of miles each year to take part in such contests as the South Street Eisteddfod at Ballarat.

Committed to the belief that "music is an adornment of life", religious orders which founded schools in remote localities in the early days provided private music lessons for gifted young persons of the area and encouraged them to study for examinations in music prepared by boards in England. Talent was recognized and individuals were encouraged to believe in their ability and to work hard to develop it.[3]

Pioneer conditions fostered the need for co-operation and the custom grew up in large and small communities of staging farewell concerts to raise money to send promising young artists abroad for further study. Newspaper accounts of more than fifty years ago refer to events of this sort given either by groups or under the patronage of a public figure like the wife of a governor or a famous personage like Dame Nellie Melba. The importance of the money raised in this way cannot be overestimated considering the cost of travelling 12,000 miles to London or a capital on the Continent, and of maintenance during a considerable period of study.

The sense of responsibility for making the most of the opportunity which such money provided, and for proving worthy of the confidence that had been placed in them, helped many young singers to muster the courage required to leave family, friends and an established way of life for the loneliness, competition, and impersonality of a sophisticated metropolis where they had to prove themselves at every step. Successful artists often remarked to the authors: "I felt I had to work hard and 'stick it out' after people had invested so much in me". This feeling persists among those who are still struggling to get a toe-hold and they keep on working despite the obstacles they encounter and the sacrifices required. Endurance and individual initiative are qualities that stand them in good stead as they did their forefathers who settled and developed the new continent.

The large sums of money which are awarded today to the winners of the commercially subsidized aria contests in Adelaide, Canberra, Melbourne and Sydney would seem to be meeting in a corporate way the same need of aspiring young artists for a means of financing their musical education. The contests attract much the same kind of community interest as did the earlier locally sponsored fund-raising events like farewell concerts. In Melbourne, for instance, seats for the annual *Sun* Aria Final at the Town Hall are at a premium and many people attend year after year and follow with interest the subsequent careers of the contestants. Appearing on one of these occasions in an attractive setting before so large an audience is a valuable experience in itself for an aspiring young artist.[4]

The "Mobil Quest", a weekly radio programme sponsored by an oil company from 1949 until 1957, seems to have owed much of its initial success to the traditional interest of the Australian public in contests and to their dependence at that time on the radio as an important source of entertainment. A third factor however, appears to be of even greater significance when we keep in mind the purpose of the quest, i.e. "to bring to the attention of the public the best vocal talent available in the Common-wealth", and the requirement that each contestant sing an operatic aria.[5] Brass bands and itinerant street "orchestras" that found their way to the Outback in the early period of settlement usually played operatic arias as part of their standard repertoire and these were hummed later in the homes of those who had stood around to listen outside a general store or in front of a local hotel. In larger, but still quite remote communities, as well as in the capital cities, visiting opera companies from abroad and world-famous recitalists appeared frequently and left behind pleasant recollections of the enjoyment provided by the music they had played. Melba had stimulated interest of this sort through the inexpensive concerts she gave as well as by her opera seasons in Australia.

Public knowledge and appreciation of good music in Australia also owe a great deal to the influence of a number of British and Continental musicians who settled here. They utilized their previous training and experience to enlarge the horizons and improve the taste of people who would not otherwise have come in contact with music of high quality. Their wide experience also made it possible to recognize talented individuals who might otherwise have gone unnoticed, since the local residents often lacked criteria by which to judge fine performances.

Natural as well as cultural factors have been held important in the development of good voices. The climate of Australia has been likened to that of Italy, another country famous for her singers. Attention has been called to the similarity of Australia's location south of the equator to Italy's position north of it. It is interesting to note that the areas of Australia which have a "Mediterranean" climate include the sites of Adelaide, Melbourne and Perth[6] — cities from which a high percentage of singers have come. Donald Brook in his book, *Singers of To-day,* refers to the fact that "atmospheric conditions can exert a great influence on the voice". He quotes Muriel Brunskill, the English contralto who visited Australia in 1935 as saying that she found the climate of

England not beneficial, adding: "On the other hand, singing in Italy and Australia is a perfect joy; one's voice always seems to be in splendid form in both of these countries". It is also said that the climates of both countries are conducive to relaxation and have a favourable effect on "timbre".

The process of selective migration may also have played a part by bringing to settle in this once remote part of the world the adventurous, the self-reliant, and the hard-working who are not daunted by what might seem insuperable obstacles to the fulfilment of their ambitions. Reference is sometimes made, too, to the supposedly characteristic "Australian jaw" that is said to bear relationship to other physical attributes that contribute to superior voice production. People cite group photographs of Australian members of Covent Garden casts of the middle 1950's which unintentionally reveal striking similarities of a distinctive jaw line.

No-one claims to have a definitive answer to the question, "Why has Australia produced so many outstanding voices?", but a sensitive observer of the Australian scene can discern influences that seem to have been conducive to the cultivation of an interest in music and to the development of talented performers.

NOTES.

[1]Horner, J., "A Short History of Music in South Australia", *Australian Letters,* Vol. II. No. 4. March 1960.

[2]It is realized that this custom is not unique to Australians, but the fact appears to have real significance in this context because so many artists interviewed by the authors remarked spontaneously: "My mother always sang" or, "We used to sing at home. Both my father and mother had good voices". Many had grown up in areas where the demands of the frontier were pre-eminent and might have been expected to call forth other kinds of expression.

[3]The importance of this influence was brought out in interviews when artists were asked, "Were there any teachers or others who were aware of your talent and helped you to develop it?"

[4]The Australian Broadcasting Commission recognizes the importance of public appearances for young artists and awards such opportunities to the winners of its "Concerto and Vocal" competitions.

[5]No commercial enterprise would sponsor a programme that was not assured of large numbers of interested listeners. In Australia there was widespread interest in operatic music, which obviously is not true in many parts of the world.

[6]A description of Mediterranean climate on page 27 of the *Life Pictorial Atlas* (New York, 1961), is followed by the statement, "only two per cent of the earth's surface enjoys this balmy climate".

Cynthia Johnston as Violetta and Maurine London as Annina in the 1962 production of La Traviata

Nellie Stewart as Marguerite

2

Opera in Australia

AUSTRALIA HAS HAD a long tradition of interest in opera, as Hugh Hunt, the first director of the Elizabethan Theatre Trust, recognized when he stated in the initial report published in the Australian Theatre Yearbook in 1957,

> The ground for the creation of an Australian theatre, opera especially, had been well prepared in advance. Experimental seasons of home-grown operas ... had been presented in each of the states {and} commercial theatre organizations, in particular the long established firm of J. C. Williamson, had shown a record of opera, ballet and drama importations unsurpassed in the British Commonwealth.

Although there had been sporadic efforts to produce operas in Australia as early as 1834, William Saurin Lyster is said to be the man chiefly responsible for stimulating a sustained interest in opera. He arrived in Australia in 1861, having come from Ireland via the United States. For the next twenty years he continued to organize and import opera companies. Among the individuals Lyster brought to Australia and who remained to enrich its musical life, were the conductor, Alberto Zelman, Sen., and the popular singer, Armes Beaumont. He is credited also with having provided valuable opportunities for local singers to join his company from time to time.

These early visiting opera companies met with an enthusiastic response from audiences everywhere, not only in urban areas but also in small communities. H. Brewster Jones, writing in the *Australian Musical News* in 1936 recounts,

> In 1861, Adelaide, with a population of 18,000 supported a season of grand opera lasting sixteen weeks. Even those difficult and spectacular operas, *The Huguenots* and *The Prophet* (Meyerbeer), were presented by the Lyster Opera Company in all their magnificence in 1866. In that year

nineteen operas were staged in one season. These visits of opera companies continued for a number of years, and enthusiasm ran so high that one company travelled to Tanunda in German wagons with all its scenery and performed for the benefit of the local inhabitants.

The article continues: "I know about this personally, for it was my wife's grandfather, a pupil of Schroder-Devrient, who arranged for this trip, and who sang one of the main roles in the Tanunda performance". This statement not only confirms that opportunity was provided for local singers to take part in the productions of visiting opera companies but suggests the interesting musical background of some of the local inhabitants.

Martin Simonsen — the grandfather of Frances Alda and a former court violinist to the King of Denmark — who had begun an active musical career in Sydney as early as 1865, with his wife the singer Fannie Simonsen, presented several seasons of Italian grand opera between 1887 and 1895. For these he imported Italian singers and a conductor, Roberto Hazon, who stayed on in Australia for a number of years and made a considerable contribution to the development of the musical life of Sydney. In a recent book on the Australian Theatre George Lauri says: "Simonsen does not deserve to be forgotten. For he, no less than his predecessor (Lyster) spent his life in pursuit of an ideal — to give to Melbourne grand opera interpreted by the finest singers obtainable". Another company, headed by Annis Montague and Charles Turner, also presented several seasons of opera between 1881 and 1884.

Another early producer of importance was George Musgrove, a former associate of J. C. Williamson, who presented several opera companies between 1900 and 1907. He brought out Gustav Slapoffski from the Carl Rosa Company in England to be the conductor; Slapoffski stayed on and became most active in the musical life of Australia. The first productions were in English but the last season was one of German grand opera for which he imported German and Italian singers for the principal roles. It was Musgrove who managed Melba's concerts in 1902 when she returned to Australia for the first time since her triumph in Europe. In these concerts she incorporated the arias from grand opera that made her audiences eager to hear her in full scale operatic performances. This opportunity was to be provided in 1911 through the collaboration of Mme Melba and the Williamson firm.

The activities of J. C. Williamson from the time he came to Australia in 1874 led up quite naturally to the presentation of his first Italian grand opera company in 1893. Soon after Williamson established himself in Australia he secured from D'Oyly Carte the rights to produce the authorized version of Gilbert and Sullivan operas. The first production was *Pinafore,* at the Theatre Royal in Sydney. This opened on November 15, 1879, with Williamson himself playing the part of Sir Joseph Porter, and his wife, Maggie Moore, singing the role of Josephine. There followed many seasons of Gilbert and Sullivan in Melbourne and Sydney and other cities of Australia, and in New Zealand. Australians whose performances in early productions are still remembered included Howard Vernon, George Lauri, Edwin Kelly, Hugh Ward, Nellie Stewart and Dolly Castles. Marie Bremner, Strella Wilson, Viola Wilson, Gladys Moncrieff, Charles Walenn and Richard Watson appeared in revivals given many years later.

The enjoyment derived from attendance at these early performances may well have prompted many to attend Williamson's later productions of grand opera. The following statement made by Norman Tucker, Director of the Sadler's Wells Opera Theatre, when speaking before the Royal Society of Arts in London in 1962, suggests this possibility:

Since we played *The Merry Widow* a few years ago — and now Gilbert and Sullivan — a different kind of audience has been coming to the theatre to see these pieces and some of them, at any rate, having enjoyed an operetta in an opera house, are willing to try the experience of grand opera.

"Studley Hall", the Pinschof home at Kew, where students of the Melbourne (later Melba) Conservatorium rehearsed scenes from opera

9

Two seasons of Italian opera — in 1893 and 1901 — were presented by the Williamson firm before their 1910 offerings of "Opera in English", which are said to have done more than any other to popularize grand opera. It was during this year that Amy Castles, the Australian prima donna, and Rosina Buckman of New Zealand, sang leading roles in *Madame Butterfly* and *La Boheme*. These productions also helped to prepare the public for the first Melba-Williamson season of 1911 which brought to Australia an excellent company of singers including John McCormack. This season was acclaimed as setting a new standard of operatic production in the Commonwealth.

In 1912 Thomas Quinlan arrived in Australia with a triple cast, a large chorus and a fifty-piece orchestra that had had successful seasons of opera in England and South Africa. Among the principals were John Coates, the English tenor, and Lalla Miranda who had left Melbourne some eighteen years before for Europe. The company returned to England at the end of the 1912 season but Quinlan returned the next year with a reconstructed company and presented the first Australian performances of Wagner's *Ring Cycle*.

In 1916 Benjamin Fuller presented the Gonzalez Company for the first time and in 1919 Frank Rigo organized an opera company which after a short season in Australia went on to tour New Zealand.

Before the Williamson firm again collaborated with Mme Melba in 1924 they produced a season of grand opera in English in 1919. Included in the company were the Australian singers Amy Castles, Nellie Leach, Elsie Treweek, Leah Myers and Fred Collier. Pauline Bindley appeared as Polly Peachum in their 1923 presentation of *The Beggar's Opera*.

To prepare for the second Melba-Williamson season of grand opera, Mme Melba, her manager John Lemmone, and Nevin Tait, head of the Williamson office in London, went to Italy where they organized a company that was brought to Melbourne to work on a score of Italian and French operas. Besides the principals, who included the Australians John Brownlee and Browning Mummery, there were "twenty-four Italian tenors and basses to match thirty Australian feminine choristers". Two of the Italian principals of 1924, Toti dal Monte and Apollo Granforte, were extremely popular in Australia and returned for later engagements including the third and last season presented jointly by Mme Melba and the J. C. Williamson Company in 1928. In 1932, a year after Melba's death, the Imperial Grand Opera Company was organized by the Williamson firm. For this they imported several principals from Europe, including John Brownlee, to strengthen the primarily local casts. Besides Eleanor Houston, who sang leading soprano roles, the Australians included two women who were soon to begin careers abroad, Joan Hammond and Mollie de Gunst.

10   In 1934-35 Sir Benjamin Fuller presented a grand opera season in

Fritz Hart
Photo: Athol Shmith

connection with celebrations to commemorate the centenary of Melbourne. Under the batons of Maurice D'Abravenal and Richard Ainsworth fifteen operas were given during a seven months period which included ten weeks in Sydney. Besides Florence Austral the primarily imported casts included Muriel Brunskill, Browning Mummery, Walter Widdop, Frederic Collier, Thea Philips and Horace Stevens; Joan Hammond appeared as one of the Valkyrie maidens. There were two more Williamson Italian grand opera seasons in 1948 and 1955. Of these the former was the more successful. Nevin Tait made several trips to Italy to select principals for the company while Australian choruses and dancers were trained in Melbourne. In addition, six local singers (Eleanor Houston, Jean Campbell, Wilma Whitney, Colin Thomas, Lorenzo Nolan and Maxwell Cohen) were selected to play important roles if needed. This 1948-1949 season ran continuously for fourteen months in Australia and New Zealand; the company was transported by plane from city to city.

Through the years J. C. Williamson had had a number of associates. In the early days, he, Arthur Garner and George Musgrove, formed what was known as "The Triumvirate". Together they "brought a scintillating procession of world stars to Australia for eleven years". The Triumvirate dissolved in the early 1890's and Williamson carried on with George (later Sir George) Tallis and Hugh J. Ward (actor, talent scout, and producer) as partners. By

11

1900 E. J. Tait was treasurer of "the Firm" in Melbourne. When Williamson died in Paris in 1913, E. J. Tait and Hugh Ward continued as managers. Meanwhile the concert firm of J. and N. Tait, organized in 1907 with the help of an older brother, Charles, had been operating as part of the Williamson organization and bringing to Australia outstanding artists like Clara Butt, Emma Calve, and Amelita Galli Curci. In 1920 J. C. Williamson Theatres, Inc., amalgamated with J. and N. Tait under the Williamson name, with all four Tait brothers as managing directors. In 1961 when Nevin Tait died, Sir Frank Tait, the only surviving brother, assumed control of the organization, sharing its management with the long-time executive directors in Melbourne and Sydney, Claude Kingston and Harald Bowden. Sir Frank Tait died in 1965 shortly before the end of the Sutherland-Williamson Opera Season which he had arranged.

Experimental Seasons by Local Opera Groups

Of the many organizations that had presented "experimental seasons of home-grown operas" before 1956, it is possible to describe only a few.[1]

For more than fifty years Melbourne had been the scene of a number of "experimental seasons" of amateur productions of high level. Not long after

The Princess Theatre, built to George Musgrove's specifications

Marshall-Hall founded the conservatorium on Albert Street in 1894 he engaged Madame Elise Wiedermann Pinschof, a former European opera principal, who had come to Australia as the wife of the Austrian consul in Melbourne, to take charge of vocal training. Soon the custom was established of presenting regular public performances of scenes from opera. These were later described in the student magazine by one of the participants:

A most enjoyable side of the operatic work was the many happy rehearsals held at "Studley Hall", the lovely Pinschof home overlooking the river at Kew. The whole company would generally travel there together and in the large ball-room of this stately home Madame and her three daughters, Carmen, Elizabeth and Louise, would help the students in every possible way. The result was an excellent interpretation (both musically and histrionically) of the chosen scenes.

A performance was presented each year at one of the large theatres such as Her Majesty's or the King's. Among programmes collected from various sources I find one of "The First Performances of Opera by Students", held at the Alexandra Theatre, Melbourne, on 20th December, 1898. Operas chosen were *The Marriage of Figaro, The Merry Wives of Windsor, Alcestis* (Marshall-Hall) and *Der Freischutz*. Each succeeding year the list of both operas and artistes increased considerably. A very distinguished performance of a later date was that of Evelyn Scotney in the well-known scene from *Lucia,* when her brilliant voice was cheered to an echo. Carmen Pinschof[2] also added to her fame in the role of "Carmen", which she performed with a visiting grand opera company. Another memorable occasion was the performance of that future celebrity, Florence Fawaz (Austral) in the scene from *Der Freischutz* when her glorious voice made a triumphant entry into that musical sphere where later she became so famous.[3]

When Fritz Hart, himself a composer of operas, became director of the Albert Street Conservatorium in 1914, he began to produce complete operas and continued to do so for the next twenty years.[4] So favourably impressed was Melba by the quality of these performances that she volunteered to train the opera students in her own famous method of voice production. This she did during the frequent intervals between 1914 and 1920 when she resided at Coombe Cottage, her home near Melbourne.[5] When she returned to London she presented to the conservatorium a statement which read: "I leave all my pupils at the Albert Street Conservatorium in the hands of my Lieutenants, in whom I have absolute confidence; and I wish it to be recognised that the vocal tuition they receive is completely in accordance with my own methods".

The close relationship between activities at the Albert Street Conservatorium and the musical life of Melbourne was described in another article:

The Conservatorium had always been noted for its Opera School. Between 1915 and 1931, under the stimulus of Dame Nellie Melba's personal interest, and the driving force of a Director who was an experienced producer and conductor, it rose to its greatest heights, and the annual performances were eagerly looked forward to by the musical public. During that time, six of Fritz Hart's own operas were produced, as well as works by Purcell, Gluck, Mozart, Flotow and Donizetti and Thomas Dunhill's amusing comedy *Tantivy Towers*. In 1927, the year of the Beethoven Centenary, the first complete presentation in Australia of *Fidelio* was given with success.[6]

Soon after Fritz Hart left Melbourne in 1934 the Australian National Theatre Movement was founded by Gertrude Johnson, one of Melba's former pupils at the conservatorium. She had just returned from England and the continent where she had been singing coloratura roles for fifteen years. Although Miss Johnson's primary purpose in founding this movement was "to provide work for our young artists to enable them to get the experience that so many of them go abroad for", the productions themselves provided the public with an opportunity to become familiar with the works of contemporary as well as classical composers. In addition to the *Tales of Hoffman* presented before Queen Elizabeth II, during the royal visit in 1954, the repertoire for that year included first performances of *Amahl and the Night Visitors* by Menotti and Benjamin Britten's *Albert Herring* as well as such standard works as *Hansel and Gretel, La Traviata* and *Madame Butterfly*. *The Consul* in which Marie Collier — later a leading soprano at Covent Garden — became so well known, was also given repeat performances.

In Sydney the New South Wales State Conservatorium played an important role in encouraging an interest in opera. Soon after Dr Edgar Bainton became director in 1934 he arranged for the establishment of an opera department under the direction of Roland Foster, a member of the faculty, who had come to Australia originally with Dame Clara Butt and Kennerly Rumford.[7] Regular productions of opera began under the direction of Hilda Mulligan who had studied with Puccini and sung in opera in Italy. Interest in the presentation of operas was stimulated by the fact that two directors of the Conservatorium were themselves composers. *The Pearl Tree* by Dr Edgar Bainton, director from 1934 until 1948, and *Judith* by his successor, Sir Eugene Goossens, were both given public performances at the Conservatorium with Joan Sutherland appearing in the latter.

Programme of the 1921 International Celebrity Concerts in London

The Undersigned Artists Will Positively Appear at the forthcoming

International Celebrity Subscription Concerts

Directors : Lionel Powell & Holt, 6 Cork Street, London, W.1

Signed Sealed and Delivered by

Tetrazzini	*Luisa Tetrazzini*
Rosina Buckman	*Rosina Buckman*
Stella Power	*Stella Power*
Edna Thornton	*Edna Thornton*
Bielina	*Stefan Bielina*
Peter Dawson	*Peter Dawson*
Dinh Gilly	*Dinh Gilly*
Maurice D'Oisly	*Maurice d'Oisly*
Adela Verne	*Adela Verne*
Josef Hofmann	*Josef Hofmann*
William James	*William James*
Kreisler	*Kreisler*
Kubelik	*Jan Kubelik*
Bratza	*M. Bratza*

I·C·S·C

Three other groups originating in the vicinity of Sydney stimulated an interest in opera and provided valuable opportunities for talented young singers. The activities of the National Opera founded by Clarice Lorenz, were the most extensive and helped to launch the careers of Ronald Dowd and Margreta Elkins later of Covent Garden and of Angela Arena a principal in Italian opera companies. The Rockdale Municipal Opera Company and the Sydney Opera Group were also "nurseries" in which a number of future Elizabethan Trust opera singers received their early experience.

In South Australia, the Elder Conservatorium in Adelaide presented a number of "experimental seasons" beginning in 1925. The high quality of the singing in these amateur performances is suggested by the fact that a number of the participants later appeared in principal roles at Covent Garden and Sadler's Wells.[8] When the late Professor John Bishop,[9] became director of the Elder Conservatorium in 1948, he encouraged public performances of all kinds that he thought would enrich the musical life of the community. Thus Adelaide became the site for the opening of the First Elizabethan Trust opera season in 1956, and two years later for the first major Festival of Arts to be held in Australia.

Radio presentations of opera by the Australian Broadcasting Commission, from 1941, should also be noted as an important educational force in familiarizing audiences with standard operatic works and interesting them in attending subsequent stage performances. The ABC's efforts over the years to build fine orchestras made it possible for them to provide the Elizabethan Theatre with instrumentalists of high calibre, an indispensable adjunct to successful operatic productions. During this period the ABC had also been helping to develop an experienced operatic conductor, Joseph Post, whom it released to the Trust to act as Musical Director for the first season.

NOTES.

[1]Others include activities sponsored by the Queensland Government, the Arts Council of New South Wales, the Adult Education Boards of Western Australia and Victoria, and the National Theatre and Fine Arts Society of Tasmania.
[2]Carmen Pinschof later sang professionally as Carmen Pascova in the United States with Mary Garden's opera company in Chicago.
[3]Parkinson, V. C. E., "Mme Elise Wiedermann and the Opera School", *The Melba Conservatorium Magazine*, No. 12, 1945.
[4]Later the English tenor, Clive Carey, an associate of Lilian Baylis at Sadler's Wells presented additional seasons of opera while acting as director of the Melba Conservatorium from 1941-1944.
[5]Subsequently this conservatorium was renamed the Melba Conservatorium in her honour.
[6]Campbell, M., "Fritz Hart. F.R.C.M.", *The Melba Conservatorium Magazine*, No. 16, 1949.

[7]Foster, R., *Come Listen to My Song.* Sydney, Collins 1949.

[8]Producers included Clive Carey, who started these presentations as an extension of the activities of his opera class; Arnold Matters who had returned to Australia after an operatic career abroad; Max Worthley who later became internationally known as an opera and oratorio singer and William R. Cade who had studied the violin in Germany and played in the Beecham Opera Company Orchestra.

[9]John Bishop, Mus. Doc., O.B.E., F.R.C.M., was distinguished by the consistency with which he brought music and the arts to the attention of political, civic and university authorities and the general public in a fresh, attractive and challenging manner. In the opinion of his colleagues he was able to do this by reason of his particular combination of knowledge, artistic integrity, imagination, courtesy, humour, persistence and administrative ability.

Born in Adelaide he studied piano at the University Conservatorium there and in 1922 was awarded the Elder Overseas Scholarship for three years post-graduate study at the Royal College of Music, London. In 1929 he became Conductor of the Choral Union and the Philharmonic Orchestra in Wellington, N.Z. and while there organized the first Children's Orchestral Concerts and festivals of local compositions. He went to Melbourne to join the staff of the University Conservatorium in 1934 and later took the post of Music Master at Scotch College where he remained from 1936 to 1947. He had a firm belief in the importance of providing school children with the broadest musical experience possible and to this end founded the Victorian Public Schools Music Association, the Summer Music Camps and the Australian Youth Orchestra.

In 1948 he was appointed Elder Professor of Music at the Adelaide University and Director of the Elder Conservatorium. Three years later he became the first Australian to receive a year-long fellowship from the Carnegie Corporation, New York, to investigate music education overseas. His long range aim was to give the Australian music student as good a quality of musical experience at home as he could obtain by going overseas. By far-sighted planning and deployment of staff he brought into existence the first Australian University resident String Quartet and later a resident Wind Quartet. He instigated the creation of a lectureship in composition designed to bring to Adelaide each year for a period of six months a well-known overseas composer to stimulate musical composition in Australia.

At the time of his sudden death in London in December, 1964, he was chairman of the Australian Committee for U.N.E.S.C.O. and was abroad engaging artists for the 1966 Adelaide Festival.

18   *Marshall Hall — a portrait by Tom Roberts*

3

Musical Traditions and Pioneer Activities

AUSTRALIA'S LOVE OF singing has its roots in the traditions the early settlers brought with them. Its development into talented expression is due to nurturing by individuals who came somewhat later, well equipped by experience and training to develop natural ability into high level performance. Writing of the history of music in South Australia, John Horner calls attention to the fact that colonization of that state constituted the transplantation of an advanced civilization and illustrates this by quoting from the diary of a young girl who arrived in Adelaide in the winter of 1839. Her first entry states: ". . . lived in a tent formed by pieces of canvas thrown across some poles". Two years later she wrote: "Miss Williams gave Helen and me our first lesson in music". By this time it was already possible to receive instruction in the bush villages along the Torrens River, not only in playing the piano but also the harp. A Mr Bennett taught organ, piano and violin on Grenfell Street in Adelaide in 1839 and as early as 1841 "238 violins and bows were being offered for sale for prices ranging from ten to fifteen guineas each", presumably with the expectation that there would be a demand for them.[1]

Both English and German settlers brought musical traditions with them and the year 1859 witnessed the coming together of representatives from both groups when the Gawler Institute of South Australia offered prizes for an Australian national song; Mrs C. J. Carleton, an English immigrant of 1841, won first prize for her verses "Song of Australia" and Carl Linger, who had emigrated from Germany in 1849, won the competition for setting it to music.

The large number of German Lutherans who settled some forty miles from Adelaide in the Barossa Valley in the 1840's brought with them a love of brass bands, choirs and musical associations, many of which persisted until the outbreak of the First World War when throughout Australia all things German tended to become suspect. Interest in musical activities persisted, however, and both the Tanunda band and liedertafel concerts continued to be well attended when these organizations made their annual public appearances. In 1961 the choral society was still under the leadership of its long time conductor, Fritz Homburg, who was then seventy-five years old. His interest in male choirs, he said, began during his student days at the Elder Conservatorium of Music when he was a member of the Adelaide society. The Tanunda Liedertafel in 1961 comprised forty men between the ages of twenty-four and seventy from all walks of life, including doctors and farm labourers. It owned a large library of German lieder (some brought to Australia by the original settlers of the Barossa Valley), many English part-songs, and some Russian songs. Recordings of the group are still popular and are broadcast frequently on the national network of the ABC.

The English choral tradition was probably responsible for the fact that many choirs often burst their church bonds and blossomed into Choral Societies of oratorio dimensions and for popular interest in the programmes of a group like the late Norman Chinner's "Adelaide Singers". Male choirs have flourished in all states; the Orpheus Society in Hobart has had an uninterrupted history since 1877, the Melbourne Philharmonic Society was founded in 1853 and the Royal Victorian Liedertafel in 1868. Comparable groups existed in Sydney under the direction of well-known musicians, many of them having come to Australia for the first time as the conductors of visiting opera companies.

Another tradition found expression in the lives of the men of the Outback. Roger Covell called attention to this in an article he wrote in recognition of the Queensland Centenary.[2] He also alluded to the intangible and persuasive aspect of musical experience.

> Music is in the air. It can live as a softly-hummed tune or even as a thought in the mind. That is why a history of music in Queensland can never be a mere record of public performances.
>
> The first white man's music in this State came in the memories of the early convicts, soldiers, and settlers. Words and tunes of folk songs, street ballads, and popular theatre ditties from England, Scotland and Ireland—particularly Ireland — survived discomfort, pain, fear, and an ocean crossing. Some of them were probably used as unconscious charms to lessen home-sickness, or to summon up an image of well-loved scenes.
>
> But gradually the songs changed to fit a new land. Passing into currency by ear alone their words and melodies altered. Singers began to make up new songs in the old styles. Many were first sung by drovers and shearers (the two great singing classes of the Outback). The shearers sang them around a campfire, often to the accompaniment of concertinas and guitars (on the coast) from at least the 1860's onwards. The drovers sang them quietly as they rode around their cattle to quieten them at night and perhaps more rousingly when they reached their favourite pub.

One of the old droving songs, "Farewell to the Ladies of Brisbane", which began life as a variation on a British seamen's song, traces through its verses the route of a one-time cattle trail, from Toowong through Caboolture and Kilcoy to Taromeo and Yarraman Creek and then on to Nanango. Most of these traditional songs are good to sing; they would not have survived otherwise.

Many Australians owe their familiarity with operatic airs to the music they heard played by the local bands that were a feature of the early life of communities even in remote areas. The English authority on bands, Dr Denis Wright, says:

Wind bands came to Australia through the military and defence forces during the early years of the nineteenth century. The civilian excursions into brass band music came about in two ways: settlers from Britain and other European countries brought instruments with them and soon started to form small groups; bandsmen discharged from the forces drifted into industry and quite naturally augmented the number of available players for the numerous bands associated with public and private enterprises. Both in schools and amongst the civil population bands rapidly increased. This increase was stimulated in the 1860's following the Queensland gold-rush and in Western Australia as well; as new townships sprang up, so did the bands. The people had to make their own music or go without; they were very isolated, often some hundreds of miles from a city ... In Western Australia the eastern goldfields produced two outstanding bands: Boulder City and Kalgoorlie. At one time the Boulder City Band contained a whole family of seven brothers who had migrated to the goldfields after having played in the Hillgrove Band in New South Wales.
Some of the most successful of the early Australian small bands were made up of Germans; these were often itinerant groups, roaming from place to place, making a scanty living by playing in the streets or at local dances ...

A counterpart of these bands were Italian street orchestras. Lyng, writing on non-British immigrants in Australia, refers to

... scores of street orchestras which up to the outbreak of the war (1914) in conjunction with German bands, filled the streets with music and, in a pleasant manner, relieved the prose of city life. The Italian street-bands of from two to three stringed instruments always including the picturesque harp and occasionally supplemented by the flute, generally took up their positions in front of hotels where, for the modest sums collected from   21 floating audiences, they rendered gems from operas and ballads by the world's greatest composers.[3]

Dr Wright notes:

As late as the 1920's the brass band world clung to the old type of operatic selections as their mainstay. Following the general pattern of the already established band contests, the music chosen as tests at Ballarat from the inception of brass band classes (in 1900) right up to 1922 consisted of operatic or one-composer "selections" such as "Gems from Meyerbeer", "Lucretia Borgia", "Weber's Works", and "Semiramide".

The music played by these groups must have had considerable influence in familiarizing people throughout Australia with music from opera. Indeed, one of the most distinguished figures in the current musical life of Australia testifies to the fact that his own introduction to Wagner was listening to a rehearsal of the Prelude to *Tristan and Isolde* by St Augustine's Orphanage Band, Geelong, when they were preparing for the famous South Street competitions in 1922.

Irish tradition found its expression primarily in the musical activities of the religious orders that established convents — often in remote areas — during the nineteenth century. In these religious communities were nuns of considerable musical attainment; they brought with them the convent tradition that music is "an adornment of life" and worthy of cultivation. From the earliest days not only was singing taught in classes but a good deal of private tuition was given. It is interesting to note that many of the well-known musicians of today who grew up in Western Australia were educated in convents, among them Eileen Joyce, Catherine Goodall, Katherine Mansfield and Lorna Sydney.

As pointed out earlier, nuns often did more than teach music; they were able to recognize talent and when they found it, they helped their pupils to believe in themselves and to work hard to develop their gifts. Many secular teachers all over Australia played similar roles, of course, but in many remote areas the only qualified music teachers were members of religious orders.

Teachers, generally, encouraged pupils to take examinations prepared by boards in London and to compete for awards which could take them abroad to one of the Colleges of Music for further study. Percy Brier of Queensland was the first recipient of a three-year travelling scholarship offered by the local committee of the Trinity College of Music. He became the first Australian Fellow of the College and later an Associate of the Royal College of Organists.[4]

The generally high quality of choirs in Queensland is due largely to the influence of musicians who, born and educated abroad, settled in widely

Ballarat at the time of the first eisteddfod in 1855

separated towns. Percy Brier speaks of R. T. Jeffries as "the first real pioneer of music in Queensland"[5] and describes the influence that he and his three talented daughters exerted on the musical life of Brisbane organizing concerts and introducing new music. An excerpt from an article on the *Musical Union*[6] gives some idea of Mr Jeffries' contribution in the way of raising people's aspirations and encouraging them to enter upon more complex undertakings:

"Early after his arrival in Brisbane (from London, in 1871) Mr Jeffries suggested the performance of a complete oratorio. Hitherto the most that had been attempted had been isolated choruses or numbers from oratorios or masses or cantatas. There was a disposition to think anything more elaborate was quite impossible. Mr Jeffries assured them that it was not impossible, and it was not long before *The Messiah* was put into practice . . . The performance of *The Messiah* on April 25, 1873, forever set to rest any doubts as to the practicability of rendering an oratorio in Brisbane. It was the first time Handel's great work had ever been heard here, and that circumstance alone invested the occasion with deep interest."

By the next year, 1874, a Melbourne newspaper was calling attention to Mr Jeffries' accomplishments and to the fact that it was the second largest musical society in the colonies, surpassed only by the Melbourne Philharmonic Society.[7]

George Sampson, Jeffries' successor as conductor of the Musical Union, had studied with Sir George Risely and Harford Lloyd and been a well-known organist and conductor in England. For fifty years after his arrival to become organist of St John's Anglican cathedral in 1898, Sampson was very influential in the musical life of Brisbane. Not only did he found a symphony orchestra which eventually became the nucleus of the Australian Broadcasting Commission's Queensland Orchestra, he also secured instruments and music for the players.[8]

Before the end of the century, the musical society, the local choir, and the eisteddfod were playing a prominent part in the communal life of a number of Queensland towns.[9] Among these was Rockhampton. Louis D'Hage settled there about 1886 and made unique contributions to the musical life of that community. He had been educated as a violinist at the Vienna Conservatorium and during this period had had the opportunity of hearing many of the great European musicians of this era including Joachim, Brahms and Bruckner. He had come to Australia with a seventy-five piece orchestra conducted by Alois Wildner, a professor of the Royal Conservatoire in Leipzig. This body of musicians had been recruited in Vienna to play at the Melbourne Exhibition of 1880 and was known popularly as the "Strauss Band".

After fulfilling its contract and making a tour of the principal cities of the Commonwealth the orchestra disbanded. Some of the players decided to remain in Australia, among them D'Hage, who went to Rockhampton. Shortly after his arrival he became conductor of the orchestral Orpheus Club and led it for more than twenty-five years.

Two articles which appeared in the Rockhampton *Morning Bulletin* at the time of his death in April, 1960, provide a picture of D'Hage's impact on that community. One article points out that

> ... Apart from the high standard of entertainment his Orpheus Club concerts gave to the local community, the reputation Rockhampton gained for its musical taste served as a magnet for most of the great names in the concert world. Melba, Ada Crossley, Clara Butt, Amy Castles, John McCormack and many famous instrumentalists came to sing and play here — at a time when the population was well below 20,000.

The second article indicates the important part D'Hage played in discovering talent, providing good basic training, and giving informed guidance in the direction of securing additional education. It also gives a glimpse of the high level of talent that was discovered during the early period, even in remote communities.

24   It refers to D'Hage's "renown for the success of his pupils", and states:

He discovered Alma Moodie, the infant prodigy from Mt Morgan, who was only five years old when she came under Mr D'Hage's notice. On his recommendation she was sent to Brussels at the age of seven. At twelve she set musical Europe "ablaze" with her playing and at sixteen went on a world tour with Max Reger, eminent composer. At the opening of the new Festival Hall in Cologne, Hans Pfitzner, who conducted the Festival, wrote a special violin concerto dedicated to Alma Moodie.

Another of Mr D'Hage's pupils to achieve international fame was Molly Hourigan. She had already attained a high standard when, at the age of eighteen, she left Rockhampton to take lessons at the Royal Conservatorium, Brussels. Two years later she won the Grand Prix against all competitors.

Turning from Queensland to Melbourne, the phrase "ever since the time of Marshall-Hall" is still heard among singers, though this dominant figure in the musical life of Australia died as long ago as 1915. The authors were fortunate to meet in 1961 J. Sutton Crow, who had been a student and friend of Marshall-Hall and provided them with a copy of an article he had written some years before.[10] We reproduce some of it here with the permission of the author and of the magazine:

George William Louis Marshall-Hall, son of a London surgeon, was born in 1862. From his youth, he manifested a strong bent for music, and at the age of sixteen published a book of songs. He studied at the Royal College of Music, London, under Sir George Grove and Sir Hubert Parry, after which he travelled much in Europe. In 1891, he came to Melbourne as the first occupant of the Chair of Music in the University. He was regarded as a musician of exceptional ability, and also possessed an unusual command of the pen, in addition to which he spoke fluently in German, French, Italian and Spanish.

Numerous statements could be quoted which reveal the inner nature of the man. In 1891, in his inaugural address as first occupant of the Chair of Music at the University of Melbourne, he said: "Music to a musician is a language by which, even more definitely than by speech, it is possible to express every emotion, simple or complex . . . The lofty passions which lead to acts of heroism, the human sympathy which should be the foundation of morality and justice, he is enabled to let stream through his heart, creating within him noble impulses . . . Such is the meaning of music to me, and my energies will be chiefly devoted to making this meaning clear to others." When he first occupied the Chair of Music, there was no Conservatorium and no established orchestra. In 1892, although he had had very little 25 experience as a conductor, he, with the assistance of the late Mr George Allan of Allan's music house, organized an orchestra, and conducted his first concert in the Melbourne Town Hall. The programme included the Beethoven Fifth Symphony, which work always appealed immensely to him, and the production of which may perhaps be regarded as outstanding amongst his finest efforts. The success of this concert led to the creation of an organization headed by Dr (later Sir) James Barrett, Sir John Mackey, Carl Pinschof, Madame Wiedermann, and Dr Felix Meyer which resulted in the establishment of the Marshall-Hall Orchestra. Concerts were given more or less regularly. Those with any knowledge of orchestral affairs in the city will know of the difficulties with which a management was faced in those days in welding a body of players into shape. Instrumental players were either employed in theatres, or were busily engaged in teaching, and because of the uncertainty of engagement and the inadequate remuneration could not be relied upon to attend orchestral rehearsals regularly. Such problems in these early years appeared almost insuperable. For over twenty years this rugged and virile personality laboured untiringly to create a deep musical appreciation in this city, and to establish a full symphony orchestra. As occupant of the Chair of Music, Marshall-Hall was convinced that in addition to the lectures he delivered it was essential to establish a practical School of Music.

In 1894, the University decided to establish a conservatorium; and the institution known as the University Conservatorium of Music came into being in February, 1895, with the Ormond Professor as its Director.[11] It was the first conservatorium established in the British Empire within a university.[12]

In 1935 at the dedication of a new wing of the University Conservatorium to the memory of Marshall-Hall, Mrs Herbert Brookes unveiled a plaque on which were inscribed the words, "His Soul Was Aflame with Music". Sir James Barrett, in the address which followed, spoke of Marshall-Hall as "An artist to the tips of his fingers; with little desire for business details, he yet, by his driving force, clarity of insight and knowledge of human nature, created a great educational institution.

"He founded an orchestra with great traditions, and, above all, he altered the attitude of the people of the State to his art".

The influence of two other musicians from abroad, Mme Wiedermann and Fritz Hart, is apparent in the above account. Other communities were also fortunate to have settle in their midst well-trained musicians who were able to judge talent by world standards and to exercise musical leadership. Together they constituted a powerful force in developing the natural interest and musical ability which awaited them.

Eisteddfodau and other competitions

Competitions have played an important part in encouraging the development of musical talent in Australia, a fact to which the biographies in later pages will bear witness. According to the *Australian Encyclopaedia,* the idea of holding eisteddfodau or musical and elocutionary competitions, was brought to Australia by Welsh immigrants during the second half of the nineteenth century. The earliest was that organized by Welsh miners at Ballarat, Victoria, in 1855,[13] but this seems to have been an isolated effort. The next known eisteddfod was held at Newcastle in 1875, again a spontaneous effort, probably promoted by the Welsh coalminers there.

In an old volume in the library of the Mechanics' Institute in Ballarat it is recorded that "The Welsh Eisteddfod has become an established institution in Ballarat . . . These festivals date from the year 1855, and they have done much to foster and evoke musical talent, not only amongst the natives of the principality and their children but among all classes of citizens. Vocal and instrumental music, poetry and oratory are all subjects within the programmes, and the best masters are employed as the awarders of the prizes offered for success".

In a history of Ballarat written in 1935 by Nathan Spielvogel there is an interesting account of how the South Street competitions began, which illustrates the initiative, ingenuity and self-reliance of early settlers as they found ways to express their interests.

"In 1879 a dozen studious youths attending night classes at the Dana Street School initiated a debating club. Encouraged by their teacher, J. C. Charles, they rented a room in Skipton Street, collected a few hundred books and formed a library. They met regularly and under the direction of a young enthusiast, W. D. Hill, they prospered. In 1890 this society began a series of competitions with a prize list of £50. And so, modestly, was inaugurated the famous South Street competitions."[14]

The 1956 announcement of the Grand National Eisteddfod of Australasia, as these competitions came to be known, gives June, 1891, as the date when they started and refers to it as the time when "Ballarat discarded the gold of the earth for the gold of the human mind and voice and took its place among the cultured nations of the world".

In Queensland eisteddfodau first appeared about 1885. The Brisbane Eisteddfod, which was later to become one of the most extensive in the Commonwealth, grew out of earlier musical celebrations of the birthday of St David, the patron saint of Wales; the other, at Gympie, comprised competitions among choirs in the afternoon and a concert in the evening. At first these events were local in composition but gradually inter-city rivalry was introduced; so was the Welsh custom of moving the eisteddfod in a circle so that festivals

Ada Crossley. One of the singers attracted to Rockhampton in the time of Louis D'Hage

were held in different communities in a fixed order. Because Queensland communities tended to be widely separated two eisteddfod councils were formed at the turn of the century.[15] Besides their co-ordinating function their objectives included "the fostering and promoting in worthy ways, the love of music and literature and the establishment of scholarships or bursaries to aid the development of musical, artistic and literary talent".

In 1908 two Queensland choirs travelled over a thousand miles to take part in the South Street competitions at Ballarat. When they won first and second places, the attention of the other states was called to the high quality of choral singing in Queensland and other Queensland choirs became interested in fuller participation in the eisteddfod movement.

The City of Sydney Eisteddfod was launched in 1933 under the joint auspices of the Citizens of Sydney Organizing Committee and the Music Week Committee of New South Wales. Professor Roland Foster of the Conservatorium was president of the latter and a leading figure in promoting the idea. From the beginning the newspaper, the Sydney *Sun,* sponsored an aria contest, and soon Australia could boast of two important *"Sun* Arias", one in Sydney and one in Melbourne, both of which offered large prizes. The Melbourne contest was the result of a decision in 1934 to present the finalists in the Ballarat competitions at a concert in the Melbourne Town Hall instead of continuing to sponsor contests that had been established ten years before in three Victorian cities: Ballarat, Bendigo and Geelong (where the competitions were known as the Commun na Feinne). Writing of the importance of such contests in 1931, Thorold Waters, music critic of the Melbourne *Sun* and one of the instigators of the aria contests, said: "Such a heritage of lovely voices as Australia possesses is worth putting to the best use. As surely as Italy itself this continent should develop into a head centre of opera."[16] When Roland Foster was an adjudicator at the 1928 competitions at Ballarat, he remarked that from the singers who had come before him he thought it would have been possible to select the principals and chorus of a complete opera.

Besides the famous *Sun* Aria contests held in Sydney and Melbourne, there are less well-known vocal competitions held in connection with eisteddfodau in smaller cities. Many who ultimately win first place in one of the big contests begin as entrants in smaller competitions. Rosina Raisbeck, who grew up in Newcastle, N.S.W., recalls that the opportunity to compete in the eisteddfod in her home community encouraged her to work hard and the success she achieved there stimulated her to seek further training in Sydney. Later, after winning the *Sun* Aria there in 1946, she went to London and soon was engaged to sing at Covent Garden where she remained for a number of years.

Participation in the City of Orange Eisteddfod was the first step for Tello Siciliano, winner of the 1959 *Sun* Aria in Melbourne. He had entered the competitions in the New South Wales community because there he would be permitted to sing arias he knew only in Italian. One of the judges, Linda Phillips, a well-known adjudicator from Melbourne, recognized his talent and encouraged him to learn to sing his repertoire in English and thus qualify for the Melbourne contest the next year. This he did and used his prize-money to go to Milan where he won a scholarship at the Verdi Conservatorium and became a protege of an old Italian maestro. Contestants often travel great distances to enter events in the capital cities. A number of New Zealanders compete each year and it is not unusual for one of them to win; Heather Begg and Noel Mangin are two examples.

The personal interest shown in contestants by the staff of the sponsoring bodies has been an important factor in their continued success. Miss Gunn, in Sydney, for instance has acted as a clearing house of information about individuals who have remained abroad for years and have been quite successful but about whom not much is known locally. For twenty-five years Dot Jones, who assisted the late Mr H. Pacini, general manager of the Melbourne *Sun,* to establish the *Sun* Aria and later arranged the finals at the Melbourne Town   29

Hall, helped many a finalist to find the right teacher abroad or suggested names of promising young singers to visitors seeking worthy candidates for scholarships. It was she who arranged for auditions by the noted French teacher, Dominic Modesti, who wished to provide one scholarship and ended by granting five to study with him in Paris. The biographies of all these appear among accounts of contemporary young singers now established abroad.

Commercial enterprises, too, have played an important part in promoting an appreciation of good music and offering to young singers an opportunity to be heard and to earn prize money which could be used for further training. Besides those which provide prizes at eisteddfodau, several firms have sponsored large-scale competitions of their own. Of these, the activities of the Vacuum Oil Company are among the best known. After presenting a radio programme, "Opera for the People", for two and a half years, during which productions of well-known operas featured such singers as Elsie Morison, David Allen and John Lanigan (all of whom later were engaged by Covent Garden), the company decided, in 1949, to broaden its scope with a new contest, "The Mobil Quest". The avowed purposes of this programme were "to encourage Australian artists, and assist them in their singing career, and to provide entertainment for all sections of the community". It was also designed to create a greater appreciation of good music among the Australian public. For each broadcast there was a studio audience, many of whose members saw for the first time singers performing with a symphony orchestra. The music was under the direction of Hector Crawford who conducts many of the "Music for the People" concerts in the Myer music bowl, Melbourne.

Large cash prizes were offered and a complex system of heats was worked out for the preliminary contests. Later, nationwide tours were arranged for the winners. The biographies of winners Ronal Jackson, Joan Sutherland and Donald Smith and of second-place winners, Robert Allman, John Shaw and Margreta Elkins, appear in later pages. Margaret Nisbett, the 1951 winner, later sang with the Sadler's Wells Company in England before returning to Australia with her young son and appearing regularly in operas on television. Elizabeth Allen sang at Covent Garden after winning in 1953 and appeared in the Sutherland-Williamson International Grand Opera Season in Australia in 1965. The 1955 winner, Marjorie Conley, was beginning a most promising career when striken with a fatal illness. Heather Begg and Robert Bickerstaff, second-placegetters in 1956 and 1957 respectively, have also sung at Sadler's Wells where the latter has been featured as one of the promising new artists.

Among other finalists in the Mobil Quest who have chosen to make music their career in Australia and/or New Zealand are Allan Ferris, William Smith, Maureen Boyce, Raymond McDonald, Joyce Simmons, Neil Warren Smith, Brian Hansford (after some seasons in Germany) and Nance Grant who won in 1957. Some of these have sung regularly with the Elizabethan

Theatre Trust, others like Brian Hansford and Nance Grant, usually appear in recitals or as soloists with symphony orchestras.

NOTES

[1]Horner, J., "A Short History of Music in South Australia", *Australian Letters,* Vol. 2, No. 4, 1960.

[2]"Queensland's Rousing Folk Songs", Brisbane *Courier Mail,* March 18, 1959.

[3]Lyng, J., *Non-Britishers in Australia,* Melbourne, Melbourne University Press, 1935.

[4]"Percy Brier's Activities", *Australian Musical News,* January, 1926.

[5]Brier, P., *Pioneers in Music in Queensland,* The Musical Association of Queensland, Mimeo, 1962.

[6]Jubilee issue of the *Queenslander,* 1909.

[7]It was described as "having an effective strength of 190-160 vocalists, and an orchestra numbering over thirty . . . has just closed its second year, and since its formation a year ago has . . . rendered the following works: Handel's *Messiah,* Mendelssohn's *Elijah,* Romberg's *Lay of the Bell,* Sterndale Bennett's *May Queen,* several of Mozart's productions, Haydn's *Creation* and Mendelssohn's *St Paul.* At the present time it has Handel's *Judas Maccabeus* under rehearsal".

[8]During the time he served as conductor Sampson persuaded the City Council to buy instruments for the orchestra because they were difficult for individuals to acquire. Because symphonic music was hard to borrow or to hire he purchased scores himself and thus built up a valuable collection which he later turned over to the ABC as the Sampson Library.

[9]Lynch, K., *Cultural Developments in Queensland, 1880-1930,* unpublished thesis, University of Queensland, 1959.

[10]*Magazine* of Past and Present Students' Association of the Melba Conservatorium. Twelfth Anniversary number, 1945.

[11]Marshall-Hall was authorized to establish a conservatorium on condition that it be self-supporting and not dependent on the University for financial support.

[12]At the time, the university could not house the new institution, but a temporary home was established in the Queen's Coffee Palace in Carlton. A little later, the conservatorium was removed to the building of the Victorian Artists' Society in Albert Street, East Melbourne. It was unfortunate that Marshall-Hall's duties as Ormond Professor of Music were terminated in 1900. In the following year, the university arranged to transfer the conservatorium to a building in the university grounds, and the newly appointed occupant of the Chair of Music, Professor Franklin Peterson, became its new director. Professor Marshall-Hall, however, with the assistance of his numerous friends and a substantial portion of the staff, decided to establish a conservatorium of his own in the Albert Street Building, and a great number of the students from the University Conservatorium joined his conservatorium.

[13]Withers, W., *History of Ballarat,* 1887.

[14]Spielvogel, N., *History of Ballarat,* 1935.

[15]Brier, P., *Short History of Music in Queensland,* privately printed.

[16]The *Sun News-Pictorial,* May 6, 1931.

MELBA
by Joan Lindsay

We present, as a frontispiece to this chapter, the following excerpt from Joan Lindsay's book Time Without Clocks. *It is a better portrait of Melba than any photograph or painting we have seen. With deft strokes of the pen Lady Lindsay portrays the woman she knew and we see the complex personality illuminated*

A GOOD DEAL of what Melba herself would have called 'damn nonsense' has already been written about that remarkable woman — a complex personality who on paper has so far failed to come to life as a human being for thousands of Australians born too late to have seen and heard her for themselves. It isn't easy of course to draw a convincing posthumous portrait of a person who looked sometimes like a Roman Emperor, sometimes a frail feminine Mimi. Actually this dual role calling for masculine horse sense and feminine charm might be said to have run through Melba's whole personality whether on or off stage. It helps I think to explain why she was loved, hated and often misunderstood. Melba could swear like a bullock driver, was courteous and truly kind to people she liked, and enjoyed being rude to people she didn't like when she felt they deserved it. Listening to Melba for the first time was an emotional experience beyond everyday living. The first pure notes of 'Chanson Hindoue' as she stood looking straight before her with loosely folded hands — she appeared to have no special concert mannerisms — stilled a vast audience to frozen attention as at the call of a far-off magic bird. And as she sang to them 'Home Sweet Home' magnificent in a jewelled tiara, transforming the hackneyed air into a thing of delicate beauty, a genuine love for these, her very own people, welled up in her heart.

As Nellie Mitchell the young Australian who had battled her way to stardom she had always remembered and loved the little township of Lilydale and it was here within a few miles of her father's limestone quarry that she had built her Australian home. At Coombe she was relaxed, houseproud, fond of her cockatoo and the dogs, enjoyed the good country food and talking to her Italian gardener. The glorious voice was no casual gift from Heaven. Its ultimate perfection was developed by will-power, self-sacrifice and gruelling years of hard work. When she was no longer young the lines of that desperate struggle for perfection and even for recognition could sometimes be seen in her face. It was a strong, clear-cut face, dominated by the large luminous eyes. They were eyes that recognised quality wherever they saw it — in hats, food, jewels, antique silver and glass. She knew instinctively when to buy and sell shares, whether a business was sound or a human being a humbug and could appreciate a frothy musical comedy far removed from her own line of country so long as it was good theatre.

34　　　　　　　　　　　　　　　　　　　　　*Nellie Melba*

4

Nellie Melba

FOR FORTY YEARS the pure and silvery voice of Nellie Melba made her an undisputed Queen of Song during the "Golden Age of Opera". After her voice was stilled on February 23, 1931, she lived on as a legend in operatic circles throughout the world and in her native Australia as a warm human being.

In order to understand the person behind "The Voice", as she often referred to herself, it is necessary to see her as the child of an enterprising Scottish pioneer in Australia and as a native daughter who loved the freedom of the life there during the second half of the nineteenth century. As Marie Narelle, one of her contemporaries, said in an interview in which she spoke of her own early childhood experiences, "I have recalled them because I think that the pre-eminence of Australian voices is not the outcome so much of climate or any exterior influence, but of our character. It is the Australian personality that has made the Australian voice. We are a natural people . . . free in all we do and say and think and it is that freedom, I believe, that makes us good singers".[1]

Melba's maiden name, Helen Porter Mitchell, conveys some of the strength of the woman who was said by her contemporaries to have had such high intelligence and acumen that she could have been successful in whatever field she chose. Having chosen music she needed all her other gifts of mind and courage to bring to fruition the native talent that her early life had fostered. Her capacity for hard work, her imagination, courage, perseverance and concentration, all were placed at the service of the amazing gift with which she had been born.

But Melba had far more than a voice, even though it was a voice which for quality, flexibility, purity and sheer lasting power, will probably never be excelled. She had a personality which carried across the footlights of the biggest opera houses in the world and, as a young woman, an austere type of beauty which compelled the admiration, when it did not excite the affection, of audiences.

35

John Thompson, of the Australian Broadcasting Commission, said at the time of her centenary:

> It would be a poor compliment to a great personality to pretend that Melba had no failings. She was ambitious, proud, domineering and she was sometimes ruthless. She was capable, too, of great kindness and generosity . . . an indefatigable worker . . . a woman of great intelligence . . . she had all the unconventionality and all the authority of a genius, who knew she was a genius. She succeeded, unlike most creative artists, in leaving her mark on the musical life of her native land where she is still a living force, thanks to the teachers she taught and the performers she helped and trained.[2]

Another view came from her accompanist, John Lemmone, who described her as

> . . . dynamic, forceful, compelling — but a woman, human and sympathetic. Fiery temperament she had, but it was the fire of a woman with a big mind, big ideas and a personality seldom found more than once in an age. [She was] a strange mixture of human woman and dynamic personality. She always had her way, and always she seemed right. Dame Nellie was a woman of an age; it took a man to understand her.[3]

Helen Porter Mitchell was born on May 19, 1861 in Richmond, then a semi-rural suburb adjoining the infant city of Melbourne. The daughter of a Scottish pioneer, she spent her formative years in a primitive country where society was still in a state of flux after the greatest gold rush in history.

Migrating from Forfar, Scotland, in 1852, her father, David Mitchell, arrived in Australia during a momentous period. In less than two years the immense gold discoveries of 1851 transformed Melbourne from a raw settlement serving as entrepot for the pastoral district of Port Phillip into the capital of the new colony of Victoria.

In 1834 Melbourne consisted of a single house. When Mitchell first saw it eighteen years later, Hobson's Bay was crowded with ships abandoned by crews who were digging for gold. Like most new arrivals, Mitchell joined the gold seekers, but he soon tired of washing for colours along the bush creeks. Returning to Melbourne, he became a building contractor — a well-timed move when a fourth of the population was living under canvas.

Time and place were made for a man of his energy and enterprise. Moreover, he built to last. The quarries and cement works he established are still in operation, while bricks made in his works form part of buildings standing today. In addition to his other enterprises he became a large landowner. Before his death in 1910 he saw Melbourne grow from a mining port into a substantial modern city with a population of more than half a million.

His daughter Helen was the eldest of four girls in a family of seven. The tide of immigration still ran strong while she was a child but as the first effervescence of the gold discoveries subsided, the Victorian mining camps either disappeared altogether or evolved into regular towns.

Music flourished, both as public entertainment and private hobby. The "musical evening" became standard home entertainment, and the ability to play an instrument, usually piano or violin or flute, was a passport to social success. One of the first questions asked about newcomers to a district was "Are they 'musical'?" Musically, the Mitchells were well abreast of their contemporaries. David Mitchell's rugged exterior concealed an excellent bass voice, while the ramifications of his business did not prevent his playing the violin and harmonium. It would not be easy to find a modern magnate so accomplished.

His wife played the piano, violin and harp, while two of her sisters who were regular guests at "Doonside" had excellent voices and possessed musical knowledge "quite exceptional for amateurs". Thus Nellie grew up in a musical atmosphere. Among her earliest memories were crawling under the piano to listen while her mother played, and sitting on her father's knee on a Sunday afternoon while he amused himself at an old harmonium. Later an organ was installed in the drawing room and there were many opportunities to hear well-known visiting musicians, among them the pianist Mme Arabella Goddard who made an outstanding impression on the girl.

Nellie loved to sing and had a habit of going about the house humming to herself. When she was only six years old she appeared at a public concert singing two ballads in the authentic Scottish dialect taught to her by her grandmother. She was a high-spirited child, not at all interested in dolls and picture books, and indifferent to any studies except music. She was sent to a boarding school for several years with the hope that she would receive the discipline her family thought she needed. Later she attended the Presbyterian Ladies' College in Melbourne which was only a short ride from home in one of the four-horse omnibuses for which the city was becoming noted. Here she was a day pupil and studied with Mme Ellen Christian, an English contralto who had been a student of the renowned teacher Manuel Garcia, brother of the famous Mme Malibran. In an interview many years later Mme Christian said,

At that time her youthful voice boasted a sweetness in the lower register by which it resembled the violin tone of Kubelik in legato passages, a fact revealed to me years later while listening to a phonograph record. As 'Melba' she lost the timbre in question under the training necessary to acquire the top notes characteristic of the coloratura repertoire.[4]

37

An Australian musical evening in Melba's time

Nellie's friends remembered her as an expert in the art of whistling popular tunes, an activity sometimes credited with having helped to develop the exceptionally fine breath control for which she was famous at the height of her career. During the lunch hour at the college, while her classmates gathered for sociability, Nellie spent her time practising on the organ, an instrument to which she was much attracted throughout her lifetime.[5] Dr A. E. Floyd, the English organist who came to St Paul's Cathedral in Melbourne in 1911, recalled in an interview fifty years later that on numerous occasions when she was home on a visit Melba would come to the big church and ask him to play for her.

Exactly when Nellie Mitchell determined to adopt music as a career is uncertain. Obviously her father gave her no encouragement. No doubt he was very proud of her accomplishments as singer and pianist, of the invitations she received to appear at private parties and musicales and of her position as organist at Scots Church. Mitchell himself had built this big church as the headquarters of Presbyterianism in Victoria. However the thought of his eldest daughter becoming a public entertainer was quite another matter.

Evidently Nellie had a musical career in mind when about 1880 she began taking lessons from Pietro Cecchi, a former member of one of Lyster's opera companies who had established himself as a teacher in Melbourne. Had her father been in favour of this step, he would probably have paid for the lessons. As it was, Cecchi apparently agreed to wait for his money until she could afford to pay for them out of her earnings. Before that could happen, however, the death of her mother and a younger sister started a train of events which turned the Helen Porter Mitchell of 1881 into the Dame Nellie Melba of history and legend.

So intense was the girl's grief at her mother's death that she ceased to be her gay and out-going self and her father began to worry about her health. Since he was scheduled to take a business trip to Queensland, 1,500 miles away, he suggested that Nellie and her sister Annie accompany him in the hope that the steamer trip and a change of scene and climate would benefit them. He was financially interested in a property in the Mackay district of North Queensland where in the 1870's the importation of labourers from the islands north of Australia had lifted the sugar industry into a state of prosperity.

Mackay sprawled along the estuary of the Pioneer River. At first glimpse, the town which was to have so decisive an influence on her life must have seemed peculiarly romantic to the girl from Melbourne — tropic skies, mild winter days, the off-shore islands with their palms, coral reefs and white beaches, the dark-skinned Kanakas working in the canefields, the sugar schooners in the river, the exotic birds, flowers and insects, and the general air of leisure which reminded American visitors of life in the old South.

The sugar growers had developed a social life mainly centred on the School of Arts, where Nellie Mitchell found her services much in demand as singer and pianist. On October 15, 1882, she wrote to Cecchi, naively informing him of her success at two concerts: "The ladies up here are all jealous of me. I was encored twice for each song and they hurrahed me and threw me no end of bouquets".[6]

Some of the younger women may have had an even stronger reason for their jealousy. In December Nellie left Mackay for Brisbane to marry Charles Nesbitt Frederick Armstrong, twenty-three year old son of an Irish baronet and manager of the Mirani sugar plantation. The marriage took place in the manse of the Ann Street Presbyterian Church, on December 22, 1882. The wedding party which rattled up from the wharf in a four-wheeled cab consisted of David Mitchell, Annie Mitchell and the best man, Arthur Herman Feez, afterwards a well-known Queensland barrister.

Described as a tall, handsome, young Irish gentleman, Armstrong was known in Mackay as 'Kangaroo Charlie'. Whatever the implications of this nickname may have been, he was certainly very unlucky to marry a girl so utterly unsuited for life on a North Queensland sugar plantation. If the pair had any common interests, they did not extend beyond social activities, sex attraction, youth and horses. Temperamentally, they seem to have been far apart. Normally, Nellie Mitchell was high-spirited, impulsively generous, and filled with the joy of life. Armstrong appears to have been quick-tempered and moody.

Once they were married the riding, driving, yachting and dancing came to an end, and the social life of the remote little port disintegrated in the steamy heat of the rainy season. Existence became a battle against humidity, 39 insects, snakes and boredom. The situation was made more difficult when Nellie became pregnant almost immediately, and Armstrong proved to be chronically hard-up. By the time her son was born on October 16, 1883, Nellie Armstrong had decided to return to Melbourne. She wrote to Cecchi that she would like to study for opera but that she would have to earn money at the same time, adding, "There is nothing to detain me now that Mr Armstrong is agreeable".[7]

She had studied both singing and piano but it was as an instrumentalist that Nellie Armstrong was most frequently invited to appear at private gatherings. Soon after her return to Melbourne she played at a reception given by the Marquis of Normanby, then Governor of Victoria. Between piano solos she sang to her own accompaniment and must have felt greatly encouraged when the cosmopolitan Lady Normanby said, "Child, you play brilliantly but you sing better. Some day you will give up the piano for singing and then you will become famous".[8]

Appearances at concerts in Sydney and Melbourne during the next two years led to the growth of her reputation as a singer. Of her performance at a benefit for Herr Elsasser, the former conductor of the Melbourne Liedertafel, on 17th May, 1884, the critic of the *Australasian* wrote "She sings like one out of ten thousand". Two days later the Melbourne *Argus* reported:

> Mrs Armstrong (nee Mitchell) was the only non-professional singer present, but we are glad to think that she was moved to give of talent, as well as good-will toward the object aimed at, because she both surprised and delighted her hearers. She chose the elaborate cavatina, "Ah fors e Lui", from the second act of the opera *La Traviata.* She commenced with something like hesitancy of manner, but as she proceeded this evidence of nervousness wore away and she developed such a high, clear and flexible soprano voice, and such well-trained method as a vocalist, that all hearers who remember the best performances of the opera in this city were caught in the charm that belongs only to good singing, so the kindly and accomplished singer, when she came to the end of her song, instead of receiving only that modified approval that greets the best of amateur effort, was awarded, with good reason, the enthusiastic reward of the accomplished artist. This performance was quite an unexpected treat. It is right to mention here Signor Cecchi was Miss Mitchell's teacher.

This occasion was notable also for the fact that it marked the first appearance on the same programme of Nellie Melba and John Lemmone, the flautist[9] who was to become her life-long associate and general manager.

In 1885 the theatre manager George Musgrove paid Nellie her first professional fee, a modest £20, for singing at a series of concerts. Then for a time she was soloist at the Roman Catholic Church of St Francis, and made a concert tour with the Australian violinist Johannes Kruse. The next year David Mitchell was appointed a commissioner to the Indian and Colonial Exhibition in London and decided to take his daughter and grandson with him. It is said that he hoped that this trip would serve to rid his daughter of the ambition to become a great singer and that if she were not well received in London she would be content to return to Australia and settle down to domesticity.

Before they left home an incident occurred which disturbed Nellie deeply. When it was announced that she was to go abroad her teacher, Signor Cecchi, submitted a bill for about £90 to cover twenty months of tuition and threatened to have her luggage impounded if it were not paid immediately.

Melba about 1890

She raised the money by giving a concert that netted £60 and borrowed the rest from friends. Subsequently, she never mentioned any artistic indebtedness she might have felt towards Cecchi although Thorold Waters described him in his book as "the very man to locate the glowing, pearly rarity of Melba's voice and to make the most of it". Five years later, in 1891, Fanny Simonsen wrote in the Italian publication *Il Mondo Artistico* of her surprise at Melba's failure to express a word of appreciation of the man who she declared had laid the foundation for the diva's career. Whether Melba's silence would have continued if Cecchi had not died the next year is a matter of conjecture. We do know, however, that Melba held no grudge against him because she wrote him a friendly letter a few months after her arrival in London telling of the artists she had heard and of an occasion on which she sang. She gave him her London address and signed herself, "Your old pupil, Nellie Armstrong".

When she set out for London she took with her letters of introduction to several influential people in the musical world but she received little encouragement. Sir Arthur Sullivan advised her, as he did all young singers, to study for a year and then return with the hope of receiving a small part in one of his operas. Brimsmead, the manufacturer of fine pianos, noted that the timbre of her voice was almost as pure as that of one of his instruments but he made no overture to help her. The society teacher, Alberto Randeggo, was not the least interested in an unknown singer from a remote part of the world known only for its wool, wheat, minerals and cricket players.

Despite her lack of success in securing the assistance of those in a position to help launch a career the young Mrs Armstrong's early weeks in London were not wasted. By June she had heard not only the singers Adelina Patti, Christine Nilsson, Emma Albani, Zelia Trebelli, Charles Santley and Edward Lloyd, but also the violinists Sarasate and Halle, and the pianist Vladimir de Pachman whose wife, Marguerite, was New South Wales-born Maggie Oakey, one of Australia's first piano virtuosi. Apparently the only individuals to recognize her great gift were Vert, the concert agent, who tried hard to secure engagements for her, and Wilhelm Ganz, the German pianist and song writer. Having heard her sing "Ah, fors' e lui" in a manner which he thought could not have been bettered, Ganz arranged for her to appear at a dinner for the Royal Theatrical Fund, presided over by Augustus Harris. Known in the world of the theatre as "Augustus Druriolanus", Harris was soon to take over the direction of the Royal Opera House, Covent Garden, and loom large in the subsequent career of Nellie Melba.

At the dinner, her singing of "Ave Maria" made so deep an impression that Ganz arranged an audition with Carl Rosa, but he forgot the appointment. Nellie thereupon picked up her son and left for Paris armed with a letter to the redoubtable Mathilde Marchesi, who she hoped would undertake her training.[10] The success of their first meeting has become history. Having

42

heard her sing, Marchesi dashed out to call to her husband, *"Salvatore, enfin j'ai trouve une etoile!"* Madame was right. She had found a star of such magnitude that the years have not dimmed the memory of its brilliance.

It is evident that Nellie Melba always considered that Marchesi had laid the foundation for her success, and treated her with deep affection all her life. Subsequently Madame herself stated that her chief contribution to her celebrated pupil's vocal progress was in teaching her to sing pianissimo. Cornelius Reed, while discussing the art of the bel canto wrote:

> Marchesi, who claimed the celebrated Melba as her pupil, never 'built' that great voice, or provided it with the flawless technique for which the prima donna was so justly renowned, simply because the nine months of study Melba had with her prior to making a sensational debut was too short a time to do more than polish the technique.[11]

Discussing Melba's probable reasons for seeking out Marchesi, George Bernard Shaw referred to the "advice as to style, habits, phrasing and pronunciation, stage business and tradition, which make eminent professors of singing so useful to pupils who already know how to sing".[12] He failed, however, to mention another essential service Marchesi was able to render. Her influence in the international world of music was so great that any student of hers could be sure of being heard by influential people and under favourable conditions.

On the last day of December, 1886, Nellie Mitchell-Armstrong disappeared from the record, and Mademoiselle — soon Madame — Melba appeared in her place. The transformation occurred at one of Marchesi's "matinees musicales" held at her home in the Rue Jouffroy. According to Melba, the name originated with Marchesi who felt that to sing as Mrs Armstrong would be a handicap. Among the guests in the Rue Jouffroy that afternoon was Moritz Strakosch, the Hungarian pianist, conductor and impresario. As the husband and manager of Carlotta Patti and one of the teachers of her sister Adelina, Strakosch was an authority on sopranos. Having heard Melba sing "Caro nome" he took her aside and persuaded her to sign a ten year contract which virtually gave him control of her actions for the next decade. Doubtless Melba was delighted to think that her vocal career had begun at last, but she soon realized that the contract was much more to Strakosch's advantage than to hers. If it guaranteed her against poverty until the year 1896, it likewise prevented her from taking advantage of better opportunities that might present themselves in the future. One of these opportunities occurred a few months later when Joseph Dupont, principal conductor, and Lapissida, a director, of the Theatre de la Monnaie, Brussels, called on Marchesi in search of a soprano. They auditioned several of her 43 students and then asked, "Where is the Australian?" After hearing Melba sing they immediately offered to engage her for the forthcoming season, their terms being three times Strakosch's figure. Melba's heart sank when she realized that the contract she had signed precluded her acceptance of their offer, but Marchesi felt sure that Strakosch would understand how much the chance in Brussels meant to her and be generous enough to release her.

Strakosch, however, did not intend to let himself be talked out of his legal rights by Marchesi. Loudly denouncing what he called Melba's ingratitude, he assured her that he would not permit her to appear at the Monnaie or anywhere else except under his management. That he meant what he said was apparent when she reached Brussels only to find that he had taken out an injunction to prevent her entering the theatre. Dismayed, she returned to her hotel, flung herself on her bed and lay there all day wondering what she could do.

Her release came in a manner thoroughly operatic. Evening brought Lapissida bounding up the stairs calling "Strakosch est mort!" Death, breaker of all contracts, had come to Strakosch that afternoon. It was 9th October, 1887.

Four days later, Melba made her operatic debut at the Monnaie as Gilda in *Rigoletto*.

Although the operas of the time were lavishly staged and costumed, so little importance attached to the histrionic side that apart from a brief and chilly audition at the Paris Opera, Melba had never been on the stage of a theatre until the hurried rehearsals for her debut at the Monnaie. But if her acting displayed shortcomings, her looks at the age of twenty-six delighted the most captious, while her singing of the role of Gilda made the night memorable in the history of the Brussels opera house.

This performance was followed by equally fine appearances as Violetta and Lucia. The enthusiasm of her audiences increased with each production until it touched something like frenzy when she sang the title role in Delibes' *Lakme* on 8th March, 1888, and a month later Ophelie in the *Hamlet* of Ambroise Thomas. Leo Delibes felt that her interpretations were invested with a magic and poetry far loftier than the ordinary "triumph" of vocalization. He told her, "In a sort of reverie I heard your ideal voice interpreting my work with a superhuman purity. It gave me the keenest and most delicious impression I have ever known in hearing anything I have written".

Brussels critics acclaimed her as "a new and brilliant star" and described her voice as "a revelation, unique in quality, with a remarkable trill and perfect technique". Melba's trill was subsequently remarked on wherever she sang. She once wrote "I was born with a natural trill",[13] and her American accompanist, Samuel Harwell, said it was the most beautifully executed ornament he had ever heard.

44

Melba's trill . . . her marvellous crescendo in the Mad Scene in *Lucia,* remains a vocal feat. It began pianissimo. It grew steadily stronger and stronger, more and more intense and at last . . . that vast auditorium which is the Metropolitan Opera House of New York, just vibrated with its wonderful fortissimo of crystalline purity. What a thing to have heard![14]

The trill remained with her always. In the late 1890's, Anton Siedl wrote:

The trill in her case is of quite fabulous sostenuto; for instance, she has at her command a long powerful crescendo on the highest notes that is without parallel, and yet performed with a clearness and certainty which simply excite astonishment and are at the same time soft, clinging and cajoling.[15]

Many years later Beverley Nicholls persuaded Melba to meet Professor A. M. Low, inventor of the audiometer, an apparatus for photographing sound with which Low made a photographic record of her famous trill. This was reported to be so uniform that it might have been drawn by a geometrician.

During Melba's first Brussels season, the inadvisability of tying herself up to Strakosch for an entire decade was clearly shown when she was asked to appear at Covent Garden, now under the direction of Augustus Harris. In his "Golden Age of Opera",[16] Herman Klein records that Harris had no burning desire to engage Melba, and did so only after considerable persuasion on the part of some of the wealthy and socially powerful ladies connected with the Covent Garden Syndicate. From Melba's point of view, the most important was the immensely influential Lady de Grey, who became her patron and remained her friend for life.

Despite her Brussels success, Melba's Covent Garden debut on 24th May, 1888, was not a triumph. The audience was enthusiastic but small and critics referred more to her powers of acting than to the unique quality of her song. One of them did state that her voice was the best to have been heard since Patti's, but the *Athenaeum* reviewer, after acknowledging her fine performance, added, "But we do not for a moment imagine that Mme Melba will ever hold the highest position in her profession".[17] With the applause of Brussels still ringing in her ears Melba, after three performances at Covent Garden, asked to be released from her contract. Augustus Harris reluctantly agreed to do so adding, "In a little time they will clamour for Melba above all others and, by gad, they will pay for her, too".[18]

After another season at Le Theatre de La Monnaie, Melba made her debut at The Paris Opera on 8th May, 1889, in the role of Ophelie in Thomas' *Hamlet.* This was a great success despite a number of mishaps at the opera house which made it necessary for her to appear with a Hamlet she had never seen before and without having had a single rehearsal with the orchestra. August Vitu, critic of *Le Figaro,* spoke of her success in the early part of the performance and of "a triumph after the Mad Scene which literally moved the listeners to frenzy". He referred to her as the most delicious Ophelie since Christine Nilsson, and added

> . . . Madame Melba has a marvellous soprano voice, equal, pure, brilliant, and mellow, remarkably resonant in the middle register, and rising with a perfect pastosita up to the acute regions of that fairylike major third. That which ravished us was not alone the virtuosity, the exceptional quality of that sweetly timbred voice, the exceptional facility of executing at random diatonic and chromatic scales and trills of the nightingale, it was also that profound and touching simplicity and the justness of accent which caused a thrill to pass through the audience with those simple notes of the middle voice, 'je suis Ophelie'.[19]

Echoes of this great occasion soon reached the other side of the world. "Now that we are basking in the reflected glory of Mrs Armstrong", wrote a correspondent to Melbourne *Punch* in June, 1889, "you will be specially interested in hearing further of the Australian diva. I was fortunate in hearing Madame Melba on her first appearance in Paris as Ophelia. After her scene with Hamlet and the Queen, the curtain had to be raised three times, but her greatest triumph was achieved in the Flower Scene when, amidst the enthusiastic cheering of a critical Parisian audience, the curtain had to be raised again and again, even the ladies joining in the rapturous clamour".[20]

Melba's Paris season produced offers from Madrid and Berlin as well as a letter from Lady de Grey urging her to give Covent Garden another chance. Fully aware now of her own powers, Melba saw to it that nothing was left undone to assure her success this time. She appeared as Juliette, singing Gounod's opera in French with the great tenor Jean de Reszke as Romeo and his baritone brother, Edouard, as Friar Lawrence. When the curtain rose on 15th June, 1889, the big opera house was full and in the audience were Edward, Prince of Wales, and the Princess Alexandra.

An additional reason for this being an important occasion for Melba was that it marked the fulfilment of a long cherished ambition to sing with Jean de Reszke whom she had first heard when a student, in a performance in Paris with Adelina Patti. It also marked the beginning of a long association with the two brothers which continued for the rest of their lives and made their performances together so noteworthy during the "Golden Age".

After subsequent performances as Juliette and as Marguerite the London public recognized that Melba was indeed the British Queen of Song and this she remained until her last performance at Covent Garden on 6th June, 1926.

Melba about the time she returned for her first Australian tour

Every night she sang was a "Melba Night" and tickets were at a premium. All over Europe people were clamouring to hear her. The Czar of Russia invited her to make a series of appearances with the de Reszkes at the Imperial Opera in St Petersburg in February, 1891. She accepted and was acclaimed whenever she sang; on the night of the farewell performance, a group of   47

Russian youths spread their coats on the snow for her to walk on. Czar Alexander the Third added to her already mounting collection of jewels a diamond necklace which was insured for the equivalent of one hundred thousand American dollars when it was exhibited at a benefit in Melbourne in 1963.

After a noteworthy debut in *La Traviata* at Palermo, Italy, in the spring of 1892, Melba appeared at Covent Garden on 5th July with Jean de Reszke in the opera *Elaine* which had been dedicated to them by its composer, Hermann Bemberg. Of this opera George Bernard Shaw wrote:

> I am obliged to *Elaine* for one thing in particular: it reconciled me to Mme Melba, who is to all intents and purposes a new artist this year. I find Madame Melba transfigured, awakened — in sum, her heart, which before only acted on her circulation, now acted on her singing, giving it a charm which it never had before. The change has completely altered her position; from being merely a brilliant singer, she has become a dramatic soprano of whom the best class of work may be expected.[21]

In the autumn of 1892 Melba appeared in *Aida* for the first time. Although critics noted that she displayed great energy as an actress and faultless diction she felt that the role was not suited to her voice and subsequently dropped it from her repertoire. Her initial experience with *Otello* at about the same time was quite different and the role of Desdemona became one of her favourites. The following spring, at the request of the composer, she created the role of Nedda in Leoncavello's *I Pagliacci,* with Fernando de Lucia singing the title role. The opera was received so enthusiastically that it was presented thirteen times in two months. Sir Henry Wood, who played for her rehearsals, recalled that her scale and arpeggio technique were perfect. "Her notes were like a string of pearls, touching, yet separate, strung on a continuous vocal line of tone that was never marred nor distorted."[22]

One of the most vividly-remembered events in Melba's career was her first appearance at La Scala in March 1893, in the role of Lucia. Italian audiences seldom welcomed foreigners and Melba had a hostile reception in Milan, where anonymous letters threatened her with dire consequences should she have the temerity to appear. Halfway through the Mad Scene however, the audience realized that they were hearing a singer who could rival even the beloved Adelina Patti and at the end of it they greeted her with an ovation seldom equalled in the annals of this historic opera house. The Italian press next day commented on "the marvellous felicity of her production, the seduction of *timbre,* the finished art and the pureness of intonation". Her position in Italy was established and she went on to appear in Turin, Genoa, Florence and Rome.

Melba first appeared at the Metropolitan Opera House in New York in 1893, in the distinguished company of Emma Calve, Emma Eames, Lillian Nordica, Sophia Scalchi, the de Reszke brothers, Fernando de Lucia and Pol Plancon. Although she had been singing for only five years Melba's technique and tone production were noted as being unusually natural. Of her debut as Lucia on 4th December the critic H. E. Krehbiel wrote in the *New York Tribune:* "She moved with the greatest of ease in regions which her rivals carefully avoided." W. J. Henderson of the *New York Times* reported that he had never heard another voice just like Melba's stating, "Its beauty, its power, its clarion quality differed from the fluty notes of Patti. It was not a better voice but a different one. It has been called silvery, but what does that signify? There is one quality which it had and which may be comprehended even by those who did not hear her, it had *splendour.* The tones glowed with a starlike brilliance. They flamed with a white flame. And they possessed a remarkable force which the famous singer always used with continence. She gave the impression of singing well within her limits".

Two nights after the performance of *Lucia* Melba appeared as Ophelie in Thomas' *Hamlet* and a week later, on 11th December, as Nedda in the Metropolitan's first performance of *I Pagliacci.* These were roles that had brought her great acclaim in Europe. On 12th January, 1894, she sang the incredibly difficult part of the Queen in *Semiramide,* one of the unusual operas presented by Joan Sutherland during her Australian tour in 1965. *Tannhauser* and *Romeo and Juliette,* both sung in French, completed her repertoire during the first year in New York. Her appearances at the Metropolitan's Sunday evening concerts infused new life into them.

Writing of that season's Metropolitan Opera Company tour of major cities of the United States, Quaintance Eaton[23] refers to Melba's triumph in Chicago, singing Marguerite in *Faust,* as being "as complete and instantaneous as was Sembrich's in 1884". An article in the periodical *Interocean* at about this time speaks of her as "gifted by nature with a graceful personality, queenly figure, expressive eyes", and after noting the phenomenal purity of her voice adds, "we have a new goddess of song".

Melba proved herself to be a great showman as well as a great singer when she appeared as Rosina in *The Barber of Seville* in San Francisco on the eve of the Spanish Civil War. The sinking of the battleship *Maine* had aroused antagonism to all things Spanish and the diva sensed this feeling in the audience. Taking advantage of her privilege to utilize an aria of her own choosing in the "Music Lesson" scene, Melba sang "The Star Spangled Banner" and brought an electrified audience to its feet.

After appearing with the de Reszke brothers in two triumphant opening nights at the Metropolitan — *Romeo and Juliette* on 16th November, 1894, and *Hamlet* on 19th November, 1896 — Melba launched forth on what

As Rosina in The Barber of Seville

Oscar Thompson later referred to as "a celebrated if somewhat disastrous excursion . . . when forsaking the velvet of her coloratura she attempted the declamation of Brunnhilde".[24] Melba sang this role in the opera *Siegfried* against her own better judgement and the advice of Mme Marchesi.

Despite the fine support she received from her friends the de Reszkes and other members of the cast she disappointed the audience and critics alike and afterwards was forced to rest her voice for three months.[25] The morning after the performance H. E. Krehbiel, in a review in the *New York Tribune,* quoted from the Psalms, "there is one glory of the sun, another of the moon and another of the stars; one may not have all three. Mme Melba should have been content with her own particular glory". Another critic addressing the singer herself wrote, "Your voice is like a piece of Dresden china. Please do not smash it". Melba's own comment was characteristically frank, "I've been a fool. I'll never attempt that again".

The composers Delibes, Gounod, Massenet, Thomas and Verdi all helped Melba prepare roles in their operas. Thomas called her the "Ophelie of my dreams"; To both Massenet and Joachim, the violin virtuoso, she was "Madame Stradivarius"; and Saint Saens named his opera *Helene* for her. The reputations of these composers had all been made before Melba appeared on the scene; Puccini, on the other hand, was somewhat of a controversial figure, musically speaking, when she went to Lucca in 1898 to study *La Boheme* with him. At the time considerable prejudice existed against him in the higher musical circles; even in Italy many regarded him as a purveyor of cheap sentiment. Melba, however, expressed the belief that he was the coming composer and it is scarcely an exaggeration to say that it was she who established *La Boheme* in the standard repertoire. After singing the role of Mimi in Philadelphia she persuaded the Covent Garden Syndicate to mount the opera. It received its first London performance on 19th May, 1899, with the diva as Mimi, Fernando de Lucia as Rudolfo and the sprightly Zelie de Lussan as Musetta. Six months later it was presented at the Metropolitan Opera House in New York and has never lost its world popularity.

Few singers have become as closely associated with a role as Melba did with Mimi. Many people thought Puccini wrote *La Boheme* for her, yet she did not appear in it until she had passed her thirty-seventh birthday and was by no means physically ideal for the role of the consumptive young model of the Montmartre tenement. Nor did the gifted Caruso, with whom she sang it for the first time at Monte Carlo in 1902 remotely resemble a starving poet of 1830 vintage. None the less, the famous pair became symbols of grand opera as no others have before or since. Many people have testified to the eerie effect of her singing in the duet at the end of the first act. As Mary Garden described it, "The note came floating over the auditorium of Covent Garden. It was Melba's throat, it left Melba's body, it left everything and came like a star and passed us in our box and went out into the infinite . . .".[26] How greatly Melba's singing of Mimi aided the popularity of *La Boheme* is a matter of history. Many people, however — some of them her greatest admirers — regretted that she clung to the role for nearly thirty years.

Some commentators have asserted that Melba never encouraged anyone who might be able to challenge her supremacy and made sure that she was never adequately supported by a first-rate Musetta. Whether or not this is completely true she found a summary way of dealing with the Austrian soprano Fritzi Scheff who was endowed with unusual histrionic ability. Percy Colson who was present at a performance of *La Boheme* at Covent Garden early in 1903, recounted that during the second act while Fraulein Scheff was singing the "Waltz Song" and preparing to take the high 'B natural' at the end, "a clear angelic voice in the wings landed on it with effortless

51

ease and sang the rest of the phrase with her". The audience whispered "Melba" and after the curtain fell Neil Forsyth, the manager, announced that due to an indisposition, Fraulein Scheff would not be able to continue with her role but that Madame Melba had kindly consented to complete the evening by singing the Mad Scene from *Lucia di Lammermoor*. Fraulein Scheff was described as expressing "the extremity of displeasure" and the following day was on her way back to Vienna.

Melba frankly admitted to Herman Bemberg that she could not bear any other artist on the same programme to get as much applause as she. It must have disturbed her then, even to share the honours of the evening with Emma Calve, when, in 1895, the Metropolitan first linked *Cavalleria Rusticana* to *I Pagliacci* and created the famous double bill. Calve sang Santuzza while Melba followed with Nedda making a marvellous evening for the audience but not necessarily for the two stars. Fortunately their orbits, though coming dangerously close, bisected each other only when "as a special courtesy to the management" Melba sang Micaela to Calve's Carmen.

Fritzi Scheff did not emerge from her encounter with Melba as well as did the celebrated Italian baritone, Titta Ruffo, who went to England in 1901 to sing at Covent Garden. He was billed to substitute for Antonio Scotti who was too ill to sing Rigoletto to Melba's Gilda. To Ruffo's astonishment the diva refused to appear with him, on the ground that, at twenty-four, he was too young to be cast as her father. Ruffo, however, had good cause to believe that the real reason was the ovation he had received from the orchestra and chorus at the dress rehearsal at which Melba had refused to sing. Giving full rein to his Tuscan temperament, the infuriated Ruffo told Higgins, the director, what he thought of Covent Garden and, presumably, of Melba. So pungent were his remarks that Higgins threatened legal action, whereupon Ruffo fled to Italy. Years later, when he was one of the leading baritones of the world, Melba stopped in Naples on her way back to Australia. Having heard him in *L'Africaine* and *Hamlet* she offered to appear with him at the San Carlo. This was Ruffo's opportunity, and he made the most of it by requesting the director to give Madame Melba his compliments and to inform her that she was now too old to sing with him.

In 1902 she returned to her native land for the first time since leaving it sixteen years before. Great changes had taken place. The Federation of the six colonies had transformed Australia from a geographical abstraction into a new nation of which Melba, now an assured woman of forty one, was the best-known representative. She had arranged with George Musgrove to organize a concert tour for her and his former partner, J. C. Williamson, suggested that she should appear afterwards in *La Boheme* with a small Italian opera company he was then recruiting. If anyone in Australia had any doubt about the heights to which David Mitchell's daughter had risen, they became fully aware of where she stood when Williamson announced that he could not meet the diva's terms, which, among other stipulations, called for £400 a performance, the engagement of the costly tenor Albert Saleza, and French pitch in the orchestra.

Reaching Australia by way of Canada, Melba began her first Australian concert tour in Brisbane on 14th September, 1902. Everywhere she received the kind of welcome which up to that time had been reserved for the rare visits of royalty. When she sang at the Melbourne Town Hall, traffic in Collins and Swanston streets was practically suspended and police had to fight all evening to get the cable trams across the intersection and the carriages to and from the hall. Musgrove, who had paid Nellie Armstrong £20 for a series of concerts seventeen years before, handed Nellie Melba a cheque for £2,350, her share of the proceeds for a single night's performance.

After the concert tour, Melba gave Australians a glimpse of what Williamson had deprived them of, when she appeared at the Princess Theatre, Melbourne, and the Theatre Royal, Sydney, in scenes from *Faust, La Traviata* and *Rigoletto.* In these excerpts, which were complete with costumes and scenery, she had the assistance of several members of George Musgrove's Opera Company, including Louis Ahrens, the tenor, Lempriere Pringle, the Tasmanian basso, and Madame Slapoffski, the soprano, whose husband, Gustav, conducted the orchestra. She left Australia to the plaintive strains of "Wull ye no come back again?" and with the knowledge that her absence had made her not less, but more an Australian than she had ever been.

In 1907 and 1908 Melba did some of the finest singing of her career during the two seasons she appeared at Oscar Hammerstein's new opera house in the Manhattan Center in New York. The previous autumn Hammerstein had spent much time and effort trying to persuade her to become a member of a new company he was forming but she had steadfastly declined his many offers. On one of these occasions after Melba had withdrawn from an interview Hammerstein scattered £4,000 in bank notes on her living-room floor before leaving. Melba, still uncommitted, banked the money in Hammerstein's name but later, impressed by what she called his "pluck" in attempting this operatic venture, she accepted a very favourable contract with him.[27]

Her first appearance at the Manhattan Center was in *La Traviata* on 2nd January, 1907. The house was sold out and Hammerstein was so delighted that he met Melba at the stage door and had her stand on the stage behind the huge curtain to listen to the dull roar of conversation in the crowded house. As the curtain rose Melba was greeted with thunderous applause, quite contrary to the custom of this period. As soon as her voice rang out with its famous bell-like clarity Melba knew that she and Hammerstein had won at least temporarily the battle to establish a second opera centre in New York City.[28] Reviewing the performance in the *New York Times* Richard

Aldrich wrote: "Her vocalism has its old time lusciousness and purity, its exquisite smoothness and fullness; Mme Melba's singing of Violetta was a delight from beginning to end". Of her performance on 11th January, in *Rigoletto,* with Bonci and Renaud — a costly and delicate casting of three famous artists — John Pitts Sanborn, another well-known music critic, wrote: "The voice of Madame Melba is sculptural; it has the qualities of physical form. The voluptuous large body of her voice takes shape in the air . . . she can lay out a note as a painter lays colour on his canvas, so that it stays there . . . as if it had and would always exist".

The mutual interest which Melba and Hammerstein shared in presenting *La Boheme,* notwithstanding the many attempts of the management of the Metropolitan to prevent it, is an interesting story but cannot be recounted here. On the morning after the performance of this opera — 2nd March, 1907 — the *New York Times* reported, "She (Melba) sang the music more beautifully than she had anything else this season in New York". This was the opera in which she also gave her last performance of the season and after which, as an encore, she sang the Mad Scene from *Lucia.* Melba had originally agreed to sing at ten performances but had extended the number to fifteen and had declined all offers to appear elsewhere in New York City. A farewell

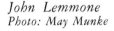

John Lemmone
Photo: May Munke

54

statement was issued to the press the day before she left for Europe, which stated in part: "I have never enjoyed any season in America as much as the one now closing . . . I am proud to have been associated with Mr Hammerstein in his launching of New York's new opera house . . . His pluck appealed to me from the first, and I leave, as I came, his loyal friend and admirer."[29]

Melba had filled the theatre every time she sang, and had helped to rescue the reckless Hammerstein from bankruptcy; but all her efforts could not establish his opera house permanently. After what his son Arthur called "four years of torture", he sold out to the Metropolitan, one of the conditions being that he was not to produce opera again in New York for ten years. This condition, alone, speaks for the strength of the competition Hammerstein's venture had offered to the older establishment on Broadway.

Between her two seasons with Hammerstein and after her last performance at the Manhattan Opera House, Melba made short trips to Australia, one of them to be with her father on his eightieth birthday. She returned to London, however, in time to celebrate her twentieth year at Covent Garden at a charity matinee on 24th June, 1908, at which she and Emmy Destinn raised £2,000 for the London Hospital. She sang the first act of *La Traviata* and Destinn the first act of *Madame Butterfly*.

From 1906 to 1908 Melba had divided her time between the United States and Australia and had taken no part in the Covent Garden seasons. She was vacationing on the Riviera in the autumn of 1907 when Tetrazzini made her sensational debut there. However, by 1909 when audiences began to clamour for her return she agreed to appear for single performances of operas in her repertoire for her usual fee of 500 guineas. This was also the amount she was receiving at the height of her career for private appearances at the homes of wealthy patrons in London and New York. Hostesses sometimes invited her to their parties hoping that she would sing without a fee. But as one Australian writer pointed out, "No one ever bustled David Mitchell's daughter out of her due". When a hostess approached her saying, "Surely, Madame, it is no trouble to sing a little song", she would reply: "No more trouble than to write a little cheque".

It was also in 1909 that Melba was able to fulfil a long-held wish to sing to her countrymen in the remote areas of the Outback. Incidents frequently occurred on this tour which revealed how much her appearances meant to people in isolated areas. One evening Melba was seated in the ante-room of a hall in a small town when she felt a draft from a window that John Lemmone, her manager, had closed a few minutes earlier. Looking out she saw two urchins crouching in the rain hoping to hear at least part of the concert. She invited them inside and after the performance said to them in jest, "Now boys you owe me a guinea each". The younger one came forward with a smile and said, "Madame, we owe you much more than that".

55

A similar sense of indebtedness had been expressed during Melba's first visit in 1902 by Professor Marshall-Hall. In a welcoming address he said:

> You represent to us all the possibility, the promise, the glamour of that rich imaginary world which each one secretly in his heart of hearts dreams attainable . . . you represent more than a particular person . . . you represent an idea . . . Your living presence has compelled this immature, partially cultured, somewhat unintellectual city to dimly feel for a moment the presence of art, the supreme manifestation of joyous strength.[30]

After Melba's return to London in 1909 the plan to take her own opera company to Australia began to take shape. With representatives of J. C. Williamson and Company she visited the musical centres of Europe to select outstanding artists.[31] When John Lemmone returned to make final arrangements for the season in 1911 he asserted that at fifty years of age Melba's voice was as fresh as ever. He quoted Dr Milson Rees, the eminent Harley Street specialist who had peered down nearly every musical throat in Europe, as saying that Melba's vocal cords were the most elastic he had ever seen and that her voice would never grow old. Melba had hoped that Caruso would be a member of the company but he declined because of the long journey and in his stead came the twenty-six year-old Irish tenor John McCormack, who was promised a concert tour after the opera season in order to make the trip worthwhile financially. The company opened at Her Majesty's Theatre, Sydney, on Saturday, 23rd September, 1911 with *La Traviata*. The demand for tickets was enormous. Scalpers who bought up places in the Gallery at seventy-five cents, were able to unload them at a profit of anything up to 1000 per cent.

At that time, the Gallery had not been dignified by any such title as Upper Circle and reserved seats were not issued for that elevated region. Patrons of "the gods" — originally so called because they were perched beside the mythological deities usually frescoed on theatre ceilings — sat on hard backless benches, their feet wedged between the people in front. Expert packers jammed them together in a solid mass, not an inch of space being wasted. Uncomfortable though this was, it developed a feeling of unity which helped to detonate the explosions of enthusiasm which were a feature of live theatre in its greatest days.

The premiere of the first Melba-Williamson opera company was a series of such demonstrations, culminating in an immense ovation at the finale, when the diva was left standing alone on a stage knee-deep in flowers. Those who had heard Melba before agreed that her marvellous voice had not deteriorated, despite her fifty years. Oddly, J. C. Williamson himself did not witness her triumph. While she was on her way to Australia, he left for

Europe, their ships crossing in the Indian Ocean, so that the task of keeping the opera season running smoothly devolved on George Tallis and Hugh J. Ward. At the time, it was said that although Williamson had steeled himself against losing money on the season, his heart quailed at the thought of facing Melba if it failed.

It did not fail, although Melbourne did not respond as Sydney had done. The original plan had been to play eight weeks in each of the capital cities, but although tickets for the Melba nights in the Victorian capital were always sold out, attendance at other performances fell off to such an extent that the diva cancelled the last eleven nights of the Melbourne season and moved the company back to Sydney. This was the only time many Australians had an opportunity to hear the diva in the roles for which she had become celebrated — Lucia, Mimi, Gilda, Marguerite, Ophelie, Julietta, Desdemona and Violetta. When she had sung Desdemona in *Otello* during the previous season of the Boston Opera Company Melba was said to have "triumphed by the sheer perfection of her singing and the unearthly quality of her voice. At the completion of the 'Ave Maria' the audience rose in a body to applaud".[32]

The 1911 Melba-Williamson season of grand opera was considered enormously successful. Despite production costs of £4,000 a week the partners were reported to have split a profit of £30,000, an enormous sum in light of the purchasing power of money at that time. Cynics who suggested that the diva had been interested primarily in the prospect of large financial returns ignored the fact that at this time she was one of the world's wealthiest artists. If making money had been her principal objective she could have made it more easily from a concert tour without any of the worries of an opera season. She had told a reporter for the Melbourne *Argus* on 16th February, 1910, "It is my greatest ambition to be able to present grand opera in Australia on the same line as it is presented in the great opera houses of the world . . . When I have appeared in grand opera here my highest ambition will have been realized". To this end she wished to appear in her best roles supported by other artists of high calibre. Before leaving for London she gave a concert in March, 1912, to raise money to erect the concert hall which bears her name at the Melbourne University Conservatorium. One of the titles she valued most highly was earned during this period when she sold a flag for £2,100 at a concert for Belgian Relief and was called "The Empress of Pickpockets".

On 22nd May, 1913, John McCormack appeared with Melba in a special performance of *La Boheme* to which he referred later as, "The memorable occasion when she celebrated the quarter of a century of professional life at Covent Garden", adding "it must always be reckoned amongst the great events of my life. I had the honour of being Rudolpho. I never witnessed such a demonstration. It was a splendid tribute to a marvellous woman and incom-

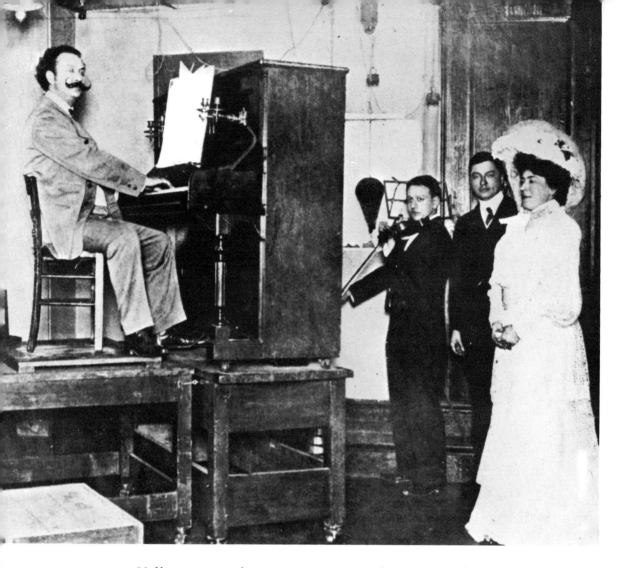

Melba at a recording session. Between the years 1904 and 1926, she made more than 150 gramophone records

parable artist. I believe — in fact, I know — that I sing better with Melba than with any other soprano . . . It is an inspiration".

That same season Melba also appeared in *La Boheme* with Caruso when he returned to Covent Garden for the first time after an absence of seven years. Of this performance a review next day stated: "They sang as if truly inspired." Early in 1914 she appeared in Paris with the Boston Opera Company and later toured the United States and Canada with Jan Kubelik, the violinist returning to London for the closing of the opera season at Covent Garden.

The outbreak of war in August 1914 was a great blow to Melba, who had closer contacts with Europe than any other Australian had ever had. Returning to Coombe Cottage, her home at Lilydale near Melbourne, she turned it into a headquarters from which she organized concerts in aid of the Red Cross, travelling all over Australia to make personal appearances. She extended her activities to New Zealand, Canada and the U.S.A., and according to the *Sydney Morning Herald* of 24th February, 1931, she raised more than £100,000 for patriotic purposes.

During this period Melba also devoted much time and attention to training voice students at the Melbourne Conservatorium in Albert Street.[33] She had become interested in this institution because operas were being produced there regularly and the singing was of high quality. One day she sent for the director and inquired abruptly, "Fritz Hart, what would you do if I offered to come to the Conservatorium and teach singing?".[34] Of course Hart was delighted and the students had many memorable experiences, some of which are described in an article in the student magazine.[35] On one of these occasions, after a student had sung the aria from *Herodias,* "Dame

This portrait was said to be one of the singer's favourites

Nellie, who had been pacing the broad middle aisle during the performance, swung round suddenly and said 'Sing it this way: Il est bon, il est doux.' A thrill went through us all as she painted those two short phrases with just the lovely tone colour she desired. They will remain in the memory of all those who heard them".[36]

Melba's work with individual pupils was described in 1965 by Miss Ethel Walker, librarian for J. C. Williamson's in Sydney. She recalled that,

Melba had the most dynamic personality and, great as she was, found time to impart to us Australians much of her wonderful knowledge . . . She would hear me sing and give me advice and, believe me, Melba could teach you more in ten minutes than many could in six months (or ever) . . . When I met her later in New York where I was playing and showed her the good notices I had received for my part as Teresa in *The Maid of the Mountains* she said she was proud of me. Melba liked people to stand on their own feet and fight for themselves.

The diva's method of teaching was an extension of that of the renowned Garcia which she had learned from his pupils Mme Ellen Christian and Mme Mathilde Marchesi. Melba was said to have been "an indefatigable worker who tired out everyone in the studio but herself. She left fresher than she came although she appeared habitually at an early hour and expected students to report on the dot for their lessons". Shortly after her death, John Lemmone wrote:

On her frequent returns from abroad, Melba's first visit was always to the Conservatorium. I have known her to arrive in Melbourne in the morning — after two years' absence! — and be at the Conservatorium in the afternoon. She frequently spent from 9 a.m. until lunch, giving gratuitous lessons. Had you seen her there, with her enthusiasm, her kindly encouragement, you would have forgotten your Melba of the theatre in your love of Melba the helper.[37]

The important role she played in recognizing and encouraging the development of talent wherever she found it is illustrated by the story of her encounter with Lauri Kennedy, the cellist. He says,

I shall never forget Melba. Indeed it is to her that I owe my career and whatever success and position I have achieved. In 1919 I was playing, with several others, at a little concert arranged by Fritz Hart at the Albert Street Conservatorium in Melbourne at which Melba was present and I little dreamed that this day was to be the turning point in my life. I cannot remember the details of the concert which pursued the even tenor of its course, but I sat down to play in all modesty. When I had finished, bedlam broke loose. I dimly remember Melba standing up in the middle of the people, shouting, "Bravo! Bravo! Encore! He must play an encore". Still in a daze, I was confronted with the great lady. She said: "What are you doing here! You have a great talent and a career before you. You must go abroad!"

These words had a great impact on the young artist:

When I got home that day, I sat down to think things out. I had, up to that time played quite-naturally, taking it for granted, and never thinking there was anything remarkable in what I could do.[38] Melba had now, however, started new thoughts in my head. If such a great artist thought I had talent, and made such a fuss, I reasoned, perhaps I could become a great player and make my name in the world.[39]

Melba was in the United States continuing her Red Cross concerts after the Armistice, when she was called to London to take part in the peace celebrations. In 1918 she was made Dame Commander of the newly established Order of the British Empire, the equivalent of a knighthood. Later she made a tour of the English provinces and opened and closed the 1920 opera season at Covent Garden, in *Romeo and Juliette*. After the war Melba's appearances in Australia became more frequent.[40] In 1923 she was back in London singing at a benefit performance for Mme Albani and in *La Boheme* with the British National Opera at Covent Garden as a gesture of support for the many Australians who were singing with this company.

Roland Foster relates an interesting incident concerning a visit Melba made to the New South Wales Conservatorium. As was his custom, the Director Henri Verbruggen took charge of the Diploma class on Monday afternoons and gave strict instructions that under no circumstances was he to be disturbed. An insistent demand by Melba sent a messenger up to announce her but the diva had to wait. When Verbruggen finally appeared she said jokingly, "Henri, this is a nice way to treat the Queen of Song", to which he replied with a smile, "But I am King of the Conservatorium and the King can do no wrong".

Melba's immense personal popularity was partly due to her high regard for her public, no matter what they paid at the box office. Gallery patrons long remembered her admiration for their fortitude in waiting hours for theatre doors to open and then sitting on hard benches until the performance started.

More than once during the 1911 season she arranged with a nearby   61 caterer to have afternoon tea sent up to the early comers while at the final performance she ascended in person to the "gods" and thanked them so warmly for their appreciation that the packed multitudes felt they had made a real contribution to the success of the occasion. During her visit in 1921 Melba announced in December that owing to the disappointment expressed by many who had been unable to afford the minimum price of a guinea a seat required at her earlier concerts she had decided to give a series at which no seat would cost more than five shillings and sixpence. When she heard that speculators had bought up tickets for the first concert of the series and sold them at higher prices, she stationed herself outside the box office when bookings opened for the later ones and saw that no one bought more than enough for his own personal use. History records many instances of artists hoping wistfully for a rush on the box office, but Melba provides the sole example of a star trying to restrict the sale of tickets. In the end she check-mated the scalpers by increasing the number of concerts until more than 70,000 people in Melbourne and Sydney had heard the diva at phenomenally low cost.

In 1924 Melba brought another opera company to Australia in conjunction with J. C. Williamson Ltd. The post-war absence of German, Australian and Russian artists was compensated for by a strong contingent of Italians, including the celebrated soprano Toti dal Monte, who became immensely popular as did Apollo Granforte and Dino Borgioli.[41] Once more Melba was heard in *La Bohème* and proved that her voice, unimpaired at sixty-three, was still capable of filling the theatre with the famous floating high C.

The Melbourne season closed with another performance of *Bohème* for the benefit of the Limbless Soldiers' Association. By auctioning boxes and seats total proceeds reached £18,000. That performance also marked the inauguration of broadcasting in Victoria; the complete opera was transmitted from station 3AR giving the few hundred radio owners of Victoria a share in the historic occasion.

Melba spent most of 1925 in England completing her recollections which were published under the title *Melodies and Memories*.[42] Then, in anticipation of giving a farewell concert at Covent Garden, she made a last tour of other English cities. The official farewell took place on June 8, 1926, and was a brilliant event. The programme opened with Melba singing Act II of *Romeo and Juliette* under the baton of Sir Percy Pitt; Vincenza Bellezza conducted the rest of the programme which included Act IV of *Othello,* and Acts III and IV of *La Bohème* in which three other Australian singers, John Brownlee, Fred Collier and Browning Mummery appeared with her. The greater part of this performance, including Melba's farewell speech after the final curtain, was recorded by Mapleson. Of this occasion John Brownlee wrote:

As Marguerite de Valois, 1896

How can one describe such a night, when the whole of England, from the Royal family down, had come to pay homage to another kind of queen? The atmosphere was charged almost beyond endurance, and at the end of it all the ovation, with all its overtones of love, affection and adoration, as only the cold English can bestow them upon those whom they worship.[43]

On December 7 of the same year Melba gave a final performance of *La Bohème* at the Old Vic to augment the funds being raised by Lilian Baylis to establish opera at the Sadler's Wells theatre. The Musetta of the occasion was the Australian soprano Gertrude Johnson, who later was to train so many young Australians for roles with the Sadler's Wells company.

Eventually the sands of farewell tours and last appearances ran out. In 1928 Dame Nellie brought her third opera company to Australia. It was long remembered for introducing *Turandot* and *The Love of Three Kings* to Australian audiences, and for the magnificent presentations of *Aida* with

63

Anna Surana in the name part and John Brownlee as King of the Ethiopians. The diva herself said farewell to the operatic stage in Sydney in August 1928, forty-two years after her debut in Brussels. In November she made her last Australian appearance in a concert in Geelong. After this she returned to London.

On her final visit to Covent Garden, the scene of many triumphs, she seemed to have a premonition of her death because she is said to have shivered suddenly and said, "I can see ghosts here. There are Caruso, Forsyth and others of the past". Then she broke down and wept inconsolably and said she would never return. At about this time her splendid health began to fail. Returning to Australia by ship she was taken gravely ill in Cairo and on reaching Sydney was taken to St Vincent's hospital where she died on 23rd February, 1931, in her seventieth year.

After a funeral service at the Scots Church, Melbourne, long associated with the Mitchell family, Melba was buried in the Lilydale cemetery near her beloved Coombe Cottage and in sight of the beautiful Dandenongs. At the end of the burial service the Melbourne Liedertafel sang *The Long Day Closes* and after a brief silence a chorus of Australian song birds rose from the nearby gum trees. They sang a fitting requiem to the passing of a great Australian.[44]

Melba's centenary in 1961 was celebrated in many ways in different parts of the world. A Homage to Melba Committee in Melbourne organized a memorial exhibition; Australia issued a special commemorative postage stamp, and Angel Records of London released a Melba disc in their "Great Recordings of the Century" series. On November 22, 1962, a stained glass window designed by Brian Thomas was installed in the Musicians' Memorial Chapel in St Sepulchre's Church, London, portraying a medallion of Melba with full length figures depicting her favourite roles on either side.

Roland Gelatt reviewing Joseph Wechsberg's book *Red Plush and Black Velvet*[45] in 1961, provided an excellent picture of Melba as a prima donna. He wrote:

> She began with an incomparable voice. For this we have the testimony not only of ear witnesses who heard her in person, but also of the recorded legacy she left us[46] . . . most notably two actual-performance recordings, one made from the stage of the Metropolitan Opera House on primitive cylinder equipment in 1901, the other made from the stage of Covent Garden with benefit of microphones at Melba's farewell in 1926. It is hard to say which is more incredible, the recklessly brilliant coloratura on the early cylinder or the serene purity of tone and magical legato of the 65-year-old veteran. Certainly you will not hear her like today.

Melba's voice was not the only element that gave her stature as a prima donna. She was good looking; she had the air and bearing of a great personage, and she was given to saying and doing exactly as she pleased. Her forthright tongue and her penchant for young men were the talk of Europe. She was also rich . . . and Melba did not boggle at spending as lavishly as she earned.

Melba, a film produced in Hollywood in 1952, although considered entertaining by a large segment of the American public, seemed far from an acceptable picture to those familiar with the facts of her life. Evan Senior the Australian-born editor of *Music and Musicians* ended a review with the statement, "No, I do not have to wonder what Melba would have to say about *Melba.* Her command of blistering invective far outshone anything I could summon up for the purpose. She would have blasted the whole film from its wide screen."[47] A far better portrayal was the radio serial *The Melba Story,* first broadcast over a nationwide hook-up in Australia in 1946 with Glenda Raymond, a leading Melbourne soprano, playing the title role and singing many of the operatic arias associated with the diva's career.

The best portraits, however, probably are those that lie embedded in the living memories of those who knew her well. Freda Barrymore, a Tasmanian journalist, wrote: "Had I met Melba against any other background than Coombe Cottage, Lilydale, I doubt that she would have appeared to be the same person. When I saw her later in London, Paris and America it always seemed to me that only in her Australian home was she the real woman as well as the artist. She was much happier there and less sophisticated, more interested in simple things".[48]

John Brownlee, Melba's most illustrious vocal protege, recalls: "She could be graciously warm or uncompromisingly frigid; tolerant to novitiates, she liked to queen it over her equals. Outwardly austere, Melba never wore her heart where it could be seen. She went out of her way to make contacts for her proteges. She was almost fanatical in her attempts to foster young talent and was never happier than when surrounded by a group of young ambitious singers, who were sincere in their attempts to strive for a professional career".

Melba was the first of a distinguished line of singers whose fine voices and strong personalities have brought Australia to the attention of the world as a cradle of musical talent.

NOTES

[1]*British Australasian,* April 19, 1906.
[2]Thompson, J., *On Lips of Living Men,* Melbourne, Lansdowne Press, 1961.
[3]The *Sun,* Sydney, January 24, 1932.
[4]*Sydney Morning Herald,* 1927.

[5]Reid, M., *And the Ladies came to Stay,* Melbourne, Presbyterian Ladies' College, 1961.

[6]Waters, T., *Much Besides Music,* Melbourne, Georgian House, 1951.

[7]Ibid.

[8]Murphy, A. G., *Melba,* London, Chatto and Windus, 1909.

[9]John Lemmone was considered one of the greatest flute virtuosi of his time but he was closely associated with Melba for so long a period that his achievements as an artist in his own right were often overlooked.
He was born in 1861 at Ballarat, Victoria. When he was a child his father bought a penny whistle and offered to give a fife to the first of his three young sons who learned to play a tune on it. John won the contest but practised so persistently that the family forced him out of the house and on to the common to play. One day, when passing a pawnbroker's shop, he spied a flute in the window and determined to have it. Not possessing the required 12/6 he dredged a small quantity of gold from the creek that flowed through the town and became the proud owner of his first flute. Years later he said "I have since had special instruments made for me by the best makers of flutes in the world but somehow none has equalled this in my regard. It was my whole world. It moulded my destiny and the walk in life that I would sincerely follow again".

[10]In her memoirs Marchesi wrote: "The wife of the Austrian Consul in Melbourne gave her a letter to me. This lady was Mme Elise Pinschoff (nee Wiedermann) one of my former pupils and for several years a distinguished opera comique singer". — Marchesi, M., *Memoirs,* London, Harper Bros., 1897.

[11]Reed, C. L., *Bel Canto — Principles and Practice,* New York, Coleman & Ross, Co., 1950.

[12]Shaw, G. B., *Music in London, 1890-1894,* Vol. 2, London, Constable & Co., 1932.

[13]*New York Herald Tribune Magazine,* May 28, 1961.

[14]Duval, J. H., *Svengali's Secrets and Memoirs of The Golden Age,* New York, Robert Speller and Sons, 1965.

[15]Murphy, op. cit.

[16]Klein, H., *Golden Age of Opera,* London, Routledge, 1933.

[17]*Sydney Morning Herald,* 24th February, 1931.

[18]Murphy, op. cit.

[19]Ibid.

[20]Some of the French papers with hostile inclination made themselves ridiculous in the eyes of cultured citizens of that city by writing that they did not want "Aborigines" in the classic music halls of Paris. Continental journalists were always rather baffled by Australians. If not aborigines, what were they? Twenty-five years before, Sydney-born Lucy Chambers had been referred to as a "creole" by the newspapers of Florence.

[21]Shaw, op. cit.

[22]Wood, H., *My Life of Music,* London, Gollancz, 1946.

[23]Eaton, Q., *Opera Caravan,* New York, Farrar, Straus, Cudahy, 1957.

[24]Thompson, O., *The American Singer,* New York, The Dial Press, 1927.

[25]Why Melba ever essayed a role so patently unsuited to her voice and temperament was not clear. Perhaps she wished to prove that she could equal any other singer in versatility as well as surpassing most in vocal quality.

[26]Garden, M., and Biancolli, L., *The Mary Garden Story,* New York, Simon and Schuster, 1951.

[27]Colson, op. cit.

[28]Sheehan, V., *Oscar Hammerstein I,* New York, Simon and Schuster, 1956.

[29]Sheehan, op. cit.

[30]Murphy, op. cit.

[31]Among these were Mme Jeanne Wayda, the Countess Eleanora de Cisneros and Rosina Buckman. The men included the tenors Ciccolini and Juesnel, bass baritones Edmund Burke, Alfred Kaufman and Andreas Scandiani. The principal conductor was Angelini and the producer Frank Rigo.

[32]Eaton, Q., *The Boston Opera Company, Its History,* New York, Appleton Century Company, 1965.

[33]This was later to be renamed in her honour and to have £8000 bequeathed to it by her for a scholarship to be used "in the search for a successor".

[34]Hart, F., "Words from Honolulu", *Melba Conservatorium Magazine,* No. 5, 1938.

[35]Sutton, V., and Tregear, W., "Those Were the Days", *Melba Conservatorium Magazine,* No. 12, 1945.

[36]Editorial, *Melba Conservatorium Magazine,* No. 10, 1943.

[37]The *Sun,* Sydney, 24th January, 1932.

[38]This is an attitude encountered among many Australian artists. When it was mentioned to Sir William McKie in his study at Westminster Abbey he considered for a moment and then commented, "That is a very interesting observation; I had never thought there was anything extraordinary in what I had done before I came to England".

[39]Kennedy had never received any instruction on the cello. He had learned to play by studying each evening by candlelight under the stage where the Kennedy Concert Company had performed earlier and while the others packed in preparation for moving on to the next town the following day.

[40]In 1919 she gave a concert with the Australian violinist, Leila Doubleday and others at the Sydney Conservatorium and when John Lemmone became ill she quickly arranged a benefit performance for him which raised more than £2,500. In 1921, after an extensive tour of the United States she gave another series of concerts in Australia with Lemmone as flautist, and Una Bourne as pianist; several concerts were also given in conjunction with the New South Wales State Orchestra under the direction of Henri Verbruggen who later became conductor of the Minneapolis Symphony Orchestra.

[41]Sixteen operas were presented, among them *Andrea Chenier* for the first time. The Australian singers were Vera Bedford, Doris McInnes, Rita Miller, Rosa Pinkerton, Anita Roma, Strella Wilson, Vida Sutton, Roy Dunn and Alfred O'Shea (brought back from Europe by Melba). Later in the season Eileen Castles joined the company. Frank St Leger, one of the conductors, had been Melba's accompanist, and later became an administrator of prima donnas and legers at the Metropolitan Opera House.

[42]Published by Thornton, Butterworth, London, 1925.

[43]*Saturday Review* (New York), 25th December, 1954.

[44]*Walkabout,* Vol. 27, No. 5, May 1961.

[45]*The New York Times Book Review,* 17th December, 1961.

[46]Between the years 1904 and 1926 Melba made over 150 recordings, more than a third of which, it is said, were never released. Of the royalties on these records which were sold for a guinea each (which at the time was roughly equivalent to five American dollars, half went to the singer. Referring to this income Peter Dawson once remarked in a radio interview, "Imagine how the wool grew while she slept".

[47]*Music and Musicians,* London, September, 1953.

[48]"The Great Melba", *Women's Weekly,* Sydney, May 6, 13, 20, 27, 1957.

Amy Sherwin

5

Melba's Contemporaries

AMY SHERWIN, soprano

A YEAR BEFORE MELBA left Australia a Sydney writer[1] prophesied that she would some day equal the achievement of Amy Sherwin who was at that time (July 1885) singing at the Promenade Concerts in London. There were many who were sceptical, for the reputation of the "Tasmanian Nightingale" was already assured. For many years it was generally accepted as a fact that she had sung Lucia at Covent Garden four years before Melba did.[2]

Amy Sherwin was born on March 23, 1855, at "Forest Home", the homestead her father had built in the wild Huon Valley of Tasmania near what is now known as Judbury. The little girl grew up in the bush and received her first piano and singing lesson from her mother. Later she became a pupil of Frederick Augustus Packer, an accomplished Hobart organist who broadened Amy's musical horizons and fostered her love of opera and oratorio. All the members of the Sherwin family were musical and took part in entertainments in Hobart and Launceston and in concerts held in the old barn at Inlet Farm near their own property, but Amy was the only one who sang professionally.

Her talent was recognized early by William Russell, a former conductor of the Covent Garden orchestra. She made her first public appearance as Puss in the pantomime *Puss in Boots* which he produced, then took the part of Little Zillah in an operetta *Zillah* which he had written. This performance took place in Del Sarte's Rooms, Hobart.

There are several versions of Amy's operatic debut. One claims that it was in the role of Norina in Donizetti's *Don Pasquale,* with the visiting Pompei and Carlo Royal Italian Opera Company at the Theatre Royal, Hobart on May 1, 1878. Another, published in an article in the *Strand Musical Magazine* when she was singing in London states that she was introduced to Pompei in Hobart; that he heard her sing, gave her instruction and offered her a prominent position in the company for a tour of the mainland and New Zealand; that she accepted the offer and made her debut in Melbourne as Lucia. In spite of these conflicting reports as to where she actually made her debut, it is quite probable that she sang Norina in Hobart as a prelude to the more difficult roles she tackled on the mainland. Besides the role of Lucia she also sang those of Maritana and Leonora in *Il Trovatore* in Melbourne and at the Royal Victoria Theatre, Sydney. In July, 1878, she was associate artist in the concerts given in Victoria by the Scandinavian lieder singer Emblad and his wife, a Melbourne-born pianist.

We hear of her next in New Zealand, where on December 14, 1878, she was married to Hugo Gorlitz, a Sydney concert manager. Early in the following year she and her husband went to San Francisco and there she sang *La Favorita* and Violetta in *La Traviata* as a member of the Strakosch company.

The San Francisco correspondent of the Melbourne *Argus* reported that her Violetta was "warmly commended by the press. She proved that her voice had a greater range than the other two prime donne soprani of the company".[3] When the season finished she opened at the Grand Opera House on June 9 as Josephine in a *Pinafore* company assembled by Gorlitz and Fred Lyster.

Miss Sherwin appeared in New York in a small part in *Elijah* in September and during the first few months of 1880 sang at a number of concerts in New York and Boston. Of these performances three are of particular interest — a concert at which she was soloist with the Brooklyn Philharmonic Society under the baton of Leopold Damrosch; a concert at the Lincoln Hall, Boston, with the Theodore Thomas Orchestra in January, and a performance as Marguerite in a concert version of Berlioz' *Damnation of Faust* conducted by Damrosch in February. This was the first presentation of the work in Britain or the United States. The critic of the *New York Times* reported that "she sang tastefully and is a singer of promise".

In May, 1880, Amy Sherwin was the principal soprano at the Fourth Biennial Cincinnati Musical Festival. The musical director was the aforementioned Theodore Thomas and the celebrated Italian tenor Italo Campanini was one of the soloists. The critic of the Cincinnati *Enquirer*[4] had much to say of her debut.

> She refused to appear until [the conductor] came to escort her. It was courtesy due her as a lady . . . Her solo was a beautiful aria from Rossini's *William Tell*. Her voice is a peculiar one, but full of melody. She sings with great expression and soul, and is really dramatic in her style. In appearance she is slight and girlish looking . . . Her manners are simplicity itself, therefore she is captivating and charming . . . Her hair, which is of a dark brown shade, was arranged low on her neck with a single blush rose at the

side. She wears her front hair parted at the side like a boy, and frizzed, an odd but becoming style.

For the remainder of that year and part of the next she continued to sing in the United States. Then she went to England where Hans Richter was one of the first to recognize her ability. Soon her name was appearing in the programmes of the most important London concerts. She was the leading lady vocalist in Sims Reeves' farewell tour, and was a great favourite at the Patti concerts at the Royal Albert Hall.

Toward the end of 1887 Madame Amy Sherwin, as she was then, returned to Australia for the first time. In Melbourne she met John Lemmone and engaged him as a member of a concert party she was arranging for a short tour. In his memoirs Lemmone states that this tour was very successful and that at its conclusion Mme Sherwin, "who had a brilliant career as a concert singer . . . had ambitions to become a grand opera star and formed a company of her own. All great singers, however, are not great actors; consequently, the season was not the success anticipated".[5] To recoup her losses the concert party was re-organized, this time for an extended tour of the East. The party left Melbourne after the Centennial Exhibition of 1888 on the opening day of which she was one of the soloists in Frederick Cowen's *Hymn of Praise*.[6] She also sang in a performance of Beethoven's *Ninth Symphony* later in the season. The Eastern tour met with great success, the artists visiting Colombo, India, Singapore, Hong Kong, China and Japan. The party broke up in Japan in June, 1889, after visiting all the main cities and Amy Sherwin returned to England.

A cable received in Melbourne in February, 1890, reports that she appeared in Berlin in *Faust* and *Les Huguenots*, but her ventures into opera were few and she continued to build up her reputation as a concert singer in England. We read of her re-appearance at the Patti Concerts in November, 1892, with Sims Reeves, Mme Albani, Santley and Mme Patey; and from the same source comes the comment: "Mme Amy Sherwin's position on the concert platform may be compared in interest with that of Mme Melba who figures as the leading Australian vocalist on the operatic stage."[7]

It was from Southampton that she set out in 1896 for a tour of South Africa with a party which again included John Lemmone. They travelled the length and breadth of the colonies under conditions which were often difficult and gave numerous concerts. A tour of Australia with Arthur Deane, Barton McGuckin and Rivers Allpress followed late the next year and extended into 1898. A tremendous reception awaited the singer in Hobart where her enthusiastic admirers unharnessed her horses and hauled her carriage through the streets.

On returning to England she fulfilled many concert engagements. She

71

sang with the London Philharmonic Society, at some of the celebrated Crystal Palace Concerts, at the Richter Concerts at St James' Hall and at the Promenade Concerts at Queen's Hall. In 1902 she toured Australasia with the violinist Jan Kubelik and in 1906 made her last visit to her native land. Soon after her return to London she retired from active concert work to devote her life to teaching and to her invalid daughter who was completely dependent upon her for support. She died there on September 20, 1935.

The *Australian Encyclopedia* states that ". . . she was optimistic and without any sense of business and her last years were clouded by a struggle with sickness and poverty".[8] Because of this the Lord Mayor of Hobart tried to relieve the situation by raising a fund on her behalf a year before she died. In Australia she was remembered for her "richly sweet voice" and in London "as the wittiest of Australian singers and the easiest of hostesses".[9]

AMY SHERWIN — CHRONOLOGY

1855	Born in Huon Valley, Tasmania.
—	Sang at local concerts and in pantomime *Puss in Boots* produced by William Russell.
—	Sang Little Zillah in Russell's *Zillah*
1878	
May 1	Debut at Hobart Theatre Royal as Norina in *Don Pasquale* with The Royal Italian Opera Company (Programme of the Cincinnati Festival). Later toured with company in N.S.W., Victoria and New Zealand.
—	Sang Lucia, Maritana and Leonora (*Il Trovatore*) in Melbourne and at Royal Victoria Theatre, Sydney. *(Strand Magazine,* Nov. 1892, and Orchard, *Music in Australia.)*
July	Sang at Emblad concerts in Victoria (Orchard). To New Zealand with Pompei company.
Dec. 14	Married Hugo Gorlitz in Dunedin.
1879	
April	Sang *La Favorita* in San Francisco with Strakosch company (Cincinnati programme).
May 27	Violetta in *La Traviata* with Strakosch (Launceston *Examiner,* 18th July, 1879).
July 9	Opened in San Francisco as Josephine in *Pinafore* — company assembled by Gorlitz and Lyster (*Examiner,* op. cit.).
Sept.	Small part in *Elijah,* New York (Cincinnati programme).
1880	
Jan. 23	Soloist at Aronson's Sunday Concert (Odell, *Annals of the New York Stage, vol. X).*
Jan. 25	Soloist with Brooklyn Philharmonic under Leopold Damrosch. She sang "Ah Perfidio". Adolphe Fischer on same programme (Odell).
Feb. 8	Sang "Cavatina" *(Der Freischutz)* and "The Surprise" (F. Gabriel) with Theodore Thomas Orchestra, Lincoln Hall, Boston (Odell).
Feb. 14	Sang Marguerite in *The Damnation of Faust* in concert form under Damrosch (Odell). Review of rehearsal, N.Y. *Times,* Feb. 13.

Feb. 15	Sang Booth Theatre, New York, with pianist Theresa Carreno supporting artist (Odell).
Mar. 14	Soprano soloist in Rossini's *Stabat Mater,* St Stephen's church (Odell). Repeated 21st March.
Mar. 30	Concert at Steinway Hall with Adolphe Fischer (Odell).
Apr. 11	Sang in Gounod's *St Cecilia Mass,* probably at St Stephen's (Odell).
May 18-21	Cincinnati Festival. Sang (in order of concerts) "Selva opaca" *(William Tell); Missa Solemnis* (Beethoven); *Gotterdammerung,* Act 3, Scene 1; "Vane, vane" *(Robert the Devil); Missa Solemnis. See* Festival programme.
Dec. 27	Saalfield Concert, Steinway Hall, soloist (Odell).
1881	
Feb. 20	Saalfield Concert (Odell).
Apr. 22-23	Gluck's *Orpheus* with Brooklyn Philharmonic. Anne Louise Carey was also a soloist (Odell).
1882	Studied at Frankfurt with Stockhausen, at Paris with Madame Hustache, and with Georgio Vannuccini and Ronconi *(British Musical Biography).*
1883	Debut at Drury Lane, London in *Maritana* (Wallace) with Carl Rosa company (as above).
1884	Promenade and Richter concerts at the Crystal Palace.
1885	Provincial concerts.
1886	Concerts and oratorio in England *(Daily Telegraph,* Sydney, July 27, 1889).
1887	Concert tour in Australia with John Lemmone.
1888	
Aug. 1	Sang in opening concert of Melbourne Centennial Exhibition under Frederick Cowen and later in the *Ninth Symphony* (Orchard).
Oct.	Re-formed concert party and left for tour of east, visiting Colombo, Calcutta, Singapore, Hong Kong, Shanghai, Kobe, Nagasaki, Yokohama and Tokyo. Tour completed June, 1889 (Lemmone).
1890	*Faust* and *Les Huguenots* in Berlin (Orchard); leading vocalist on Sims Reeves' last tour *(Strand Magazine,* Nov. 1892).
1892	
Nov. 18	Re-appearance at Patti concerts at Royal Albert Hall with Sims Reeves, Albani, Santley, Patey.
1896	South Africa tour (Lemmone).
1897	Australian tour with Arthur Deane, Barton McGuckin, Rivers Allpress.
1899	Sang with London Philharmonic Society in England and at Promenade concerts.
1902-3	Toured Australasia with Jan Kubelik.
1906-7	Short Australian tour; retired from stage and concert platform.
1935	Died in poverty, 20th September at age of eighty.

MARIE NARELLE, soprano

Marie Narelle, "The Queen of Irish Song", was born Mary Ryan at the Combaning Sheep Station near Temora, New South Wales, in 1870. Both her parents were Australian-born of Irish lineage. She had a happy girlhood, full of interesting experiences. When her father took part in the gold rush she and her brothers "used to follow the wash-carts to the sluice and pick up gold nuggets that had dropped on to the road", later converting them into money with which they bought "candy, cookies and all sorts of things". When later they lived in small towns, Mary sang at concerts for the benefit of local charities and became a well-known amateur throughout the Monaro district before the family moved to Sydney and then later to a dairy area on the south coast of New South Wales. While in Sydney she attended St Vincent's College, Potts Point, where she studied voice with Mme Christian, a former professional singer and pupil of the great Garcia.

She married while still very young and was soon faced with the necessity of supporting herself and three small children. Singing seemed to be what she could do best, so friends suggested that she make this her career. One of them, the Reverend Charles Hunerbein, who, Narelle wrote in an unpublished autobiography, "had given Melba her first concert tour of New South Wales", undertook to help her by providing some insight into the classics and assisting her to build a repertoire.

Finding that there were few opportunities for singing engagements in Sydney at that time she returned to the country where she taught pianoforte and singing. In this same autobiography she wrote: "Many pupils came to me at my studio in Candelo but a greater number I had to visit at their homes. The only means of getting to them was on horseback until later on I could afford to buy a sulky in which I travelled back and forth to Bega where I had a great many pupils and made sufficient money to keep myself and three children".

Then occurred the event which proved to be the immediate forerunner of her concert career and which she referred to as "the turning point in my life." She was invited to sing at the consecration of a church in Cobargo where she had originally been organist and choir master. "The bishop", she wrote, "was impressed by the quality of my voice and persuaded me to return to Sydney where he would use his influence in getting me pupils and concert engagements."

Her immediate response was to engage a studio at Palings, a centre of musical activity in downtown Sydney, because, to use her own words, "If a hand is stretched out to me I take it". At the same time she never forgot those who helped her. She was especially appreciative of the generosity of her cousin Kate Heffernan and her husband, William Bourke, who cared for her

74

children for five years and made it possible for her to accept the engagements which were offered soon after her arrival in Sydney.

It was about this time that she adopted the name Narelle. When asked about its origin, years later, she told reporters:

My name is pure Australian, Narelle was a Queen of the Moruya tribe of aborigines who inhabited the Murrumbidgee Valley where my father had lived. When I was quite a child they used to tell me legends about her, of the days when she and her people were great in the land. And I got to fashion an idea in my mind of how she must have looked. So when I was starting out in life and wanted a name for programmes and posters I chose hers as a sort of talisman.

Marie Narelle

Narelle's first big opportunity came when she substituted for a European artist on a tour that had been arranged by John Lemmone. Lemmone was loathe to engage an unknown artist like Narelle for so important a tour but no one else was available and her friends guaranteed him against loss. The tour proved so successful that it was the beginning of a series that continued for several years. These tours often required her to be away from Sydney for six months at a time while she toured all of New South Wales and the island state of Tasmania. The rigours of these trips were great since they were made by coach and often required numerous changes of horses and frequent stops "to scrape off the red mud that stuck to the wheels and brakes and clogged the horses' hoofs".

Between trips the young singer studied with two Italian voice teachers who had come to Sydney with visiting opera companies, Senors Steffani and Hazon. Under the baton of the latter she made her Sydney debut at the Town Hall with the amateur Philharmonic orchestra in June of 1901, singing "Mon Coeur S'ouvre a ta Voix" from *Samson and Delilah*. So enthusiastic was her reception that she was soon offered future engagements in other states. Subsequently the Irish patriot, William O'Brien, who was visiting friends in Sydney, heard her rendition of Irish songs and invited her to sing at the closing of the forthcoming Cork Exhibition which the European favourite, Mme Albani, was scheduled to open. Narelle accepted this invitation and, after a Farewell Concert in Sydney, set out for the British Isles in 1902.

Soon after her arrival in London Narelle was able to resume study there with her former Sydney teacher, Senor Steffani. He helped her to develop her upper register and to improve her production. Four years later when interviewed in Australia she spoke of the absolute perseverance and determination that had been required at that time to achieve "ordered breathing, a free lip, and a jaw cured of stiffness". Her first appearance at the Cork Exhibition was made just three weeks after she reached Great Britain. It was on this occasion that Michael Davitt made an often quoted remark that "It took an Australian to teach the Irish how to render their own songs". It was not long after that she appeared before enthusiastic audiences in St Andrew's Hall, Glasgow, both in *The Messiah* and in recitals of Scottish songs. The ability to reach the hearts of both the Irish and the Scots was noted twenty years later when the Detroit Labor News reported "It was a lesson in art to hear Mme Narelle in the songs of two races, 'Loch Lomond' and 'The Minstrel Boy' ".

She appeared in London on June 6, 1903, at a benefit concert in the Royal Albert Hall before a large audience including the Prince and Princess of Wales. The manager of this concert had been reluctant to include an unknown singer among the many scheduled favourites that included Ada Crossley and Clara Butt. He agreed to do so, however, when a friend, Agnes Murphy, who was also Melba's secretary, offered in exchange for this favour to make all the arrangements for a forthcoming tour of an artist under his management. The young singer said later, "All the other artists had their followings in the audience. I knew only two persons. I walked on to the platform in silence but after my song I was recalled many times". As an encore she sang Tosti's "Goodbye" which had been written originally for Mme Melba, in whose box the composer was seated that afternoon. It is said that when he turned to Melba and remarked, "That is the finest interpretation of my song I have ever heard", the great diva was not pleased.

In a review of The Irish Ballard Concert given at St James Hall that same year it was pointed out that "for Miss Narelle to have wrested the honours of the evening from such an array of popular stars (Messrs Santley, Ben Davis, Plunkett Greene and Mme Kirkby Lunn) was a very notable achievement". Many other engagements followed throughout the British Isles. In Ireland she was heard by a gentleman who was selecting artists to appear at Ireland's Exhibit at the World's Fair that was scheduled to open in St Louis on 30th April, 1904. He invited her to be the Prima Donna at the Blarney Castle Theatre which was designed to present the cultural aspect of Irish life. Twelve days after receiving the invitation she set sail for the United States, accompanied by a number of Irish boys and girls who made up the rest of the cast. The engagement lasted seven months and audience enthusiasm was so great that Narelle was often forced to give several performances on one day. Immediately after the close of the Exposition in November, 1904, she was engaged for a tour of Boston, Philadelphia, and other major cities in the northeast. En route from St Louis she suffered an ear infection from a cold contracted on the train but with characteristic fortitude she was able to fulfil her engagements by having the ear lanced each night. When she arrived in New York she collapsed but having had the good fortune of being introduced to the family of Jimmy Walker, she was nursed back to health by his mother; and the future Mayor of New York City played her accompaniments during her convalescence.

As soon as she was well Narelle had many engagements in the city that brought her in contact with a number of interesting people. After one concert Victor Herbert, who had been in the audience, thanked her for having sung "Rory O'More" which he said he had not heard since he was a little boy in Ireland when it was played to him on the flute by its composer, his grandfather, Samuel Lover. Thomas Edison, who was experimenting at the time with a little wax cylinder but had not been able to make good recordings of the soprano voice, asked Mme Narelle to sing for him. When her records proved successful and were released for public distribution Edison presented her with one of his first phonographs and engaged her for further collaboration, an association that lasted nine years. She was also invited by President Theodore Roosevelt to come to the White House where he talked with her about

77

Australia and "seemed pleased when I was able to answer his questions".

Early in 1906 Frederick Shipman, the American concert manager, approached Narelle concerning a concert tour of the world under the title of "Queen of Irish Songs". Unable to secure as a supporting artist her young friend, John McCormack, who was then studying operatic roles in Italy, she engaged a French-American tenor, Chester Fentress, who later proved to be very popular. When they arrived in Sydney in June (1906) they were joined by the pianist, Miss Brandon Usher. Narelle's reception throughout Australia, where she appeared in all the large cities and in many remote areas, was exceptionally enthusiastic. In Sydney where three concerts had been scheduled originally, seven had to be arranged and the attendance was reported to have "exceeded that at any previous occasions in the Town Hall with the exception of Mme Melba's first concert" four years before. In both Melbourne and Sydney she was presented with illuminated scrolls by committees of Irish citizens in appreciation of the way she "had revolutionized the old conception of the nature and genius of Irish Music". The ladies of Brisbane presented her with a brooch in the form of a Southern Cross made of Queensland sapphires and gold. This was a particularly appropriate gift because Narelle often spoke of herself as "A Daughter of the Southern Cross". When she sang in Canada three years later, a Toronto newspaper referred to this Australian tour as "an experience of a kind that comes to few persons" pointing out that she had travelled thousands of miles through a country where a great singer had never appeared before. "In many places some of the audience had travelled for three days — often on camel-back — to hear her . . . she even went to the Western gold fields where houses were sold out weeks before she arrived and late-comers were forced to sit on empty cases or to stand during the entire performance."

After a tour of New Zealand and return engagements in Sydney and Melbourne, Narelle set out again for London by way of the Far East and Europe. En route she gave recitals in the major cities of the Orient and later appeared at a number of concerts on the French Riviera before going to Paris for a season. She was back in London by the Spring of 1909 singing there and touring other parts of the British Isles. In 1910 the New York *Musical Courier* announced that Mme Narelle would take up residence in the United States. The following year she and John McCormack toured the United States giving joint recitals before capacity audiences in all the major cities. "Standing-room only" was available on the nights at Carnegie Hall in New York and at Symphony Hall in Boston as well as in Philadelphia, Detroit and smaller cities.

Marie Narelle had given John McCormack his first opportunity to sing at a public concert when she invited him to appear with her at Rathmine in County Athlone, on 27th October, 1902, after she had been asked by a friend to give him an audition. Years later he presented her with an autographed photograph of himself in the costume of Rudolpho in *La Boheme,* inscribed "To Marie Narelle, one of the first to encourage poor me". She had the ability to identify talent and was instrumental in furthering the careers of a number of young singers.

Critics praised the purity of Narelle's voice and its delicate shades of expression, referring also to her great dramatic ability, her bright platform manner and her good looks. The wide compass of her voice, with a range of three octaves, made it possible to sing the classic arias of Gluck as well as the dramatic coloratura of Bellini's "Casta Diva". Customarily her programmes included compositions of Tschaikovsky, Halevy, Verdi, Ponchielli and Puccini. She sang these so well that a critic for the New York *Tribune* was prompted to comment in a review of a ballad concert in 1910, "Never before has an artist of Marie Narelle's calibre willingly put aside the glamor of an operatic career to become an exponent of the stirring and lovable ballads of the people". He did not know that soon after arriving in London in 1902 Narelle had realized that "in order to win success among so many excellent singers" she would have to specialize and "do some one thing better than anyone else could do it". "Naturally", she said in an interview given some years later, "my thoughts turned to the music I loved which I could sing from my heart, the beautiful Irish ballads". Students of folk music in college communities like New Haven, Connecticut, the site of Yale University, were quick to recognize the importance of "curious old airs" like the 700-year-old "Oh, Native Music" that were included in her programme and which had been among her early discoveries in Ireland. She told of having found almost untouched "a great treasure trove of Gaelic peasant songs that had been handed down for many generations". She had asked a Gaelic scholar to collect some of these for her but soon discovered that this was impracticable. "It was almost impossible to set down on paper their curious ornamentation and the regular rhythm that seemed to leap and answer to the wild passionate pulse of the people. . . . One must hear the old songs sung, understand the folk, be in tune with their temperament and in sympathy with their joys and sorrows."

Marie Narelle had all these attributes and the Irish appreciated her. Her sympathy led her in the early days to take an active part in benefits for the independence movement and to sit through long debates in Parliament on the Irish question. The fiery way she sang the rallying cry in "O'Donnell Aboo" suggested her to the sculptor, Charles Mulligan, as the model for the Spirit of Ireland to stand behind the seated figure of John Finnerty in the statue he was designing for Garfield Park, Chicago. The mayor of Dublin had presented her with a gold replica of the Brooch of Tara inscribed in Gaelic, the ancient language she began to study as soon as she arrived overseas. Michael Davitt's comment that her pronunciation was "pure and genuine" pleased her as much as the critics' praise of her fine enunciation of the four modern languages in which she also sang. In 1906 before she left New York for her first tour of Australia a group of wealthy Americans, including James Fortune Ryan, made her a gift of a valuable emerald and diamond bracelet; "perhaps for the sake of the memories which had been awakened in them by the old familiar airs", she said.

In 1911 Mme Narelle married Harry Currie, Chief Electrical Engineer of the New York Central Railroad. After this, as Mme Narelle-Currie, she gave many benefit concerts but made fewer regular tours. Most of these were in company with her two daughters, Kathleen and Rita. Kathleen was an accomplished pianist who in 1910, while she was a student at the Ursaline Academy in Armidale, New South Wales, had won the first Emmaline Wooley Award for three years' study at the Royal Academy of Music in London. Narelle's other daughter, Rita, was a coloratura soprano who had studied with Mme Gilly in Paris and subsequently had an independent career.

From the time of Currie's death in 1934 until her own in 1941, Narelle lived in London with her daughter, Kathleen, who was married to H. Newton Quinn. When in 1925 Reginald Narelle took his mother on a visit to Australia she was persuaded by E. J. Carroll, the impresario, to give a number of concerts in New South Wales and Queensland with a party that included two instrumentalists from the Moscow Conservatory. On this tour, which lasted seven months, her voice was adjudged to be "still fresh and beautiful". At a reception held in her honour in Sydney on 30th October, 1925, Sir Henry Braddon, one-time Australian Trade Commissioner and later President of the English Speaking Union, paid tribute to her generosity to the many Australian troops who had passed through New York during the first World War when she had placed her home at their disposal as a kind of club. He spoke of her as a great ambassador for her country. "Wherever she goes," he said, "there is an immediate enthusiasm for Australia".

LALLA MIRANDA, soprano

When Lalla Miranda left Melbourne early in 1894 Melba was already well established abroad, but by 1908 the names of both singers appeared as principal soprani at Covent Garden with the notation that Mlle Lalla Miranda was on loan from the Paris Opera. Like Melba, Lalla Miranda began her musical career in Australia as a pianist, appearing first in Geelong in 1886 and then several times a week as a soloist in concerts at the Melbourne Centennial Exhibition of 1888 with Fannie Hewitt of Tasmania as one of her associate artists. A chance appearance in 1890 as soprano soloist in the Schumann Cantata *Paradise and the Peri,* when she substituted for the regular

Lalla Miranda

soprano, called the attention of critics to her fine voice and she began the serious study of singing under the tutelage of her mother, who, as Annetta Hirst of Dundee, Scotland, had had an established reputation as a soprano in Britain and had been a favourite with Queen Victoria. The idea of Lalla having a vocal career seemed natural enough because her father, David Miranda, was a singer and had appeared as principal tenor at Covent Garden in 1866 during the Mapleson era.

Lalla joined the Turner Concert and Operatic Company in 1891 and soon was said to be Melbourne's favourite soprano and one of the most talked of singers in Australia.[1] The purity of her voice, its extensive range — middle C to E in alt — and her charming manner and attractive appearance all contributed to her popularity. She was described as "petite, spirituelle, with flashing dark eyes and a bright smile".[2] On 7th April, 1894, she was tendered a Complimentary Farewell Concert at the Melbourne Town Hall and left soon afterward to study overseas. Before going to Paris she went to Dundee, where her mother's family was very active in musical affairs and where she received many reassuring appraisals of her talent. It was to Scotland she returned in February 1895 to make her first public appearances in Europe at the Scottish Orchestral Concerts under the baton of George Henschel. Reviews of these performances mentioned her "irreproachable technique" and her "perfect trills and shakes".[3]

She had hoped to study with Mme Marchesi in Paris but when this was not possible she became a pupil of Mme Richard to whom she was introduced by the composer Massenet. Mme Richard had at her house in the Rue Prony a small theatre and so had at her disposal all the means necessary for the training of students for the operatic stage. She was delighted with her pupil and told a correspondent of the Melbourne *Age* in November, 1894: "She has a beautiful light soprano voice, *une vraie voix d'oiseau* . . . She vocalises to perfection, and is very intelligent and studious . . . She possesses, in fact, all the elements which lead to success".[4]

After her debut in Scotland, Lalla Miranda returned to Paris and for a time studied with Mme·De Garetti, another well-known teacher of the period. Then in 1898 she made her operatic debut in Europe at the Royal Court Theatre at The Hague, in the role of the Queen in Meyerbeer's opera *Les Huguenots*. During the next two years she sang frequently at La Monnaie in Brussels and began to appear in the sort of distinguished casts which were to prove characteristic of her career. At La Monnaie her associate artists included the tenor Van Dyke, the French baritone Renaud and the distinguished American contralto, Louise Homer. Here she created the role of the Fairy Queen in Massenet's *Le Cendrillon* and appeared as Ophelie in *Hamlet*. In 1900 she made her Covent Garden debut as Gilda in *Rigoletto* with Bonsi, Scotti and Mme Homer, and sang the Queen in *Les Huguenots* with Saleza, Plancon, Edouard de Reszke and Edyth Walker, another American contralto.

Miranda did not sing in London again until 1907 when her mother and her sister, Beatrice, were resident there, as she said that the climate did not agree with her. She sang, instead, at many of the important opera houses on the Continent, among them Paris, Bordeaux, Nice, Monte Carlo and Lisbon. A highlight of this period was her performance as Gilda at the opening of the Ostend Opera House on 13th August, 1905, when she and Caruso sang the principal roles in *Rigoletto* in the presence of the King and Queen of the Belgians, the Arch-duchess of Austria and other royalty. In 1907 she sang Gilda again at Covent Garden and Zerlina in *Don Giovanni* with Emmy Destinn and John McCormack, alternating her appearances there with her commitments as a member of the Paris Opera. In 1909 she took part in the Italian season at Covent Garden when she sang many roles, opening in Gluck's *Armide*. Soon after she sang Michaela in a Gala Performance of *Carmen* with an all-Spanish cast[5] which took place at Covent Garden in the presence of the King and Queen of Spain. Then, in September 1910, she opened the Manhattan Opera season for Hammerstein in the role of Lucia. In 1911 she returned to London to sing Michaela in *Carmen* with Mme Kirkby-Lunn and Dolores, *Lakme* with John McCormack and Edmund Burke, and Violetta with McCormack and Sammarco.

82 Miranda was now under permanent contract to the Paris Opera but was

released in 1912 to join the Quinlan Opera Company for a season in Melbourne and Sydney. She was enthusiastically received in both capitals, but especially in Melbourne where many people still remembered her fine voice. The Lord Mayor, Cr Davey, gave a reception for her at the Town Hall soon after her arrival and Melba, whose own opera season had been so successful only the year before, sent her a large basket of roses and chrysanthemums together with a message of welcome back to her native city. On the first night "she was given an ovation greater even than that extended to Melba, and was buried in floral tributes when the curtain fell".[6]

When the Quinlan season ended Lalla Miranda returned to Paris where, shortly before the outbreak of the war, she was presented with the Legion of Honour. In 1918 she became a member of the Carl Rosa Company[7] appearing with it only at infrequent intervals. However, she continued to sing in Paris and the French Provinces, Spain, Portugal, Brussels and Holland where she was a favourite and friend of Queen Wilhelmina. She died at her sister's home in Edinburgh in 1940, at the age of sixty-six.

ADA CROSSLEY, contralto

Ada Crossley, one of the first Australians to achieve a reputation abroad as an oratorio artist, left Melbourne the same year as Lalla Miranda. She was born in South Gippsland in 1874 when that part of Victoria was a wilderness where pioneers battled for a living; her father had hacked out a selection near the tiny township of Tarraville. With the possible exception of Amy Sherwin, Ada Crossley had a wilder and more picturesque birthplace than any other singer.

When she was a small child her father transported a wooden-framed piano up the Tarra Valley on a bullock dray — the only piano in hundreds of square miles of bush. Taught by her mother, she learned the rudiments of music before she could read. Later, she was taken in hand by a bush teacher who predicted a great future for her. By the time she was fourteen, she was the star of every concert within range, not only as a singer but also as a pianist. In 1888 the celebrated Sir Frederick Cowen visited Melbourne to conduct the symphony orchestra at the international exhibition held to celebrate Australia's first hundred years. The Crossleys sought Cowen's opinion of their daughter's ability. Brushing aside her pretensions as a pianist, he told them that he had rarely heard a youthful contralto of such beauty and purity. If her voice were not ruined by faulty training, she might go a long way.

At that time Fanny Simonsen, the former Lyster prima donna, was one of the best coaches in Australia. When she took charge of Ada Crossley she declared she had found an ideal pupil. Never having had a singing lesson, the girl from the Tarra Valley had nothing to unlearn. Quiet and dignified beyond her years, she so dedicated herself to her work that Alberto Zelman, who gave her lessons in piano and harmony, said that his idea of heaven was "a crate of Chianti and a dozen pupils like Ada Crossley". When the Reverend Dr Charles Strong seceded from Scots Church and founded the Australian Church, his choir master engaged Ada as soloist. The congregation increased in number as many people came specially to hear her.

In 1892 the young contralto made her first public appearance with the Melbourne Philharmonic Society as soloist in *Elijah*. Critics agreed that a contralto of such quality had not been heard in Australia for many years. Before the century ended the London *Punch* was to refer to her as "Miss Southern Crossley, an antipodean contralto, whose organ has the luscious richness of a Carlsbad plum combined with the translucent purity of rock crystal".

Within two years of her Melbourne debut Ada Crossley was one of Australia's favourite platform singers. But her opportunities were limited and the depression of the 1890's restricted the musical horizon. In 1894 she tossed a coin to decide whether to go to England or to stay at home. She went to London, where, provided with additional funds by the Crossley family of Yorkshire, she studied the art of oratorio with Sir Charles Santley and, later, voice with Mme Marchesi in Paris. Mme Marchesi told a correspondent for the Melbourne *Age* late in 1894: "Miss Crossley has a splendid contralto voice, there is no doubt as to her success. She is very intelligent . . . a hard worker . . . and I consider her one of my best pupils".[1] She made her London debut in 1895 at the Queen's Hall, but her big opportunity came when she substituted at a moment's notice for Clara Butt at a concert in Manchester and thus appeared before an additional segment of the British public.

In 1898 she again made an unexpected appearance which attracted favourable attention when she substituted for a missing contralto at a performance of Mendelssohn's oratorio, *Elijah* being conducted by Sir Arthur Sullivan. Learning that the scheduled singer was absent Sir Arthur asked, "Where is Ada Crossley?" When told that she was in the audience Sullivan said "Fetch her up" and, as he expected, she sang the part admirably. In November of this same year she appeared in a concert at the Royal Albert Hall with Melba and the Australian violinist, John Kruse.

With Sir Charles Santley she established a record by singing *The Messiah* and *Elijah* at Manchester for twelve years in succession, while her annual tours of Britain were regarded as musical events. Roland Foster, later of the New South Wales Conservatorium, knew her well in her early days in England and considered that she was unsurpassed in oratorio — even by Clara Butt. He heard her first at Liverpool in *The Messiah*, and noted that when she sang "He was despised" people in all parts of the hall were visibly moved.[2]

Ada Crossley in 1903

Numerous performances at concerts, in oratorios and as a singer at festivals in the British Isles won Ada Crossley acclaim as one of the greatest contraltos of her day. She was often commanded to sing before Queen Victoria and was a member of the famous Festival Quartette of which the other members were Mme Emma Albani, Edward Lloyd and Sir Charles Santley. Her voice, a pure lyric contralto was described as "not only delightfully even, but uniquely beautiful".

When she made her American debut in Mendelssohn Hall in New York City on 6th February, 1903, a critic from the *New York Times* spoke of her fine contralto voice and intelligent method of singing, noting that her voice was "an effective organ of low range and dark colour" and that such voices are rare. He wrote: "Her method is good, her enunciation admirable and her singing intelligent and sincere . . . She sang the songs in antique manner with dignity, fine poise and style". Her programme consisted of four groups of songs: Old Italian — selections from Giordani and Scarlatti; Old English — Purcell; Lieder — selections from Schubert, Brahms, Grieg and Strauss; and modern songs in English by Sir C. Villiers Stanford, Francis Allisten and Ethelbert Nevin. People marvelled at her remarkable chest expansion and were charmed with her generosity in giving encores, often referring to her as "Ada of the Voice". While in the United States that year she made the first recording for the Victor Gramophone Company's Red Seal Celebrity series.[3]

During the next five years Mme Crossley returned to Australia twice with concert parties that included Percy Grainger.[4] When asked in 1960 to comment on Ada Crossley as he had known her, Grainger told of having met her first in England about 1902 when he was twenty years old.

She was then at the height of her artistry and fame, and I, as an Australian taking pride in Australia's achievement in the arts, rejoiced greatly in her successes. She had a glorious voice and rare interpretative gifts in every style of music that she essayed. She was equally at home in an aria such as Bach's "Schlage doch, gewunschte stunde" and in one of the popular or sentimental ballads of the day. In 1903 she engaged me as an assisting artist to be part of the touring company with which she was to give about 300 concerts in Australia, New Zealand and South Africa.[5] In those days a great star, if a contralto, was surrounded by a "concert party" consisting of a soprano, a tenor, a bass, a violinist, a pianist, and an accompanist. The enthusiasm aroused by Ada wherever she sang was positively frenetic, and I must say she played up to it with unflagging liveliness and energy. But what seemed to me the most remarkable side of her nature was her ability to remain always a kindly, helpful, appreciative and democratic Australian. I never heard an unfriendly or harsh remark about any of her assisting artists pass her lips. In my own case her appreciative encouragement was dearly prized.

Ada Crossley was one of the first persons sought out by other Australian artists when they arrived in London and their biographies include frequent references to her hospitality and helpfulness. Her home in Cavendish Square was always open to them and she used her prestige to introduce many of them at recitals in London. In 1905 she married Dr Francis Muecke, an Adelaide-born throat specialist practising in London, and retired professionally in 1913. She continued, however, to sing at charity concerts until her death in London on 17th October, 1929. The *Daily Telegraph* of London noted that although Mme Crossley had retired from the concert platform some years before "there still lingers a memory of the striking beauty of her voice, with its strange smoothness of quality, and of the almost equally fine natural production".

KATE ROONEY and ELLA CASPERS, contraltos

Two other Australian contraltos of the period also became well-known concert artists and oratorio singers in England. Kate Rooney and Ella Caspers, although separated in age by a generation, were similar in many ways in background and early experience. Both born in N.S.W., they grew up with sisters and brothers who had good voices and were encouraged by their parents to play musical instruments and to sing. Both started their musical education in convent schools — Miss Rooney at St Vincent's, Potts Point, and Miss Caspers at Goulburn — and both studied with Mme Christian who had been a well-known oratorio singer before she became a nun, her last appearances having been made in 1889 with Charles Santley in three performances of Elijah with the Sydney Symphony Society conducted by Signor Hazon.

In 1905[1] Mme Christian founded the Garcia School of Music at Potts Point to honour her former teacher at the Royal Academy of Music, London, on the occasion of the one hundredth anniversary of his birth.[2] This soon became a centre to which young singers came to learn his famous method of voice production.[3] Asked twenty years later whether many had become famous Mme Christian replied: "The majority of the students of high promise who passed through my hands either had no ambition for a public career, or having it, retired early on their marriage.[4] The best known of those who made a name on this side and in London were Kate Rooney, Carrie Lancely and Ella Caspers".

Ella Caspers was noted for fine diction, subtle powers of tone colouring, and a voice with an unusually wide range (from low D to A in alt.), often referred to as "The Golden Voice". She appeared at a concert in the Sydney Town Hall when only thirteen and came to the favourable attention of many prominent musicians of the day, among them Rivers Allpress, Gerard Vollmer, Signor Hazon, Mme Dolores and Dame Clara Butt. Clara Butt said of her: "I have heard many beautiful voices during my tour through Australia, but Ella Caspers has a place all by herself". No wonder, then, that she was selected to be the featured vocalist at the inaugural concert of the New South Wales

Above: Ella Caspers

Kate Rooney

Conservatorium in 1915 when she sang "Il est doux" from Massenet's opera *Herodiade.* This was shortly after her return to Australia when the outbreak of World War I forced the cancellation of a tour of the United Kingdom which she was scheduled to make as the sole supporting artist to Fritz Kreisler.

She had gone to England originally to accept an Exhibition Scholarship awarded by the Royal Academy of Music, her trip to London being made possible by the music-lovers of Goulburn, Albury, and Sydney, who tendered her complimentary concerts. Singing fluently in German, French and Italian, she soon became a well-known soloist at Boosey Concerts and in oratorio and classical concerts. She also appeared with leading artists of the day at the Albert Hall and Queen's Hall. When John Lemmone first heard her sing in London he said: "Ella's unique voice is more beautiful than ever". Her best remembered appearances are in *The Dream of Gerontius, Elijah, The Messiah* and as Ruth in Sir Arthur Sullivan's *Golden Legend* at the Crystal Palace where she sang with an orchestra and a chorus of 1,000 voices.

Kate Rooney was also tendered a Farewell Concert before leaving for Europe in 1903 but she had already earned most of the necessary funds, not only by her appearances in oratorio with the Sydney Philharmonic Society and a series of tours through the country districts of N.S.W., but by selling paintings, sketches, and newspaper articles while attending the university. Her talent as a painter and black and white artist won recognition in Sydney and she was awarded the first prize of £250 in a competition sponsored by the Art Gallery.

Before settling down to study with Charles Santley she visited the Continent and sang for Manuel Garcia — now nearly 100, but still considered the world's greatest authority on the human voice. In London she continued to support herself as an artist and writer, having the distinction of being on the staff of *Punch*. She appeared weekly at the Prom Concerts and through the good auspices of Lady Chandos Poole, who had encouraged her originally to come to London, received many engagements to sing at drawing-room parties.

She made professional tours of Great Britain, France, Germany, Spain and the Channel Islands before returning to Australia in 1909 for an extensive and successful concert tour. An early tour of Ireland was made at the same time that Marie Narelle was appearing there. Both Australians were received with special enthusiasm because of their Irish backgrounds and their ability to interpret traditional Irish songs. In appreciation each was presented with a replica of the Brooch of Tara by civic authorities.

HORACE STEVENS, bass

Nowhere are the effects of the English choral tradition more evident than in the quality of the Australian male singers who have appeared in Britain and the United States. The success of men like Horace Stevens, Peter Dawson and Malcolm McEachern illustrates how the sound musical training given to boy choristers fostered their talents and laid the foundation of many a distinguished oratorio and concert career.

Mary Ellen Christian

Horace Stevens was born in 1876 at Windsor, Victoria, but did not begin his career as a professional singer until after World War I when he was heard by Sir Henry Wood in London. The great conductor advised him to abandon his dental practice in Melbourne for the concert platform; he claimed later that Stevens was the only man he had ever advised to give up a successful career in one field in order to pursue another in music.

Stevens made his debut as soloist with the Queen's Hall Orchestra in 1919 and sang his first Elijah at Birmingham under the baton of Sir Henry

Horace Stevens

Wood in the same year.[1] The next day the London *Morning Post* critic hailed him as "the greatest Elijah since Sir Charles Santley". Soon he gained the reputation of being the world's finest exponent of the role. Sir Edward Elgar, in an interview published in 1931, described Stevens as "the greatest Elijah the world has ever known, not excepting Santley",[2] and Santley himself predicted that Horace Stevens would be his successor and gave him his own score of the oratorio. Although Stevens sang the role many times during his long career his interpretation never grew stale. The *London Musical Courier* discussing the quality of his performances in 1930, said: "He never sings a word in public without special preparation, no matter how often he has sung it before, so that each time his singing has a fresh outlook and makes a vital appeal".[3] These words applied not only to his Elijah but to every performance he gave. He sang *The Messiah* "with a vivid force of conviction",[4] and engagements with all the leading choral societies in Britain testified to the greatness of his art. His large repertoire included Brahms' *Requiem,* Bach's *St Matthew Passion,* Handel's *Samson* and Bantock's *Omar Khayyam.*

Stevens created the role of Hiawatha when Coleridge-Taylor's trilogy was performed in operatic form at the Royal Albert Hall in 1924 and afterwards sang many roles in opera with the British National Opera Company. He was acclaimed for his performances as Wotan in *Die Walkure* and as Hans Sachs in *Die Meistersinger* which placed him in the front rank of Wagnerian singers. Stevens lived every role he sang. He was a "delightful" Falstaff; his "virile singing lifted the part of the High Priest in *Aida* to a level of outstanding merit"; his impersonation of Mephistopheles in Gounod's *Faust* was compared to that of Placon; in *Prince Igor, Tannhauser* and *Der Fliegende Hollander* he always showed the same impressive quality.

In 1927 came his first American tour, during which he met with success everywhere and was proclaimed "one of the greatest singers of our time". The Chicago *Daily Journal* said of his Elijah: "He knows the value of a reverent pianissimo in sacred music, and knows when to take restraint off and when to apply it". The Cincinnati *Commercial Tribune* commented on "his genuine bass trill, quite a novelty, and something quite odd in vocal pyrotechnics". Stevens returned to Melbourne in 1934 and devoted his great talent to promoting the cause of music in his own country. Early in 1936 he took part in the first performance of the Australian Opera *Auster* by Alfred Hill. He became a member of the staff of the Melbourne University Conservatorium in 1938 and in 1939 became conductor of the Royal Victorian Liedertafel, a post he held till his death in 1954.

His achievement in opera was as great as that in oratorio. It was said of him: "Wotans inferior to his have walked the stage of Covent Garden in German seasons, and if evidence were needed in support of Sir Thomas Beecham's claim that we had British singers equal to those of any other nation, it was here".[5] He did not reach these heights by chance. Behind his beautiful voice and impressive appearance was an active, alert intelligence which spurred him on to strive always for the perfect performance.

PETER DAWSON, bass

Peter Dawson's fine voice and genial manner made him one of the best-known ballad singers of his day. His ambition was to become an oratorio singer and in 1899, at the age of seventeen, he started to take lessons from C. J. Stevens, the founder and conductor of the Adelaide Choral Society. Dawson's father who had been a Scottish sea-captain before he established an ironmongery business in South Australia, did not approve of this although he had given all five sons and four daughters the advantage of a good musical education. However when Peter won the bass solo competition at Ballarat in 1900, his family's opposition began to lessen and his teacher advised him to go to London to study with Charles Santley. He set out in 1901 and after a talk with Santley went to Glasgow for six months of preliminary training by F. L. Bamford. At the end of this period he sang again for Santley and was accepted as a pupil. Santley took a great interest in him and in 1904 invited him to join a concert party including Santley and Mme Albani for a tour of the West Country. He made his first professional appearance at the Guildhall, Plymouth, and critics praised him then, as later, for his fine diction and phrasing.

About this time, Dawson, who had a bass range from E flat to D, was persuaded by Professor Kantorez, a Russian teacher in London, that it could be extended. Soon he was reaching top A flat and was quite satisfied to be a bass-baritone. His teacher, however, assured him that, if permitted to do so, he could make him into the finest tenor of his age![1] Not long after this Dawson began to make a series of recordings which were to provide the basis for his world-wide reputation as a ballad singer. In 1904 he was invited by the Edison Bell Company to make his first phonograph record — the song "Navahoe" — for which he received one pound. More recordings for Edison and other companies followed and in 1906 he signed a year's contract with His Master's Voice which guaranteed him £25. This marked the beginning of an association which lasted for half a century.

Meanwhile, Dawson had begun to record Scottish songs under the name of Hector Grant. During a break in a recording session one day he had been overheard imitating Harry Lauder singing "I love a Lassie" and was asked by HMV to record songs of this type under an assumed name. As the summer season was approaching and this was a lean period in the concert world, he decided to try it. The recordings were so popular that Dawson, dressed in

"Hector Grant"

Dawson the oratorio singer

costume, was soon appearing as Hector Grant in music halls. On some occasions he appeared on the same programme under both names. "Hector Grant" was so convincing that years later when Dawson told Harry Lauder that there had never been such a person, Lauder refused to believe it.

Having made one successful impersonation, Dawson tried others. He recorded light popular songs under the name of Frank Danby, music hall hits as Will Strong, and as J. P. McCall, composed rollicking baritone songs, some of them musical settings of poems by Kipling. Discussing the reasons for his success as a recording artist, Dawson said: "I always put diction, or if you prefer, enunciation, in the forefront of any rendition. I have, from the beginning, studied the lyric of a song until I knew it. In this way I 'lived' every song I recorded — no matter whether it was a trivial or a classical number".

In 1909 he returned to Australia as a member of Amy Castles' Concert Party on a five-week tour. They sang in all the capital cities of the six states and in sixty-one country towns as well. Travel conditions in some of the rural areas were described in letters from Dawson to his wife, Nan. On 17th November he wrote: "The roads were . . . chock full of pot-holes, and in many cases we had to crash over big protruding roots of gum trees. And we were rattled, bumped, flung and jolted about quite helplessly. . . . The drag was drawn by five fine horses and you can imagine the clouds of dust that enveloped us the whole way . . . the effect it might have on our throats was giving us a lot of worry".

After this tour Dawson returned to London where he continued to sing and to record. During both world wars he gave his services generously entertaining troops both in Australia and England. After the First World War he made many concert tours of England, one as a member of a small company of artists giving the newly-instituted International Celebrity Concerts designed to bring opera to the people. Two other members of the party were Rosina Buckman and the pianist, William James.

Radio brought a new audience. He made his first broadcast at a reception at Australia House, London, in 1931 and thereafter took part in regular BBC programmes and broadcasts from the radio stations of countries he visited. In 1947, when he was more than sixty-five, he made eleven recordings, twenty-seven BBC broadcasts and nearly one hundred concert appearances. In 1949 Dawson took as his accompanist on a tour of New Zealand a young pianist, Geoffrey Parsons, who had won the City of Sydney Eisteddfod piano championship in 1943 and whose advanced musical study was begun and continued entirely on scholarships awarded by the Australian Musical Association, the State Conservatorium of Music and the Australian Music Examination Board. Parsons had won the ABC Concerto and Vocal Competitions in 1947 and subsequently played concertos many times with the Sydney Symphony Orchestra. The impetus to go abroad stemmed from Peter Dawson's promise to give him the opportunity to act as his accompanist in England the next year if he could find a means of getting there.[2]

Peter Dawson died in Sydney in 1961, aged seventy-nine. He had begun his career as an effective oratorio singer and towards the end of his life wrote: "I did not waste any of the instruction so patiently given to me by Sir Charles Santley". He was acknowledged to be a good interpreter of lieder[3] but he found his widest audiences among those who delighted in the vigorous, lively and often sentimental ballads sung in a forthright and manly style.

MALCOLM McEACHERN, basso cantante

The internationally famous oratorio singer Malcolm McEachern was born in the same section of N.S.W. as Ella Caspers, with whom he later appeared in concerts and oratorios, notably, *Elijah, The Messiah, The Creation, Judas Maccabeus, Samson* and *The Golden Legend.* He made a number of recordings for the Vocalian and the Aeolian Company in London, his ones of Mozart being specially popular.

McEachern came to the attention of Melba when she was on a concert tour of Australia a few years after he had made his debut as a singer. He later appeared with her frequently in concerts in many places, especially in London, and sang with her in opera in Australia. His rich bass voice which had a range of three octaves from low C to top F was acclaimed wherever he sang. Much has been said of the value of physical activities in the development of singers; Malcolm McEachern's interest in football and boxing probably

Malcolm McEachern

95

helped him to acquire the excellent physique which enhanced his platform presence.

In 1916 he married the pianist, Hazel Doyle, who became his accompanist, and they set out almost immediately on a two-year world tour which included Commonwealth countries and eighteen cities of the United States. An American review in December, 1919, stated:

Stalwart Malcolm McEachern made the florid and exacting bass solo parts stand out with more than usual prominence. His opening recitative was taken at a faster tempo than commonly heard; and his singing of the really tempestuous music of the part, in which "The Nations Rage so Furiously Together" was faster than it has ever been sung here, perhaps faster than any other human being could sing it, was a veritable study in breath-conservation and control. The soloist possesses a voice of unusual resonance, and one sufficiently powerful to fill the largest of halls.

Everywhere audiences remarked on the resonant quality of his voice, and he soon became a much-sought-after singer in London, appearing frequently at Command Performances and as soloist with symphony orchestras under Sir Henry Wood and John Barbirolli. In January 1921, The *Morning Post* of London said:

Malcolm McEachern has the finest bass voice that has been heard in England for many years. His tone is beautifully soft and round, and at the same time of great volume, and he sings with all the graceful nuance and gesture of voice that is so rarely heard.

Despite widespread recognition of his fine voice Malcolm McEachern was often quoted as saying that "singing for your supper is not one-tenth the fun of singing at it". It was natural then that he should be attracted in 1925 by the suggestion that he and B. C. Hilliam, a composer of popular songs, form a partnership, "Flotsam and Jetsam" and appear on a variety circuit. The two men met originally at the Lambs' Club, New York, in 1920 when McEachern dropped in and asked for someone to play the accompaniment for two songs. Hilliam volunteered, but it was not until five years later, in London, when Hilliam saw an announcement that McEachern was to sing at the Queen's Hall, that they renewed their acquaintance. Invited to a party, the two men improvised together and the manager for Moss Empires persuaded them to accept a booking at the Victoria Palace. This was the beginning of a twenty-year partnership which provided their listeners with much pleasure and gave them an opportunity to hear some of Hilliam's popular lyrics sung by a first-class artist.

When McEachern died in 1945, Peter Dawson said: "The world has been robbed of a master of song and one of Australia's greatest ambassadors to Great Britain".

FRANCES ALDA, soprano

Frances Alda, about twenty years younger than Melba and equally enterprising, has been described as one of the most striking figures in an era that ran to colourful prima donnas. For two decades she was a leading soprano with the Metropolitan Opera Company in New York at a time when it included such outstanding singers as Bori, Eames, Easton, Farrar, Matzenauer and Hempel. As the wife of Gatti Casazza, the impresario at the Metropolitan, she presumably was able, also, to exercise some influence on the selection of artists. It has been noted that after Alda came to the Metropolitan Melba seldom appeared there. That a feud existed between the two Australian prima donnas is well-known; Melba consented to join Hammerstein's new venture only when she was assured that Alda would not be a member of the company.

Born in New Zealand, Alda grew up in Melbourne where she lived with her mother's parents, Martin and Fanny Simonsen, after her mother died when she was only four years old. Music was in her blood. She said in her biography that her father's parents had left England "with few more possessions than a violin and a baby or two" and we know that her father, Andrew Davies, was a member for many years of a J. C. Williamson opera orchestra in New Zealand. Alda's mother's family was well known for their unusual talent. Martin Simonsen, violinist and conductor, had come to Australia under the aegis of the impresario William Lyster. Her grandmother, Fanny, had been a prima donna with that company and later established herself as a teacher in Melbourne.[1]

Mme Simonsen early recognized that one of her own daughters, Frances, for whom Alda was named, had the promise of an unusual voice and after providing her with basic training she sent her abroad for further study, first to Germany and then to Mme Mathilde Marchesi in Paris. As Frances Saville, the girl fulfilled her early promise and had a distinguished career in opera in Europe and in the United States. On 7th September, 1892, she made her debut in Brussels, at the Theatre de la Monnaie, as Juliet in Gounod's opera *Romeo and Juliet*. This was followed by a series of engagements in St Petersburg, Moscow, Berlin, and Monte Carlo, and with the Opera Comique in Paris, and the Carl Rosa Company in England. She appeared again as Juliet at the opening of the Metropolitan's 1895-1896 season. Singing with Jean de Reszke she remained with this company in New York until 1900 when she went to the Hofoper in Vienna where she sang leading roles for many years.

97

Frances Alda

Alda was only seven or eight when her aunt went abroad to study and her imagination was probably kindled by the accounts of her progress. The child was taking piano and violin lessons at the time but, as she had announced to her grandmother on the night she arrived in Australia, she "wanted to sing". This her grandmother would not permit her to do until her voice had matured. So she took things into her own hands and secured engagements as a juvenile in the pantomimes that were so popular at the time. Her striking beauty, titian hair, irrepressible personality and charming voice soon attracted managerial notice.

In 1897, when she was fourteen, she got her first chance as a singer, appearing as a member of the chorus in a spectacular extravaganza called *Matza,* set in ancient Egypt and put together by J. C. Williamson himself, with considerable assistance from his scenic artists and stage carpenters who were called upon to reproduce such phenomena as the flooding of the Nile at Memphis. The title role in this bizarre production was originally played by a popular English comic opera artist named Flora Graupner but when she became ill the role was given to the fourteen-year-old in the chorus who then adopted the stage name of Frances Adler.

When *Matza* closed she went straight into the next production, a pantomime which, though called *The Forty Thieves,* owed little to the Arabian Nights. As the singing and dancing Fairy Queen she played opposite the acrobatic Hugh Ward who leaped in and out of trap doors in the role of the

Demon King. After touring with a juvenile opera company she appeared as a soloist in vaudeville under the genial auspices of Harry Rickards, an English comedian who founded an extensive circuit of variety theatres in Australia. Probably no one in the audiences who heard her warbling "The Honeysuckle and the Bee" or "The Sunshine of Paradise Valley" recognized her musical endowment or had the imagination to envisage her singing a few years hence at Covent Garden where she made her debut on 24th May, 1906. During this period of her life she occasionally received brief mention in the press to the effect that "little Francie Adler" pleased the patrons of the Bijou Theatre with her rendition of "I was Dreaming", or she was taken to task for improving "Redwing" with coloratura ornaments of her own. These self-appointed critics were no more aware of the girl's potential than Melbourne concertgoers had been impressed in 1884 by the quality of Mrs Armstrong's singing of difficult coloratura arias from David's *Pearl of Brazil* to the flute obligato of John Lemmone, although the performances of both these artists were soon to win world acclaim.

In 1902, a few years after the death of Fanny Simonsen, her granddaughter, aged nineteen, set out to become a great singer. Using either an inheritance from her mother which she had received when she came of age the year before, her own savings, gifts from friends, or money from all these sources, Frances was headed in the direction of her aunt's teacher, Mathilde Marchesi. She made a short stop in England but soon arrived at Marchesi's home in Paris. Alda tells in her biography how her acceptance as a pupil of Marchesi altered the entire course of her life and refers to the many times she returned to Marchesi to be coached for new roles which she sang in different opera houses throughout Europe. Marchesi was also instrumental in securing concert engagements for her in Berlin, Warsaw, Vienna and St Petersburg. It was she who christened her protegee "Alda" because she disliked the German-sounding stage name of Adler.

As was customary with young singers in Paris Alda made her debut at the Opera Comique and sang the role of Manon in which she had been coached by the opera's composer, Massenet. When her performances received no especially favourable attention from the critics she stopped her public appearances and returned to Marchesi for further lessons. Later she applied for an audition for the Theatre de la Monnaie in Brussels where both Melba and her aunt had made their debuts. Her success there was instantaneous and the reception so enthusiastic that Alda remained for two seasons at La Monnaie, singing seventy-four "Manons" and fifty-two "Marguerites". H. C. Lahee referred to her later in *Famous Opera Singers of To-day* as "the most charming Manon on the opera stage".

In 1906 she was engaged to make her Covent Garden debut in June as Gilda in *Rigoletto* with Caruso singing the title role. Her first performance 99 there, however, was several weeks earlier than planned because she was asked to substitute at the last minute for Melba in the role of Marguerite in *Faust*. During that London season she was also invited by Campanini to sing at the Verdi Festival in Parma; she immediately graduated to La Scala where she sang with a fire that stirred the Milanese as few foreigners have ever done. In 1907 she sang the title role in the premiere of Charpentier's *Louise* and later appeared with Chaliapin in Boito's *Mephistofele*. Here began a life-long friendship with Toscanini and the acquaintance which led to her later marriage to Gatti Casazza. Alda remained at La Scala for two seasons varied by engagements in Warsaw and in South America, at the famous Theatre de la Colon in Buenos Aires and in nearby Montevideo where her grandmother, Fanny Simonsen, had also sung in opera and where her mother had been born. She was then only twenty-five years old and Toscanini who was about to conduct at the Metropolitan Opera House in New York was insisting that she be engaged as a member of the Company.

Alda made her Metropolitan debut in *Rigoletto* with a distinguished cast which included Caruso as the Duke, Amato as the Jester, Louise Homer as Maddelena and Didur as Sparafucile. Newspaper critiques of this perform-ance were cool but before long her Desdemona was bringing the New York public to its feet and Lahee was writing of the "pure and limpid beauty of her voice" stressing the variety of expression in "The Willow Song" and the devout feeling of the "Ave Maria". He mentioned, too, the "beautifully pathetic and appealing little figure" she made beside the towering Leo Slezak, who sang the title role in *Othello*.

Alda sang at the Metropolitan from 1908 until her retirement in 1929. In 1910 she married the director, Gatti Casazza, sharing with him and Toscanini the glories of the regime which is still regarded as one of the most brilliant in the history of the lyric theatre. Although her repertoire included over forty major soprano roles Alda was able to boast that she had never missed a single performance for which she was scheduled. Her farewell appear-ance at the Metropolitan on 28th December, 1929, in the title role of Puccini's *Manon Lescaut* was a festive occasion. Newspaper accounts the next morning referred to "fifteen curtain calls", "fifty bouquets", etc., and to the illuminated parchment scroll from her colleagues which was presented by Antonio Scotti. This expressed "the feeling of deep regret at the retirement of so distinguished an artist and sympathetic comrade".

Alda continued her singing career through the then new medium of radio, broadcasting from a specially equipped studio in the Waldorf Astoria Hotel. In addition, she made concert tours throughout the United States, and to Australia and New Zealand. On an earlier visit to Australia in 1927, she revealed that she still retained her picturesque Australian speech. When asked by a young reporter whether she thought grand opera would ever show a profit in Australia she replied, "Stick your money on a horse, son". Doubtless she was thinking about the losses incurred by her grandfather, Martin Simonsen, and others who had produced seasons of grand opera in different parts of the Commonwealth.

By the end of World War Two Alda was among the few survivors of the glittering constellation of stars who had made the Metropolitan what it was in the legendary pre-1914 era. Her marriage to Gatti Casazza was dissolved in 1929 and in 1943 she married an old friend, Ray Vir Den, an advertising executive. She died in Vienna on 18th September, 1952. Almost until the end of her life she maintained a studio in New York where she taught promising young singers the famous methods of voice production she had learned from Marchesi half a century before.

AMY CASTLES AND HER SISTERS

On 16th March, 1899, a small but hand-picked audience assembled at Melbourne's Austral Salon, to hear a young soprano whom one of the members had discovered in Bendigo. Amy Castles was not quite seventeen; although her platform manner was gauche and unimpressive, the magnificent quality of her voice startled the members of the Salon. Next morning, the critic of the Melbourne *Argus* wrote: "Miss Castles possesses a dramatic soprano of rich volume and exquisite purity".

Both volume and purity lasted well. Twenty-one years later, the President of the Boston Symphony Orchestra declared: "All her notes are of equal beauty. The greatest compliment that could be paid to Tetrazzini at the height of her boom was that three of her high notes were almost as lovely as the corresponding notes of Miss Castles".[1] The two decades which stretched between those two comments were filled with achievement, but in many respects Amy Castles remains one of the enigmas of Australian music. Few singers began their careers with more acclaim or with more generous financial backing. Fewer still have achieved fame so young only to fade into obscurity while still apparently at the height of their powers.

Amy Castles was born in Melbourne in 1882. Both her father, a newspaper compositor, and her mother were amateur vocalists. Of their seven children, the three girls, Amy, Eileen and Dolly became celebrities. The four Castles brothers were also talented singers, George, a tenor, being a well-known professional for years. He toured with Eileen and Amy, but although prominent in Victorian concert circles before World War I, is chiefly remembered for being the Australian soldier selected to sing a solo in Rheims Cathedral on Armistice Day, November 11, 1918.

As the family moved to Bendigo in the mid-1880's the Castles children   101 spent their schooldays in the shadow of the towering poppet-heads which then dominated that city. Renowned for goldmines claimed to be the deepest in the world, Bendigo was also a centre of musical activity. The Bendigo Eisteddfod was rated among the top six in Australia. The Royal Princess Theatre was regularly visited by the comic opera companies of the day. In addition, the railways usually ran special cheap excursions to Melbourne, about a hundred miles away, when there was any special theatrical attraction, such as a grand opera season in the capital. An amateur operatic society also flourished, and the Castles family became familiar with most of the Gilbert & Sullivan works as well as *Veronique, La Poupee, Les Cloches de Corneville, La Mascotte* and other favourites from the French repertory then so popular.

Amy Castles gained her early education at the Bendigo Convent of Mercy, where she not only became a competent pianist but aroused great interest in the quality of her voice. One of her earliest teachers was E. Allan Bindley, whose daughter Pauline later achieved distinction as a coloratura soprano.[2] Under Bindley's direction, Amy played the title role in an amateur production of *Patience* and became a local star when she won the soprano section at the Ballarat (South Street) Eisteddfod of 1898. As a result, she made her Melbourne debut at the Austral Salon early the following year.

The press had never before been so enthusiastic over a new singer. "The first few notes she sang sent a thrill of astonishment through the gathering", said the weekly newspaper *Table Talk,* "Such a voice had never been heard before at the Salon, so full of melody and charm". Amy made such a sensation that a trust fund was established to further her career abroad. Her supporters wasted no time. At a benefit concert held in the Exhibition Building, Melbourne, two months later, 14,000 people paid to hear her sing, after which she went on tour to raise additional money. Bindley, her Bendigo teacher, rather resented being crowded out by notables who came forward to help the girl. Prominent among them were the Reverend Father George Robinson, a well-known Roman Catholic priest, himself a musician of considerable attainments, and J. C. Williamson. Father Robinson took a keen interest in Amy's welfare and she owed much of her initial success to his efforts. Years later she repaid his kindness with many benefactions to his church, Our Lady of Victories, at Camberwell.

For some unexplained reason Amy incurred the displeasure of the then influential Sydney weekly, *The Bulletin.* Although his paper had originally praised the young singer highly, referring to her "rich, pure, organlike voice, produced without effort", Edmund Fisher, the Melbourne editor, launched an attack on her as a "naive, countrified child who looked about fifteen though in

Eileen (left), Amy and Dolly Castles

reality at least four years older". Despite Fisher's hostility, however, Amy's tour was an outstanding success, showing a profit of over £4,000.

Reaching Paris better equipped financially than almost any of the Australian singers who had preceded her, Amy went straight to the great Marchesi, who, as Melba's teacher, was now invested with immense authority in the singing world. Contrary to all Australian opinion, Marchesi considered Amy Castles a contralto and began to train her as such. Thorold Waters, the singer and journalist, records her astonishment and dismay at this unexpected verdict which, had it been accepted, might have completely ruined the Australian girl's voice. Fortunately, Amy was not so naive as Edmund Fisher believed. Leaving the "senile martinet", as Waters irreverently called Madame Marchesi, she fled in consternation to Jacques Bouhy, the celebrated Belgian baritone, whose teaching methods were so effective that in November, 1901, she made her first London appearance at a St James Hall concert in company with both Ada Crossley and Clara Butt. Fulsome in its praise, the London press classed her with Jenny Lind, Tietjens, Patti, Melba and Calve. Touring the British cities in oratorio, she was received with enthusiasm everywhere.

The year 1902 brought Amy Castles back to Australia for a concert tour under the auspices of J. C. Williamson who, although he did not ordinarily engage in concert management, had taken a great interest in the young soprano. Although only twenty years old, Amy was now already an established artist. Sensing Fisher's prejudice, the *Bulletin* privily sent Thorold Waters to cover her first concert. His reaction, recalled many years after, was that Amy Castles was the most astonishing happening in Australian art.

> The Castles voice was endowed with almost incomparable elements of beauty. It combined the attributes of a dramatic and coloraturo soprano, able to deal equally well with the fluid "Mad scenes" from *Hamlet* and *Lucia* or the pulsating realism of a Tosca or a Butterfly. Yet this was the voice which Marchesi proclaimed a contralto.[3]

In June 1902 she gave a farewell concert in the Melbourne Exhibition Building where 20,000 people, surely one of the largest audiences ever gathered indoors in Australia, gave her one of the greatest ovations in her career. Between 1902 and 1909 she consolidated her European reputation, returning to Australia with a concert company organized by J. & N. Tait, and consisting of Peter Dawson, Anderson Nichol, Victor Buesst and Adrian Amadio. The tour began on September 30, 1909, and did not end until the middle of the following February. During that four and a half months, the party appeared in seventy-two different towns including Mount Morgan in North Queensland, Adelaide, and Hobart. Many of the places visited were small one-night stands such as Kyabram in Victoria and Narrabri in N.S.W.

and a great deal of the travelling was done by cutting across from railway to railway by horse-drawn drag at the height of one of the hottest summers in memory. Writing many years later, Peter Dawson recalled the company's arrival in Shepparton, Victoria, after travelling for five-and-a-half hours in a shade temperature of 110 degrees: "We looked like a set of dirty tramps. We were completely covered with white dust as the roads were devoid of metal and nearly a foot deep in dust. . . . The effect it might have on our throats was giving us a lot of worry".

Amy Castles came through all right, for little more than a month after the tour ended she made her debut in grand opera as co-star of a company assembled by J. C. Williamson to give Australia its first presentation of Puccini's *Madame Butterfly*. The opera was played every evening, Amy Castles alternating in the title role with the French soprano Bel Sorel. This ingenious arrangement ensured that most people saw the performance at least twice in order to decide which soprano was the better. Contemporary reports indicate that the Australian carried off the palm, although her rival was undoubtedly handicapped by having to sing in English.[4] The supporting cast was topped by Frederick Blamey as Pinkerton and the New Zealand soprano, Rosina Buckman, as Suzuki.

Amy returned to Europe under contract to the Imperial Opera, Vienna, where she spent the last two years of the Hapsburg regime as the youngest Imperial Court singer ever appointed, alternating prima donna roles with the celebrated Selma Kurtz. The outbreak of the 1914-18 war ended the dreamlike life in old Vienna. The cavalry officer to whom she was engaged was killed fighting against the Russians in Galicia and Amy left for Italy where she spent some time studying under Roberto Hazon, who had conducted the Puccini season in Australia.

After another tour of her homeland, she went to America, making her debut at Carnegie Hall in 1917. Again war disrupted her plans. When America entered the conflict she joined the great Polish piano virtuoso Paderewski and other artists in giving concerts for service men. In 1920 she became prima donna of an opera company organized under the direction of Gustav Slapoffski. With this company she appeared in her favourite role of Butterfly, as well as in *Faust, Romeo and Juliet* and *La Boheme*.[5] That season marked the termination of Amy Castles' operatic career. Thereafter she restricted herself to recitals, and soon abandoned public singing altogether.

It cannot be denied that in some aspects her career disappointed the expectations of many of her admirers. She never seemed to recover from the interruption of her career caused by World War I, and she was bound to Australia by family ties she had no thought of breaking. She seems to have lacked the drive and ambition necessary to reach the top and stay there but she undoubtedly had one of Australia's great voices. As Thorold Waters said:

"Amy's emergence into the musical world when she was seventeen was the most astonishing happening in Australian art. It had almost the reactions and reverberations of the first discoveries of gold in Ballarat and Bendigo." Her disappearance was equally surprising. After the death of her mother in 1941 little was heard of her until her own death ten years later.

Eileen Castles was scarcely known to the Australian public. After a fleeting appearance with the Melba-Williamson Company in 1911, she spent much of her time in the United States, appearing in grand opera at the Century Theatre, New York, and in various Gilbert & Sullivan seasons. During the First World War she returned to Australia and made a country tour supported by her brother George and the New Zealand pianist Harold Whittle. Her appearances with the Williamson company in 1924 and 1920 aroused great enthusiasm, particularly when she appeared as the Doll in *Tales of Hoffman* a portrayal which, said the Adelaide *Register,* was "a masterpiece in every sense."

The third Castles sister, Dolly, was very popular in Australia during the early years of the century. Like Amy, she studied in Paris under Bouhy, but concentrated on light opera and after making her debut in *Patience* in Melbourne in 1904 she played all the soprano roles in Gilbert & Sullivan with the exception of *Ruddigore.* As prima donna of the J. C. Williamson Repertoire Company in 1905, she had the distinction of playing opposite Charles Kenningham in the only professional production of *Utopia Limited* ever given in Australia. Her subsequent career extended to Great Britain, France and the United States, where as well as in Gilbert & Sullivan, she sang in operettas by Leo Fall, Jerome Kern and other popular composers of the era. In 1917 she married Dr Charles Finn, a major in the R.A.A.M.C., and retired from the stage.

ROSINA BUCKMAN, soprano

Born about 1880, in Blenheim, New Zealand, at a time when the artistic links between that country and Australia were much closer than they are today, Rosina Buckman made her first appearances in grand opera in Australia. In 1905 she had sung the leading role in Alfred Hill's opera *A Moorish Maid* in Wellington and this had brought her to the attention of the public on both sides of the Tasman Sea. She went to Sydney to sing *Maritana* when George Musgrove produced the opera at the Criterion Theatre in 1909 and the following year toured with the J. C. Williamson Opera Company singing Suzuki to Amy Castles' Madame Butterfly. In 1911 she became a member of the Melba-Williamson Opera Company, repeating the role of Suzuki and singing in addition, Frasquita in *Carmen,* Martha in *Faust* and Musetta in *La Boheme.* At the end of the season she toured New Zealand with John McCormack, who encouraged her to return to England,[1] which she eventually did.

Rosina Buckman in Madame Butterfly

After some preliminary operatic experience, Miss Buckman joined the Beecham Opera Company in 1915. She became noted for her portrayal of Aida and of Isolde of which a London critic wrote: "She infuses the part with all that unforced feeling, sincerity and genuine womanliness which are part and parcel of the artist's own nature and rank chief among the qualities which the ideal Isolde must have". Her performance of the title role in *Madame Butterfly* moved Neville Cardus to write:

Buckman's 'Butterfly' was exquisite; she was a vast size but nobody noticed it. Her voice was none other but the heart and every impulse of Cho Cho San; she sang the part on the scale of miniature pathos; and those who never heard Buckman asking Sharpless to read the letter, those who never heard her tone, intolerably trustful when she asked Suzuki to put a little carmine on her cheeks, have never heard the opera transformed . . . into a pathetic world in which Butterfly, a pretty figure from a Japanese fan, is caught in the trap of circumstance incomprehensible to her in its tragic hurtfulness.[2]

Rosina Buckman became principal soprano at Covent Garden in the 1919-20 season and repeated some of her previous successes there as well as creating the roles of Mrs Waters in Dame Ethel Smythe's *The Bosun's Mate*[3] and Nail in a new opera of that name by Isadore de Lara. She married the tenor Maurice d'Oisley in 1919 and together they toured Australia and New Zealand in 1922-23. Melba wrote of her at this time:

Rosina Buckman today represents the fulfilled dreams of thousands of young singers. By hard work and unrelenting study, she has gained a position foremost in the musical world of Europe. Great in opera, magnificent in concert work, Australians will be delighted and charmed with her. God has blessed her with a heavenly voice, which, with intelligence, experience and study has carried her through the bitter struggles of the beginner to success and fame. I know no one better fitted to carry on the great and noble tradition of music, and New Zealand may well be proud of its Queen of Song.

Shortly after this tour Rosina Buckman retired from the stage but made many recordings of her famous roles. Later she became a Professor at the Royal Academy of Music in London. She died in that city on 30th December 1948.

The special qualities of her voice were described by "Figaro" of the *Musical Opinion* in the issue of June 1920: "Miss Buckman could make her singing poignant without any explosion of its roundness of tone or any rending of the melodic line. She could refine her tone down to the faintest pianissimo without the smallest sacrifice of its evenness or colour; and by skilfully contrived crescendos, secure an effect of eloquence not to be found in the words sung". The same critic spoke of her as embodying "all the qualities of unaffected simplicity, womanly charm, and unadulterated sincerity which lend individual life to her parts".

ELSA STRALIA, dramatic soprano

Stralia was the name Elsa Fischer adopted when she first sang at Covent Garden in 1912. It served to identify her with her native land and to answer a question asked by a reporter after her first appearance at Albert Hall, "Who is this great singer and where does she come from?"

She was born in Adelaide, in 1881, the daughter of Hugo Fischer, the baritone. After the death of her mother, who had also been interested in music, Elsa and her sister were sent to a convent to be educated. "There", she said, "I learned to play and sing. These were my only hobbies. I played anything I heard and always wanted to be an opera singer". Speaking of the death of both parents when she and four other children were still quite young she recalled: "We were left alone and had to make our own careers".

When Elsa auditioned at the Albert Street Conservatorium in Melbourne she was awarded a scholarship to study voice for two years with the head of the opera school, Mme Elise Wiedermann. Following this, she joined the chorus of the J. C. Williamson Comic Opera Company and travelled with them to Sydney where she took lessons from Gustav Slapoffski who had come to Australia with a visiting opera company. He recognized the "unusual breadth, power and feeling of her singing", and believed she had a "world voice". Slapoffski, who by this time was also conductor of the Sydney Philharmonic Society, presented Miss Fischer at one of their concerts where she sang the *Jewel Song* from *Faust* and Arditi's "Il Bacio". These selections were so well received that it was suggested that she go abroad for further study. Speaking of this she said: "I gave it much thought and held many concerts and engagements to gather together the money. In 1910 I left and went to London — I was then unknown and sang under the name of Miss Else Adela". From London she went to Italy to study with Mme Falchi and made her debut at the Carlo Felice Opera in Genoa.

Returning to London, she was called upon in May 1912, to substitute for Melba who was scheduled as the soloist for a Sunday afternoon Symphony Concert in the Royal Albert Hall. Critics hailed her performance and she was asked to audition at Covent Garden. She was engaged there and given three weeks to prepare the part of Donna Elvira for a performance of *Don Giovanni* at the Royal Opera Company's forthcoming Mozart Festival. In this production she sang with John McCormack, Antonio Scotti, Mignon Nevada and the

109

Elsa Stralia as Donna Anna, 1925

world-famous dramatic soprano Emmy Destinn. Reviews of her performance stressed "excellent dramatic quality and a voice of wide range and great power, highly trained and well-developed". The next year at Covent Garden she sang Elsa in *Lohengrin,* Elizabeth in *Tannhauser,* Santuzza in *Cavalleria Rusticana,* Amelia in *Ballo in Maschera,* Leonora in *Il Trovatore* and the title role in *Aida.*

110　　　In 1916 and 1919 she also appeared in leading roles with Sir Thomas

Beecham's English Opera Company at the Drury Lane Theatre. "Singing *Aida* one night in Italian at Covent Garden and in English the following night at Drury Lane presented its difficulties", she said. She sang *Aida* so many times she wore through the soles of a pair of slave girl's sandals. She kept these for many years after her retirement as a memento.

Stralia was also praised as a concert artist and oratorio singer. She appeared with leading orchestras throughout the British Isles and a reviewer of one of these occasions reported: "The vocalist was Mme Elsa Stralia, who has a Melba voice, clear, pure, ringing and sweet — her two operatic numbers were sung brilliantly", Stralia toured as associate artist with the violinist Eugene Ysaye, the pianist Vladimir Pachmann, and the baritone Edmond Burke and gave nearly 100 concerts throughout England, Scotland and Ireland with Dame Clara Butt. During the First World War she appeared frequently as the soloist at Promenade Concerts with Sir Thomas Beecham and Sir Henry Wood and in special concerts arranged by George Robey at the Coliseum for the benefit of the Lord Mayor's Fund. So popular was she that on one occasion £14,000 was raised and 175 guineas paid for a single box.

In 1920 she was guest artist in concerts with the Lamoureaux Society of Paris and in 1922 with the New York Symphony Society under Walter Damrosch. That same year she and Richard Crooks toured the United States in concerts featuring the third act of *Siegfried*. After singing in South Africa she returned to Australia in 1924 under contract for a tour of Australia and New Zealand. During the years that followed she continued to give concerts in London and the United States. In 1927 Walter Damrosch noted: "She is never a fraction off pitch. The big voice soars and swells; her top notes can be a clarion or have the soft beauty of a woodwind. This singer is a dramatic soprano who can change to a perfect coloratura in 'Bel Raggio' *(Semiramide)* — one marvels at the top voice, anew".

On a second tour of the Antipodes in 1933 she met Adolphe Christensen in a small town in New Zealand and later married him. She retired and lived in Auckland until 1943, ten years before her death, when she returned to Melbourne to live. In recognition of the valuable assistance she had received years before at the Albert Street Conservatorium, she made provision in her will for the establishment of the Elsa Stralia Scholarship[1] to assist a girl singer of outstanding promise.

An article written at the height of her career described Stralia as ". . . gifted with a remarkably fine stage presence as well as a voice of gorgeous quality and a temperament of southern warmth; Stralia looks every inch the Prima Donna and her popularity increases with every appearance. Few singers have been so successful in recording for the gramophone and her Columbia records will provide many an object lesson for aspiring young singers and enjoyment for all who hear them".

111

NOTES.

Amy Sherwin

[1]*Sydney Daily Telegraph,* 27th July, 1885.
[2]Attempts to verify this have proved impossible but brought to light many other facts.
[3]Launceston *Examiner,* 18th July, 1879.
[4]*The Cincinnati Enquirer,* 22nd May, 1880.
[5]*The Flutist,* Vol. 7, No. 9, Sept. 1926.
[6]The other soloists were: Ellen Christian, Armes Beaumont and Otto Fischer.
[7]*Strand Magazine,* November, 1892.
[8]Vol. 8, p. 105.
[9]Todd, R. H., *Looking Back.* Sydney, Snelling Printing Company, 1938.

Lalla Miranda

[1]She appeared in *Maritana, The Bohemian Girl, The Huguenots, Robert the Devil, Dinorah, Faust,* and *Cavalleria Rusticana,* and in a concert version of *Lohengrin* with the Melbourne Liedertafel.
[2]*The Dundee Courier,* 12th February, 1895.
[3]Ibid.
[4]The *Age,* 22nd December, 1894.
[5]Lalla Miranda was the only non-Spanish singer in the cast, though her father, David Miranda, was of Spanish parentage.
[6]The *Age,* 10th June, 1912.
[7]In 1920 she sang Zerlina with John McCormack and Da Ingot in William Sommerville's *David Garrick* with William Boland as Garrick.

Ada Crossley

[1]The *Age,* 22nd December, 1894.
[2]Foster, R., *Come Listen to My Song,* London, Collins, 1949.
[3]Two of these records — Giordani's "Caro mio ben" and Hahn's "Paysage" — were issued forty years later as collectors' items on G.R.C.C. pressings. She also recorded for Pathe selections from oratorios which were transferred from cylinders to discs and are now cherished by connoisseurs.
[4]Percy Grainger was one of the few Australians who never lost his identity as such when performing in other parts of the world. Throughout a long career as a pianist and composer he remained unique as a person but recognized that achievement is not an individual matter. In an inscription at the entrance to the museum he established at the University of Melbourne, he wrote:
"Believing that great achievements in musical composition are seldom the result of a purely individualistic effort on the part of the composer, but are often the outcome of a coming together of several propitious circumstances of fructifying personalities,

I have tried, in this museum, to trace as best I can the aesthetic indebtedness of composers to each other; the borrowing of musical themes or novel compositional techniques and the culturising influences of parents, relatives, wives, husbands and friends."

⁵On the Rand, where flowers were scarce, bouquets were sent by rail from Durban, 500 miles away. In Johannesburg she was presented with a life-size silver jackal and in Kimberley with diamonds by the managers of the De Beers mines.

Kate Rooney and Ella Caspers

¹Mme Christian became a Sister of Charity in 1894, taking the name, Sister Mary Paul of the Cross. She died at St Vincent's College on May 31, 1941, at ninety-three.

²Although there are frequent short references in news items of the day to Mme Christian's appearances as soloist in oratorio performances in Melbourne and Sydney, very little information about the early life and work of this influential voice teacher is recorded. The authors of this book are greatly indebted, therefore, to Miss Jeanette Rooney, who was Mme Christian's last pupil, for introducing them to the Sisters of Charity at St Vincent's Convent who graciously made available two press cuttings that were very informative: "Deeds of Other Days" by Gerald Marr Thompson, *Sydney Morning Herald,* 1927, and "Madame Christian Interviewed" by an unidentified reporter in a 1912 copy of the *Town and Country Journal.* In the latter article she is reported to have said that Australian voices had a peculiar fullness of quality but needed to be carefully trained and "a forcing either 'up' or 'down' inevitably spells ultimate ruin. A singer cannot be made in a month or two, though some parents seem to cherish that delusion. There is much nerve-disturbing work in training voice, and inducing a 'feeling' for the best music; but there is, also, abundant compensation in noting how a God-given organ gradually becomes an unequalled instrument for the expression of feelings and ideals that else could not receive articulation at all".

³Born in Quebec, Canada, Mary Ellen Christian was brought to London as a child. There she was prepared in 1865 for the Royal Academy of Music, where she won the open competition for the Westmoreland Scholarship and was awarded the Cipriani Potter exhibition. Her voice was greatly admired by the professors for its true contralto quality, an easy production, and an immense range from D in the bass to the soprano high B. A future which would place her amongst the celebrities of the day was confidently predicted, the *Times* recognizing in her vocal style "a dramatic talent which any artist in London might envy".

During her brief London career, Saurin Lyster, the Australian operatic impresario, endeavoured to engage her for his season in Melbourne but, as she explained later, "I never had an ambition for stage experience. Lyster coaxed me into studying six operatic parts for his Italian company, but I disliked the idea of the life, and declined to sign the contract". In 1871, Mary Christian came to Australia hoping to regain her health and the voice she feared she had lost when stricken with a serious respiratory ailment after a concert at St James Hall, London. Soon after her arrival in Australia she began to appear at concerts and in oratorios. Her first tours were made with two visiting celebrities, the French violinist Jennie Claus, and the English pianist Arabella Goddard. She soon became a member of oratorio casts which usually included Rosina Palmer, the daughter of Mme Carandini; Armes Beaumont, the tenor; and "whichever baritone or bass might be available at the time in Melbourne".

⁴Kate Rooney married William Kirkham of Bath and made her home in the United States. Ella Caspers married A. A. Maloney, a dentist, of Taree, N.S.W.

Horace Stevens

[1]In 1888 Stevens sang the Youth's part in *Elijah* under Frederick Cowen at the Melbourne Centennial Exhibition.
[2]*London Daily Telegraph,* 5th November, 1931.
[3]*London Musical Courier,* April, 1930.
[4]*London Daily Express,* 17th October, 1927.
[5]*London Musical Courier,* April, 1930.

Peter Dawson

[1]Dawson, *Fifty Years of Song.* London, Hutchinson & Co., 1951.
[2]This was the beginning of Parsons' distinguished career as accompanist to many of the world's most famous vocalists in all parts of Europe and Australia. He is considered the probable successor to Gerald Moore, who was also Dawson's protege.
[3]A London critic reviewing a recital he gave at Wigmore Hall soon after his return from the tour with Amy Castles in 1910 wrote, "Hitherto I had known Peter Dawson to be a singer of note of gramophone records, but after last night I maintain that if he cared he would become one of the world's greatest Lieder singers".

Frances Alda

[1]A receipted bill given Fanny Hewitt, a well-known oratorio singer of Tasmania, indicates that in 1882 Mme Simonsen's fees were six guineas a quarter "paid in advance", and a guinea for a single lesson.

Amy Castles and her Sisters

[1]*The Green Room,* Sydney, August, 1920.
[2]Pauline Bindley won the Champion Aggregate at the South Street Eisteddfod at the age of twenty; appeared with J. C. Williamson companies; toured Australia, New Zealand and the Far East with Paul Dufault; appeared in oratorios and operas in Britain for five years as a principal in the Carl Rosa Opera Company in such roles as Gilda, Rosina, Violetta, Marguerite, Nedda, and Norma in *Don Pasquale* and did considerable broadcasting, especially from Ireland. She returned to Australia in 1931 due to the serious illness of her father.
[3]Waters, T., *Much Besides Music,* Melbourne, Georgian House, 1951.
[4]Dawson. Op. cit.
[5]Also in the company were the Australian artists Fred Collier, Elsa Treweek, Leah Myers, Browning Mummery, Strella Wilson, Charles Mettam, Patti Russell, Thelma Carter, and Amy's sister Eileen Castles, who appeared as the automaton, Olympia, in *Tales of Hoffman* and sang Musetta to Amy's Mimi in *Boheme.*

Rosina Buckman

[1]She had gone there to study at the Birmingham and Midland School of Music in 1900

but returned home before making her debut.
[2]Cardus, N., *Second Innings,* Sydney, 1950.
[3]*The Bosun's Mate* was given its premiere in 1916 but this was its first performance at Covent Garden.

Elsa Stralia

[1]Two of the holders of this Scholarship have already justified their selection as "singers of outstanding promise". Yvonne Minton, mezzo soprano, holder of the Scholarship from 1956-1959, won the £1000 Shell Aria at the Canberra Eisteddfod in 1960. This enabled her to go abroad to study in the following year. After winning the Kathleen Ferrier Prize at a Holland Internale Competition she sang in oratorio and on broadcasts in England for two years, studied at the Joan Cross Opera School and recorded for Decca in association with John Shaw and other outstanding singers. She appeared in the title role in Benjamin Britten's *Rape of Lucretia* at the City Literary Institute in London and then, on 26th March, 1965, made her debut at Covent Garden as Lola in *Cavalleria Rusticana.* This was followed by appearances there in other operas, including *Boris Godounov* in Russian in which her singing of Marina won high praise from the critics.

Joy Mammen, the previous holder of the Stralia Scholarship, was already an experienced singer in Australia before going abroad in 1958. She had appeared at the Festival of Perth in the title role of *Dalgerie* and with the Elizabethan Theatre Trust. After winning several scholarships in England she appeared as guest artist with European companies and then settled in Germany as principal soprano with the Aachen Opera. In 1965 she visited Australia to take part in the Sutherland-Williamson International Opera Company in which she alternated the title role in *La Traviata* with Joan Sutherland and played the lead in some performances of *The Elixir of Love.*

6

Singers Of The Period Between Two World Wars

JOHN BROWNLEE, baritone

The internationally renowned baritone, John Brownlee, was probably Melba's most famous protege. Born on 7th January, 1900, in Geelong, Victoria, he learned at an early age to enjoy both singing and acting; his father was a fine singer and an uncle was a well-known Shakespearean actor.

When Brownlee was only six his father taught him to play the cornet and later he played with the Geelong Municipal band under its famous leader, Percy Jones. An interesting incident occurred during the rehearsal of a new piece containing an important cornet solo. When the crucial moment arrived, the bandmaster, noticing a change in the young man's complexion and other signs of distress, asked if there was anything wrong. "Yes", replied Brownlee, "I'm afraid I cannot play this solo because I cannot read music and have always been playing by ear". The astonished bandmaster immediately set about teaching him to read at sight, an accomplishment that was invaluable for his future career.

When Brownlee was fourteen he joined the Royal Australian Naval Reserve and was trained at the Naval College, Osborne House. He once said in an interview that at that time he had hoped this might enable him to see the world but that his career as an opera singer had provided more opportunities for interesting travel than would have been possible through naval assignments. While studying to become a Certified Public Accountant, he entered the 1921 South Street Eisteddfod at Ballarat and won first place in the Vocal Championship which carried a prize of £30 and a gold medal. At this time he had had only a few singing lessons but now he began to study with Ivor Boustead, a well-known Melbourne teacher who later taught Marjorie Lawrence.

Melba heard Brownlee sing the bass solos in a performance of *The Messiah* by the Melbourne Philharmonic Society at the Town Hall in 1922. Impressed by the quality of his voice, she went back-stage to advise him to   117 consider becoming a professional singer, first going to Europe to study. A year later he was able to follow this advice and went to London. There Melba strongly urged him to go to the Continent, learn languages and study opera. She arranged an introduction to Dinh Gilly the famous baritone, who saw the potential of Brownlee's voice and immediately took him under his wing. Thus began the young man's serious study in Paris where he was able to profit from the many cultural advantages that city had to offer.

In the winter of 1925-26, Brownlee's progress was so impressive that he was invited to join the company of the Trianon Lyrique, a theatre in Montmartre devoted to operetta, which staged gala performances of opera at weekends. His repertoire was to be *Lakme, Traviata* and *Mireille.* During this season, Melba, appearing like a fairy godmother, again crossed his path. She had come to spend the winter months in Paris and was dining one night with an American friend who mentioned having heard a young "American" by the name of Brownlee, sing at the Trianon Lyrique. Melba remembered the name, but could not believe this could be her protege from Australia, so her host phoned the theatre. The origin of the young man was not settled by the phone call but the information was volunteered that he was definitely not French and that he was singing *Mireille* that same night. So after dinner the whole party went up to Montmartre to see for themselves. Melba was of course delighted to find that this was the same young man she had discovered back in Australia in 1922, but she was also a little annoyed that he had not kept her informed. She took a lively interest in his progress and studies in Paris and it was here that she invited him to sing in the cast of *La Boheme* at her famous Farewell to Covent Garden, scheduled for June 1926. Two years later he was to sing with her again in her "Farewell of Farewells" as a member of the Melba-Williamson Opera Company during a tour of Australia. They also made a number of records together, which Brownlee cherishes and shares with the public when he plays them on special broadcasts.

That short season at the Trianon Lyrique proved a memorable one for young Brownlee. His dramatic ability, as well as the beauty of his voice, established him as a great favourite with audiences. He was also exposed to the perils of the French custom in opera of speaking dialogue instead of singing recitative. At that time, his command of French fell far short of the perfection he later achieved. In retrospect he shares with the audience of that time the amusement they felt at his pronunciation of the spoken words of his roles.

Brownlee's debut in *Thais* at the Paris Opera in 1927 established his reputation as an artist of international stature. He was awarded a permanent contract with the Paris Opera and later one for the international seasons at Covent Garden. He appeared also at other leading opera houses in Europe and in South America where he sang with equal facility in French, German, or Italian. His reputation as a Mozart interpreter made him a regular partici-

John Brownlee

pant in the Glyndebourne Festivals and his interpretation of the roles of Don Giovanni and Papageno there and at the Metropolitan Opera House won special recognition.

Ernest Newman wrote of Mr Brownlee's performance in *Pelleas* at Covent Garden in June, 1930: "The Goland of John Brownlee was as great a piece of work as we have seen this season. His voice is as musical an organ as could be wished; and he seems to have, in addition, an instinctive sense of dramatic psychology and an extraordinary taste and restraint". Of his American debut in *Rigoletto,* which took place at the Metropolitan Opera House on February 17, 1938, Olin Downs said: "It was a pleasure to recognise, as soon as he appeared, a singer who had not only the routine of the part well in hand, but who has a consistently and proportionately developed conception of the character, which he reinforced with a voice of quality and style which was that of a musician". This same critic, in his review for the *New York Times* of that season's new singers stated: "Among the men came Brownlee whose authoritative and sincere presentation of his roles was needed at the Metropolitan, if only as an example of what it means really to have learned the sound traditions of celebrated baritone parts". On 16th March, 1940, another reviewer commented that "His interpretation of Scarpia, vocally and from the histrionic angle, was the crowning achievement of his career here (at the Metropolitan) to date. An adequate Scarpia must be aristocratic, polished and domineering, as well as satirical and vindictive; Mr Brownlee met all the requirements in these respects, giving a finished and well rounded portrayal". Another highlight of his career was his performance of Iago in Verdi's *Othello* when he substituted for Lawrence Tibbett at a performance in Cleveland.

In addition to appearances with the Metropolitan Opera Company in New York, Philadelphia, Boston, Baltimore and Cleveland, John Brownlee sang with the Chicago Civic Opera, the San Francisco Opera and the Rochester Civic Music Association. Concerts and recitals took him to Canada and all parts of the United States. He also appeared as soloist with leading symphony orchestras, including the Philadelphia Orchestra under Eugene Ormandy, and in nationwide broadcasts with the General Motors' Symphony Orchestra.

In recent years Brownlee has combined his vocal and histrionic talents in programmes that have been referred to as "characterised by expressiveness and clarity of diction". He has appeared as narrator in concert versions of operas such as *Macbeth* and in a special programme of Scottish songs and readings from Scottish poets. In a review of the latter, John Briggs, in the *New York Times* of May 28, 1958, wrote: "John Donald MacKenzie Brownlee, Australian-born baritone familiar to Metropolitan Opera audiences as Count Almaviva and Papageno, made his appearance at Town Hall yesterday afternoon in a new dress, the tartan of the Clan MacKenzie. The programme presented "Come to the Highlands", with which Mr Brownlee will tour the United States next season. The baritone was in good voice, and the delivery of the familiar works on his programme was simple, unaffected and quite charming". From 1957 until 1960 he broadcast a weekly programme on the Columbia Broadcasting System's network entitled "Backgrounds in Music" in which he presented many rare recordings.

Since 1941 John Brownlee has been closely associated with the American Guild of Musical Artists; he has been President since 1953, the year he was invited to teach at the Manhattan School of Music as the successor to Friedrich Schorr. When Mrs Janet Schenck, who founded the school, retired in 1956, Brownlee became the Director. As Director of the Manhattan School of Music, John Brownlee is utilizing all his talents.

His business acumen is evident in the improvements that have been made to the school's plant and in the enlistment of support from foundations interested in promoting artistic endeavours. His years of experience as a member of opera companies in different parts of the world have familiarized him with all aspects of this art. He not only directs and stages many of his school's productions but he also appears in some of them. (He sang Don Alfonso in *Cosi fan Tutti* and took part in a performance of Jan Meyerowitz's *Grandfather*

Death presented by the school's 1962 Summer Opera Workshop.) In a review of the latter for the October number of *Opera* magazine a critic reported that "John Brownlee, director of the Opera School, himself took a small but extremely impressive part and showed everyone how to communicate with an audience". His students are required to build a large repertoire and to develop the ability to learn roles quickly so that they will be ready to take advantage of any opportunities that may arise, at short notice, when they become members of professional opera companies.[1] Brownlee has also tried to solve the problem of the young performer who may need special study to remedy a lack of early musical training and be unable to read music. Instrumentalists as well as singers gain experience by performing in groups, which helps to produce orchestral players and avoids the pitfall of concentrating on solo work to the exclusion of ensemble playing. In addition to four opera productions there are six symphony concerts, a choral concert, and numerous chamber music and percussion concerts each year. Several graduates of the school are members of European orchestras and additional requests for players have come from Israel, South Africa and New Zealand.

Brownlee calls attention to the extent to which American singers, too, have become an integral part of the European operatic scene. A decade ago, for instance, only a handful of Americans sang in German opera houses but today over 500 Americans are performing in opera companies in eleven of the large cities from Berlin to Stuttgart. He lays great stress on musicianship and dramatic understanding; he thinks of opera as musical drama rather than as dramatized singing and each year students take part in the production of a play which teaches them how to convey the meaning of dialogue without the aid of music.

Having received so much of his training and early experience in Paris where he was that rarity, a foreigner in the Paris Opera, it is natural that Brownlee should be interested in presenting works in French. In 1962 these included *Werther* and *The Pearl Fishers* and in 1963 *Lakme* and *Mireille*. *Mireille* had not been produced as an opera in New York since 1918 and is the work in which he was singing at the Trianon Lyrique when Melba "rediscovered" him in 1924.

In 1965, using three separate casts, Brownlee revived Berlioz' *Beatrice et Benedict* in the original Opera Comique form with spoken dialogue in French. "Taking place in what has been called Spanish-Harlem on Manhattan's Eastside, one could still believe oneself to be in Glyndebourne or Salzburg. It was a glittering production studied to the smallest detail and splendidly carried out",[2] a reviewer wrote. The following summer he directed the Central City Festival production of Massenet's *Manon* in Colorado. "His work was of the unobtrusive sort that ranks highest in the field of direction".[3] This was in keeping with Brownlee's belief that "the unknown and unqualified factor — 121 talent — has always been the oxygen in our academic air". He looks forward to the time when improved facilities will enable the Manhattan School of Music to develop this talent in a larger and more suitable setting, a building near Columbia University being vacated by the Juillard School of Music[4] when it moves to the new Lincoln Center of the Performing Arts. This with the help of "matching" grants from the Ford Foundation, will make possible a substantial increase in size of the student body from its present limit of 650 students at the university level and 200 in the preparatory school.

Mr Brownlee has returned to Australia several times to make professional appearances. The first time in 1928 at Melba's request, and most recently in 1952. A reporter who interviewed him in Sydney on one of these trips wrote: "With those of us who have got to know him well, he leaves behind the memory of something much more real and worthwhile than the picturesque and temperamental opera star of tradition — the memory of a man robust, genial and direct, a fine man and an artist".

GERTRUDE JOHNSON, coloratura soprano

An important direct link between Melba and the internationally known young Australian singers of today is Gertrude Johnson. Soon after her return from abroad in 1935 she founded an organization to provide training and experience for young people aspiring to operatic careers. In the announcement of a concert to be given by Miss Johnson at the Town Hall on 24th June, 1935, the Melbourne *Age* stated: "She has been away fourteen years and during that time has sung in opera at Covent Garden, at concerts in the Albert Hall and Queen's Hall, London, and throughout the British Isles in important oratorio performances and at musical festivals . . . Sir Adrian Boult, Albert Coates, Eugene Goossens, Sir Hamilton Harty and Percy Pitt are among the important conductors she has sung under. Miss Johnson did much broadcast work in England and was engaged up to the time she left for Australia". The article added: "She will return to London after her visit to her own country". But Gertrude Johnson did not return to London; instead she remained in Australia to found the National Theatre Movement, for which she believes her career as a singer was but a prelude.

Miss Johnson had received her early training at the Albert Street Conservatorium under Ann Williams and Dame Nellie Melba and was one of a small group of girls with fine voices whom the great diva volunteered to teach at the Conservatorium. In an interview in London some years later Miss Johnson spoke of the far reaching effect of this association. "One morning in 1917," she said, "Melba asked me to sing 'Caro Nome' for Signor (Guido) Cacialli. I little knew that this morning was to be the beginning of my operatic

Gertrude Johnson

career. Signor Cacialli was the leading bass of the Gonzalez Opera Company then touring Australia. He recommended me for an engagement to sing Gilda, Violetta and Nedda, and was the means of getting me my first operatic engagement to tour Queensland and New South Wales." (Later Miss Johnson was also to tour New Zealand.)

Many enthusiastic reviews greeted her appearances during this period. The Melbourne *Herald* termed her Gilda "a sparkling performance", and the Melbourne *Punch* noted in its review of her Mimi: "She has the youthful beauty we connect with Mimi, a voice of charming fitting quality, stage composure most natural, and her work comes right across the footlights." The *Australian Musical News* reported: "Her singing of Lucia, especially in the Mad Scene, drove the packed audience half crazy with joy and excitement . . . a triumph I have not known in a long experience of this opera." And the Sydney *Sun* added: "Her execution in the cadenza in which she ascended with lovely purity of tone to the E in alto was brilliant." Summing up performances

123

given in Adelaide, the *Advertiser* said: "One may without hesitation class her as the success of the season."

In November, 1920, Gertrude Johnson gave a Farewell Concert at the Melbourne Town Hall, an occasion for which Sir James Barrett served as chairman. The following February she left for England, where, in her own words, "I had the good fortune to meet Robert Radford, who has been wonderfully kind to me. He asked Mr Pitt to hear me, and I was engaged to sing coloratura roles with the British National Opera Company, with whom I have performed since their formation." She was also in the cast of the first opera to be broadcast in Britain, singing Queen of the Night in *The Magic Flute.* With this company she also sang Constanza in *The Abduction from the Seraglio,* Marguerite in *Faust,* the Princess in *The Perfect Fool,* and Micaela in *Carmen.* In an article in the Melbourne *Herald* in 1923 she was quoted as saying: "It's only three years ago that I used to go down to the Prahran tram every morning and stand and wait at the corner of Chapel Street and Alma Road and wonder if I'd every really get to England; I used to close my eyes while I was waiting and think of Covent Garden until I could almost see it standing on the other side of the road. Then one day things began to happen. They kept on happening, and now I'm here, even though I'm only just beginning to believe it."

But before "things began to happen" there were hurdles to be negotiated, among them an audition in which sixty singers took part. Miss Johnson remembers that she was so nervous when her turn came that she thought she "would be unable to get through it all". Finally, however, the manager took down her address and said she would hear from him. She hoped that the suspense might be ended by a letter in the mail next day but three months passed and she had about given up hope when the letter did arrive asking her to come for an interview. As a result she was given a leading role which marked the beginning of a fruitful association with the British National Opera Company. She performed with them and gave concerts in London and also in the provinces, and in Scotland and Wales. It was a strenuous life — rehearsals in the morning, concerts in the afternoon, performances in the evening, extensive travelling — in addition to coping with the British climate, which is not easy for Australians accustomed to the sunshine and warmth of their native land. However, she endured the rigours of both weather and work and received such reviews as the following:

One of the most enjoyable parts of the concert was the singing of Miss Gertrude Johnson, an Australian soprano, and she is certainly one of the best singers we have heard here. She sang three groups of Mr (Cyril) Scott's songs with distinguishing charm; her voice is of great beauty of tone; wonderful in its purity and flexibility; she sings with perfect art, her enunciation is clear and her intonation flawless. She scored a great triumph by her splendid artistry.

On 7th December, 1926, culminating her long association with the great diva, Miss Johnson sang Musetta to Melba's Mimi in a performance of *La Boheme* — advertised as the "farewell of Dame Nellie Melba" — at the Old Vic Theatre, London, as a benefit for the Sadler's Wells' building fund. Her singing of Mozart was always much admired; at the Salzburg Festival she was lauded for her rendition of arias "in true Mozart style" and a London review of her Constanza called attention to the fact that this was "a part in which she can claim to be one of the few sopranos who can sing the difficult music in the key in which it was written by the composer for his voluble-throated sister-in-law." Miss Johnson attributed the refinement of her technique to Melba who also taught her several unusual coloratura cadenzas, but her interest in Mozart operas was stimulated originally by Fritz Hart, Director of the Albert Street Conservatorium and the man who, she says, "introduced Mozart to Melbourne." She is grateful to him for insisting that students build a large repertoire; having done so, she was ready to step into roles at short notice and to take advantage of unexpected opportunities when they presented themselves.

Soon after Miss Johnson decided to remain in Australia she attempted to arouse public interest in a cause she knew to be important. In the *Melba Conservatorium Magazine* of 1936 she wrote of the need for a National Theatre "in order to provide work for young artists to enable them to get the experience that so many of them go abroad for." She added:

> They should be able to get experience in their own country. There is a serious side to this sending of young students abroad with a few hundred pounds, more serious than appears on the surface. It is because of my knowledge of these difficult conditions that I am bringing forward this National Theatre scheme — a National Theatre could be made the home for so many branches of our artistic life — Opera, The Drama, and Ballet. It would be an outlet for Students with talent from the Conservatoriums, Dramatic and Dancing Schools.

After more than four years of unremitting effort to gain public support for the idea, Miss Johnson was able to launch a modest opera season in 1939. When she had addressed The East Melbourne Forum the preceding spring she had pointed out: "Up to the present we have exported our best brains because many of them could earn little more than a starvation wage in their own land. Surely our talented writers and artists . . . are worthy of the same appreciation as the talented cricketer and footballer . . . "

One of the first young writers to receive such appreciation from the   125

Australian National Theatre was Ray Lawler, author of *The Summer of the Seventeenth Doll*. Among the many internationally-known younger singers who received their early experience under the auspices of this movement and the direction of Miss Johnson are Marie Collier, Ronald Dowd, Elizabeth Fretwell, John Lanigan and John Shaw, all of Covent Garden; Robert Allman and Leonard Delany, who are singing in German opera houses and Lance Ingram, who appears at the Paris Opera as a leading tenor, "Albert Lance". In 1965 six former members of the A.N.T.M. Opera Company appeared in the Sutherland-Williamson International Opera Company.

In 1954, at the request of the Victorian Government, a performance of *The Tales of Hoffmann* was presented before Queen Elizabeth II. The repertoire for that year included also *Amahl and The Night Visitors, Albert Herring, Hansel and Gretel, La Traviata, Madame Butterfly* and also repeat performances of *The Consul*. For the first time the theatre presented an operetta *La Belle Helene* which included members of the National Ballet Company. Since then operettas have been an annual feature of the company's offerings, and revenue from these helps to provide an important source of income.

The range of productions since the first season in 1939 has been very wide. It would compare favourably in extent with that of any major professional opera company anywhere in the world. The opportunity to learn a number of roles in a variety of operas has proved especially valuable to singers who later auditioned at European opera houses or found themselves singing the same roles in professional companies abroad.

FREDERIC COLLIER, bass-baritone

Frederic Collier, the bass-baritone, was closely associated with Melba during the First World War when they appeared frequently at concerts in aid of the Red Cross and later when he toured Australia in her party. In 1926 he was the only Australian besides Melba in the group assembled by the Opera Syndicate in London for the international season at Covent Garden and, at the end of this season, he was invited with John Brownlee and Browning Mummery to sing in *La Boheme* at Melba's Farewell to Covent Garden.

Born in Melbourne in 1885 Fred Collier went to work in the railways when he was fourteen, confining his singing to church choirs. At twenty-one he entered a number of the vocal competitions at the South Street Eisteddfod in Ballarat and won the grand aggregate award. Soon after this he left the railways and became manager of the Melbourne office of the English music firm of Chappel and Company. For the next twelve years Fred Collier sang locally in concerts and oratorios and then in 1918 joined a J. C. Williamson

126

opera company which toured Australia and New Zealand. His wife, Elsie Treweek was also a member of this company, and Amy Castles was a principal.

In 1921 they went to England where their friend Horace Stevens helped them to establish themselves. The next year Fred Collier was one of a number of Australians to join the British National Opera Company which was being organized by former members of the recently disbanded Beecham Opera Company. He soon became known for his fine characterizations, particularly in Wagnerian roles: Klingsor in *Parsifal;* Wotan and Hagen in *The Ring;* Kurvenal in *Tristan and Isolde.* He delighted audiences as the father in *Hansel and Gretel* and sang both Valentine and Mephistofeles in *Faust.* According to critics his Amonasro in *Aida* was a unique contribution to opera, and he could sing Wagner and Puccini with equal facility. During the seven years he sang with the British National Opera Company he was associated with a number of other Australian singers including Beatrice Miranda and Gertrude Johnson. After the termination of that company he joined the Carl Rosa organization and toured Britain.

He returned to Australia in 1934 as a member of the Benjamin Fuller Opera Company which included Florence Austral and many distinguished English singers. At the end of the season he decided to continue his singing career in Australia and sang many leading roles in productions of the new National Theatre Movement, which benefited greatly from the presence of an experienced principal in casts composed mostly of inexperienced young people singing roles for the first time. He also sang in *Aida* with Marjorie Lawrence when she appeared as guest artist with the company. Until a very short time before his death in October 1964, Fred Collier was a leading member of the ABC choir and appeared in supporting roles in musical comedies.

BROWNING MUMMERY, tenor

Nothing could be written about this other Australian who sang at Melba's Farewell to Covent Garden that would provide a better picture of the man and the early influences which shaped his career, than his own account.[1]

It seems but a few years since I was working at a mechanic's bench in Australia, but those few years have brought such changes in my life that a month or two ago I had the honour of appearing in a principal part with Melba when she made her farewell to opera at Covent Garden.
As the son of a mother who had an exceptionally beautiful voice, I began to sing at an early age, and as time went on my thoughts were always on

singing. Even while I worked as a mechanic, I was under the care of a teacher; and, although I could hardly see how they were to be carried out, I had all sorts of ambitious schemes in my mind.

I sang for hours as I worked at my lathe, sometimes making so much noise that the foreman came to me and said: "For heaven's sake, stop it, or there will be a crowd outside!" But he knew all about my enthusiasm, and made every allowance.

I devoted nearly all my spare time and most of my spare cash to music, attending concerts and operas whenever I possibly could. Opera was my special favourite, and to see certain roles portrayed only increased my ambition to go and do likewise.

One day an operatic company came to Melbourne and gave a performance of *Madame Butterfly*. Luckily, I had just received my bonus at the works, and I decided to take my mother to hear it. This was the first time I had heard the opera, and when Pinkerton had sung I exclaimed to my mother: "I should love to play that part."

He was singing with Miss Amy Castles, and, strangely enough, four years later I actually appeared as Pinkerton with Miss Castles in the same company.

My introduction to opera came through the medium of an Italian company which was touring in Australia. As things had not gone too well with Italians in the cast it was decided to substitute Australians, and I was given an opportunity to show what I could do.

Of course, I was overjoyed, and in my enthusiasm I did something which more mature experience would probably cause me to shirk now; for, without any kind of rehearsal I went on to the stage and sang the principal tenor part in *Faust.* Imagine the cool effrontery of a mechanic going straight from his lathe to undertake such a task! Truly, it is inexperience that gives us confidence.

Still, I was voted a success, and before long I bade farewell to the lathe and gave myself exclusively to opera. In course of time I became a member of the Williamson Opera Company, and toured all over Australia and New Zealand.

But the desire of all Australian singers is to come to England, where, of course, the scope is much wider than in their own country. I had the same kind of ambition, and it was a great joy to me when I was able to set sail for these shores.

Then I was fortunate enough to come under the notice of Mr Percy Pitt, who gave me my first engagement with the British National Opera Company.

After touring with them, I decided to go to Italy in order to continue my studies. I returned from Italy to appear as Rudolpho in *La Boheme* at Covent Garden, with Melba as Mimi, one of her most famous roles. It was, as I have said, her farewell to opera, and the emotion and enthusiasm of that night were something that will not easily be forgotten by those who were present.

Mummery had a repertoire of thirty roles. He sang in the first broadcast of opera from Savoy Hill and appeared as Rudolpho in *La Boheme,* the first opera conducted in England by Sir Malcolm Sargent, at Birmingham in 1923. Shortly after he returned to Italy to appear as The Singer in *Der Rosenkavalier,* later singing the same role in another production with Lotte Lehmann, with Bruno Walter conducting.

After giving a series of concerts and many broadcasts in Great Britain Mummery returned to Australia in 1928 as Principal Tenor in the Melba-Williamson Opera Season. Subsequently he went to the United States, gave concerts in New York, and was associated for two years with the National Broadcasting Company. One of his interesting experiences during this period was participation in the first successful relay of a concert by wireless, from the Roxy Theatre in New York to Admiral Byrd's Camp at the South Pole, during Christmas 1931. After spending another two years in London broadcasting with the BBC and singing with Evelyn Laye in the motion picture version of *Evensong,* he returned to Australia and again appeared in opera as a member of the distinguished cast of The Fuller Grand Opera Company in 1934. Later he made several tours of Australia and New Zealand as a Celebrity Artist and taught in Melbourne for many years before retiring to live in Canberra.

ETHEL OSBORN, soprano

When Melba visited the New South Wales Conservatorium in Sydney in 1918 she asked permission to test "the girl from Brisbane", about whom she had heard so much, and whom she had already heard sing in a radio broadcast. As Roland Foster, the girl's teacher, told the story:

> Dame Nellie seated at the piano began singing up the scale with Miss Osborn. They continued together past the high C to D, E and F at which Melba stopped. Ethel Osborn, however, completely absorbed in the activity, continued on to B Flat in altissimo.

It seemed natural to her to be able to sing high notes; she came of a family in which the men for generations had had unusually fine tenor voices, and she had been singing ever since she could remember. When she was only seven, an inspector from the state education department, testing the children in school, had found her to be the only one who could hold the difficult   129 interval from high "Doh" to "Fa". Later her teacher was impressed by her ability to sing the high C in Elgar's *The Fallen.*

E. R. B. Jordan, the outstanding Brisbane choral director, encouraged the girl to go to Sydney for further study. He offered to help her financially if necessary, but she didn't wish to accept help, and worked in her sister's sheep-station, often in temperatures of 128 degrees, scrubbing eleven wooden floors a week. By saving all she earned she was able to go to Sydney to study.

Between 1920 and 1924 Ethel Osborn appeared as soloist in Sydney, and also toured Queensland and New Zealand. The Sydney *Daily Telegraph* referred to her as "undoubtedly one of the foremost sopranos Australia has produced". The *New Zealand Times* said: "Ethel Osborn, who was named 'the Tetrazzini of Australia' by the late Sir Walter Davidson, has no necessity to shelter under the name of the great prima donna; her own work is her best recommendation".

Another New Zealand review, referring to an accomplishment revealed in her encores, wrote: " 'the Kookaburra' and 'Little Gray Dove' showed Miss Osborn to be an astonishingly faithful mimic of birds".

In 1924 Melba was again in Australia with an Italian Opera Company. She heard Osborn sing at a concert and, impressed by her easy production and exceptionally good breath control, she asked the young woman whether she would like to sing in opera.

Melba had wished to give her an opportunity to sing Lucia during this company's tour, but Toti Dal Monte had priority for the role and the opportunity for Ethel Osborn to sing it did not eventuate. Dame Nellie did arrange, however, for the young singer to be present at all the remaining performances of the opera season, and to receive operatic coaching from the conductor, Signor Schiavoni.

Ethel Osborn went to London in 1926 with Dame Clara Butt, after the latter, during a visit to Australia, invited her to "come to England and sing with me at the Royal Albert Hall". She and her husband, John Gilmour, arrived two days before Melba gave her last concert and during the meeting which ensued the diva told Osborn of her plans to form an opera company of world standard comprised of Australian artists who were capable of singing in many languages. Before leaving she encouraged the new arrival "to study Siegfried, Die Walkure, Otello and Faust" in preparation for this. The company, however, never materialized, because Dame Nellie suffered an illness soon afterward.

A month after arriving in London Ethel Osborn was scheduled to appear at a concert at the Royal Albert Hall. Before beginning rehearsals with the orchestra she was asked to sing an aria for the conductor, Sir Landon Ronald. She sang it in the florid Italian style she had been taught by Signor Schiavoni and was told that no British orchestra would accompany her unless she took out "all that rubbish". This seemed like an impossible task with so little time before the performance, but Ethel Osborn worked around the clock and returned to sing without any of the embellishments which in the eyes of Sir Landon had marred her performance of the day before. This is an ordeal which she still remembers. She attributes its successful outcome to the early discipline of her Brisbane teacher, E. R. B. Jordan. It is one of the early experiences which prompted her to remark: "Australians need better preparation before they go abroad. It is not enough, and it may not even be desirable, to give them money which they may not know how to use wisely. They need 'briefing' on what to expect, and to have contacts made for them overseas, so that they will not be exploited by incompetent teachers and agents who make big promises." She recalls Melba's words: "Although very little in the way of vocal study may be needed most of them need at least two years coaching in repertoire, languages and acting."

Miss Osborn's first performance with the London Symphony Orchestra elicited special headlines in the London papers: "New Australian Star"; "Another Australian Discovery"; "Remarkable New Soprano"; and "New Soprano's Success". She seemed to be on the brink of a spectacular career but she was a very loyal and ingenuous person. When Dame Clara Butt, whom she considered a benefactor, suggested that she sign up for three years as an assisting artist on that lady's provincial tours, she did so, and dropped out of sight of London audiences.

When Roland Foster of the New South Wales Conservatorium met Sir Landon Ronald some time later he was asked: "What became of that remarkable soprano of yours whom I conducted for a year ago at the Albert Hall? Has she gone back to Australia?" When Foster explained that she had been away touring, the distinguished conductor commented "As an assisting artist she is just the tail to somebody else's kite and the kite gets all the attention. An individual recital following the Albert Hall debut would definitely have put her on the map. At that stage in her career one London engagement would have been worth twenty in the provinces."[1]

Ethel Osborn did, nonetheless, have a successful career in the British Isles for over twenty years. She was a soloist in oratorios and cantatas, sang on the concert stage and from the BBC studios, appeared with provincial choirs and in Sir Henry Wood's Promenade Concerts. She sang operatic arias, songs by contemporary composers and even provided the voice for performances of "Aesop's Fables" in the early days of television. During the war years in London, she volunteered for service with the Evacuation Department and much of her music and other personal possessions were destroyed when a bomb hit the home of a friend where they had been stored for safe keeping.

In 1951 she returned to Brisbane where she now prepares candidates for examinations of the Australian Music Examinations Board.

STELLA POWER, soprano

While she was in Melbourne during the war, Melba, always on the alert for a successor, took a special interest in Stella Power who was then studying at the Albert Street Conservatorium. She arranged for her to make her debut at the Auditorium under the well-known Tait management, where she was billed as "The Little Melba". Stella Power was said at the time to reveal a light soprano voice of wide compass and the loveliest undertones. Critics were favourably impressed with the quality and calibre of her voice and were unanimous in predicting a brilliant future for her.[1] She made a fine impression at a concert of the Madrigal and Chamber Music Society in the same year, when she received tumultuous applause for her singing of Donizetti's "Regnata del Silenzo" and Rossini's "Bel Raggio". She was said to have a "good endowment for coloratura work, the proper temperamental qualifications and a just appreciation of dramatic values". Her voice was delightfully clear and liquid, her production was good and her tones "beautifully poised and balanced."

Later in 1917 Melba, who had gone to the United States, cabled Stella Power to join her there. A farewell concert in the Melbourne Town Hall was very well attended and an enthusiastic reception given to her singing of The Mad Scene from *Lucia.* She and her teacher, Mary Campbell, left Melbourne in November and arrived in San Francisco a month later. Melba was there to meet them. She had arranged a full tour of engagements for her young protegee, among them performances with the orchestras of Philadelphia and Boston. A review of her singing with the Boston Symphony Orchestra in May stated: "Miss Power warrants well the interest of her celebrated patron. Hers is a voice notable for its fineness of texture and extreme range." Another critic said: "Her voice is lovely, full and resonant, superb in colour and of excellent timbre. It is extremely pliable and responds to any demand put upon it by its charming and unaffected possessor."[2]

During February 1918 Stella Power toured the United States with the violinists Ysaye and Mischa Elman and then went to California to sing with Melba. The next few months were busy ones for the young singer. She sang at many concerts and the critics gave her high praise. One commented on her "unusual range and quality — mezzo in the lower tones but most truly and sweetly soprano in its highest reaches."[3]

When she returned to Melbourne in June, 1918, she was welcomed home at a concert at the Auditorium. The audience showed tremendous enthusiasm. "The liquid freshness of her voice is enhanced by the added brilliance of her style and the ease and finish that comes with travel, experience and study", said one review. In August after another Farewell Concert she left Melbourne for England where, as "The Little Melba", she made her debut under Sir Landon Ronald at the Royal Albert Hall. The London Press was enthusiastic: "She grasped the mystery, at least in good part, of Mme Melba's evenness of voice — the liquid purity of the high notes, which is remarkable, a smoothness of phrasing and the breath control", said one reviewer.

Stella Power made several tours of English provincial cities during the next three years. A concert at Blackpool in which she appeared also marked the first appearance in England of the Australian cellist, Lauri Kennedy, fresh from his tour of North America with John McCormack. Early in 1921 Melba arranged a tour of Norway for her — to be followed by concerts in Scotland where she had been well received the previous year. In 1922, she made appearances at the Chappel Ballad Concerts at Queen's Hall and in the International Celebrity Series in London. These were followed by thirty-five concerts on a tour of England with Kubelik.

At the end of 1923 Stella Power returned for performances in Australia and soon afterward entered into a ten years' contract with John Murray Anderson to appear in the United States in scenes from operettas. At the conclusion of her contract, Miss Power returned to Australia and toured for the ABC. With the advent of the war she retired from the stage and devoted her time to her family.

EVELYN SCOTNEY, coloratura soprano

One of Melba's early protegees was Evelyn Scotney, a gifted coloratura soprano, who was born in Ballarat, home of the famous South Street competitions. Even as a child she revealed the promise of an outstanding voice and as a young girl soon attracted attention when appearing at student concerts; later she won scholarships at the Albert Street Conservatorium where she was a pupil of Mme Elise Wiedermann. In 1910, soon after she had graduated from the Conservatorium, Evelyn Scotney entered the Eisteddfod at Ballarat and won a number of awards. Shortly after, when singing at a mayoral reception for Lord Kitchener in Melbourne, she was heard by Melba who was so impressed by the young singer's voice that when she left for Paris two weeks later she took Scotney with her and arranged for her to study with Mme Mathilde Marchesi. After Mme Marchesi had auditioned the girl she turned to Melba and exclaimed: "Where have I heard this voice before?" She had noted the strong resemblance to Melba's own voice which was apparent to all who heard Scotney sing.

After studying with Marchesi in Paris she continued her studies in London and, later, in Rome with Tosti. In 1911 Henry Russell, the impresario, offered her an engagement in the United States with the Boston Opera Company. Called on suddenly to deputise at a concert for Tetrazzini, who was indisposed,   133

Scotney gave such a brilliant rendering of the Mad Scene from *Lucia* that the critics commented on her voice as "[having] astonishing range, power and beauty. The upper tones were round, edgeless, and of a remarkable bell-like quality. In their amplitude and haunting beauty they are comparable to the voice of Melba." There followed a three-year contract with the Boston Opera Company and on the occasion of her operatic debut in *Lucia* she again received high praise. Critics spoke of "the ease with which the voice soars", and of its "power, clarity and brilliance."

In a recent book two outstanding Boston critics[1] of the period are quoted as referring to Evelyn Scotney's appearance in *Thais* as "the surprise and delight of the evening," and praising her singing of the roles of Lucia, Gilda, Violetta and Olympia. Her voice was described as unusual, "extraordinarily pure and crystalline in the upper reaches", "excellent in florid passages and possessing a trill uncommonly good for her age." Another critic said: "Her singing of the Bell Song from *Lakme* exhibited rare proficiency in music of the florid, decorative order and showed her a past mistress of coloratura."

Miss Scotney married another member of the Boston Opera Company, the American basso Howard White and later appeared with him in concert tours of the United States and Australia. She credited him with providing guidance and help which aided her in developing into a mature artist. (White died soon after the couple returned to the United States from an Australian tour near the close of World War I.)

In 1920 Mme Scotney joined the Metropolitan Opera Company and during that season appeared regularly with Caruso as Adina in *L'Elisir d'Amore* and as The Princess in *La Juive*. As The Queen in *Le Coq d'Or* her rendition was considered especially outstanding. Following her performances at the Metropolitan in New York, she toured the United States, Australia and the United Kingdom, singing in the International Celebrity Concert series and in guest performances of opera in English with the Beecham Opera Company. Critics on these occasions referred to her as ". . . singing with a perfection of art and beauty of tone which earned her an enthusiastic ovation", using such phrases as "exquisite voice", "consummate skill", and "accomplished artist".

In London in 1926 Miss Scotney married B. H. Russell, well known in trans-Atlantic shipping circles, but continued her career in opera, concert, and broadcasting until the outbreak of World War II. Like a number of other gifted persons Miss Scotney has several talents; she is not only a fine pianist but has also achieved success with pencil and crayon.

CLARA SERENA, contralto

134   Clara Serena, a descendant of German pioneers named Kleinschmidt who

settled in Lobethal, South Australia, in the 1840's, was about to begin an international career as a dramatic contralto when World War I broke out. She met Melba when she returned from England where she had been studying at the Royal College with Henry Blower and Visetti. She was giving recitals in Melbourne and was invited to sing at three of Melba's concerts for the Red Cross. In 1918 the *Australian Musical News* commented on her "even and mellow tone, splendid physique; and the admirable breathing which enables her to deliver the highest notes with thrilling volume and richness". A year after her return to Australia, she married the pianist Roy Mellish who became her accompanist for the rest of her professional career.

Her musical education had begun in 1908 when the Waite family of Adelaide arranged for her to enter the conservatorium of the University in that city; she had been discovered by friends of theirs who heard her singing in her aunt's home at Outbank as they chanced to pass by. Later she won a scholarship for a second year at the Conservatorium and then the Elder Overseas Scholarship for three years study at the Royal College. Before she began her studies there, Miss Elizabeth Waite took her on a tour of the Continent so that she might attend performances at Bayreuth and elsewhere to hear famous singers in roles which she hoped to sing some day.

In 1922 she returned to London with her husband and met Ada Crossley, who by this time had retired from public life. So interested was she in Serena however, that she presented her at a recital in Wigmore Hall in 1923 and sang three duets with her. The London critics were unanimous in their praise; one wrote: "She answers the oft repeated question, where are the great singers?" All agreed that a singer of rare quality had arrived. She possessed a most unusual voice, having a range of three octaves, reaching to top B flat. She was also an excellent linguist and able to sing roles in four languages: German, French, Italian and English. Of a performance with the British National Opera Company at Covent Garden on 11th June, 1923, a critic wrote: "In a new British work, Rutland Boughton's *Alkestis,* Clara Serena in the title role displayed a full, clear voice and invested the music with real interest".[1] During the International Seasons of 1928, 1929 and 1931 she sang at Covent Garden as a guest artist in the roles of Amneris, Delilah, Erda and Waltraute. She also appeared in numerous performances of oratorios, especially *The Messiah* and *Elijah* and in the title role of *Solomon.* In 1928 at the Queen's Hall she sang this part with the Royal Philharmonic Society at a performance before King George and Queen Mary. For more than fifteen years she appeared as soloist with leading orchestras under the direction of the outstanding conductors of the day, singing operatic excerpts and lieder from the standard German repertoire, as well as modern works by English, French and American composers. In 1924, for instance, she sang "Hecuba's Lament" by Holst with the female chorus of the Philharmonic Choir under Charles

Kennedy Scott's direction, and later "Der Erlkoenig" by Schubert with the BBC orchestra conducted by Sir Henry Wood and "Gerichter Gott" from Wagner's *Rienzi* with the Scottish Orchestra conducted by Albert Coates. In 1932 she and Florence Austral sang a duet from *Die Gotterdammerung* at a concert by the Halle Orchestra. One of the numerous recitals which she gave with local choral groups in the smaller cities of the United Kingdom and Ireland was the Schubert Memorial Concert in Sunderland in 1928 — the centenary of the composer's death.

Serena's career was again interrupted by the outbreak of the Second World War. This time, however, she remained in England and did not return to Adelaide until 1951.

DOROTHY HELMRICH, mezzo soprano

While many of the singers of this period who achieved an international reputation did so on the operatic stage, Dorothy Helmrich was primarily a recitalist. W. J. Henderson called the song recital "the highest test of ability in singing", and wrote: "there one must display not only temperament and dramatic intelligence but voice of the finest timbre, tones of the purest and roundest quality, perfect attack".[1] Marie Narelle's concerts in the early part of the century demonstrated this as did Dorothy Helmrich's song recitals in later years.

While studying with Stefan Mavrogordato at the New South Wales Conservatorium in Sydney, Miss Helmrich met Lady Alice Cooper, an Australian resident in London, who was home on a visit. After hearing Miss Helmrich sing at a concert at Government House, Lady Cooper invited her to go to London for further training under her patronage. This made it possible for Miss Helmrich to attend the Royal College of Music and pursue further studies of lieder and opera with Sir George Henschel at the London School of Opera, and interpretation with Plunkett Greene. During vacations she went to Munich to study German.

As soon as Henschel heard her sing he predicted a career as a lieder singer. So appreciative was he of her talent that he acted as accompanist for her debut in Wigmore Hall. She, in turn, took very seriously a well known statement of his: "To have a choice of becoming an artist in the true sense of the word, the student should from the outset strive for none but the highest ideals, and resist the temptations which the prospect of popularity and its worldly advantages — may place in his way".

Newspaper accounts of her appearances in Australia, years later, when she was one of the two Australian soloists selected for the first season of the newly instituted Australian Broadcasting Commission's Celebrity Concert Series in 1936, indicate how closely she subscribed to these sentiments. When

Dorothy Helmrich
Photo: Athol Shmith

interviewed in Brisbane she said: "I would rather sing to an audience of ten people who are sincere in their love of music, than to a hundred who are there because they think it is fashionable". A Sydney reviewer noted: "It is the complete effacement of self to the greater glory of the composer which explains half the secret of the art of Dorothy Helmrich. The other half of the secret is her impeccable musical taste, both in her choice of items and the singing of them". Reviewing a concert of hers in Melbourne, Thorold Waters wrote: "Such an intellectual and sincere, yet at the same time deeply

137

emotional, outlook on song as Dorothy Helmrich's is needed to rectify the whipped-up craze for stereotyped prettiness".

Before returning to Australia for this tour she had been acclaimed as a singer of the first rank by leading music critics in London, New York, Boston, Amsterdam, Brussels, Paris, Berlin, Warsaw and Stockholm. The following quotations from reviews in German and Polish papers are typical. Max Marschalk in the *Vossiche Zeitung* of Berlin wrote: "Dorothy Helmrich is a singer of the first rank" and Alfred Einstein of the *Berliner Tageblatt* referred to her as "a singer of distinction, knowledge and charm of presentation". Mormus in the *Kleines Journal* commented: "In all she sang one recognized the experienced singer who more than most gave evidence of excellent breath control. In the high voice she forms exquisitely beautiful tones and the low voice is sonorous. She sang in Italian, French, English and German, and her interpretation throughout showed both taste and understanding".

Warsaw reviews were equally enthusiastic. The *Kurjer Poranny* said:

Miss Dorothy Helmrich gave us a beautiful rich programme last night. She has a beautiful mezzo-soprano voice and in a long programme of lieder proved the fullness of her musicality, artistic taste and technique. Miss Dorothy Helmrich is an Australian, and a compatriot of Melba, one of the great singers of the latter half of last century — but Miss Helmrich's art is altogether different. The voice is clear and voluminous, the quality is velvet, and the colour very warm; at the same time, this beautiful voice is technically excellent — of remarkable subtleness, which permits the artist to present each melody with its particular expression.

In addition to recital work, Miss Helmrich appeared as soloist with many famous English orchestras, including the Queen's Hall with Sir Henry Wood, the BBC Symphony with Sir Adrian Boult, and the Worcester Orchestra with Sir Edward Elgar; also with such orchestras on the Continent as the Scheveningen with Neumann, the Finnish State with Schneevoight, and the Symphony Orchestra at Gottenberg. In the early 1930's Miss Helmrich represented British Composers at the Contemporary Music Festival at Salzburg, and at the Anglo-American Music Conference at Lausanne. Addressing the Sydney University Musical Society in 1936 she said: "The impression that the English are not a musical race is dying out in Europe. Modern British music is gradually percolating through to the Continent, and really good music which is being written in England is beginning to be appreciated by Europeans — people in Germany, Poland and Sweden in particular are very enthusiastic about it".

Miss Helmrich went back to Europe at the end of the celebrity tour for the ABC but returned to Australia five years later. In December 1941, having completed a tour of India, Singapore, Java and New Zealand she reached Australia just three days before Japan entered the war. She then toured again for the ABC and, departing from her established custom of singing songs only in their original language, gave a series of recitals in English of the great song cycles of Schumann, Schubert, Brahms and Mahler using the translations of Sir Robert Garran, which he had dedicated to her.

Shortly after, she joined the staff of the New South Wales Conservatorium of Music where she has taught a number of students who have gone on to sing in opera in England and in Finland; others have appeared successfully in Gilbert and Sullivan operettas and in oratorio. Having worked with the Arts Council of Great Britain, Miss Helmrich was enthusiastic about the possibility of forming a similar organization in Australia. She soon organized C.E.M.A. (the Council for Encouraging Music and the Arts) and in 1943 took a plan for cultural development in Australia, especially in rural areas, to the directors of both federal and state Post-war Reconstruction Departments. Requests for financial aid to implement the scheme all received the same answer: "No money has been allocated for cultural development". She then turned to other possible sources of support; this came first in 1945 from the N.S.W. Department of Education through the Advisory Board on Adult Education. Gradually, the idea of having rural arts centres took hold. After four delegates to an agricultural conference which she addressed became interested in the idea of having artists sent to their towns other requests followed. She then visited communities in remote areas of the state and new centres were founded. By 1950 twenty towns were participating and the Council was receiving £5000 a year from the Department of Education.

As early as 1947 it was apparent to Sir Angus Gillen of the British Council, who was revisiting Australia, that this was a movement to be encouraged — and Dorothy Helmrich was invited to go to England under the auspices of the British Council to study repertory theatre and allied activities. While in London she visited her former concert manager who presumed that now that the war was over she was ready to resume her career. It was difficult to convince him that she was serious when she said she had found a more absorbing and satisfying occupation.

Her interest in this enterprise was based on a conviction that, "the more mechanised life becomes, the more vital is the need for establishing live theatre and the allied arts on a firm progressive basis in both city and country. . . . Only thus can a national culture worthy of the name be nurtured. Decentralization is considered to be one of Australia's foremost cultural necessities". From 1943 to 1950 she laid the groundwork for the far flung organization of Arts Council Branches and Centres. A gift by The Joint Coal Board in 1950 had made possible the first Mobile Theatre Unit; by 1965 four travelling theatre units were covering, each year, an area almost half the size of Australia   139 and serving over 100 centres and towns as far north as Darwin. In this way remote areas as well as large centres see artists from the East and Europe.

An outstanding early achievement of the Arts Council was the staging in Sydney in 1950 of the world premiere of the Australian ballet *Corroboree* — the music for which was written by the native born composer John Antill — and its subsequent restaging in all capital cities for the jubilee celebrations in 1951. That same year saw the Australian premiere of Benjamin Britten's *Let's Make an Opera* under the auspices of the Arts Council. After performances in Sydney, Canberra and Brisbane, it was presented in country centres, using the original cast and sets.

Since 1956 the Arts Council has sponsored Summer Schools of Dramatic Arts in Sydney and Brisbane. Country drama festivals, week-end drama schools, art exhibits and lunch-time lectures on the arts are also held at many country centres. An important phase of the Arts Council's activities everywhere has been to provide school children with experience in all branches of the arts; by 1965, 200,000 children were seeing plays, operas, ballets and puppet shows at regular intervals in New South Wales alone. Dorothy Helmrich has always believed that ". . . beginning with the child we can encourage and build a nationally-minded and well-informed culture for tomorrow".

BEATRICE MIRANDA, dramatic soprano

Since Melba's debut at Covent Garden in 1888 Australians have played prominent roles in opera in Britain. Beatrice Miranda was not only a member of the Beecham Company and a prima donna of the Carl Rosa and the British National Opera Companies but in her later years was a producer of grand opera in Edinburgh and the founder of the Scottish National Opera.

She was born in Melbourne about ten years after her famous sister, Lalla (see page 80). She, too, was an accomplished pianist but singing was always her first love. She made her first appearance as a solo vocalist at a concert given by Una Bourne at Glen's Music Rooms, in December 1903, a critic remarking on this occasion that she was "the possessor of a rich, effective dramatic soprano voice, suited rather to the operatic stage than to the concert platform".[1] Nevertheless it was as a concert artist that she toured Victoria for the next two and a half years with the Turner Company, all the leading critics of the day pronouncing her to have "a magnificent voice of the rarest purity and sweetness". She made her farewell appearance on 3rd May, 1906, in "Opera di Camera" at the Melbourne Town Hall singing the role of Agnus in *Der Freischutz* and was the star of the evening.[2] A month later she and her mother left for London.

140   Her debut there at a concert given by her teacher, Mme Minna Fischer,

brought Beatrice to the notice of William Boosey who engaged her for the 1907-08 winter season at Queen's Hall. Her career as an opera singer began in 1909 when she sang at Covent Garden with the Carl Rosa Company in *I Pagliacci* and *Rigoletto.* Thereafter she appeared with this and the Beecham Companies. A performance of *Aida* with the Carl Rosa group at Hammersmith won her "unstinting praise from the critics for her voice and dramatic instinct".[3]

When the British National Opera Company was organized by former members of the Beecham Company in 1922 Beatrice Miranda was one of its principal sopranos. She sang *Aida* at its first performance in Bradford and during the same season, *Tosca* and the Marquess in Offenbach's *Goldsmith of Toledo,* the former being a bi-lingual performance with Hislop and Dinh Gilly. Miss Miranda was especially admired in Britain as an interpreter of Wagner.[4]

Her best role was Isolde but critics wrote of her as a superb Brunnhilde, a notable Sieglinde, and a commanding Elisabeth, and she was said to be equally at home as Elsa.

In 1924 she and her husband, the singer Hebden Foster, moved to Edinburgh and opened a teaching practice there. She continued to sing in opera and at concerts, always giving a high standard of performance. After

Beatrice Miranda
Photo: James Bacon

141

one recital the critic of *The Scotsman* said: "It is questionable whether quite so good a piece of Wagnerian singing has been heard before at a concert". When the Edinburgh Grand Opera Company was formed Foster became its producer, but Miss Miranda, with her charming personality and hard work, did more than anybody to put it on its feet.

The outbreak of the war in 1939 put an end to this venture but when it was over she founded the Scottish National Opera Company and, until her retirement, both produced and conducted for it. She died at her daughter's home in Buffalo, New York, in 1964.

HAROLD WILLIAMS, baritone

Harold Williams, whose career in opera and oratorio and as a recording artist established him as an outstanding figure in British musical circles for more than thirty years, was born in Sydney in 1893. Until the time of his service with the Australian Forces during World War I his chief interests had been international cricket and football. Then one evening, when he was singing for friends at a home in Sheffield, it was suggested that he apply for discharge in England and go to London to undertake the serious study of music.

When he made the decision to follow their advice he had no financial resources so he had to work during the day and study singing in the evening with a professor from the Royal Academy of Music. After eighteen months of this routine he was advised to try himself out on the concert platform. Using the £350 in pay he had received when he was mustered out of service, he arranged to give three concerts at Wigmore Hall. Of the first, presented in December 1919, the London *Times* wrote that he had "a voice of noble quality, glittering, stirring, and intrepid". His subsequent appearances attracted equally favourable attention and he began to be engaged for ballad concerts. Introduced to Mr Tillett of the well-known firm of concert managers "as a friend from Australia who is a cricket fiend", Williams was "put on their books" and soon received a sufficient number of engagements to keep him busy every evening.

It was not long before he graduated from ballad concerts to opera and oratorio. With the British National Opera Company his principal roles were Wolfram in *Tannhauser* and Iago in *Othello*. In seasons of Italian and German opera at Covent Garden he appeared in the title role of *Boris Godounov* and as Mephistopheles in *Faust*. With the English Opera Company he sang a score of important roles both in London and on tour. He often sang at 'Prom' concerts, and was regarded as one of the outstanding soloists to appear during Toscanini's season at the Queen's Hall, notably in Beethoven's *Ninth Symphony*. For many years he portrayed the title role in annual performances of *Hiawatha* at The Royal Albert Hall. He came to be looked upon as one of the leading British baritones of his day and his Columbia recordings of *Elijah* with Sir Malcolm Sargent, and of *The Messiah* with Sir Thomas Beecham, were hailed both in the United States and Great Britain. The London *Morning Post* spoke of his singing of the role of the Prophet in *Elijah* as "a real study in tone colour"; the *Liverpool Post* called him "one of the most intelligent and consistent all-round singers" and the *Manchester City News* spoke of his "beautifully mellow voice, rich in quality throughout the whole range — impeccable vocal style and sense of the dramatic".

Neville Cardus, in a review of a performance of Elgar's *The Kingdom*, in the *Manchester Guardian* in 1929, wrote: "Harold Williams sang with a nobility that carried us back to the great days of oratorio". When he appeared after the war with Kathleen Ferrier in *The Dream of Gerontius* the same critic noted that "There is no greater music in *Gerontius* than that given the Angel of Agony and no one in recent years has excelled Harold Williams in this part for mingled dignity, awe and tenderness".

In 1938 Williams was chosen to sing at Westminster Abbey at the coronation of King George VI and Queen Elizabeth and in 1952, just before leaving London, he appeared in the film, *Mr Gilbert and Mr Sullivan* which was produced in connection with the festivities for the coronation of Queen Elizabeth II. From 1940 until 1946 Mr Williams lived in Australia, touring the Commonwealth for the Australian Broadcasting Commission and appearing on concerts and oratorios notably *The Messiah* and *Elijah*. In 1947 he returned to England where he was welcomed back by his agents who said: "You remind us of Kathleen Ferrier. Wherever we sent her they wanted her back again". That same year he appeared at the Edinburgh Festival and at the Three Choirs Festival. Later he was associated with Benjamin Britten in the London and Weisbaden premieres of *The Rape of Lucretia.*

Harold Williams's concert programmes always had a wide appeal as is shown by a quotation from the *Straits Times* of 28th October, 1953. Commenting on a performance at a studio in Singapore, a columnist wrote: "From Mozart to Delacroze, from the saucy charm of the Tamborin 'Bel Amanda' and the easy abandon of 'Non pui andrai farcollone amaroso' to the passionate 'More was lost at Mohacs field' the singer lived every part and ran the gamut of our emotions and his own".

After returning to Australia to live Harold Williams made many appearances throughout the Commonwealth. Reviewing a gala empire concert at the Town Hall in 1953 the critic for the Melbourne *Age* wrote: "Greatest among {the singers} was Harold Williams who sang English songs and opera arias with splendid diction and perfect phrasing, and in a voice still fresh and youthful and under admirable control". Another review referred to "breath control that joins the longest phrases" and "the infusion of mood into song", 143 and noted that "oratorio, opera, folksongs, the French romantics, ballads, are all within his grasp".

Harold Williams joined the staff of the New South Wales State Conservatorium of Music in 1952 as Professor of Singing, and since that time has been able to further the musical education of young Australian singers, among them, Raymond Nilsson, Neil Easton and Margreta Elkins, all of Covent Garden.

MARGHERITA GRANDI, dramatic soprano

Two world wars interrupted the singing career of Margherita Grandi but they merely delayed her triumphs. It was 1911 when, as Margaret Garde, she left Tasmania at the age of sixteen to study at the Royal College in London, aided by a benefit concert presented by the musicians of Hobart. In London she won the £400 scholarship which had set Clara Butt on the road to fame, and went to Paris to work with Madame Emma Calve. In 1914 she was engaged to sing at the Opera Comique. In November of that year she made her debut in Massenet's *Werther* and later in the season sang *Carmen.* As a result of these performances the Director of the Monte Carlo Opera signed her for a three-month season commencing in February 1915, when she opened in the first performance of Massenet's last opera *Amadis.*

Margherita Grandi

144

She now decided to go to Italy for further study but on her arrival was detained and kept under surveillance for the remainder of the war. At its end she changed her name to Grandi and resumed her studies, her principal teacher being Gianina Russ. It was not until 1932 that she made her operatic debut in Italy — as *Aida* at the Teatro Carcano in Milan. The following year she sang Elena in Boito's *Mefistofele* at La Scala and her reputation was established. In the next few years she sang at all the leading opera houses in Italy — Rome, Vienna, Naples — in such roles as Tosca, Aida, La Gioconda, Desdemona, Elsa (*Lohengrin*), and many others.

At the Glyndebourne Festival in 1939 Madame Grandi sang the role of Lady Macbeth. The newspapers were enthusiastic in their praise. The critic of the *Sunday Times* wrote: "She is magnificently voiced; it was thrilling to hear those notes . . . rolling out with such power and freedom". The *Observer* described her as "the Prima Donna who appears only in the dreams of producer and conductor". The *Daily Telegraph* said she "proved herself not only an exceptionally fine singer, but also a noble tragic actress". When she repeated the role at the Edinburgh Festival, the *Punch* critic spoke of the "thrilling experience" of the sleep-walking scene. Her Irish and Italian ancestry was standing her in good stead.

After the Edinburgh Festival, Grandi returned to Italy where she opened the La Scala season in *Aida* with Gigli as Rhadames and took the leading role in the Italian premiere of Richard Strauss' opera *The Day of Peace* in Venice in 1940. By this time the whole of Europe was at war and Grandi retired to the mountains where she became an active helper of the partisans, smuggling Allied airmen to safety in Switzerland. The Germans allowed her to sing in public only twice — in Rossini's *Stabat Mater* and in *La Coronazione Di Poppea* by Monteverdi at the Reale.

Once again a war had interrupted her career, but once again her artistry triumphed. She sang the Verdi *Requiem* at La Scala and, in 1947, repeated her role of Lady Macbeth at Glyndebourne. 1948 saw her again in London where she sang Donna Anna and *Tosca* at the Cambridge Theatre and made her debut at Covent Garden as Diana in the premiere of Sir Arthur Bliss' new opera *The Olympians*. Later in the season she sang the role of Leonora in *Il Trovotore*.

In the following year Grandi sang Amelia in *The Masked Ball* at both Glyndebourne and Edinburgh Festivals. Then, in 1952, she returned to Covent Garden to sing *Tosca*. She has also sung in a number of European capitals and toured South America and Egypt. Her already large repertoire was increased to include Norma, Leonora in *The Force of Destiny*, Amelia in *Simon Boccanegra* and the leading role in *La Schiano* by Gomez.

Margherita Grandi has never sung in opera in her native land, though she always wished that a tour could be arranged. She has made a number of recordings, among them *The Tales of Hoffmann* with the Royal Philharmonic Society under Sir Thomas Beecham.

FLORENCE AUSTRAL, dramatic soprano

Florence Austral was one of the outstanding singers who emerged during the 1920's. As Florence Fawaz she won both the soprano and mezzo-soprano contests at the South Street Eisteddfod in Ballarat in 1914 when the adjudicator, Fritz Hart, told her: "You are a Brunnhilde". This proved to be prophetic of the career that lay ahead because it was in this role in *Die Walkure* that, as Florence Austral, she made her debut at Covent Garden eight years later. In 1914 however, she did not understand the reference to Brunnhilde because she had not even heard of Wagner.

Florence Austral was born in a suburb of Melbourne on 26th April, 1894. Her father, a Scandinavian named Wilhelm Lindholm who changed his name to Wilson on the way out to Australia, died soon afterward and when her mother married again she took her step-father's name, Fawaz. The family was not a musical one and her encouragement to study voice came from two Melbourne teachers, Professor Constantine and George Andrews. It was the latter who had suggested she enter the contests at Ballarat. Soon after winning these she sang for Mme Elise Wiedermann, the head of the opera school at the Albert Street Conservatorium. Mme Wiedermann was favourably impressed by the "wide range and fine quality of her voice" and recommended that she be given a scholarship for the following year. From that time until Florence left for the United States four years later, Mme Wiedermann worked with her intensively at home as well as at the Conservatorium — on voice production and on operas in the German repertoire. Miss Fawaz made her first public appearance as Leonora in an excerpt from *Fidelio* in a conservatorium production of Scenes from Opera. Later when Mme Wiedermann went to teach at the University Conservatorium her pupil transferred there.

So it was that Professor Laver, the director of that institution, headed a group of citizens who contemplated giving the young singer a complimentary concert in order to raise funds to enable her to go to New York for further study. At one of their meetings a letter was read from Mme Wiedermann in which she said: "Miss Fawaz has been studying with me for the past four years and I consider hers the very best and most wonderful soprano voice I have heard — in my long career as a prima donna. I am convinced that if she can go to America she will be as famous as Nordica".[1]

The farewell concert was held on 22nd September, 1919, and Florence Fawaz left soon after to study in New York with Signor Sibella. Concerts she gave in Chicago and Boston were well received and reviewed. One critic noted

Florence Austral as Tosca, 1924

that "hers was an amazing voice, a marvellous instrument that stands supreme among the dramatic sopranos of the present generation". She was offered a contract with the Metropolitan Opera Association in May, 1920, but decided not to accept. She was very lonely in the United States and decided to go on to London where she received encouragement from the Australian, Ada Crossley, who told her: "You have one of the most beautiful dramatic soprano voices I have ever heard. In opera you must surely go to the top". When Harry Higgins of the Covent Garden Opera Syndicate heard Florence Fawaz sing he said: "If you have as much faith in yourself as I have in you, you will go far". Subsequently she competed in an audition with thirty other singers and was given a contract with Covent Garden, adopting the name of "Austral" at Higgins' suggestion. She wrote to her family at that time: "It is a most delightful feeling to have got to the top with a bound, without any wire-pulling, influence or corruption whatsoever."

On 16th May, 1922, she sang Brunnhilde in *Die Walkure* as a last minute substitute for Elsa Stralia, another Australian. This was her first professional operatic appearance. There had been time for only a brief rehearsal, and she had never sung before with an orchestra. The audience and critics were most enthusiastic; one critic however, not only said that "her voice is beautiful and her singing perfectly true" but added: "She looked at the conductor too often and she might have sung with more abandon". He did not know that she had had to wear a curass and a helmet that were too small for her and that, therefore any freer movements would have been disastrous. The *Daily Mail* reported: "In London musical circles the one topic of conversation is the pluck of Miss Florence Austral in her first appearance as Brunnhilde in *Die Walkure* and the complete success which rewarded it". There followed comparable successes as Brunnhilde in *Siegfried* and later, at the end of the season, in the *Gotterdammerung*. When the company went on tour audiences in other cities gave Miss Austral equally warm receptions.

When she opened the British National Opera Company's second season at Covent Garden in December of 1922 the critics spoke of her as "one of the most notable Aidas in recent years". Later Austral added Isolde to her repertoire and in this role her singing was referred to as "magnificent". In January, 1923, she appeared at Covent Garden in a joint programme with Melba. She sang two acts of *Aida* and Dame Nellie appeared as Mimi in two acts of *La Boheme*. In 1924 Austral was invited to participate for the first time in the renowned International Season at Covent Garden when she sang the Brunnhilde in German, receiving special commendation for her singing in the last scene of *Siegfried* and for her fine enunciation.

During the years she sang with the British National Opera Company Austral also appeared as soloist in a number of festivals. In 1923 these included the Handel Festival and the Three Choir Choirs Festival at Worcester

Cathedral. She toured England as soloist with Sir Landon Ronald's Royal Albert Hall Orchestra and appeared frequently with them in London. It was at a rehearsal performance of *Israel in Egypt* for a Handel Festival at the Crystal Palace that her rendering of "Sing ye to the Lord" moved the audience to demand an encore — an unprecedented happening. Ronald refused at first but finally had to give in and she sang the aria again.[2] Austral sang also with Sir Henry Wood's Orchestra at Queen's Hall and in Manchester with the Halle Orchestra. The next year she appeared at the Wembley Exhibition in Beethoven's Choral Symphony with the Royal Philharmonic under the baton of Felix Weingartner and at the Crystal Palace in the Jubilee of Verdi's *Requiem.* At this time, too, she was considered one of the most important sopranos making recordings of acoustic discs.

In 1925, Austral appeared at the Evanston and Cincinnati Festivals singing Brahms' *Requiem* and the difficult aria "Ocean! Thou Mighty Monster" from Weber's *Oberon.* This was the first of six extensive tours of the United States and Canada during which she gave song recitals and made guest appearances in opera under the direction of such famous conductors as Walter Damrosch, Koussevitsky, Toscanini and Bruno Walter. At the end of that year she married the noted Australian flautist, John Amadio, who later appeared with her in recitals. Critics in America had noted that she had a definite gift for lieder but London did not have an opportunity to learn this until the autumn of 1928 when she presented a programme at Queen's Hall. Don White[3] quotes a critic as saying:

> A group of Brahms and Strauss showed that she understands the difference in style between them and the operatic numbers with which she began and ended her recital. Her enormous power enabled her to sing the Zigeuner Lieder without the effort which is entailed for most singers, while Strauss' *Standchen* and *Morgen* gave her the scope for greater sweetness and tenderness than is possible in the broader style of the stage. The subtlizing influence of lieder should enrich Austral's art and add something more profound to her glorious voice and always musical way of singing.

By the time she appeared in another International Season at Covent Garden in 1929, after an absence of five years, the illness which was to cripple her completely was beginning to affect her health. The following year after the first of twelve performances at which she was scheduled to sing at the Berlin State Opera she was forced to cancel her contract on her doctor's advice. During her performance of *Die Walkure* in Berlin she had found herself unable to rise from her seat at Wotan's feet and was compelled to pull herself to a standing position by hanging on to Wotan's cloak as he stepped in front of her hiding her from the audience. Years later she spoke of having suffered from multiple sclerosis for most of her professional career and said that this had been responsible for the lack of flexibility noted in her acting by many critics who had been enthusiastic about her singing.

In 1930 Austral returned to Australia for the first time. She made a memorable concert tour, delighting audiences with the fine singing about which her countrymen had heard so much from abroad. Subsequently she toured Holland and North America with her husband. Besides giving many recitals she appeared in guest performances in opera in Philadelphia, Chicago and San Francisco. In 1933 Austral appeared again in the International Season at Covent Garden in *Die Walkure* with Lehmann and Schor, and with Schor and Melchior in *Siegfried*. The next year she accepted an invitation to sing leading roles in Sir Benjamin Fuller's Australian Grand Opera Season which was being arranged to commemorate Melbourne's centenary in 1935. The company included Walter Widdop, Muriel Brunskill and two other Australians, Frederick Collier and Browning Mummery. Between September, 1934, and the following April, Austral sang her established roles of Aida, Brunnhilde and Isolde and appeared for the first time as Tosca, Senta in *The Flying Dutchman* and Leila in *The Pearlfishers*. For all of these performances she received the highest praise from critics in both Sydney and Melbourne who commented on her "great vocal art" and "thorough knowledge of traditional Wagnerian technique".

Reviews of a series of concerts which Austral gave in Australia after the end of the Opera Season were equally laudatory. Audiences were especially enthusiastic when, as an encore, she sang the Mad Scene from *Lucia di Lammermoor*. One critic said: "She phrased the opening 'Ardon gli'incensi' with unusual warmth and richness, and the runs, trills and cadenza {the Melba cadenza} with flute were executed with flexibility and effortless ease, a remarkable accomplishment for a dramatic soprano".

Austral returned to England at the end of 1936 for a series of concerts. Then, in 1937, she went to the United States to give what was to be her last appearance there — a concert at which she sang Isolde's arias with the Minneapolis Symphony with Eugene Ormandy conducting. The review in the *Minneapolis Press* stated:

> The superb singing of Florence Austral thrilled every susceptible heart in the audience. There was a quality of glory, of enchantment, of sheer spiritual and human grief and passion that we have rarely heard equalled. Not only a singer with one of the noblest voices in the world but also a great musician.

In 1938 she appeared as guest artist in six performances at Sadler's Wells. On these occasions the audiences were enthusiastic and press reports were favourable but it was said that her voice sounded smaller than it had been.

She appeared in benefit concerts during the war and then, as her physical disability progressed, she returned to Australia in 1946.[4] The recollection of her exceptionally fine voice, however, remained with all those who had heard her sing. As Roger Covell said in his appreciation of a re-issue of some of her recordings made originally between 1927 and 1930: "The special quality of her voice... is not charm but heroism... It can stir, thrill and exalt, but it could never sound frivolous or lightly decorative."[5]

Dorothy Helmrich, the Australian lieder singer later Director of The Arts Council, said in 1960: "I first met Austral when we were students at the London School of Opera. Looking back I have the feeling of stimulation which I always felt when I was with her. She was a happy, genial person and a generous colleague — a hard worker, a good musician deeply engrossed in her art. When her chance came to sing at Covent Garden she was ready. The thrill of her Brunnhilde is still with me."

LAWRENCE POWER, tenor

Lawrence Power was one of four South Australians appearing in the opera houses of the world in the 1930's whose careers were furthered by aria contests and overseas fellowships. When he won the first Melbourne *Sun* Aria contest in 1924, the adjudicator, Alfred Hill, said: "Lawrence Power is the possessor of a world voice". A year later this Adelaide-born tenor went to Milan for further study with Maestro Peraccini and in 1926 made his debut in *La Favorita* at the little town of Lovere, winning high praise from the critics and from the critical Italian audience.

For the next five years he sang in many of the opera houses of Italy, including the Dal Verme of Milan, under the name of Lorenzo Poerio. Then, in 1930, he went to the Royal Opera House of Malta with a Company from La Scala to open a season with *Mefistofele*. During the season he also sang roles in *Boris Godounov*, *La Boheme*, *Madame Butterfly* and *Rigoletto* and won tremendous applause from the audiences. There followed appearances in Switzerland and a contract, in 1931-32, to sing four leading roles at the Royal San Carlo Opera House of Naples in a company which included such great singers as Tito Schipa and Toti Dal Monte.

The San Carlo Company engaged him as a principal for its nine months' tour of Indonesia during which he sang opposite a young American soprano, Annunciata Garotto, whom he had first met when he was singing Rodolfo and she was making her debut as Mimi. After the Indonesian tour Power was brought to America by Alfredo Salmaggi to open the 1933 Season of Popular Opera at the New York Hippodrome. There he met Garotto again and they were married. Lawrence Power remained at the Hippodrome under various

151

managements during 1933 and 1934 and sang many roles. The critics were enthusiastic about his performances. Pitts Sanborn of the New York *World Telegram* wrote: "He sang with telling effect as Rodolfo, voice of ample strength and compass."

Tours of the United States and Canada followed with Power as the leading lyric tenor. In Toronto the critic of the *Daily Star* reported: "He has a wonderfully pure tenor voice naturally lyric but dramatic in acting. Sang so superbly that he had to repeat 'E lucevan le stelle'." At this time Power added to his already large repertoire *Martha, Phoebus and Pan* and Rossini's *Moses.* Faust was one of his best roles. He was acclaimed wherever he sang it. "He makes a Faust long to be remembered. Voice is of lovely lyric quality, true and pure. He seemed to release the full beauty of his finely tempered tenor, letting it revel in its own effulgent beauty", said Mozelle Horton, the critic of the *Atlanta Constitution.*

With his wife Lawrence Power toured extensively and carried grand opera at popular prices to many of the American States. After returning to Australia just before the war, he was engaged as a celebrity artist by the Australian Broadcasting Commission and sang in the capital cities of the Commonwealth. After an illness in 1945, he was forced to retire and died in Adelaide in August, 1963.

ARNOLD MATTERS, baritone

It was Arnold Matters' success at Ballarat that brought him to the attention of Melba. He had won the *Sun* Aria Contest and seven other prizes there in 1927. Thorold Waters, editor of the *Australian Musical News,* who was present on that occasion said: "Arnold Matters from South Australia ought to

Arnold Matters
Photo: Elizabethan Trust

152

command a place in opera if all his singing is in line with that in the "Credo" from Verdi's *Otello* in which a splendid voice with bell-like tone lent itself thoroughly to the aria's dramatic cynicism and captured enthusiastic plaudits." Fritz Hart, the Director of the Albert Street Conservatorium and adjudicator on this occasion, said that he considered him the most outstanding student he had heard in twenty years of competitions. Melba engaged him to appear with her at a concert at the Melbourne Town Hall and invited him to tour New Zealand in 1928. She, like the two men, urged him to go overseas for further study and experience.

Before acting on this advice, however, he was obliged to consider the advisability of doing so. On the one hand, he was already established in the Civil Service as an accountant and on the other, he had a real interest in singing. He had continued to study part-time at the Elder Conservatorium and sang solo parts in oratorios and bass leads in concerts given by the Adelaide Bach Society under the leadership of Dr Harold Davies.

Matters went to London in 1929. Beginning in 1930 he did a great deal of singing for the BBC and became a member of the choir at Westminster Abbey. This led indirectly to his engagement in 1932 at Sadler's Wells. During the next eight years he sang principal baritone roles in most of the operas of Beethoven, Mozart, Verdi, Puccini and Wagner; among these productions were *Lohengrin, Die Meistersinger* and *Fidelio* in which Mollie de Gunst of Queensland also sang, and *Die Walkure* with Florence Austral from Melbourne.

In 1935 Matters was one of the British artists in the International Season at Covent Garden during which Beecham, Weingartner and Coates conducted. He sang there again in 1938 and 1939 repeating some of the Wagnerian roles he had sung earlier and adding new ones including Kurvenal in *Tristan and Isolde,* with Eva Turner. A decade later Matters returned to Covent Garden as guest artist for a period of four to five years.

In 1941 he had made a successful tour of South Africa before returning to Australia to join the Armed Services. He was posted to entertainment and welfare work and so was able to continue singing in concerts and in broadcasts of operas in which he took principal roles and directed performances. In 1944 he appeared during a brief season of opera in Sydney. After the war Joan Cross invited Matters to return to Sadler's Wells where he remained until 1954, singing a number of roles, among them *Simon Boccanegra* and *Falstaff* for which he won great acclaim. Later he appeared as the Pilgrim in Vaughan Williams' *Pilgrim's Progress,* Lord Hamilton in Lennox Berkeley's *Nelson,* and was in the premiere of Benjamin Britten's *Gloriana.* Altogether Arnold Matters had sixty roles at his command.

In 1954 he began teaching at the Elder Conservatorium in Adelaide, broadcasting operas and concerts, appearing as guest artist in the ABC 153

Celebrity Series, and producing operas at the Conservatorium and for the Australian Elizabethan Theatre Trust.

RICHARD WATSON, bass

Richard Watson's name is so closely associated with productions of Gilbert and Sullivan operas that many people are unaware of his varied experience. Going to England in 1926 as an Elder Overseas Fellow, he spent three years at the Royal College of Music and then became principal bass at Covent Garden for both the International and English seasons. He also sang in oratorio in London and in English provincial cities, recorded for Decca and His Master's Voice, and sang at recitals and in opera performances for the BBC. He interrupted his stay at Covent Garden in 1933 to devote himself for the next four years to singing the works of Gilbert and Sullivan — first with the D'Oyly Carte Opera Company in England and later with J. C. Williamson companies in Australia and New Zealand.

In 1937 he returned to England and resumed his activities at Covent Garden. Returning to Australia in 1940 he gave recitals for the ABC and became principal bass with J. C. Williamson companies. In 1944 as Teacher of Singing at his alma mater, The Elder Conservatorium of Music, he began to produce operas in conjunction with the ABC at the Tivoli Theatre in Adelaide and to give recitals there and in Melbourne and Perth. For five years after the end of World War II Watson again appeared as principal bass with the D'Oyly Carte Company in London and in a number of American cities including New York and continued to make Gilbert and Sullivan recordings. From 1951-1955 he acted as Director of the Regina Conservatory of Music at the University of Saskatchewan in Canada and, besides teaching singing there, he produced grand operas, served as Director of the Western Canadian Music Board and as Examiner in Music in three Canadian provinces. But his real love was Gilbert and Sullivan, so he accepted an offer of the J. C. Williamson Company to take charge of preliminary productions and to appear in bass roles in a current series of these operas in Australia and New Zealand. Upon returning to Adelaide he resumed his duties as Teacher of Singing at the Elder Conservatorium and joined the organization known as the Gilbert and Sullivan Society of South Australia which presents an opera annually.

RUTH NAYLOR, soprano

Ruth Naylor, after winning the Elder Overseas Scholarship in 1929, went to the Royal College of Music to study with Clive Carey and spent her vacations in Berlin, Munich and Salzburg. On completion of the course there, she was engaged by Sadler's Wells to sing a variety of roles. On 18th June, 1934, she sang Musetta at the Royal Opera House in the performance of *La Boheme* in which Grace Moore made her debut; John Brownlee and Ezio Pinza were among the other members of the cast. Of her singing of the same role on 28th July, a critic wrote: "Miss Ruth Naylor of Adelaide, was an irresistible Musetta in *La Boheme.* She had sung the part in English at the Sadler's Wells Theatre so convincingly that none doubted her ability to attain the higher standard at Covent Garden in the Italian version." Of her performance as Rosina in *The Barber of Seville* a few months later, Herbert Hughes wrote in the *Saturday Review:* "Miss Naylor can both sing and act, act with her hands and her eyes and her feet, with her whole body. She sings dead in tune and her voice has not the least suspicion of a wobble. Consequently not only the big scene in the third Act, upon which Rosina must stand or fall, but all her scenes were delightful. She is a veritable acquisition here."

Among the many operatic roles she sang at Covent Garden and the Sadler's Wells Theatre, her favourites included Susanna in *Figaro,* Desdemona in *Othello,* Sophie in *Der Rosenkavalier,* Musetta in *La Boheme* and Rosina in *The Barber of Seville.* In 1938 she sang Adele in *Die Fledermaus* at Covent Garden for the first time and when this opera, under the title *Gay Roselinda,* was presented after the war for a long run at the Palace Theatre in London, Miss Naylor sang the same role opposite another Australian, Cyril Ritchard. Soon after this she retired to her home in Norfolk to indulge her hobby of raising roses.

When she appeared during the war in Gounod's *Romeo and Juliet* with the Dublin Operatic Society on 15th September, 1943, a critic wrote: "Ruth Naylor won the audience at once by her singing of the Waltz Song in Act I and by her graceful acting. Her voice sounded fresh and pure, with easy production and flexibility."

Besides appearing in opera and operetta, Miss Naylor sang frequently in oratorios presented at the Queen's Hall and Albert Hall, and in Paris and Brussels. Included in an extensive repertoire of oratorios were classical works by Bach and Handel and modern works including Sir Edgar Elgar's *The Apostles* and Vaughan Williams' *Sea Symphony.*

MARJORIE LAWRENCE, dramatic soprano

The story of Marjorie Lawrence would provide a libretto as dramatic and inspiring as that for any opera in which she sang. At the height of a meteoric career she was stricken with paralysis, a tragedy which she met with the strength and courage worthy of her pioneer heritage. The Lawrences, a musical

155

family, lived at Dean's Marsh, Victoria. Marjorie's father could boast of a fine baritone voice; her mother played the church organ and all four brothers and two sisters sang in the choir. Even after they married and started their own farms, the young Lawrences continued to sing in the choir and to play and dance at local socials. They were all musical. Lindsay possessed a fine bass voice; Edwin was a good tenor and played the piano. Cyril also played the piano and sang, and George played the violin. Sister Eileen sang a little, too.

Marjorie was the fifth in a family of six and was only two years old when her mother died. The toughening process of growing up motherless in a large family dominated by male members was excellent conditioning, she says, for her "subsequent experiences in the competitive hurly-burly of an opera singer's career". Another favourable influence was the abundance of outdoor life — plenty of fresh air, hard work, and horseback riding. One of the delights of her girlhood — and a happy release from farm chores — was to ride full-rein across the sheep paddocks singing operatic arias at the top of her voice. Marjorie already enjoyed a local reputation for her voice, and was featured in solos in both the school and church choirs. The latter was enriched by three other members of the Lawrence family — Marjorie's brothers. They also sang with her in concerts organized locally by the minister of the Dean's Marsh Church of England, the Reverend Alex J. Pearce, who not only played the organ and directed the choir, but was a knowledgeable musician. He taught Marjorie a repertoire of religious music, including the cantatas of Bach and the oratorios of Handel and Mendelssohn, as well as how to control and discipline her phenomenally powerful voice. Under his influence she began to take singing seriously and decided to go to Melbourne to study.

At this time the family lived on a farm near Winchelsea, a larger town than Dean's Marsh, where Mr Lawrence built a home comfortable enough, he hoped, to keep his family together. He was adamant in his belief that his daughter's singing should be restricted to the local community and remain on an amateur level. So Marjorie bided her time till her eighteenth birthday, when she was free to do as she pleased, meanwhile preparing to support herself by taking sewing lessons from the local dressmaker, Ada Boddington. Her planning and dreaming were complicated by her first romance, which she took very seriously, but which she put second to her ambition for a singing career. So, with Eileen and Cyril as co-conspirators, she departed for the city at dawn one quiet morning. With her went Cyril, their own and Eileen's savings, and the hope of obtaining a job in Melbourne. Although finding the job didn't prove too difficult, holding it did. In a clothing factory she was asked to sew on electric machines, with which she had had no experience, and when a sympathetic manager offered to let her sew on buttons by hand she was unable to compete with practised operators. Marjorie then turned to housework.

Marjorie Lawrence
Photo: Delar

As Tosca, 1938

While working as a domestic servant in return for bed, board, and the use of a piano, she studied with Ivor Boustead, who had been John Brownlee's teacher and who agreed to teach this girl who hit a high C the first time she sang for him. Months of hard work and study followed, with Boustead so convinced of Marjorie's talent that he entered her, as a contralto, for every vocal contest for which she was eligible in the musical competitions at Geelong. He also wrote to Marjorie's father stressing the likelihood of her winning. On this basis the elder Lawrence agreed to allow her to continue her studies should she prove successful at Geelong. In a joyful family reunion, he welcomed her home for Christmas, but her thoughts were on the approaching contests.

Winning the *Sun* Aria at Geelong was the beginning of Marjorie Lawrence's spectacular international career. Less than a year later, in October, 1928, she was on her way to Paris. John Brownlee, now a star of the Paris Opera, recommended she study with Cecilie Gilly, an endorsement which so impressed her father that he agreed to subsidize her Paris lessons, but only if she took a chaperon with her. Since her married sister was unable to leave home, the choice was her old friend, Mrs Boddington. As their ship carried her away from family and friends, Marjorie had a premonition that she would never see her beloved father again. Her spirits were soon lifted, however, by the excitement of her first sea voyage and the prospect of Paris.

The Marjorie Lawrence who gazed in awe and incredulity at the Paris Opera House on the day of her arrival in the city was indeed a far cry from the sleek, sophisticated diva who was to make her debut there five years later. During that time she changed from a gauche, dowdily dressed young country girl into a svelte, brilliant artist. But, these were five years of struggle, disappointment, hard work, and financial austerity. True to his word, John Brownlee arranged for an audition with Madame Gilly, who quickly recognized the exceptional beauty of Marjorie's natural voice, which she classified as a dramatic soprano rather than a contralto. She agreed to accept Marjorie as a pupil; but before beginning the long, hard grind of scales, exercises, and musical "drudgery" that often discouraged her eager-for-success young student, she had to find an acceptable French family for her to live with. This family, the Grodets, although somewhat impoverished was impressively pedigreed, and well able to provide the girl from the Australian hinterland with a knowledge of French language and culture as well as with the warmth, understanding, and support she needed during her difficult days.

Difficult days were many under the strict regime of Madame Gilly, who, because she considered Marjorie one of her most promising pupils, made her work rigorously to master interpretation and delineation and to build up an operatic repertoire. This relentlessness benefited Marjorie in more than one way; not only did she master languages, acting, and new roles, but it proved to be good therapy for her when she received the sad news of her father's death. The friendship of Henri and Mimi Grodet, the son and daughter in the family with whom she was living, also served as an antidote to her intense grief at the loss of the man who overcame personal and financial obstacles to bring up his children single-handed. Later, when her brother Lindsay, as head of the family, decreed that they could no longer afford to support Marjorie, the Grodets again rallied to her cause, letting her stay on with them and lending her the money she needed because they were certain of her eventual fame and success.

Madame Gilly had already permitted her to sing at one or two concerts and had declared a moratorium on the insolvent girl's lesson fees because she, too, was sure of her pupil's future. Fame and success had their tentative beginning with Marjorie's professional debut at the Monte Carlo Opera. The thrill of seeing her name emblazoned on posters across the opera house was magnified by the enthusiastic reviews she received after her performance as Elisabeth in *Tannhauser*. One reviewer proclaimed her debut to be as sensational as those of Chaliapin and Caruso. Almost as welcome as the critics' encomiums was a note from one of Marjorie's idols, Clara Butt, who wrote: "My dear . . . You will be one of the greatest".

The Monte Carlo success led quickly to an audition with Jacques Rouche, director-general of the Paris Opera. Marjorie triumphed here not only through vocal artistry but by the use of strategy in selecting one of Ortrud's arias from *Lohengrin,* music for which the Paris Opera company had no competent singer. A contract was promised shortly, but when the organization's reigning prima donna applied pressure against it Marjorie decided to sign with the Lille Opera. Here her artistic development was furthered by a romance with her leading man and the discriminating tastes of provincial audiences. Operatic audiences in the provinces were notoriously hard to please because they knew their operas thoroughly and were quick to note a mistake. Subsequent provincial appearances convinced Marjorie Lawrence that opera could not establish itself in any country without a training ground such as the smaller opera houses provide in France, Italy and Germany, where knowledgeable audiences, she says, "refuse to be dazzled by star-spangled casts or to be fobbed off with the second-rate".

Upon her return to Paris she found herself in the enviable position of being sought out by two companies, the Paris Opera and the Opera Comique. The Paris Opera had always been her goal, and she made her debut there in 1933. Her premiere performance, as Ortrud in *Lohengrin,* elicited such thunderous applause that the conductor was unable to abide by the house rules to continue with the music without pause. There followed Brunnhilde in *Die Walkure* and *Gotterdammerung,* Salome in *Herodias,* Aida, and Rachel in *La Juive* — roles calling for a powerful dramatic voice of wide range and flexibility. By the end of 1934 she was among the most highly paid artists on the opera roster, and was receiving offers from the New York Metropolitan Opera, the Vienna Staatsoper, and Covent Garden. She was enjoying not only fame but financial independence; after many years of skimping she was now able to pay off her debts and establish herself as the prima donna she was. She had her own apartment, leisure time, a rewarding social life, and the respect and admiration of her public. She was cast to sing with world-famous singers whenever they stopped at the Paris Opera on international tours.

In 1935 she accepted one of many offers, and was on her way to the Metropolitan Opera in New York. With her went her friend Mimi Grodet and her brother Cyril, who had bolstered her morale in Melbourne and had later come to Paris to be her personal manager when her career became an actuality. Her first impressions of New York were kaleidoscopic: she was captivated by the city, dismayed by the steam heat, delighted with the Automats (where she ate her meals until advised that this was not *de rigeur* for an opera star), and disappointed with the external facade of the 'Met'. But the interior well matched the grandeur of her beloved Paris Opera House, and the reception she had on her opening night enhanced the brilliance and beauty of the "Diamond Horseshoe". Of her Brunnhilde in *Die Walkure* Olin Downes of the *New York Times* said: "The audience was taken by storm and a burst of applause interrupted the performance". Samuel Chotzinoff of the *Post* said: "Young, slim, and personable, the new soprano gave to Brunnhilde a youthful charm and motion. From a dramatic standpoint, her Brunnhilde was the most effective that the Metropolitan has seen in years." The critics were unanimous in their praise, and Marjorie Lawrence became a Metropolitan "regular", appearing with such all-time greats as Lauritz Melchior, Ezio Pinza, and John Charles Thomas. Among her triumphs two performances stand out: Strauss's *Salome,* the Metropolitan's "sensation piece" for the '37-'38 season, and *Gotterdammerung,* in which she actually rode a horse into Siegfried's funeral pyre. Undoubtedly when she leaped astride Grane singing Brunnhilde's soaring paean in the Immolation Scene the audience was as enraptured by her equestrian as by her vocal ability. Horsemanship came naturally to a farm-bred girl from the Australian Outback, but she had to work for weeks on Salome's Dance of the Seven Veils. Her Salome was physically and emotionally taxing but artistically rewarding, as the reviewers recognized. It was called "a remarkable feat for a singing actress . . . a Salome that had no rival".

Critics also lauded Marjorie Lawrence's appearances on the concert platform, where the impressive power of her top notes as well as her marked ability for dramatic interpretation had drawn such praise as that of Pitts Sanborn, who commented on a concert opening with "Divinites du Styx": "Miss Lawrence's voice is really of the phenomenal sort, and one hopes the reminder of a contralto past will never be lost in a soprano present. The vitality of her singing is no less remarkable and with it goes uncommon artistic authority." In November of that year (1938), he wrote: "Those qualities, that set Miss Lawrence apart from and above most other contemporary singers distinguished her recital yesterday afternoon . . . throughout, her buoyancy of spirit, her enormous vitality and her compelling magnetism were constantly in evidence, and in such things as the Gluck recitative and in Moussorgsky's *Trepak,* her ability to communicate mood and her dramatic expression were breathtaking."

With her reputation for Wagnerian roles firmly established, Marjorie Lawrence was signed to sing them in the composer's native country. Singing *Die Walkure* in German at the Zoppot Waldoper, in a majestic outdoor setting, was one of the most unforgettable experiences of her career, but it was tempered by the tensions, suspicions, and tyranny of the police state which she saw developing around her. Despite her fervent desire to sing at Bayreuth, her conscience would not permit her to return to Germany while the Nazis were in power. She looked forward to the unrestricted freedom of Australia, where she had been booked for her first concert tour since leaving her native shores.

Everywhere in Australia her reception was tumultuous. The most important of these concerts to her, personally, was the one at the Globe Theatre in her home town of Winchelsea — built by her father and filled with people who had known her when she was a girl who milked cows and did farm chores. Of her concert in Sydney in August, 1939, a critic wrote: "The Town Hall rocked on its foundations with the thunders of appreciation. On leaving the concert complete strangers congratulated one another on being present. Marjorie, in her white chiffon, looked about as heavyweight as a bit of thistledown, and therefore all the more amazing is her voice of heroic, of triumphic, quality."

The season of 1940-41 marked the high point of Marjorie Lawrence's career. She was in demand everywhere for broadcasts, concerts, opera. Critics said of her: "Her timbre is magnificent and the production as remarkable for its smoothness as it is for its volume . . . [She] belongs to a class of artists who sang in another era when the Nordicas, the Fremstadts, and Lilli Lehmanns graced our stages." Only eight years after her Monte Carlo debut she was riding the crest of the wave, and to make her happiness complete she met and married Dr Thomas King, the man whose love and dedication helped her later to recuperate from her tragic illness. They were married in March, 1941, and had a few happy months in a house on Long Island before leaving for Mexico City where Marjorie had an engagement with the newly-formed national opera company.

It was while she was singing Brunnhilde in *Die Walkure* — a role in which she had distinguished herself for the youthful vigour she imparted to her delineation of the daughter of the gods — that fate ironically deprived her

161

of this physical well-being. She was stricken with poliomyelitis and suffered the agonies of pain, fever, and paralysis before the malady was diagnosed and her husband decided to take her to Hot Springs, Arkansas. During her weeks of treatment there they bought a house in the hills which they both enjoyed so much that it became their permanent retreat. Pain-racked, depressed, and often despondent, Marjorie could not entertain the idea that she might be paralyzed permanently. With her strong will, indomitable fortitude, and the steady devotion of her husband, she travelled to Minneapolis to place herself under the care of her fellow Australian, Sister Elizabeth Kenny. Under the Kenny method her muscles began to come slowly to life but she had to face the bitter realization that it might be a long time before she could appear on a stage again.

The fact that it was only about a year and a half later that this was possible attests to her unflagging determination. Her first public appearance was in a wheelchair at a concert in Minneapolis, where the audience applauded warmly as she was rolled on to the stage. A few months later she was soloist at a Christmas service in her husband's family's church in Miami, where she had been. taken for the warm Florida sunshine. By continuing to practise by strengthening the muscles in her chest, stomach, and back with her singing, and by realizing that when she sang she forgot all but her music, Marjorie was ready for her "wheelchair comeback". She started with a broadcast with Andre Kostelanetz, a charity concert, a Metropolitan Opera Guild luncheon (where she was guest of honour and was commended by her fellow artists for her courage), and various patriotic and servicemen's events. When she returned to the concert stage in a New York Town Hall recital in 1942, the press greeted her with the same enthusiasm they had lavished on her in her Metropolitan Opera days. There followed many concert engagements, to which she was accompanied by her husband and a collapsible wheelchair he had devised. One typical review was that of Robert Lawrence:

> Whatever praise is due the soprano springs not from a natural desire to applaud her for the gallant fight against paralysis that she has made, but from the tremendous advances in understanding and vocal grandeur that she has achieved since last heard here in a performance of *Walkure.* The text was projected with exemplary clearness; the quality of tone was big and thrilling; the emotional penetration moving in the extreme.

The singer herself believed that her great love, opera, was out of the question until she could walk again but she reckoned without the ingenious planning of several stage managers. The 'Met' arranged for her to sing Venus in *Tannhauser* sitting on a divan; Sir Thomas Beecham had her sing *Isolde* in Montreal, entirely in sedentary positions and as Amneris in *Aida* at the Cincinnati Summer Opera she was carried on and off stage on a palanquin, befitting an Egyptian princess.

In addition to her own fight to overcome adversity, Marjorie Lawrence wanted to help others do the same, and despite the discomforts and inconveniences involved she undertook a tour of the Southwest Pacific in 1944 to entertain wounded and disabled troops. It was a gruelling, but helpful experience. She saw so many maimed war victims that she began to consider her own infirmity in a new light. She was further inspired by a visit to the White House to see Franklin Delano Roosevelt the man who had overcome polio and done "a task beside which mere singing paled as paltry and of little consequence".

Upon her return to New York she was again asked to entertain troops, this time in occupied countries. Again she put lucrative bookings behind her and with her husband, set sail for Europe. They visited many war-ravaged cities, held a happy re-union with old friends in Paris, and she gave a "command performance" for Queen Elizabeth and Princesses Elizabeth and Margaret. Before returning to New York in August, 1945, Marjorie was signed for a concert tour of the British Isles, which had a chilly start in an unheated Albert Hall but soon warmed up as the audience expressed their enthusiasm. Meanwhile her war effort continued unabated — at the request of General Lucius Clay, she sang for American and Russian troops in Germany, and for activities in France she was awarded the Diamond Cross of the Legion of Honour. While in Paris she returned to the Paris Opera to sing Amneris with many of her old colleagues.

Marjorie Lawrence was figuratively on her feet again, but one more goal remained: to stand literally on her feet. Again, her husband's ingenuity enabled her to accomplish this. He devised a platform to which she could be strapped while singing. The work which she was to sing in this contraption — *Elektra* — was by her own evaluation the most strenuous, most difficult music ever written for a singer. Constant practice and her now ironbound determination made it possible for her to overcome the hazards and when she sang *Elektra* with the Chicago Symphony Orchestra under Artur Rodsinski in December, 1947, she sang it standing up. Her vocal endowment, physical stamina, and sheer ruggedness combined to produce one of the great triumphs of her career.

The story of her courage and artistry during these years is told in her book, *Interrupted Melody,* which was published in 1949 and released as a motion picture in 1955. The next year Miss Lawrence became Professor of Voice at Newcomb College of Tulane University where she remained for four years. Since then she has been associated with the Opera Workshop of the University of Southern Illinois which conducts a summer session on her ranch at Harmony Hills in Hot Springs, Arkansas. Grateful students established the Marjorie Lawrence Endowment Fund to provide, in her name, wheel-chair   163 facilities for handicapped persons attending performances of the Metropolitan Opera Company, at its new home at the Lincoln Center in New York City.

NOTES.

John Brownlee

[1]A number of graduates of the Manhattan School of Music have been successful. In this respect, seven are singing with opera companies in Germany and France and three are members of the Metropolitan in New York, the best-known of whom is Ezio Flagello.
[2]*Welt der Musik,* 28th May, 1965.
[3]Irving Kolodin, *Saturday Review,* New York, August 7, 1965.
[4]Ernest Hutcheson, the precocious Melbourne pianist, was Dean of this institution from 1927 until his retirement in 1937.

Browning Mummery

[1]"Mechanics' Bench to Covent Garden", in *Music Masterpieces,* November, 1925.

Ethel Osborn

[1]Foster. Op. cit.

Stella Power

[1]*Musical News,* January, 1917.
[2]The range of her voice was from the B below middle C to F and G in alt.
[3]*The Spokesman Review,* Spokane, Washington, 14th March, 1918.

Evelyn Scotney

[1]Eaton, Q., *The Boston Opera Company.* Quotations from Henry Taylor Parker of the *Evening Transcript* and Philip of the *Boston Herald.*

Clara Serena

[1]Quoted in Rosenthal, *Two Centuries of Opera at Covent Garden,* London, Putnam, 1958.

Dorothy Helmrich

[1]Marchesi, M., *Marchesi and Music,* Harper and Bros., London and New York, 1898. (Introduction by W. J. Henderson.)

Beatrice Miranda

[1]Melbourne *Punch,* 3rd December, 1903.
[2]*The Musical Monthly,* 1st June, 1906.

[3]*Australian Musical News,* January, 1916.
[4]Ernest Newman used photographs of her performances to illustrate his libretto for Wagner operas.

Florence Austral

[1]Then the leading soprano at the Metropolitan Opera House.
[2]Brentnall, T., *My Memories,* Melbourne, Robertson & Mullens Ltd., 1938.
[3]*Record Collector,* London, Vol. XIV, No. 1 & 2.
[4]She taught at the New South Wales Conservatorium in Newcastle until 1959.
[5]*Sydney Morning Herald,* 10th April, 1965.

166

Joan Hammond
Photo: Elizabethan Trust

7

Singers of the Post War Periods

WORLD WAR TWO interrupted the careers of many Australians as well as singers of other countries. The European debuts of some were delayed and others who were just gaining a toehold abroad returned home and remained there; a few stayed in England and occupied themselves with activities connected with the war effort. The first eleven singers whose European careers began in the early post-war period are representative of the latter group and include a few whose talent and birth date made it natural for them to emerge on the world scene at this time. Together, however, they constitute a group different from the "flock" of young people who went abroad later stimulated by the experiences they had had as members of the Australian National Theatre Movement in Melbourne or the National Theatre of New South Wales, cash prizes won in the Mobil Quest and other commercial radio programmes, and scholarships offered by teachers abroad. As in earlier periods, Sydney and Melbourne *Sun* Aria winners are represented in the post-war period as well as successful candidates for newer nationwide awards like the Shell Aria in Canberra, the Australian Broadcasting Commission's Concerto and Vocal Competitions, and the government's Rehabilitation Scholarships. Since the foundation of the Elizabethan Trust to commemorate the Royal Visit of 1954 many have sung with the federally-subsidized Elizabethan Trust Opera Company, which provides opportunity to appear in opera in Australia and to earn money while doing so.

JOAN HAMMOND, soprano

Joan Hammond, one of Britain's best-loved sopranos, was awarded the O.B.E. in 1953 and the C.B.E. in 1963 for services to music. Born in Christchurch, New Zealand, in May 1912, she came to live in Sydney at an early age — and during an active school career won prizes for her singing, became   167 leader of the school orchestra and excelled in sport, especially swimming and golf. It was natural, then, that to support herself during her student days she should turn her sporting interests to good use, becoming sports writer for several Sydney newspapers and the golf editor of one of them. She herself was three times winner of the New South Wales Golf Championship.

Her first ambition was to become a solo violinist but an accident that injured her left wrist prevented this and she became a student of voice at the New South Wales Conservatorium of Music, though she continued to play the violin as a member of the Conservatorium orchestra and with the Royal Philharmonic Society. As a student she had the experience of appearing as vocal soloist on a tour made by two members of the staff, the duo pianists Frank Hutchens and Lindley Evans.

After she had received her Diploma from the Conservatorium Miss Hammond was engaged by a J. C. Williamson Italian Grand Opera Company to sing secondary roles in Australia and New Zealand and the distinguished European members of the company encouraged her to undertake further study abroad — a suggestion that had been made earlier by Lady Gowrie, the wife of the then Governor General of Australia. In 1935 Miss Hammond's fellow golfers raised a fund of £2,000 thus making it possible for her to go to Europe the next year to continue her education in Vienna and Italy. She made her London debut in *The Messiah* in 1938 and was engaged to sing leading soprano roles at the Vienna State Opera beginning in the autumn of 1939. In the summer she went to London for what she expected to be a short visit in order to sing at the opening night of Sir Henry Wood's promenade concerts. However, war broke out soon afterward and Joan Hammond "joined up" as an ambulance driver and whenever possible gave concerts for the troops in camp and for civilians in air-raid shelters. She sang at mid-day concerts at the National Gallery and at the Royal Exchange, and under the auspices of E.N.S.A. and C.E.M.A. made trips to service units in Germany and the British provinces.

In 1942 she joined the Carl Rosa Company with which she remained until 1945, singing leading roles in the operas of Gounod, Verdi and Puccini. Of these performances Harold Rosenthal wrote: "Among the brighter spots of the Carl Rosa wartime seasons in London were the appearances of Joan Hammond. This artist with her Italian-sounding voice, and on the stage a real prima donna personality, brought something of the atmosphere of grand opera to these performances".[1]

During this period Joan Hammond made a number of recordings and one of them in particular became a great favourite with the general public. It was "O My Beloved Father", from Puccini's *Gianni Schicchi*. She had recorded "Vissi d'Arte" from Act II of *Tosca* and when the question arose as to what should appear on the other side of the disc, she suggested this little-known aria. When the record was released it proved to have great appeal for many for whom the Tosca selection held little interest and is still a popular choice. Miss Hammond has been called upon many times to sing it as an encore at her concerts.

In 1946 she returned to Australia and New Zealand for a long recital tour for the ABC. She then went to Vienna, and in 1947 was the first British artist to appear at the Vienna State Opera since the war. In that year she also visited South Africa where she gave a number of recitals, appeared as soloist in orchestral concerts and made many broadcasts. In 1948 came the first of a number of appearances at Covent Garden where she has sung the title roles in *Aida, Tosca* and *Madame Butterfly* and the leading soprano roles in *Il Trovatore* and *Fidelio*. In 1950 Miss Hammond made her first appearance at Sadler's Wells in *Don Carlos*. Soon afterwards she sang in *Eugene Onegin* in Barcelona and in 1957 was the first British soprano to sing in Russian on a Russian stage when she made a concert and opera tour of the Soviet Union. She has performed in many other cities of the world and sings in five languages — German, Italian, Russian, French and English. Her operatic repertoire consists of more than twenty principal roles and her concert programmes include lieder and the works of modern English composers. Before her retirement she was in great demand as soloist in the oratorios of the Christmas and Easter seasons.

Miss Hammond's competence and versatility have been put to the test often. In February 1952, for instance, she was asked to sing *Aida* at Covent Garden at a few days' notice. Whilst engaged in refreshing her memory of the English translation she received an urgent request to fly to Amsterdam to substitute for a Dutch soprano who had been scheduled to sing the same role in Italian. In order not to confuse her lines she postponed her review of the Italian libretto until after the Covent Garden performance but, nonetheless, was able to sing the part two days later in Italian before an enthusiastic Amsterdam audience.

Joan Hammond returned to sing in two seasons of the Australian Elizabethan Trust Opera — In 1957 in the roles of Desdemona and Tosca and in 1960 those of Salome and Madame Butterfly. These performances did much to further the success of Australia's new venture in the field of opera.

She has always been grateful for the help she received in the early years of her career. During her 1960 tour she gave two very successful concerts the proceeds of which she donated to a fund to send an Australian women's golf team abroad. In London she gave a benefit concert in the Festival Hall to establish a scholarship at the Opera School where she had been a student.

Miss Hammond's English home is a sixteenth-century cottage in Buckinghamshire, thirty miles from London. There she has been able to enjoy the country life she loves, looking after her dogs, cats, chickens and pet birds, gardening and taking long walks. However when a heart ailment forced her retirement in 1965 she decided to commission the building of an elaborately appointed house seventy miles from Melbourne, at Airey's Inlet near Anglesea.

LORNA SYDNEY, mezzo soprano

An audition with Lotte Lehmann when the famous lieder singer was visiting Western Australia in the middle 1930's proved to be the turning point in Lorna Sydney's career. Before this, she had not only been studying singing and ballet but at sixteen had played the Grieg Concerto with the Perth Symphony Orchestra and previously made her debut with a visiting Italian opera company appearing as Nedda and Santuzza on the same evening. While continuing her music studies after graduating from the University of Western Australia she taught in convent schools where she composed operettas for her young pupils to perform.

When Mme Lehmann heard Lorna Sydney sing she was so impressed by the girl's voice and musicianship (which had been cultivated by her father, a cellist, conductor and composer, and her grandfather, who was a pianist and singer) that she recommended further study in Vienna. Perth citizens, inspired by the great singer's enthusiasm, raised money by public subscription to make this possible. Lorna went to Vienna and was soon studying under Lehmann's direction with the finest teachers of singing and repertoire. She was to make her debut at the Berlin State Opera when war broke out and she was immediately interned by the Nazis. Her hopes of an operatic career seemed at an end.

In 1946, however, Lorna Sydney made her debut as Carmen at the Vienna State Opera and was the first English-speaking singer ever to become a permanent member of the company. She has forty-seven roles in her repertoire which include operas by Gluck, Verdi, Wagner and Richard Strauss, and has to her credit the third highest number of performances of Carmen at the Vienna Opera where another of her best roles is that of Clytemnestra in Strauss' *Elektra* which she also sang with the New Orleans Opera Company in the United States. Miss Sydney remained a permanent member of the Vienna Opera for more than twenty years and still makes occasional appearances there. She is also prominent as a lieder singer and has made successful concert tours of Germany, Italy, France, the United States, East, West and South Africa as well as Australia. In the United States she has appeared with many leading orchestras, including the Philadelphia Symphony Orchestra under Eugene Ormandy. After a concert at the Town Hall in New York City during the 1955 season critics spoke of her as "the possessor of an exceptional voice which can be let out in triumphant flourishes", and of the "exquisite colour, the

Lorna Sydney

drama and the intimacy of her voice and interpretation". She received praise, also, for her portrayal of Herodias in the English version of Richard Strauss' *Salome,* a production by the NBC Television Opera. Another outstanding performance in 1955 was Prokofieff's *The Love of Three Oranges* at the opening of the New York City Center Opera Company. Since 1959 Miss Sydney has made five visits to her home state of Western Australia where she has done a series of recitals on television called "Presenting Lorna Sydney". She announces the programme and sings excerpts from Bach and operatic composers.

She is widely known for her recordings of Handel, Bach, Brahms, Schumann and Mahler and her recording of Mahler's "Youth's Magic Horn" was for two years among the top ten vocal records recommended by the *New York Times.* In 1965 she began to conduct two-day sessions at colleges in the United States; on the first day she gives a lieder recital and on the second discusses the music with the undergraduates.

Lorna Sydney is the fortunate possessor of a magnificent stage appearance, outstanding dramatic talent and thorough musicianship. Her voice has been highly praised by the critics of many countries, described by *The Christian Science Monitor* as: "A voice of extraordinary range and beauty and great expressiveness".

EMILIE HOOKE, soprano

Another Australian singer to benefit from the advice of Lotte Lehmann is   171

Emilie Hooke, the 1932 Melbourne *Sun* Aria winner, whom Mme Lehmann auditioned in London where she had gone in 1935 to study with Sir Henry Wood.

Mme Lehmann sent her to Leon Rosenstock, her own teacher in Vienna, and from there the young singer followed the musical trail to Milan where she lived for a while with Luisa Tetrazzini while studying with Arangi-Lombardi. After appearing in some operatic performances in Italy she went on to the famous old opera house in Zagreb, Yugoslavia, where she became a principal soprano. Just as she was getting a firm footing in central Europe, war broke out and she had to leave. She returned to England and joined the New London Opera Company at the Cambridge Theatre where she appeared in *Tosca* and *La Boheme,* and also at Glyndebourne, Sadler's Wells and Covent Garden. With Benjamin Britten's English Opera Groups she sang in *The Rape of Lucretia* and *Albert Herring.* Emilie Hooke was the first British artist to give a recital in Berlin after the war; she had appeared with the New Zealand conductor, Warwick Braithwaite, at one of the German spas and then flew on to Berlin in the airlift to give recitals to Allied troops stationed there.

After a short stay in South Africa where she went to appear in opera, her husband died and she again returned to London where she has since established a reputation in recitals and in broadcasts on the BBC Third Programme. Emilie Hooke is particularly renowned for her services to contemporary music in Britain where she has given many first performances of Webern, Berg, Dallapiccola and many others. She says that her interest in atonal music developed as she studied under Sir Henry Wood "to become a musician as well as a singer". She has also made a number of recordings of contemporary music for HMV and Decca.

KEN NEATE, tenor

Lotte Lehmann also helped to further the career of Ken Neate who was born in Cessnock, N.S.W. She introduced him to Bruno Walter in New York at the time he was about to abandon the search for the opportunity he believed awaited him when he left Australia in 1940. After the great conductor heard Neate sing he recommended him as understudy to Charles Kullman of the Metropolitan Opera Company. He appeared with this distinguished group at a gala performance of *The Magic Flute* in 1941 and later sang at the Montreal Festival under the baton of Sir Thomas Beecham, meanwhile fulfilling radio engagements with American and Canadian networks.

When the United States entered World War II, Neate joined the Royal Canadian Air Force with which he served for three years. At the end of the war he was auditioned by David Webster and Karl Rankl for the new Covent

Garden Opera Company that was being organized. Given a contract immediately, he made his debut in England as Don Jose in *Carmen* in 1946 and appeared later that year as Tamino in *The Magic Flute* and The Singer in *Der Rosenkavalier*. During the five seasons he remained at Covent Garden, he sang leading tenor roles in operas by Gounod, Mozart, Puccini and Verdi. Then he moved to the Continent where he sang in major Italian opera houses and with touring companies in Spain. After returning to Australia in 1955 for a J. C. Williamson season of grand opera he went back to Europe and sang Romeo in Gounod's *Romeo and Juliet* at the Paris Opera and Cavaradossi in *Tosca* at the Opera Comique in 1956. At the Bordeaux Festival that year he created the title role in Tomasi's opera *Sanpero Corso* and sang this part again at the Holland Festival. His appearance in Radio Italiano's television production of Puccini's *La Fanciulla del West* followed. Since then Neate has divided his time among engagements in France, Germany and Italy and concentrated on the more dramatic roles in the languages of these countries. In 1958, for instance, at Karlsruhe, West Germany, he sang Florestan in Beethoven's *Fidelio* and the title roles in *Tannhauser* and *Lohengrin*.

When Joan Sutherland made her sensational first appearance as Lucia at Covent Garden in 1959, Ken Neate agreed to return to London to sing the role of Edgardo on short notice and without rehearsal. That same year he appeared again in London as a member of the international cast engaged by the BBC for the performance of Mahler's *Eighth Symphony* at the Albert Hall, to mark the centenary of the composer's birth. In 1960 he appeared as principal tenor with the Australian Elizabethan Theatre Trust in *The Magic Flute*, *Rigoletto* and *Madame Butterfly*. Since returning to Germany in 1961 he has specialized in Wagnerian roles, making special appearances at Bayreuth and at the Teatro Giuseppe Verdi in Trieste.

SYLVIA FISHER, soprano

Completely unknown as a singer outside Australia, Sylvia Fisher arrived in England in 1947. Two years later she was a leading soprano of the Covent Garden Opera Company. Her performance as the ageing Marschallin in *Der Rosenkavalier* has been compared favourably with that of Lotte Lehmann and her Isolde has deeply moved opera-goers who imagined they would never enjoy *Tristan und Isolde* after Kirsten Flagstad's retirement. Sylvia Fisher's achievement is particularly remarkable as she happens to be the most gentle and retiring of prima donnas, who might easily have been worsted by keenly ambitious rivals. It is the combination of a voice of compelling beauty and a supreme sense of musicianship that made her a world celebrity.

She was born in South Melbourne, Victoria. Her father, an Englishman, 173

Sylvia Fisher

died when she was a very young child and it was left to her mother to encourage her small daughter's interest in music. She took her to concerts and impressed upon her the importance of really understanding music if she meant to be a singer. At the convent school she attended in Kilmore, a country town some miles from Melbourne, the nuns fostered her talents and gave her every opportunity to sing and play the piano. One day they took her to a modest house in the bush to sing for a crippled athlete, who had been bed-ridden for forty years. As the little girl finished her first song, the man turned to the nuns with tears in his eyes: "Mark my words," he whispered, "this child will become famous, because she sings with her soul".

At the age of seventeen Sylvia Fisher enrolled at the Albert Street Conservatorium where she took the Diploma Course and studied singing with Mary Campbell. Her only appearance in a stage production of opera in Australia took place in 1932 when, as a student, she sang Hermione in a performance of Lully's *Cadmus and Hermione* at the Comedy Theatre, Melbourne. In 1936 she won the Melbourne *Sun* Aria Contest. Concert engagements followed and she embarked on a career as a singer. She had by this time completed her Conservatorium course and begun to study with Adolf Spivakovsky, who had recently taken up residence in Melbourne. She studied with him for twelve years and credits much of her success to his teaching. When her first Covent Garden success in *Fidelio* was hailed in London in 1948, she cabled him, "Thank you, thank you".

174

For fifteen years Sylvia Fisher broadcast regularly with the Australian Broadcasting Commission — lieder recitals, oratorio, opera. She sang Elsa in *Lohengrin,* Donna Anna in *Don Giovanni, Aida, The Messiah,* Verdi's *Requiem, Israel in Egypt,* Beethoven's *Ninth Symphony* and *Missa Solemnis,* Bach's *Mass in B Minor.* By 1946 she was acclaimed all over Australia as probably its finest soprano. Several times she had endeavoured to make arrangements to go overseas but each time circumstances prevented this. In 1947 she decided that she must not delay any longer and booked a passage on the *Orion* due to leave in October. The ABC gave her two farewell concerts, one in Melbourne and one in Sydney. Of the Melbourne concert a critic wrote:[1]

It was . . . an unforgettable recital . . . It was more than vocalising; it was real singing that reflected the generous proportions of her artistic mind and the rich resources of a mature personality. One is not called upon to say that of many singers in Australia today, and it is a deeply moving experience to hear in a great voice the signs of an equal greatness of imagination, of artistic sincerity and intelligence.

When Sylvia Fisher left for London, she took her own piano, because Boyd Neel who had been visiting Australia, had told her that the war had taken a serious toll of good instruments in Britain. She carried a letter of introduction from Mme Marie Rambert to David Webster, a director of Covent Garden. The year that followed was a difficult one for her. In Australia she had become accustomed to having her name constantly before the public but in London she was unknown and ignored. She continued to work at her singing and applied for auditions at the BBC and Covent Garden. The BBC engaged her for a series of lieder recitals, but although the management of the Opera House were impressed by her voice they were afraid to take the chance of employing her. Finally, however, after five auditions, she was scheduled to appear in a new production of *Fidelio* in 1948 and was an instant success. The critics were enthusiastic in their praise: "An outstanding singer with a true Covent Garden voice, sustained and thrilling in its resonance," wrote the *Daily Telegraph.* After this she became a member of the permanent company and worked and studied harder than ever.

At first her parts were small — the Third Norn in *Gotterdammerung,* the First Lady in *The Magic Flute* — but all the time her acting was improving and in 1949 she was given the role of Countess Almaviva in *The Marriage of Figaro.* She made such an impression with "Dove sono" that "the house broke in with well-intentioned but ill-mannered applause".[2]

Now that she had achieved a place in the front rank of dramatic sopranos Sylvia Fisher had to work doubly hard as her roles during this period testify. Wagner became her forte. She sang Elsa in *Lohengrin,* Gutrune,

175

Brunnhilde and Sieglinde in *The Ring,* Isolde in *Tristan und Isolde,* Elisabeth in *Tannhauser,* Senta in *The Flying Dutchman* and also Agathe in *Der Freischutz.* Kostelnicka in *Jenufa* and Ursula in *Mathis der Maler* were also in her repertoire.

In The Ring Series of the 1950 season Miss Fisher's Sieglinde was hailed as the greatest since Lotte Lehmann. The critic of the *Musical Times* wrote of a performance with Kirsten Flagstad: "Listeners will long remember the thrilling effect of the contrast between Sieglinde and Mme Flagstad's heroic Brunnhilde in the third act of *Die Walkure.* In March 1952,[3] Miss Fisher repeated the role at the Teatro dell' Opera when she made her Italian debut during the Rome International season under the direction of Dr. Erich Kleiber.

When Flagstad retired from Covent Garden Sylvia Fisher succeeded to her roles: appearing first in 1953 as Isolde which had not been sung there by a British artist since Eva Turner, and later in 1957, as the first British Brunnhilde since the war. For Isolde she went to Berlin to be coached by Frida Leider who had sung with Lauritz Melchior in many memorable *Tristan* performances between the two world wars. Miss Fisher was now described as "a singer of real distinction . . . The intelligence and understanding she brought to every phrase were memorable, and as a whole her creation of the role was beautifully conceived . . . vocally, both in power and colour, and dramatically, she was outstanding."[4] The same critic reported in 1954: "Vocally she spanned the role as never before, with new reserves of power . . . Few [Isoldes] are so consistently beautiful."[5]

Perhaps Miss Fisher's greatest impersonation is that of The Marschallin in *Der Rosenkavalier.* When she first sang the role in 1949 the *Times* critic said: "By sheer beauty of singing she makes the dramatic point of youth and age in purely lyrical terms". Again she was compared with the great Lotte Lehmann and her voice was said to be "in its way equally as beautiful". Of a performance of this opera in 1954 we read: "Sylvia Fisher's Marschallin seems to grow in stature and perfection in each season".[6] In 1955 Evan Senior said: "She has sung some fine performances as the Marschallin but nothing finer than this . . . It was singing of breathtaking beauty and of sincere musical interpretation".[7] And when in June 1964, she sang the role at the Opera House, Manchester, a critic remarked: "Miss Fisher's long admired Marschallin still gives us many memorable phases; how impressive she was in the last act".

In 1957 she sang the title role in Puccini's *Turandot.* This opera, wrote one critic: "contains one of the most exacting dramatic soprano roles in all opera . . . Sylvia Fisher's first essay in the part of the Chinese princess was a triumph. [She] has already proved her versatility and her notable dramatic talents, but I never fail to be excited by the way in which the drama of each role colours her voice differently".

176   However, it is not only in Wagnerian and other nineteenth century

operas that Sylvia Fisher triumphs. She created the role of Cressida in Sir William Walton's *Troilus and Cressida* in 1954 and has won unstinted praise for her characterizations in the operas of Sir Benjamin Britten. She is Ellen Orford in *Peter Grimes,* Lady Billows in *Albert Herring* (a role in which she "displays a highly developed sense of comedy that one had never suspected"[8]), Mrs Grose in *The Turn of the Screw* and The Chorus in *The Rape of Lucretia.* In Janacek's *Jenufa* she "tended to dominate the stage whenever she was present and her Kostelnicka was a tragic figure of iron strength".[9]

Operatic success in Britain has not been the full extent of Sylvia Fisher's achievement during the years since she arrived unknown in London in 1947. Her repertoire also includes a very large number of German Lieder, English Art Songs, Australian songs and the songs of many other nations, including Russia, all sung in their original language. She sang in her first Promenade Concert shortly after her Covent Garden debut and her concert performances since have included the Bach *B Minor Mass,* Beethoven's *Missa Solemnis* and *Ninth Symphony,* the *Requiems* of Verdi and Brahms, and, under the baton of Sir Thomas Beecham, Delius' *Mass of Life.* In Italy she has sung Sieglinde in Rome, Gutrune in Bologna and Isolde in Sicily — all with German casts — and at concert performances with Sir John Barbirolli and the Halle Orchestra at Ravello. Her debut in Germany came when she sang Ellen Orford in the Wiesbaden production of *Peter Grimes.*

She has made two visits to Australia — a three-month recital tour in 1955 which included solo appearances with all the leading orchestras, and, in 1958, guest appearances in the Elizabethan Theatre Trust's productions of *Peter Grimes* and *Fidelio.* She returned to England after this tour by way of the United States where her performance in *Jenufa* with the Chicago Opera Company received special notice. In 1964 she sang the role of Lady Billows in a recording by Decca of *Albert Herring* with Peter Pears, April Cantelo and Owen Brannigan. This was her first recording and she received special commendation for the part she played.

Sylvia Fisher was married in 1953 to the violinist, Unbaldo Gardini of Bologna, and together they have created a home which is renowned for its Italian hospitality. She never forgets her early life in Australia, however, and is always ready to help young compatriots in London.

STANLEY CLARKSON, bass

Like Sylvia Fisher, Stanley Clarkson had been singing professionally in Australia for a number of years before he went to England in 1947. He was born in Sydney in 1905 and as a boy sang alto in his church choir. When his voice broke he began lessons with Rex de Rego and then entered the Sydney

Stanley Clarkson

Conservatorium to further his studies under Spencer Thomas. Here he made his debut in opera as Sarastro in *The Magic Flute*.

From 1930 he appeared as a vocalist in many choral and orchestral performances while working as a linotype operator on Sydney newspapers. In 1938, however, he turned to singing as a full-time career. He soon became a popular vocalist with the Australian Broadcasting Commission, took part in many recitals and oratorios, and was in great demand for grand opera broadcasts. There were many of these at that time — *Tannhauser, Don Giovanni, The Magic Flute* — and Stanley Clarkson sang all the bass roles. His only experience in opera in the theatre consisted of two appearances in *The Magic Flute* and the role of the Old Yogi in the world premiere of Dr Edgar Bainton's *The Pearl Tree* in 1942.

After Clarkson arrived in England he sang oratorio at the Leeds Festival, Wells Cathedral and York Minster. In 1948 he joined the opera school and had vocal and dramatic coaching from Arnold Matters and Clive Carey in London before becoming a member of the Sadler's Wells Company. Norman Tucker, Director of Sadler's Wells wrote after Clarkson's sudden death in 1961:

I well remember the occasion of Stanley Clarkson's audition at Sadler's Wells . . . He sang arias from *The Magic Flute* and *The Seraglio,* and we were all impressed with the noble quality of his voice and with his platform presence. I asked him to come to see me to discuss joining the company as a principal bass. At first he was reluctant to do so, as his operatic experience in Australia had been very small and he feared that having come to England at the age of just over forty, he might not find it easy to establish himself in a new career.

His first role was The Bonze in *Madame Butterfly,* and afterwards he appeared in more than twenty-two principal roles — Dikov in *Katya Kabanova,* Friar Lawrence in Sutermeister's *Romeo and Juliet* (both first performances of these works in England), Lord Minto in the world premiere of Lennox Berkely's *Nelson,* Angelotti in *Tosca,* Mephistopheles in *Faust,* and in the great comedy successes of Mr Gruff in *The School for Fathers,* Alidoro in *Cinderella* and Basilio in *The Barber of Seville.* Basilio was his last role.

Stanley Clarkson also sang with the Bach Society, the Royal Choral Society and the Halle Concert Society. He was bass soloist in Sir John Barbirolli's first performance of the *Messiah* in Sheffield and for its first televised performance with the Huddersfield Choral Society under Sir Malcolm Sargent. In the film *Melba* he made his screen debut as Mephistopheles in the Faust sequences. In 1956 he returned to Australia for an eight-months' tour with the Elizabethan Theatre Trust, during which he gave 108 performances and flew some 38,000 miles in the interior of the country.

At Sadler's Wells he was greatly respected by the younger singers and always helpful to them. Norman Tucker expressed the feeling of all Stanley Clarkson's associates when he said at the time of Clarkson's death: "We shall miss him very much".

ROSINA RAISBECK, dramatic soprano

Rosina Raisbeck is a third Australian who went to London in 1947 after having had considerable experience as a singer at home. She was born in the Eisteddfod city of Ballarat but as a girl moved to Newcastle. Since one of her grandmothers had been a singer in Italy she thinks it natural to feel that roles in the Italian repertoire suit her best. Her biggest public successes, however, have been in Wagnerian operas, as Senta in *The Flying Dutchman,* Elsa in *Lohengrin,* and Elizabeth in *Tannhauser.*

She took part in music club recitals in Newcastle and competed in local eisteddfodau. In 1942 she entered the New South Wales Conservatorium of Music in Sydney where she remained for five years. She sang with the opera

179

group there in *Tales of Hoffmann* in 1944 and in Edgar Bainton's *The Pearl Tree*. For more than three years while she was at the Conservatorium she was one of the most prominent contralto soloists in the state. In 1947 she won two important vocal contests in Sydney: the Concerto and Vocal Competition of the Australian Broadcasting Commission and the *Sun* Aria.

She then made a concert tour of New Zealand and after returning sold all her possessions and went to London with her husband, James Laurie, whom she had married in 1943. She carried with her a letter of recommendation from Sir Eugene Goossens, then the Director of the Conservatorium in Sydney. Soon after her arrival in London she was auditioned at Covent Garden and given a contract. This was the beginning of a five year period as a member of the Royal Opera Company. She made her debut at Covent Garden in 1947 as a mezzo-soprano, singing Maddelena in *Rigoletto*. Later, on the recommendation of Sir Thomas Beecham, who considered her best suited for dramatic soprano roles, she sought the help of the well-known teacher, Dina Borgioli, with whose assistance she successfully made the change. In February 1950 she made her debut at Covent Garden as a soprano, singing Ortrud in *Lohengrin*, and later, in the same season, Senta in *The Flying Dutchman*. Her other major roles were Leonora in *Il Trovatore* and Amneris in *Aida*. In oratorio she often

Rosina Raisbeck

180

appeared as soloist in Mendelssohn's *Elijah,* Verdi's *Requiem,* and Beethoven's *Ninth Symphony.*

In 1953 Rosina Raisbeck became a freelance artist. The next year she was invited to go to Australia with Benjamin Fuller's Italian Grand Opera Company but was unable to accept because of the impending birth of her son. For a few years after this she permitted herself to enjoy just being a mother and to indulge in her hobbies of interior decoration and dress designing. In 1958 she sang with the Sadler's Wells Company the parts of Senta in *The Flying Dutchman* and Elizabeth in *Tannhauser.* Subsequently she appeared with them as Kabanicha in *Katya Kabanova* and with John Cameron in the British premiere of Dallapiccola's opera, *The Prisoner,* in 1961. Since returning to Australia with her son in 1962 she has sung in two musicals under the management of Garnet H. Carroll and has taken part in broadcasts and television productions.

JOHN CAMERON, baritone

John Cameron, the baritone who appeared with Rosina Raisbeck in *The Prisoner,* is also well known as an oratorio singer. Although he is the only professional musician in his family, his parents and the other members have a more than amateur interest in singing; his brother Don is well known in Sydney as a member of a quartet of businessmen known as the "Singing Baritones".

After four years in the Australian artillery John Cameron became a member of the Army Education Service and gave recitals for the troops in New Guinea. Immediately afterwards he entered the Sydney Conservatorium on a rehabilitation scholarship and quickly gained recognition as a concert and oratorio singer. In 1948 he won the Australian Broadcasting Commission's Concerto and Vocal Contest; toured Australia and New Zealand with the National Opera Company of New South Wales and sang with the National Theatre Company in Melbourne. The following year he went to Britain and made his debut as Germont in *La Traviata* at the Royal Opera House. He remained with the Covent Garden Company for three years as a principal baritone but later became a freelance artist appearing in concerts and oratorios including *Elijah, The Messiah, Samson* and *The Dream of Gerontius* in London and on the Continent. He appeared with the Glyndebourne Opera in Bach's *Idomeneo* and in *Alceste* and sang before the Queen and the Duke of Edinburgh at a Royal Concert in the Festival Hall. As a guest artist at Sadler's Wells he achieved great success as Figaro, created the role of Sydney Carton in the world premiere of Benjamin's *Tale of Two Cities,* and the title role in the premiere of *The Prisoner.*

181

John Cameron

In 1955 Cameron gave recitals in India and returned to Australia to appear as guest artist for the ABC. The following year he was a member of the Elizabethan Trust Opera Company and sang the roles of Figaro, Papageno and Guglielmo in the Mozart bicentenary which was the focus of the Trust's inaugural season. Since that time he has appeared in concerts at the Brussels Exhibition, at Munich's 800th Anniversary Celebration, and in the Edinburgh, Leeds, London and Three Choirs Festivals; he has made films, recordings[1] and numerous broadcast and television appearances in Paris and London. He sings in Russian, German, French and Italian.

In 1962 he moved to the Continent where he sang principal roles with the Oldenburg Opera Company in Germany and appeared elsewhere on the Continent; in Prague he was heard in Britten's *Requiem*. From time to time he returned to England to make guest appearances with Sadler's Wells in *The*

Mines of Sulphur and *Gloriana,* to make special appearances for the BBC in the programme *My Songs Go Round the World* and to sing at Festivals like that of the City of London. Of his performance there in July 1962, Howard Taubman of the *New York Times* wrote: "John Cameron is an appealing Jack Point, he can act and for a change is a clown who can sing".

ELSIE MORISON, soprano

There have been many great Australian singers, but none has been more affectionately regarded than Elsie Morison. It has been said that she has "the ability to project a lovely and lovable personality across the footlights to the hearts and minds of the audience".[1] Wherever she sings, be it in opera, oratorio or as a soloist with a symphony orchestra, her artistry is apparent. She is equally at home in compositions of Handel or Mozart, of Stravinsky or Poulenc.

On one occasion, after she had sung "I Know that My Redeemer Liveth", Sir John Barbirolli stopped the playing of the Halle Orchestra, turned to the audience and said: "I have heard that aria sung many times but never so beautifully as we have just heard it".

Elsie Morison owes much to her mother's early musical guidance and to the continued interest and help of Clive Carey who taught her first in Melbourne and later in London. She began to study the piano when she was eight but did not take up singing seriously until she was sixteen. Her mother, who was a music teacher and a singer, encouraged the musical activities of her three children but would not permit her daughters to "strain their voices" by trying to sing while they were too young. When Elsie was eighteen she won the Melba Scholarship for three years' study at the Albert Street Conservatorium.

At the Conservatorium she received a good musical background and training for opera, including stagecraft, under the direction of Clive Carey, once director of Sadler's Wells Opera in London and professor of singing at the Royal College of Music, but then living in Melbourne. She also continued the study of piano under Ida Scott, the well-known Melbourne pianist. Towards the end of her course she made her debut in oratorio at the Melbourne Town Hall in a performance of *The Messiah* with the Malvern Choral Society under the direction of Herbert Davis.

After the completion of her Diploma at the Conservatorium the people of her native city of Ballarat raised money to help defray the expense of going abroad for further study at the Royal College of Music in London. She has always been grateful for this community interest and when she returned for a concert tour of Australia in 1960 she donated part of the proceeds of her first concert there to the founding of the Elsie Morison Singing Prize for Sopranos to be awarded annually at the South Street Eisteddfod and the rest to the Ballarat Orphanage.

At the end of her first year in London Miss Morison won the Queen's Prize and an exhibition that provided additional funds for her musical education. Then came the first of several appearances before the Queen, Princess Elizabeth and Princess Margaret. Her first public appearance was at the Royal Albert Hall in a performance of Handel's *Acis and Galatea* and soon afterward she sang with the Royal Choral Society under Sir Malcolm Sargent. In 1948 she was invited to join the Sadler's Wells Opera Company and for the next three years sang a variety of roles which included Nanetta in *Falstaff,* Lauretta in *Gianni Schicci,* the title roles in *Hansel and Gretel* and *The Snowmaiden,* Gilda in *Rigoletto,* Fiordiligi in *Cosi Fan Tutte* and Susanna in *The Marriage of Figaro.* However, the concert platform attracted her and after the 1951 season she virtually gave up opera for it. Then, in 1953, she was engaged by the Covent Garden management, although there were those who said her voice was not large enough for the house. She sang Mimi and then Micaela — and not only did her voice fill the theatre easily, but she proved to be the most touching and sincere Mimi since Victoria de Los Angeles.

In 1953 Miss Morison became a permanent member of the Covent Garden Company and added to her repertoire Pamina, Antonia in *The Tales of Hoffmann* and Marenka in *The Bartered Bride.* By this time she was also becoming most popular for her exquisite oratorio singing and was in such demand for this and concert work that she decided in 1958 to become a freelance artist in order to meet such engagements in England and on the continent. She has continued, however, to appear as guest artist with both London opera companies. She sang the leading role of Blanche in Poulenc's opera *The Carmelites* when it was first produced in England at Covent Garden with a cast that included six Australian singers, and Euridice in Gluck's *Orpheo.* Another of her outstanding guest performances at Covent Garden was in 1961 when she appeared as Marzelline in Otto Klemperer's production of *Fidelio,* a role for which she had been highly praised two years before at Glyndebourne. She had joined the Glyndebourne Festival Opera Company for the first time in 1953 for a production of *The Rake's Progress* and sang the same role, Anne Truelove, with the Sadler's Wells Company when they put on a new production of this Stravinsky opera in 1962. The critic in *Opera* described her singing of the role as "meltingly beautiful". In that year she appeared in the 'Wells' production of Delius' *A Village Romeo and Juliet* — which was first seen at the Bradford Centenary Festival and later in London — as Ilia in *Idomeneo* with Ronald Dowd, and as the Composer in *Ariadne auf Naxos.*

The Elizabethan Theatre Trust brought Elsie Morison to Australia as a guest artist for its 1957 and 1960 seasons and in 1964 she came with her

184

Elsie Morison

husband, Rafael Kubelik, when he toured as an ABC Celebrity Conductor. She gave some special concerts at which she was acclaimed by local audiences.

Elsie Morison has made many recordings with HMV, Columbia, L'Oiseau Lyre and Deutsche Gramophone and has sung under the direction of most of the distinguished conductors of the day, from Beecham to Solti. She has recorded the soprano roles in some of the Gilbert and Sullivan operas under Sir Malcolm Sargent and took part in the opera sequences of the film *The Gilbert and Sullivan Story.*

At the peak of a distinguished career Miss Morison displayed characteristic modesty when she told students at the Melba Conservatorium that she felt she still had much to learn about the art of singing.

WILLIAM HERBERT, tenor

Like Sir William McKie who was Master of Choristers and Organist at Westminster Abbey from 1946 until 1963, William Herbert, one of the

United Kingdom's leading oratorio tenors during the same period, was born in Melbourne and benefited from association with Dr A. E. Floyd, organist and choirmaster at St Paul's Cathedral, who had come to Melbourne steeped in the English choral tradition absorbed at Kings College Chapel in Cambridge and at Winchester Cathedral where he was assistant organist. It was Dr Floyd who taught the young Bill Herbert how to develop the fine diction which English critics noted whenever they reviewed his recitals.

Herbert comes from a large family of five boys and four girls who used to gather round the piano on Sunday evenings to sing under the leadership of their Welsh father who had a splendid voice. Before going to England in 1947 at the age of twenty-seven, he had had extensive musical experience which he found to be a great advantage. He had made his first appearance as soloist in *The Messiah* with the Victorian Symphony Orchestra when he was eighteen and a year later appeared in the same oratorio with the Melbourne Philharmonic Society. From then on he fulfilled engagements throughout Australia with choral and musical societies and was under contract to the ABC, appearing as soloist with orchestras under the direction of most of the world famous visiting conductors.

Soon after arriving in England, Herbert began to make frequent appearances at the Promenade Concerts at the Royal Albert Hall and to broadcast for the BBC on their three services and to appear on television. At the Royal Albert Hall he sang in the first 'Prom' performance of the *Dream of Gerontius* for which people seemed happy to stand for the required hour and a quarter. Other choral works in which he appeared frequently were Haydn's *Creation,* Beethoven's *Ninth Symphony,* Handel operas, Mozart litanies and Monte Verde vespers. He was well known throughout the British Isles and on the continent, singing frequently in oratorios with Kathleen Ferrier. He often took part in the Three Choirs and the Edinburgh Festivals and in those at Cambridge, Canterbury, Leeds and Norwich, and in the Welsh International Eisteddfod. During the Festival of Britain he sang in the inaugural concert at the Royal Festival Hall and also in the first Royal performance of the St Cecilia's Day Concert.

On the continent William Herbert was particularly well known for his singing of the Evangelist in Bach's *St Matthew Passion.* He also appeared with the Dutch Handel Society and in recitals in the major cities of Germany, Holland, Belgium, Denmark, Spain and Switzerland and was one of four British singers chosen to take part in the 1958 United Nations celebrations in Geneva where a concert was broadcast on a world-wide network beamed to ninety-eight countries.

Between 1950 and 1959 William Herbert visited Australia three times as a celebrity artist under the auspices of the ABC, stopping off en route to give concerts in Iran and New Zealand. In 1963 he became Professor of Voice

William Herbert

at the University of Western Australia and continued to give recitals which contributed to the musical life of the city of Perth. He has recorded *The Messiah* for Nixa and Bach cantatas for Decca, and made many recordings for L'Oiseau Lyre.

MAX WORTHLEY, tenor

From the time Max Worthley was a child he wanted to be an accomplished singer and he was able to achieve this ambition in spite of many interruptions — including five and a half years spent as an infantryman in the Middle East, New Guinea and Borneo during the War. He knew he had reached his goal in 1961 when he was invited to become a member of the Deller Consort. This virtuoso group organized by Alfred Deller has a world-wide reputation for specializing in the singing of medieval, renaissance and baroque music, much of it *a capella,* and for programmes made up entirely of selections from the great but largely forgotten literature of madrigals, motets and part-songs.

Of one of their performances at a French spa in 1963, Irving Kolodin   187 wrote in the *Saturday Review* on 20th October: "Closing the eyes, one could imagine Deller and company in a Tudor castle in which six voices had the impact of six times as many." When the group's recording of *Alexander's Feast or the Power of Music* was reviewed in the *New York Times* on 31st January, 1965, Howard Klein said: "Mr Worthley's tenor — a flexible, compact English voice of brilliance and intensity — makes for joy in the vibrant music."

Under the auspices of the Musica Viva Society of Australasia the Deller Consort toured Australia and New Zealand in 1964 and appeared at the Adelaide Festival in March of that year. In addition to taking part in the programmes of the consort Max Worthley sang the title role in twelve performances of *The Play of Daniel* and gave a recital of twentieth century British music accompanied by the composer, Anthony Hopkins. This included a new song cycle, *Prayers from the Ark,* which Hopkins had written especially for Worthley. In the opinion of John Horner of the *Adelaide Advertiser,* "Mr Worthley's biggest number was the *Seven Michelangelo Sonnets* by Britten, of which he gave a splendidly understanding account — he has his own private brand of golden pianissimo as he showed us in 'E'en as a lovely flower' (Bridge) and other pieces."

Max Worthley's appearance at the Adelaide Festival was in the nature of a homecoming. As a boy he had sung in a local choir and been a pupil of one of the city's best-known teachers, Mrs Hermann Kugelberg, the wife of a cellist who at one time had been an associate of Brahms. From an early age Max Worthley had had his heart set on becoming a professional singer. Although — for financial reasons — he was forced for a while to become a bank clerk, he continued his musical studies, part-time, at the Elder Conservatorium and graduated at the age of twenty-one. He sang at numerous orchestral concerts and in broadcasts, some of which were made with Percy Grainger when the latter was doing a series for the ABC in 1934. He continued to work in the bank until the war broke out in 1939.

In 1947 Worthley was able to go to London to begin six years of advanced study, during which time he made many appearances throughout Britain and the continent in oratorio and opera, and broadcast more than three hundred times for the BBC. He played the title role in *Albert Herring* at the Festival of Britain during one of his seasons with the English Opera Group, appeared as guest artist at Covent Garden in the roles of The Captain in *Wozzeck,* and Basilio in *The Marriage of Figaro,* and starred in the world premieres of Britten's *Let's Make an Opera* and Benjamin's *Prima Donna.* During the revival of *Let's Make an Opera* in 1963 he played again the roles he had created thirteen years before.

In 1953 Worthley returned to Australia because of the illness of a member of his immediate family. For the next three years he taught at the Elder Conservatorium of the University of Adelaide and again toured the

Commonwealth for the ABC. During this period he also gave concerts independently, in Singapore and Malaya. When the Elizabethan Theatre Trust organized an opera company in 1956 he became one of its principal tenors singing in Mozart operas with the visiting artist, Sena Jurinac, with Elsie Morison in Smetana's *The Bartered Bride* and as Rodolfo in Puccini's *La Boheme*. In a review of the Melbourne Mozart season the critic for *Canon*, wrote in December, 1956: "Max Worthley sang with clarity, purity, and impeccable taste. His Ottavio, save perhaps for Miss Jurinac, was clearly the major achievement of the performance [of Don Giovanni] and it would be hard to say whether his solo arias or his contributions to the ensemble were the more valuable." Of his performance in *The Magic Flute* it was said: "Max Worthley brought out a splendidly formed Tamino — his singing was a delight throughout the opera."

In 1958 he returned to The Elder Conservatorium where he produced Donizetti's *The Elixir of Love* and Mozart's *The Magic Flute.* That same year he married a New Zealand pianist and soon afterward went abroad to pursue his long standing interest in lieder. He enrolled at the Goethe Institute in Rothenburg and studied German in Frankfurt — and in 1959 appeared in a concert version of *Die Schone Mullerin* in Weisbaden. Early in 1960 he returned to England to work on a series of programmes for the BBC Third Programme. These included the first radio performances of Hindemith's motets and Phyllis Tate's *Phoenix and the Turtle.* Ever since his first stay in England Worthley has been extremely active with the BBC, recording about twenty different programmes a year, many of which are broadcast a number of times.

Max Worthley
Photo: Elizabethan Trust

189

He has also appeared on television as Don Alva in Meyerbeer's *L'Africaine* and in the tenor role of Delius's *Fenimore and Gerda.* His straight recital programmes have included works by Monteverdi, Purcell, Quilter and Warlock. On the lighter side he has appeared in concerts featuring selections from operettas by Strauss, Lehar and Offenbach, and has sung before huge and enthusiastic audiences in smaller English cities in a summer series of Gilbert and Sullivan programmes presented annually by The Royal Liverpool Philharmonic Orchestra, conducted by Stanford Robinson.

Oratorios have always constituted an important part of Worthley's musical activities and he has sung in most of these works by Bach, Handel and Haydn and in Beethoven's *Ninth Symphony,* appearing with such distinguished musical organizations as The Halle Orchestra, conducted by Sir John Barbirolli, and the London Choral Society under the direction of John Tobin.

Concerts with the Deller Consort frequently take Max Worthley to the continent and in 1964 he sang with them for the first time in the United States.

RONAL JACKSON, baritone

By winning the first Mobil Quest in 1949, Ronal Jackson was not only able to realize his ambition to secure further training for himself, but he also gained an understanding of "world standards" which he applied later when training others in Brisbane.

Born at Bathurst, New South Wales, Jackson grew up in a musical family. The Jackson household was a musical one — the mother played the piano and two of the boys violin and trombone respectively. Ronal was a boy chorister at the Church of England. He had none of the usual waiting period while his voice settled, as it did not break but merely dropped to baritone.

At the Canterbury High School, Sydney, where he received his education, Ronal was particularly interested in the natural sciences and dramatics, but on leaving he went into the real estate business. When World War II broke out, he entered the Army Medical Corps and during his service sang at Australian and American Army concerts and with the ABC Military and Dance Bands. After the War, he studied voice at the Sydney Conservatorium on an Army Rehabilitation Scholarship. In 1948 he won the ABC Concerto and Vocal Competition and in 1949 the first place in Mobil Quest, a new contest run by an oil company, which carried a substantial cash award. This enabled him to go to Europe for further study and experience.

After a period of study in London, Jackson toured England and Ireland for two years with the Carl Rosa Opera Company. Then he was awarded the Richard Tauber Scholarship and went to Vienna. This seems to have been the turning point in his career and the beginning of a love of German opera and lieder which caused him later to refuse a Covent Garden contract in favour of a return to Germany. During his second year in Vienna, he was invited to tour Southern Rhodesia with Sir John Barbirolli and a Covent Garden Company and on his return to join the Company in London. There he sang the role of Marcello in *La Boheme* — a production in which Ljuba Welitsch sang Musetta. After this he made several guest appearances with the Welsh National Opera Company.

It was now that Jackson refused a contract at Covent Garden and returned to Vienna where he fulfilled several operatic engagements before going to Kiel Opera House where he remained for two years, making guest appearances at Hamburg, Bremen and Lubeck. From Kiel he went to the Wuppertal Opera. There he built up his German repertoire and sang in a number of neighbouring cities, including Dusseldorf, Cologne and Essen.

Ronal Jackson returned to Australia with his family in 1960 to sing the leading baritone roles in the Elizabethan Trust's opera season. He stayed in his native land and made operatic appearances in Hobart and Perth, as well as giving concerts in Melbourne and Sydney. There followed roles in television opera productions and the leading part of Joey in Garnet Carroll's production of the American musical *The Most Happy Fella*. He sang with the Trust again in 1962 and soon afterwards was appointed head of the Opera School at the Queensland Conservatorium in Brisbane. In 1963 he returned to the Trust and has continued to appear in this way with the Elizabethan Opera Company as frequently as possible.

His pastimes include painting, photography and the renovation of antique furniture.

UNA HALE, soprano

Una Hale, another Covent Garden principal who appeared as guest artist with the Elizabethan Trust Opera, had the advantage of coming under the guidance, at an early age, of Hilda Gill, who had gone abroad to study singing with the great Elena Gerhardt and Reinhold von Warlich before becoming a member of the Faculty of the Elder Conservatorium at Adelaide University.

As a child Una Hale was ashamed of the big strong voice that made her conspicuous when she sang with other members of her class but she loved to sing and taught herself to play the piano, practising at home when she thought no one was listening. Her mother noticed this and finally asked Hilda Gill to hear Una sing and to give an opinion of her voice. Miss Gill recognized the fine quality of the girl's voice and agreed to work with her on its development, and on diction, which she knew to be so important for singers. She later encouraged Una to think of going abroad to study, and to make every effort

Una Hale

to win scholarships that would further her hoped for career in opera.

In 1946 Una Hale won the South Australia ABC Concerto and Vocal Competition held in Adelaide. Soon after this her father, a clergyman, accepted an invitation from a church in Hampstead and the family moved to London. There Una was awarded a two year opera scholarship at the Royal College of Music. At the end of the course she joined the Carl Rosa Opera Company and was soon singing leading roles. A review of one of these early performances in *The Stage,* London reads: ". . . Shining through all was the clear and sure singing of Una Hale, as Marguerite, with its admirable enunciation. Her gradations from simple joy to despair were made with considerable variety and lyrical beauty".

In 1949, Una Hale sang as a guest at the Royal Opera House, Covent Garden, in the first post-war production of *Carmen* and after consolidating her career and reputation during the next few years, joined Covent Garden under contract in 1954. She has had notable successes. She was the first British artist to sing the role of Cressida in *Troilus and Cressida* and she achieved the unusual in singing both Musetta and Mimi in *La Boheme*. She has also sung other roles as widely different in style as the Countess in *The Marriage of Figaro* and Eva in *The Mastersingers*. Beside appearing as a principal in a number of other Wagnerian operas she has interpreted such modern roles as that of Ellen Orford in *Peter Grimes*. Her career at Covent Garden has provided many rewarding opportunities and enabled her to study both in Vienna and Berlin. In addition she has sung at Benjamin Britten's Aldeburgh Festival, at the Ingestre Hall performances arranged by Lord Shrewsbury, and at the Gulbenkian Festival in Portugal.

In 1960 Una Hale married Martin Carr, the Stage Director of the Royal Ballet. He and their young son accompanied her when she returned to Australia for the first time to appear as leading soprano for the 1962 Australian Elizabethan Trust Opera Season. Of one of her performances, a critic wrote: "Una Hale as Ariadne might well have been the singer Strauss had in mind when he created the part. This was great singing in a really grand opera manner".

KEVIN MILLER, tenor

Kevin Miller and his wife, Peggy Fearn, are also graduates of the Elder Conservatorium of the University of Adelaide and are remembered there for their exceptionally fine voices. Miller studied with the late Clement Q. Williams and his wife with Hilda Gill. At first Miller was a baritone but when he was twenty his voice changed to tenor. A year later — as a member of the Australian National Theatre Company in Melbourne — he began singing principal roles in operas by Mozart, Rossini and Vaughan Williams, while during the day he worked as a trustee clerk.

When he returned to Adelaide he operated a grocery store which he owned and attended the conservatorium at the University. He gained further experience by touring Australia under the auspices of the Australian Broadcasting Commission, appearing in public and studio performances. In 1951 he won a Jubilee Scholarship which made it possible for him to go abroad and between 1952 and 1955 he studied with Borgioli in London and for eighteen months at the Accademia Santa Cecilia in Rome. During this time he toured extensively in Italy and Germany, learned to speak both Italian and German and developed an interest in archaeology.

On his return to England Miller sang at Glyndebourne, first in 1956 as Pedrillo in *Il Seraglio* and then in 1957 as Scaramuccio in *Ariadne auf Naxos*, returning to Australia to participate in the Elizabethan Theatre Trust's first

Kevin Miller
Photo: Elizabethan Trust

opera season between these performances. He also sang with the Welsh National Opera, the Dublin Grand Opera Company, "Touring Opera, 1958" and the Carl Rosa Company before joining Sadler's Wells in 1959. Here his ability to act and sing character roles such as Basilo, Pedrillo and Count Almaviva in the Mozart operas, Bamiro in *Cinderella,* Vanya in *Katya Kabanova,* The Spy in *Andrea Chenier,* Niegres in *The Merry Widow* and the title role in *Orpheus in the Underworld,* won the approval of critics.

He sang Orpheus again in 1962 when the Sadler's Wells Company brought the production to Australia. Earlier in that year the Company went to Germany and Kevin Miller sang the Auctioneer in *The Rake's Progress.* Critics again praised his acting as well as his singing. In 1964 his chief roles were in Francis Burt's *Volpone* and as Ottakar in Strauss' *Gypsy Baron.*

ALBERT LANCE, tenor

When Lance Ingram became principal tenor at the Paris Opera, he changed his surname because French people thought it improper for him to be known as "ungram" which suggested a "light weight". Known as Albert Lance, he became one of Europe's outstanding tenors.

He was born in Menindie, South Australia, in 1925, the son of Roland Ingram, of Western Australia, and Eleanor Mary Bush, who had come to Australia from England after the First World War. When he was nineteen his mother encouraged him to take singing lessons from Greta Callow of the Adelaide College of Music and soon after this went to Melbourne where, at twenty-one, he won a singing competition held at a coffee lounge: the first prize was a week's singing engagement. That week grew into months and soon he was singing on radio and in vaudeville. He was known as "The Australian Street Singer" and "The Voice in a Million". In 1951 he auditioned with Gertrude Johnson, the founder of the National Theatre Movement, and she invited him to join the Company. He made his debut as Cavaradossi in *Tosca* and then sang in *La Boheme* and *Madame Butterfly*. In 1954 he sang the role of Hoffmann in a performance of *The Tales of Hoffmann* before Queen Elizabeth and the Duke of Edinburgh and afterwards, with several other singers, was presented to the Royal couple.

Lance Ingram had entered several of the competitions which were conducted on radio but had never been fortunate enough to reach first place — although he did very well in the Mobil Quest. When he was heard in 1954 by Dominique Modesti, the French teacher who was visiting Melbourne with his Australian wife Norma Gadsden, he was offered a two-year scholarship in Paris. He was delighted, but did not have the money to make the trip. How-

Albert Lance

195

ever, a radio announcer, John McMahon, urged him to enter a competition organized by a floor-covering company. He sang the aria which had gained him his initial opera contract — "Celeste Aida" — and won first prize. He left immediately for Paris.

There he studied for fifteen months, and under Modesti's guidance entered the Paris Opera Comique where he was given a twelve months' contract with a three-year option. His debut, as Albert Lance, in a first performance of a new, modern French work given before a performance of *Tosca,* won him instant success and praise from the critics. The renowned, hard-to-please Emile Duillermoz described his work as "Magnifique . . . pure . . . lumineuse. A brilliant vocal power that fascinated the house".

Within eleven months Lance made five major Parisian debuts at the Paris Opera — *Tosca, Butterfly, Boheme, Werther* and *Faust.* He recorded *Tosca* and *Butterfly* for Pathe Marconi, and a recital "Albert Lance" for Columbia, all in French, a language he did not know before going to Paris. In 1958 he sang *Rigoletto* in English at Covent Garden with Joan Sutherland as Gilda, and in the same year *The Masked Ball* in Italian. The critics were unanimous in their praise. Clarendon said: "Albert Lance now rivals the best Italian tenors of our epoque". About the same time Lance sang in the now-celebrated Maria Callas Gala at the Paris Opera.

In 1959 there was a change in the administration at the Paris Opera and he was chosen to re-create the role of Don Jose in a new production of *Carmen.* The critics were ecstatic. One claimed: "We could almost say that this is not so much a *Carmen* as a very fine opera entitled Don Jose thanks to Albert Lance". Another wrote: "I cannot think of a finer choice in the whole of France than Albert Lance for the role of Don Jose". At a gala performance of the opera to mark the state visit to France of Nikita Khrushchev, General De Gaulle said to Lance: "I am again happy to applaud your magnificent talent".

Later Lance was given the tenor role opposite Renata Tebaldi in a new production of *Tosca* presented to commemorate the centenary of the joining of the Province of Savoy to the French Republic. *Tosca,* like *Carmen,* had never been produced at the Paris Opera, always having been performed in French at the smaller Opera Comique. This made the third work in which he had created the major role, illustrating the high esteem in which the Australian singer was held. He appeared regularly throughout France and in Switzerland, Belgium, Portugal, Spain and at Covent Garden, and sang with some of the best Russian singers in Moscow, Leningrad and Kiev.

When not singing, Lance likes to occupy himself with his hobby of painting. He is a keen amateur and founded the Art Salon de l'Opera which has regular exhibitions. He is married to a French pianist and has a small daughter.

June Bronhill

JUNE BRONHILL, soprano

Like Joan Sutherland, June Bronhill won the Sydney *Sun* Aria contest in 1950 and has sung *Lucia* at Covent Garden, but she is now best known for her appearances in *The Merry Widow, The Gypsy Baron, The Cunning Little Vixen,* and *Orpheus in the Underworld.*

June Bronhill was born June Gough but changed her name to a contraction of Broken Hill, her native city which raised a considerable sum of money to send her to England for further study in 1952. Two years later she made her debut at Sadler's Wells where she won recognition as Adele in *Die Fledermaus,* Gilda in *Rigoletto* and Norina in *Don Pasquale.* Her Covent Garden debut was made in 1959 in the title role of *Lucia di Lammermoor* for which her coloratura voice was well suited. Her success as The Merry Widow in Franz Lehar's operetta, produced in 1958 by Sadler's Wells, had been so great, however, that subsequently she had little time to devote to grand opera although she still hopes to be able to do this some day. June sang the role of

197

The Merry Widow in more than 200 performances during two London engagements in 1958 and 1960 and on a tour of the smaller English cities during the same period. In the autumn of 1960 she went with the company to Australia but returned to London in January, 1961 to sing Zerbinetta in the first performance there in English of Richard Strauss' *Ariadne auf Naxos*. She received high praise from the critics, especially for the ease with which she handled the difficult vocal pyrotechnics required by the role. A reviewer in *Opera* magazine in March, 1961, said: "June Bronhill tackled the role of Zerbinetta with a downright professional competence that reaped its reward in the ovation that followed her big scene. Not only can she manage the notes (in itself a feat) but she contrives to throw-off the whole fiendishly difficult thing in a spirit of coquettish zest". Miss Bronhill has also sung leading roles at Sadler's Wells in *Martha* and *The Magic Flute* (as The Queen of the Night); in Menotti's *The Telephone,* and in *Orpheus in the Underworld.*

Despite her ability to handle operatic roles with great success she was persuaded by the producer Garnet Carroll to return to Australia in 1962 to sing the lead in the Rodgers and Hammerstein musical, *The Sound of Music.* This had long runs in Sydney and Melbourne and June Bronhill was as popular in this production as she had been in *The Cunning Little Vixen* and *La Vie Parisienne* in London. She remained in Australia until 1964 when she returned to Sadler's Wells to sing Saffi in Johann Strauss' operetta, *The Gypsy Baron.* Her husband, Richard Finney, a New Zealand born television producer, and their infant daughter accompanied her.

Soon after returning to England, Miss Bronhill began rehearsals for the lead in a new production, by her husband, of the musical version of the *Barretts of Wimpole Street,* entitled *Robert and Elizabeth* with a score by the Australian, Ron Grainer. It has proved very popular with London and Australian audiences.

RAYMOND NILSSON, tenor

Raymond Nilsson, who was loaned by Covent Garden to Sadler's Wells to play opposite June Bronhill in *The Merry Widow,* won the Sydney *Sun* Aria in 1939. He is a tenor of Swedish ancestry, born at Mosman, Sydney, in 1919. His mother was a well-known singer who had studied with the leading teachers of her day in London. He was educated at Brighton College, England, and at the University of Sydney, where he took an Arts degree in 1943. After war service with the Second A.I.F., he joined the resident teaching staff of the Sydney Church of England Grammar School and was for some time tenor soloist at St. Andrew's Cathedral, Sydney. He studied singing at the New South Wales State Conservatorium under Harold Williams and Madame Matthay,

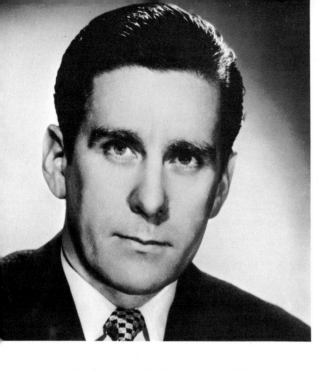

Raymond Nilsson
Photo: Elizabethan Trust

and subsequently obtained the Licentiate of the Royal College of Music.

Even as a student at the Conservatorium, Raymond Nilsson was notable for his keen intellectual capabilities as well as for his musical insight. Undoubtedly the former played no small part in the success of his "characterizations" when once he had embarked on his operatic career. This was delayed, however, because war was declared on the day following his success at the City of Sydney Eisteddfod. At last, in 1947, encouraged by Eugene Goossens, he left for England after a farewell testimonial concert tendered to him by the citizens of Sydney in the Town Hall. His success abroad has been rapid. He first appeared with the Carl Rosa Company, and later with the English Opera Group and with the Sadler's Wells Opera. In 1952 he went to Covent Garden where he sang leading tenor roles including Rodolfo in *La Boheme,* Don Jose in *Carmen,* Alfredo in *La Traviata* and Pandarus in *Troilus and Cressida.*

Nilsson has also sung in the United States, Holland and Germany, and among his German appearances was that of guest artist at the Wiesbaden Opera. He has had regular engagements in television operas throughout Britain, Germany and Holland, including principal roles in *Cavalleria Rusticana, The Saint of Bleeker Street, Carmen, Il Tabarro, Salome,* and *La Boheme.* He has broadcast in concerts from the Royal Festival Hall and the Royal Albert Hall, and has also performed contemporary works for the BBC, among them Schoenberg's *Gurrelieder,* Hindemith's *Mathis der Mahler,* Stravinsky's *Oedipus Rex* and Kodaly's *Psalmus Hungaricus.* No other Australian male singer has enjoyed higher praise than has been bestowed on Nilsson by the British press; beauty of voice, perfection of diction and phrasing, character- 199 ization, powers of interpretation—all have received the highest commendation.

After a long series of operatic successes at Covent Garden, Nilsson was "lent" to the Sadler's Wells Company to take the part of Camille in the London Coliseum season of the revised version of Lehar's *The Merry Widow* with June Bronhill in the title role. With the same Company in the same sprightly operetta, he toured Australia in 1960. This was the second visit to his homeland within two years: some eighteen months earlier he had appeared with the Elizabethan Trust Opera Company when his dynamic performance of Don Jose and his engaging interpretation of Rodolfo created a deep impression. During the same tour, he sang at the ABC Subscription Concerts and in Janacek's *Slavonic Mass*.

DONALD SMITH, tenor

Queensland tenor and Mobil Quest winner in 1952, Donald Smith is another artist whose career was interrupted by the war. He was born in Bundaberg in 1922 and began singing in light opera in Brisbane, his first appearance being as leading tenor in Edward German's *Merrie England* when he was nineteen. Several years of service with the Armed Forces during the war meant the end of serious vocal work, but after demobilization he recommenced singing in Brisbane. He appeared on all the commercial radio stations and with the ABC.

In 1947 he won a State Government Scholarship and toured Queensland with the State Government Opera Scheme. He also performed leading roles with the Brisbane Opera Society under the direction of George English. In such operas as *Maritana, The Bohemian Girl, Faust, Carmen, Rigoletto, Madame Butterfly, Romeo and Juliet,* and *I Pagliacci,* he gave excellently acted

Donald Smith
Photo: Elizabethan Trust

and assured performances. He has also sung Don Jose in *Carmen* for the National Theatre and the Hobart Fine Arts Society.

In 1952 he toured Australia in the Mobil Quest Concerts and the next year was awarded the Joan Hammond Scholarship and went abroad to study for two years at the London Opera School and in Italy. On his return to Australia, he toured with the Italian Opera Company in 1955. Apart from his operatic and concert performances, Donald Smith was a well-known radio personality in Brisbane where, for two and a half years, he conducted his own show on a local station. Before leaving Brisbane to join the Elizabethan Trust Opera Company, he performed the role of Rhadames in Sir Malcolm Sargent's concert version of *Aida* with the Queensland Symphony Orchestra. In 1958 he appeared in *The Magic Flute* and *The Barber of Seville* with the Trust, and in 1960 sang the role of Pinkerton in *Madame Butterfly.*

Donald Smith extended his experience by singing in oratorio, and was featured tenor in performances of Mozart's *Twelfth Mass,* Handel's *Messiah,* Verdi's *Requiem* and Rossini's *Stabat Mater,* also appearing at symphony concerts and recitals throughout Australia. He has toured the Commonwealth extensively for The Arts Council of Australia and the Adult Education Board in conjunction with the Elizabethan Trust. His experience in television with the ABC was highlighted by the leading tenor role in *Il Seraglio.*

Donald Smith's great opportunity came in 1962 when Joan Hammond heard him sing and was so impressed that on her return to England she arranged an audition for him at 'the Wells'. He made his debut with the company in London as Don Jose and subsequently appeared as The Duke of Mantua in *Rigoletto.* A critic[1] praised his performance as Jenik in *The Bartered Bride* for its "robust, easy tones and forthright, unsubtle stage manner". Early in 1964, another critic[2] said of his performance in a production of *Girl of the Golden West* at Sadler's Wells: "Donald Smith, as Johnston, alias Remerrez, sang magnificently. He was a fine lyric tenor with a real heroic ring to it, when required". In April, 1965 he made his debut at Covent Garden in the role of Calaf in *Turandot.* The London *Daily Telegraph* critic reported: "[He] has a fine large, evenly developed voice and a good stage presence. He had a well-deserved ovation after 'Nessun dorma', and he and Amy Shuard were magnificently effective in the heroic passages of the last act duet".

Donald Smith has three children who are all musical. His wife is a pianist and accompanies him when he is practising.

GREGORY DEMPSEY, tenor

Competitions play an important part in the lives of Australia's young singers, and Gregory Dempsey is no exception to the rule. Born in Melbourne of

Irish and Welsh parentage, he has a fine tenor voice. In 1955 he won the £1,000 Lever Award (a commercial radio award), and in 1956 was a grand finalist in Mobil Quest.

Before joining the Melbourne National Theatre in 1955, he had sung principal roles in all the well-known Gilbert and Sullivan Operas and now he sang leading roles in grand opera. Two of the parts he took at this time were Don Ottavio in *Don Giovanni* and Turiddu in *Cavalleria Rusticana.* When the Elizabethan Trust was formed in 1956, Gregory Dempsey took part in its season of four Mozart Operas. In 1957 he appeared with the company in *Tosca, La Boheme* and *The Tales of Hoffmann,* and in the 1958 season sang principal roles in *Carmen, The Barber of Seville* and *Fidelio.*

Radio and television engagements filled the intervals between opera seasons and he became a permanent member of the chorus formed at a commercial television station. In the 1960 season of the Trust, he sang the role of Monostatos in *The Magic Flute;* in 1962 an Australian opera, *Dalgerie,* was given its world premiere in Perth and he performed the role of Mundit, an aborigine. With the Trust he has also sung the roles of First Jew in *Salome,* and Goro in *Madame Butterfly,* and appeared in *Gianni Schicchi.*

After the 1962 Trust season, Gregory Dempsey went to London and joined the Sadler's Wells Company. The critic of the magazine *Opera* in March, 1963 said of his performance in *The Bartered Bride:* "The new Jenik, Gregory Dempsey, sounding as John Lanigan did some ten or more years ago, possesses a natural stage charm". The same critic wrote of a Manchester Opera House production by Sadler's Wells of *Peter Grimes:* "There is an exceptionally good Boles in the company's new Australian tenor, Gregory Dempsey, with a big voice and a big personality: it is not hard to see a future Grimes here".

Mr Dempsey's singing in both traditional and modern operas continues to receive high praise. Critics commended his performance as Baconnion in *The Mines of Sulphur* — "an heroic-villainous part of formidable challenge" — and a review of Janacek's *House of the Dead* gave "special praise to Gregory Dempsey as the youthful, extroverted, slightly irresponsible Skuratov". Other modern works in which he has appeared are the Weill-Brecht opera *The Rise and Fall of the City of Mahagonny* and *The Makropulos Case* — the latter with Marie Collier in both London and San Francisco.

BRIAN HANSFORD, baritone

Brian Hansford also won many of Australia's coveted awards beginning with the lieder section prize in the Dandenong Festival in 1954 when he was only twenty years old. "This success gave me wonderful encouragement as a singer and none whatsoever as an accountant (an occupation for which he had begun to prepare when he left school)", he says. In 1955 he was a semi-finalist in the *Sun* Aria Contest at the Melbourne Town Hall and the next year was a finalist in the Mobil Quest. Of this he says: "I toured most states with the finalists afterwards which was a great experience for a young singer . . . I can honestly say that this 'quest' gave me more through the opportunities and experience it provided than anything else at this particular stage of my career".

After winning the Dandenong Eisteddfod Aria, being a Commonwealth finalist in the ABC Concerto and Vocal Competitions and a runner up in both the Mobil Quest and the Melbourne *Sun* Aria in 1956 he won the latter with its cash award of $3,700 in 1957. This enabled him to go abroad the next year "with full intention of returning to Australia after three years of study". He went to Germany,. concentrated on voice training with the celebrated bass-baritone, Hans Hotter, and attended a master class at the Munich Hoch Schule which included study of interpretation with Gerhard Husch. In 1959 he was a finalist in the Schubert-Haydn Contest in Vienna and later won the International Vocal Contest in Munich. After these successes he was immediately engaged by the Munich State Opera Company for minor roles singing in casts which included many of Europe's top singers, and soon had the opportunity to sing main roles in *La Traviata* and *Madame Butterfly*. He appeared in a number of television productions, made numerous radio broadcasts and sang in recitals in Germany and Austria.

Since returning to Australia in 1961 Brian Hansford has been very busy appearing in operas on television and in oratorios. He has specialized in German lieder and often appeared in duo-recitals with his wife, mezzo-soprano, Dorothy O'Donohoo. The Schubert song cycle "Winterreise" is considered one of his outstanding achievements. He hopes to prove that a young Australian can pursue an international career from his home base.

LEONARD DELANY and NEIL EASTON, baritones

Of Leonard Delany, Hansford's predecessor as winner of the Melbourne *Sun* Aria, Andrew McCredie, in a review of the season of the Lower Saxon State Opera in Hanover wrote in *Opera* in April, 1965:

The first half [of the season] introduced the young Australian baritone, Leonard Delany, in the title-role of *Don Giovanni*. He had followed the familiar Australian pattern — victory in a *Sun* Aria Contest, experience with the ad hoc Sydney or Melbourne companies, then study in Italy. In Hanover and other German houses he has sung all of Mozart's major "Kavalierbariton" parts (as the Germans call them), such as Don Giovanni,

Neil Easton
Photo: Elizabethan Trust

besides Petrucchio in Goetz's *Die Widerspenstige Zahmung* and the Man in Schoenberg's *Von heute auf Morgen*. As Don Giovanni here, Delany coupled an unusually handsome figure with a sparkling vocal performance. The "Champagne Aria" was encored by a wildly enthusiastic public, a spectacle rarely seen in Hanover.

After similar musical experience — singing with the Melbourne and Sydney Opera Companies, appearances with the Elizabethan Theatre Trust Opera and at Australian Broadcasting Commission Concerts — Neil Easton was invited by Norman Tucker during his visit to Australia in 1960 to join the Sadler's Wells Company. Since his arrival in England in February, 1961, he has sung the following roles both in London and on tour: the Forester in *The Cunning Little Vixen,* Cermont in *La Traviata* and Marcel in *La Boheme.* In 1962 he sang The Dark Fiddler in *A Village Romeo and Juliet* at the Delius Festival.

GEOFFREY CHARD, baritone

Geoffrey Chard began his operatic career in 1951 when he joined the National Opera of Australia as a principal baritone. His first roles were Iago in *Otello* and The Don in *Don Giovanni,* and he also became well-known for his portrayal of Figaro in *The Barber of Seville* and Marcello in *La Boheme.* During a tour of the Company in 1954, he sang baritone leads in *Carmen,*

204

Il Trovatore, Rigoletto and *La Traviata*. Geoffrey Chard stayed with the Company until 1955 and in the following year joined the Elizabethan Trust Opera for its initial season.

Just before the season began he married Marjorie Conley, a brilliant young soprano who was a principal with the Trust Company. She had won the Sydney *Sun* Aria and was Commonwealth winner of the ABC Concerto and Vocal Competitions in 1952, and won the Mobil Quest in 1955. They toured Australia with the Trust until their son, David, was born, when they decided to withdraw from the company and concentrate on concert, radio and television work. The next couple of years were happy and successful for them, but in 1959, during a brief holiday in Surfers' Paradise following a tour of Queensland, Marjorie died suddenly from a cerebral haemorrhage.

Her husband, however, did not give up his singing, and in February, 1961, sailed for England. During the following twelve months, he sang on the concert platform, on radio and television and in performances with the Dublin Grand Opera Society and the Welsh National Opera Company. Early in 1962 he was invited back to Australia to sing leading roles with the Trust's Opera Company: Harlequin in *Ariadne auf Naxos,* Germont in *La Traviata* and Masetto in *Don Giovanni.* After the season closed he returned to London, taking his five-year-old son with him.

Geoffrey Chard is an extremely versatile singer. He has appeared on the concert platform with major orchestras and conductors for the ABC, and has given many oratorio performances, including the works of Bach, Handel, Mendelssohn, Vaughan Williams, Tippett and Benjamin Britten. He has toured New Zealand for the New Zealand Broadcasting Commission, and was chosen as soloist with the Sydney Symphony Orchestra for its first telecast. He has sung more than thirty major baritone roles in opera in Australia and New Zealand, and in 1962 sang the main role in *Die Fledermaus* with the Dublin Grand Opera Society. His home is now in England.

JENIFER EDDY, lyric coloratura soprano

The lyric coloratura soprano Jenifer Eddy won the first Shell Aria in 1955.[1] She now exercises her talents both at Covent Garden and with Sadler's Wells, and has been called by her friends "Australia's gift to the BBC", because she has appeared so frequently on their broadcasts.

She is equally at home in opera and operetta. From the time she was eleven years old she had the urge to sing and had started to take lessons in drama when she was only six. She took part in radio serials and in pantomimes, sang in the school choir and won prizes in singing at Westleigh College in Melbourne. She was not permitted to take "proper singing lessons", however,   205

Jenifer Eddy

until she was fifteen when her father's teacher J. G. Nielson let her "begin gradually". Her father, a baritone, was "very musical", Jenifer says. Her mother's sister, who was a soprano, persuaded the family to permit the girl to enter talent quests at an early age and in one of these Jenifer earned thirty shillings for her singing of "My Curly Headed Babbie".

The year before winning the Shell Aria, Jenifer began to study with Mr and Mrs Henry Portnoj, who had come to Melbourne from Vienna, and for the next four years she sang for the ABC in concerts and oratorios — notably *The Messiah* and *The Seasons* and a first performance of Horace Perkins' *Knight and Witchery* in Adelaide. In 1956 she appeared during the first opera season of the Elizabethan Theatre Trust in The Mozart Festival, singing the roles of Susanna, Despina and Papagena. In 1957 she made her debut in television, appearing on both the ABC and commercial networks in light classical selections.

In January, 1959, Jenifer Eddy arrived in London with her engineer husband David Beamish, and three months later sought an audition at Covent

Garden. She was engaged immediately to sing there in May as Frasquita in six performances of *Carmen*. Subsequently she became a principal member of the Royal Opera Company and sang a number of roles including Titania in Benjamin Britten's *A Midsummer Night's Dream,* in which she appeared not only at Covent Garden but also at the Schwetzingen Festival in Germany and at the festivals in Leeds and Edinburgh in 1961.

Other roles which she has sung with distinction at Covent Garden include The Niece in *Peter Grimes,* Papagena in *The Magic Flute* conducted by Otto Klemperer, Lisa in *La Somnambula* with Joan Sutherland, and Xenia in *Boris Godounov.* In the latter and other operas she has appeared with two other well-established Australian singers, Elsie Morison and Margreta Elkins.

In 1962 she "took time out" to have a son and the next year made her debut with the Sadler's Wells Opera Company as Norina in *Don Pasquale* and as Papagena in *The Magic Flute.* Since then she has sung Blonde in the new production of another Mozart opera, *Il Seraglio.* During the summer of 1964 she sang her first Musetta in *La Boheme* with the Welsh National Opera Company in the cities of Llandudno and Cardiff and realized her ambition to sing the role of Sophie in *Der Rosenkavalier* as a member of Covent Garden's Touring Company appearing in Coventry. Miss Eddy's singing has been described as "fresh and clear like a spring rivulet" and her voice as having "the right crystal top, without the diamond-hard quality sometimes apparently inseparable from coloratura sopranos". Other critics refer to her "excellent enunciation" and "delicious sense of comedy".

MARIE COLLIER, dramatic soprano

In 1961 a London critic[1] wrote: "Of all the Commonwealth voices that have come to our aid since the war none save that of Joan Sutherland (and she doesn't compete in this sphere) has had more lustre and sheer beauty of tone than that of the Australian soprano, Marie Collier!"

A dramatic soprano, Marie Collier was well known throughout Australia before she left in 1955 for further training in Italy. She had given more than seventy performances as Magda Sorel in *The Consul* in which she toured the Commonwealth in 1954 under the joint auspices of the New South Wales Opera Company and the Australian National Theatre of Melbourne. She had previously made her debut with the opera company of the latter organization as Santuzza in *Cavalleria Rusticana* and had appeared as Giulietta in *Tales of Hoffmann* at the Royal Performance during the Queen's visit to Australia in 1954.

Although Miss Collier admits that her success is due in part to unremitting effort she feels that chance has played a large part in determining her career. It was while working as a pharmacist's assistant that she first took up singing — when a broken arm temporarily prevented her from playing the piano as a hobby. She claims, however, that she had no deep interest in music when her singing teacher suggested she try for a bursary at the Melbourne University Conservatorium. She won the bursary and during her second year at the Conservatorium she decided to join a J. C. Williamson Company that was reviving *The White Horse Inn* and *Oklahoma!* As a result she lost her scholarship and returned to her old job as a pharmacist's assistant. By this time, however, she was very interested in singing and began to study privately in the evening with Mme Wielaert who had a studio in Collins Street Melbourne. This teacher encouraged her musical activities and eighteen months later sent her to Gertrude Johnson, Director of the Opera School of the National Theatre Movement where she attended classes after work. When she was chosen to sing Santuzza in *Cavalleria Rusticana* with the National Theatre Opera Company her employer made it possible for her to attend the daytime rehearsals by permitting her to take her annual fortnight's vacation in half days. After her successful debut as Santuzza Miss Collier decided to make opera her career.

Following her subsequent success in *The Consul* she set out early in 1955 for Milan, where she studied with Ugo Benevenuto-Giusti, who had been a friend and pupil of Mascagni in whose opera she had made her debut in Melbourne. An acquaintance in Milan called her to the attention of the Earl of Harewood, the then Artistic Director of Covent Garden. The Earl agreed to hear her sing while he was there on a visit and later recommended her to Rafael Kubelik, at that time Musical Director of Covent Garden. As soon as

Marie Collier
Photo: Elizabethan Trust

she arrived in London in the autumn of 1956, she was offered a contract with The Royal Opera Company and an Opera Singing Scholarship provided by The Worshipful Company of Musicians for three years of advanced study.

Her first roles at Covent Garden were Giulietta in *Tales of Hoffmann,* the First Lady in *The Magic Flute,* Polyxena in *The Trojans* and Musetta in *La Boheme.* Her singing of Musetta has often received special commendation. In May, 1960, Evan Senior, then the editor of *Music and Musicians,* reviewing a presentation of *La Boheme* by a distinguished cast at Covent Garden, wrote: ". . . But it was Marie Collier's Musetta that in Act II simply took the bit in her teeth and ran away with the performance in the most astonishing and effective playing and full-voiced singing of the role I have ever heard or seen. It brought the house down, and rightly; it will be a long time before anybody who saw this performance forgets it."

Marie Collier also appears frequently at the Sadler's Wells Theatre — both with the regular company and in performances by the New Opera Group. During the 1960 season she sang for the first time three title roles: Madame Butterfly, Katya Kabanova and Tosca. When she sang Tosca at Covent Garden in 1963 she was the first British artist to have done so since her compatriot, Joan Hammond, in 1954. Marie Collier has also appeared most successfully in lighter roles, especially as Concepcion in *L'Heure Espanol,* a production of the New Opera Group at the Sadler's Wells Theatre in 1961.

In 1962 she went to South America to sing with other members of the Royal Opera Company in the first performance of Benjamin Britten's *Midsummer Night's Dream* at the Teatro Colon in Buenos Aires. Later the same year she appeared as Hecuba in Michael Tippett's new opera *King Priam* both at the Cathedral in Coventry and at Covent Garden. One of her most spectacular successes was in the title role of Dmitri Shostokovich's opera, *Katerina Ismailova* which had its western premiere at Covent Garden, in the presence of the composer, on 2nd December, 1963, and was produced again in San Francisco in October of the next year. It is the story of a young, life-loving woman who is bored and oppressed by the stifling surroundings of a nineteenth century small town and finds expression in destructive and self-destructive ways. Of the London performance the *New York Times* said: "Marie Collier gave a rich-voiced, intensely acted account of the title role", and ". . . the cast is dominated by Marie Collier's strong singing and acting". Alexander Friend, reviewing the San Francisco performance for the same newspaper, wrote: "The excellent cast introduced to the United States a superb singing actress in the handsome Australian, Marie Collier".

Early in February, 1964 Marie Collier and two of her fellow countrymen played important parts in the Sadler's Wells producion of Janacek's opera, *The Makropulos Case;* Charles Mackerras was the conductor, Gregory Dempsey the tenor, and Marie Collier the principal soprano. Of her perform-   209 ance Arthur Jacobs wrote in *Opera:* "This is in a double sense a prima donna's role and Marie Collier brought to it just the right beauty, warmth and range of tone, and a compelling personality". Later that month she left for the Adelaide Festival to appear as Cressida at the request of the composer, Sir William Walton, who had been very pleased with her portrayal of this role when *Troilus and Cressida* was produced at Covent Garden in April the previous year. Critics admired it, too. John Warrach of the *Daily Telegraph* reported: "Marie Collier's Cressida is somewhat of a triumph, vocally. She has a measure of these arching lines and plenty of vocal stamina". Another review noted the "clarity of her enunciation", and ". . . the communication of sensitivity which is the mark of her best interpretations".

Ever since her first appearance as Tosca at Covent Garden on 1st February, 1963, this has been considered one of Marie Collier's best roles. Reviewing that occasion in *Opera,* Harold Rosenthal stated: ". . . she was vocally in thrilling form . . . there is no denying that this Australian soprano possesses one of the most vibrantly exciting and 'Italianate' voices now to be heard".

Frank Granville Barker spoke of her interpretation of the role as "at once tense and tender" and "{both} distinctive and dramatically valid". When she appeared as Tosca again at Covent Garden in May, 1964 it was natural that her performance should be compared with that given by Maria Callas a few months before in the same Opera House. Arthur Jacobs expressed his preference when he wrote in the July issue of *Opera:* "Let me say, boldly, that I found Miss Collier's the better sung performance".

In light of so much favourable opinion of her portrayal of the role of Tosca, it is not surprising that Marie Collier was asked to replace Callas when the great diva was forced by ill-health to cancel three of four performances of this opera scheduled for the following year. On 2nd July, 1965, The New York *World Telegram and Sun* called attention to the international importance of this by printing on its front page a large picture with the caption:

BIG CHANCE . . . Marie Collier, 34, a soprano from Australia, steps in to replace Maria Callas at Covent Garden in London — Miss Collier, wife of a construction engineer and mother of four, admitted she's afraid of the London audience because "they will expect Callas and they are not really interested in me".

The next day, however, London papers reported a "capacity audience that apparently had turned up undeterred by Callas' cancellation". Typical of the warm reviews of the performance was one by Peter Stadlen of the *Daily Telegraph* who wrote of Marie Collier's "voluminous, mellifluous top notes, delivered every time with absolute reliability". Subsequently, *The New York*

Times reported that, after hearing one rehearsal, a representative of La Scala, Milan, had presented Miss Collier with a contract to sing there.

RONALD DOWD, tenor

During more than ten years' residence in London, Ronald Dowd has been the first person to whom many young compatriots have turned for advice and encouragement when they arrived in England on the brink of what they hoped would be a successful international career.

Ronald Dowd did not begin his singing career until he was demobilized after serving during World War II. He had sung in a church choir as a boy but after leaving school he worked for twelve years in a bank before joining the army in 1941.

In 1946 he went to Japan with a civilian entertainment unit and there met Henry Krips, the conductor. Soon afterward he joined a group known as "Singers of Australia" which appeared throughout the Commonwealth under Krips' direction, singing excerpts from opera. His first operatic performance was in 1948 when he sang Hoffmann in Offenbach's opera. The production was by the Australian National Theatre Movement in Melbourne, to whose director, Gertrude Johnson, he had been introduced by the conductor Joseph Post. With this organization he undertook formidable roles in *Eugen Onegin, Fidelio, La Traviata* and *Tannhauser*. He recalls that Hans Zander (a conductor of the National Opera of Australia who had previously been associated with the Berlin Opera) said to him when he was singing with that company: "Mr Dowd, one of these days you will know what you have tried to sing". Since that time Ronald Dowd has studied and performed many roles with great success.

In 1963 his portrayal of the title role in Benjamin Britten's *Peter Grimes* was acclaimed not only in English speaking countries but also on the Continent. During the Spring Tour of Germany by the Sadler's Wells Company that year the critic of the *Suddeutsche Zeitung* reviewing the Munich performances said: "This Peter Grimes is played by Ronald Dowd whom one can call a lyrical character tenor, of convincing appearance and with an individual voice having an almost baritonal colour in the middle, but rising to a bright top, a voice which is exactly the right tone colour for the personality compounded of brutality and tenderness, a gloomy integrity and eccentric hardness — his final monologue was overwhelming". The *Munchener Merkur* spoke of "the realistic sharpness and credibility with which Ronald Dowd invests the part" and ended its review: "Much applause for our English guests and above all, Ronald Dowd". The *Frankfurter Allgemeine* spoke of the high quality of the Sadler's Wells performance and said: "On the musical side it is

Ronald Dowd

of international standard — Vocally it possesses for the main roles some splendid voices, for instance, the tenor Ronald Dowd".

When he appeared in Mozart's *Idomeneo* at the Aix-en-Provence Music Festival in July of the same year a French critic noted: "Ronald Dowd interpreted the title-role with great authority. He possesses a magnificent voice ... has the manner of a true man of the theatre and displays real conviction in what he is doing". Dowd considers Joseph Post — later Associate Director of Music for the ABC — a very important figure in the history of opera in Australia and regards him as "one of the best conductors I've ever had in any opera pit". He recalls with enthusiasm Post's conducting of performances in Brisbane, Melbourne and Sydney in 1952 when he appeared in *I Pagliacci, Tosca* and *Lohengrin* and looks back on the 1957 Sydney opening of the Elizabethan Trust's opera production of *Othello,* under the same conductor, as "most thrilling". Dowd pays high tribute, also, to Clarice Lorenz, of Sydney, who in 1950 organized the National Opera of Australia to provide opportunities for young singers to appear not only in New South Wales and Queensland but also on tours throughout Australia and New Zealand. He speaks of the importance of her vision and "the spadework she has done", of the artistic success of the production and of the debt owed by aspiring young artists to the opportunities she "doggedly supplied". He alluded also to the high standards of the joint season in 1952 of the Melbourne and Sydney Opera companies which had promised the possibility of establishing an Australian company on a permanent basis.[1]

Before leaving for London in 1956, Ronald Dowd had sung more than twenty leading operatic roles including The Poet in Arthur Benjamin's *The Devil Take Her* presented before Her Majesty, the Queen, during her Australian tour, and Herod in a concert version of *Salome* with Marjorie Lawrence when she returned to the Pacific to entertain troops during the war. He had also taken part in many oratorio performances under the direction of Sir John Barbirolli, Sir Eugene Goossens and Walter Susskind and participated in numerous broadcasts in Australia and New Zealand. It was James Robertson of New Zealand with whom he had sung *Das Lied von der Erde* who persuaded him, finally, to go to England where he was immediately offered a contract with the Sadler's Wells Opera Company. He made his debut as Canio in *I Pagliacci* and has sung Pinkerton in *Madame Butterfly* and Cavaradossi in *Tosca* as well as the title roles in *Tannhauser, Idomeneo, Oedipus Rex, Hugh the Drover* and *Peter Grimes* with the Sadler's Wells Company. Of his portrayal of Peter Grimes, critics noted: "It is no small thing to take a part written for Peter Peers and to re-establish it as one's own."

During his first eighteen months abroad he also did a great deal of broadcasting with the BBC and concert work with the Halle Orchestra under Sir John Barbirolli. In addition he sang in a number of oratorios — among them *The Dream of Gerontius,* with the Berlin Philharmonic Orchestra, during the Berlin Festival in 1956 when German critics referred to him as "an outstanding soloist who sang the cantilena of Gerontius with beautiful phrasing". In 1957 he returned to Australia for two seasons to sing the title roles in *Othello, Peter Grimes* and *Lohengrin* with the Elizabethan Theatre Trust Opera Company.

In 1959 Ronald Dowd became a freelance artist appearing at Covent Garden and Sadler's Wells, in English and European festivals, in oratorios and at 'Prom' concerts. He has also sung in Israel, both at the twenty-fifth anniversary celebrations of the founding of that country and again in 1964 on the way back from a five months ABC tour of Australia and New Zealand.

His portrayals of title roles in contemporary operas have continued to attract the favourable notice of critics. Arthur Jacobs, reviewing the first English production of the Weill-Brecht opera, *The Rise and Fall of the City of Mahagonny,* at Sadler's Wells, wrote in *Opera* in January, 1963: "Jimmy himself was given power enough in a very strong performance (including a ringing top C) by Ronald Dowd: in impact this paralleled his memorable Oedipus". He created the title role when Stravinsky's *Oedipus Rex* was presented at Sadler's Wells in the presence of the composer in 1961 and has 213 sung the part on many other occasions, both in its original form and the concert version.

ELIZABETH FRETWELL, soprano

When the Sadler's Wells Opera Company visited Germany in the Spring of 1963 both the Australians who sang the leading roles in *Peter Grimes* received high praise from critics. One of the latter, R. H. Ruppel, wrote in the *Suddeutsche Zeitung* of Munich: "In Elizabeth Fretwell . . . we get to know a dramatic soprano of the most beautiful and cultured vocal material, who, equally with Ronald Dowd, was rewarded with special applause." Another Munich critic, Greville Rothon, noted that "Elizabeth Fretwell's clear, subtly expressive, sensitive and powerful voice drew attention to her commanding, yet reticent, Ellen Orford."

Miss Fretwell joined Sadler's Wells in 1955 and soon became one of the company's leading sopranos, appearing as Musetta in *La Boheme,* Lenora in *Fidelio,* the title roles in *Madame Butterfly* and *Suor Angelica* and as Violetta in *La Traviata.* Her singing of the latter role in February, 1956 won high praise from the critics. The New Statesman reported: "Her Violetta is the best seen in London since the war — her voice is rich, warm, flexible", and The *Times* said: "She brings to the role youth, beauty, an authoritative stage

Elizabeth Fretwell

214

presence, a dramatic understanding of the role and an ample, rich voice". Seven years later, Harold Rosenthal, in *Opera,* referred to this performance again in an enthusiastic review of Elizabeth Fretwell's singing of Minnie in a revival of Puccini's *The Girl of the Golden West.* Speaking of the latter, Rosenthal called it "a triumph exceeding even her famous Violetta in 1956". Of her appearance again as Violetta in January, 1962, Arthur Jacobs wrote in *Opera:* "Elizabeth Fretwell . . . sings it very movingly with warm, well-coloured voice . . . The resulting total performance now seems to me among the best of the current opera presentations in London".

After her 1956 success in *La Traviata,* Elizabeth Fretwell made her television debut and her first appearance at a 'Prom' concert in The Royal Albert Hall, toured the English provinces, and went to Brussels with the Sadler's Wells Company to sing in *The Flying Dutchman* and *The Moon and Sixpence.* Of her Senta one European critic wrote: "We cannot praise her sufficiently for her beauty, her singing, the clear and vibrant vigour of her soprano, the incompressible ardour of her enthusiasm". Another critic thought she gave "an even better performance" in the role of Blanche Stroeve. When she appeared as Ariadne in the opulent production of the Strauss opera at Sadler's Wells in 1961, the editor of *Opera* wrote: "The Australian soprano sang truly magnificently. The voice sounded fresh and beautiful and she poured it forth in a stream of golden sound". When, the next year, she added to her considerable Puccini repertoire the role of Minnie in *The Girl of the Golden West,* the same critic noted that it "ranked among the most exciting individual portrayals seen on the London opera stage in recent years", and Frank Granville Barker in a review in *Music and Musicians* wrote: "Elizabeth Fretwell sang powerfully, securely and with considerable radiance in the title-role, acting, moreover, with such conviction and tact that she triumphed over many of the absurdities in Minnie's character".

By this time Elizabeth Fretwell had been singing in the British Isles for seven years and had had considerable artistic experience before leaving Australia. For nine years she had trained to become a ballerina but when she "grew too large" for such a career she turned to singing. She took private lessons and entered the vocal competitions at the Australasian Eisteddfod at Ballarat, winning a place among the finalists in the 1947 *Sun* Aria Contest. That year she also joined the opera school of the National Theatre Movement in Melbourne. With this group she studied acting, stage-craft, make-up and other aspects of opera as well as singing. She began as a "backstage useful" but gradually started to sing secondary roles like Cherubino in *The Marriage of Figaro* and then graduated to the major roles of Fiordiligi in *Cosi Fan Tutti,* Donna Anna in *Don Giovanni,* Elsa in *Lohengrin,* Senta in *The Flying Dutchman,* Antonia in *The Tales of Hoffmann* and the title roles in *Madame Butterfly* and *Tosca.*

215

It was in *Hoffmann* that she appeared during the Royal Visit of 1952 in a performance before Queen Elizabeth II and afterward was presented to Her Majesty. Of this occasion a critic wrote: "The honours of the evening went to Elizabeth Fretwell who sang the part of Antonia magnificently". During this period she also sang frequently for the ABC and in oratorios and concerts with leading choral societies and symphony orchestras. Some of her associates in the operatic performances at the Australian National Theatre were her future husband, Robert Simmons, Marie Collier, Ronald Dowd, John Shaw, John Lanigan, Margaret Nisbett, Neil Easton, Kevin Miller, Lance Ingram, Len Delany and Robert Allman, all of whom she was to meet again in Europe.

Soon after she arrived in London, Elizabeth Fretwell was engaged by the Dublin Grand Opera Company to sing principal roles including Aida, and Musetta. Of her performances a reviewer wrote: " . . . magnificently played and sung — a soprano of great dramatic gifts". Before returning to England she also gave a number of operatic concerts in Wales.

Following the German tour with the Sadler's Wells Company in 1963, she returned to Australia to appear as guest artist and principal soprano with the Elizabethan Trust Opera Company, singing Lenora in *Fidelio* and The Countess in *The Marriage of Figaro*. At the end of the Australian season she returned to England and Sadler's Wells. Of this company's production of *Ariadne on Naxos* on 26th March, 1964, Harold Rosenthal wrote in the May issue of *Opera:* "This . . . far eclipsed the recent performance I had seen in Munich . . . Of Miss Fretwell's Ariadne, one can only say if she were a member of a German provincial house she would be singing the role — and several others in her repertory — all over Germany . . . She was in glorious, radiant voice and looked and moved like a goddess." The same critic, reviewing a performance of *Peter Grimes* a year later wrote: "Elizabeth Fretwell's Ellen Orford seems to me the finest since Joan Cross', it was infinitely touching and human."[1]

In 1965 Elizabeth Fretwell appeared at Covent Garden for the first time as Aida and in *Il Tabarro* when she proved that her voice was more than adequate for the larger theatre. She now lives in Surrey with her husband Robert Simmons, a former baritone in the Australian National Theatre Opera Company, but who entered business when they came to England. The Simmonses and their two children at their home in the country enjoy gardening and other outdoor activities dear to the heart of Australians.

JOHN SHAW, baritone

Few singers are engaged by Covent Garden without an audition, but this

John Shaw

was the happy experience of baritone John Shaw who, in 1958, was recommended to the management by his fellow Australians Elsie Morison and Joan Hammond. Sir David Webster had asked Elsie Morison to try to find him a high baritone when she left London to appear as a guest artist in Australia, and Shaw had sung with Joan Hammond in performances of *Otello* and *Tosca* during the Elizabethan Trust Season that was just ending.

Born in Newcastle, New South Wales, the eldest of seven children, John Shaw has been singing for most of his life. Both his grandfathers were singers: his father's father was a professional, well-known throughout Australia, and his mother's father a very fine amateur. At the age of fifteen John Shaw joined a Church choir and for two of the five or six years he spent with it, studied Italian with the curate of a Roman Catholic Church in Newcastle. When he was about seventeen he began to appear in local amateur musical comedies and concerts and by the time he had become an accountant with the Broken Hill Proprietary Company he was singing professionally in his leisure hours. Then, hearing that the Victorian conductor and radio producer Hector Crawford was coming to Newcastle on tour, he wrote requesting an audition. Crawford heard him sing and recommended that he go to Melbourne to study. He took this advice and began to study with Mr and Mrs Henri Portnoj.

In 1945 he joined the Australian National Theatre Opera Company and   217 in 1949 was given a part in a production of *Martha.* During the ten years he stayed with the National Theatre he sang many roles with the company. In 1954 he entered Mobil Quest and was awarded second place at the grand final. He had many temporary "jobs" to keep him going between opera seasons, but gradually enthusiasm and hard work began to pay dividends. An Italian Opera Company that came to Australia in 1955 engaged John Shaw for all the main baritone parts — thirteen roles — in Italian. In 1956 Joseph Post, the Musical Director of the newly-formed Elizabethan Theatre Trust, asked him to be principal baritone for a season of Mozart Operas being presented in Melbourne, and in the course of the season he sang the title role of *Don Giovanni* with the visiting Viennese soprano, Sena Jurinac. During the same year he created the role of The Secret Police Agent in the first Australian performance of Menotti's *The Consul* with the National Theatre.

John Shaw had planned to go overseas in 1957 but remained, when the Elizabethan Trust again asked him to tour with its Opera Company. Nine days before leaving for London in 1958, he received a cable from Covent Garden that suggested the possibility of his singing *Rigoletto* there the following February. John Shaw has been with Covent Garden ever since and is now one of the Company's principal dramatic baritones. His repertoire comprises more than forty operatic roles, including Rigoletto, Scarpia *(Tosca),* Amonasro *(Aida),* Rodrigo *(Don Carlos),* Ford *(Falstaff)* and Tonio *(Pagliacci).* His work has won high praise from the critics. Of his performance as Marcello the London *Daily Telegraph* wrote: ". . . a magnificently uninhibited performance characterised by a splendid richness and generous volume of tone". These words could be used to describe his approach to all the parts he has undertaken, for John Shaw is a perfectionist with a passionate love of opera. Charles Reid, critic of the *Daily Mail,* described his debut as Scarpia at Covent Garden thus: "In bearing, gesture, and, above all, vocal verve and power, Mr Shaw ranks on last night's showing as one of the more eminent English-speaking Scarpias of our time if not of our century."

John Shaw has sung at Covent Garden with such artists as Victoria de los Angeles, Jussi Bjoerling, Tito Gobbi, Maria Callas and Boris Christoff and has also fulfilled various concert engagements with English provincial symphony orchestras for the BBC. For two seasons he was guest artist with the Welsh National Opera and in 1959 had great success in performances of *Andrea Chenier* with the Netherlands Opera. He made a successful debut with the Vienna State Opera in 1961 singing the role of Tonio in *I Pagliacci* and in 1963, as a measure of his increasing stature, sang in Verdi's *Force of Destiny* at the Netherlands Festival.

In May 1963 John Shaw returned to Australia as a celebrity artist for a seventeen-and-a-half week concert tour for the ABC. During this tour he appeared in the title role of *Simone Boccanegra* in the ABC television production of the opera, in performances of *Elijah* and Beethoven's *Ninth Symphony* and in recitals in all the capitals and many of the smaller cities of the Commonwealth. After the Australian tour came his American debut with the San Francisco Opera Company, whose opening production of the Autumn Season was *Aida* with Leontyne Price in the title role. Of John Shaw's performance the music critic of the San Francisco *Examiner* wrote:

"Australian baritone John Shaw . . . proved to be a vividly outstanding addition to our opera company's ranks . . . He produced a voice of dramatic emphasis, yet brainy control. His captive Amonasro had handsome presence, and was a masterly blend of barbaric thrust and authoritarian dignity."

John Shaw has moved ahead rapidly since his early National Theatre days. He is now in the fortunate position of being obliged to refuse offers from opera houses in different parts of the world because of his many commitments. He lives in Sussex, England, with his family and engages in his favourite relaxations — golf and tennis — whenever he can.

JOHN LANIGAN, tenor

John Lanigan, one of Covent Garden's most valuable singers, won the Melbourne *Sun* Aria in 1945 while he was a member of the Army Signal Corps. His teacher, Horace Stevens, entered him as a contestant on the chance that he would be able to appear in the Ballarat preliminaries and then in the final at the Melbourne Town Hall. There were many obstacles to overcome but the co-operation of his fellow soldiers in taking over his duties made his appearance possible on the final night of the contest which he won with his rendition of "The Prize Song" from *Die Meistersinger*.

Nine years before, at the age of fifteen, he had been photographed sitting next to his mother near the piano on the stage where Sylvia Fisher had won the same award. At that time he had said: "Some day I'll sing here and win that prize for you, mum." His mother, who, as Lucy Colahan, had sung in J. C. Williamson's Gilbert and Sullivan productions, thus had a keen interest in the outcome of the 1945 finals.

After demobilization, Lanigan sang principal roles with the ANTM. Six months later on 27th May, 1946, he was given a farewell concert at which he sang songs of Schubert and arias from Mozart and Verdi operas. Glenda Raymond sang "Depuis le Jour" and "Ah, fors e Lui" and other young singers and instrumentalists rounded out the programme. Margaret Schofield was the chief accompanist and Henry Portnoj accompanied John Lanigan whose voice was described by critics as "almost a true heroic tenor", 219 his high notes as "ringing", and his intonation as "very true". Soon after arriving in London that year he sang at Covent Garden and in 1955 became a regular member of the Royal Opera. He has been one of the company's stand-bys ever since, both in principal and supporting roles. Some of his best performances have been as Pinkerton in *Madame Butterfly,* the Duke in *Rigoletto,* Rudolfo in *La Boheme,* Jenek in *The Bartered Bride,* and Hylas in *Dido and Aeneas.*

SUTHERLAND'S ASSOCIATES

ROBERT ALLMAN, baritone

When casts were being assembled in Europe for the 1965 season of the Sutherland-Williamson International Grand Opera Company, Robert Allman was selected to sing baritone roles in *L'Elisir d'Amore, Eugene Onegin, Lucia di Lammermoor* and *La Traviata.*

Like so many young Australians singing leading roles in European opera houses today, he gained his first experience with the National Theatre Opera Company in Melbourne. He did not begin to study singing until he was eighteen when his aunt, who was a singer, introduced him to Horace Stevens, the well-known baritone. For a while he studied part-time, and was employed during the day as a technical salesman, but in 1952 he made singing his profession. He first appeared in concerts and oratorios and then became a member of the National Theatre Opera Company, appearing with them for three consecutive seasons in Melbourne and touring from 1955 to 1957 in their productions of *The Consul, Madame Butterfly* and *Cosi Fan Tutti* under the auspices of the Council for Adult Education in Melbourne and The Arts Council in New South Wales.

Meanwhile he had been competing in the Mobil Quest and *Sun* Aria contests and, while not winning any of the large cash awards, he had earned a reputation as a fine singer. He was therefore one of those recommended to Dominique Modesti, the Paris voice teacher, and his wife, Norma Gadsden, the Melbourne-born dramatic soprano, when they were visiting Australia in 1954 and were auditioning promising young singers for a scholarship to study abroad. Invited to go to Paris, Allman and his wife left Australia in 1955 and after studying with M. Modesti for two years he went to London.

He auditioned at both Covent Garden and Sadler's Wells and was offered engagements at both houses. After five months of guest performances at Covent Garden in 1957, he was given a regular contract for two successive

seasons as principal baritone, singing, among other roles, Donner in *Das Rheingold,* Escamillo in *Carmen,* and Schannard in *La Boheme.* During this period he also appeared in grand opera on the continent as Iago in *Otello* at The Berlin State Opera and in Hamburg, and as Tonio in *I Pagliacci* at Frankfurt. Of his German debut in *Otello* a critic wrote: "His big colourful baritone voice and noteworthy acting showed themselves, particularly in the great Credo monologue"; Another said: "Robert Allman is an acquisition to our opera, his well-grounded, cultured, voluminous voice was very striking"; And yet another: ". . . a musical singer whose voice is not only big and flexible but tasteful and well placed".

Robert Allman returned to Australia in 1959 to appear in Handel's *Messiah* with the Royal Melbourne Philharmonic Society and in the Elizabethan Theatre Trust's 1960 opera season, when he sang with Joan Hammond in *Salome* and *Madame Butterfly* and also in *Rigoletto* and *The Magic Flute.* In Melbourne he also appeared in The Silver Jubilee Arts Festival of the

221

National Theatre in a production of *Tosca*. A review of this event by Gilbert Price in *Music and Musicians,* published in London, said: "Robert Allman with his rich baritone made a telling Scarpia."

Returning to Europe at the end of the Trust season he decided to make his headquarters in Germany, because he felt that opportunities were greater there for a young singer. For two years his primary affiliation was with the Wuppertal Opera but in 1962 he accepted a five year contract as principal baritone with the Cologne Opera and a guest contract with the Vienna Volksoper. In addition to regular appearances with these companies he has made guest appearances in most of the other major opera houses in West Germany including those in Munich, Stuttgart, Dusseldorf, Hamburg, Augsburg and Essen and at the Eutin Summer Opera. Allman has specialized in Verdi roles but has also sung Scarpia and Marcello in *Tosca* and *La Boheme*, and Tonio in *I Pagliacci,* the Music Master in *Ariadne auf Naxos* and Speaker in *The Magic Flute.*

Besides his German appearances in the title roles of Simon Boccanegra, Rigoletto, Nabucco, and Macbeth and in other baritone roles in *Aida, Don Carlos, La Forza del Destino, Il Trovatore,* and *Un Ballo in Maschera,* Allman sang *Macbeth* and *Boccanegra* with Italian companies at the Strasbourg Opera. In a review of *Macbeth* in the April, 1962, issue of *Opera* magazine a critic spoke of the production as "remarkably successful, musically" and of Allman's and Varnay's success in two of opera's most difficult roles, adding: "This young baritone should have a fine career". Two years later when he sang Simon Boccanegra the critic wrote: "He really sang the formidable title part and succeeded in finding that touch of tenderness so essential to the Doge's character".

Allman returned to Australia for a second season with the Elizabethan Trust Opera Company in 1964, singing the roles of Macbeth and Escamillo in *Carmen.*

MARGRETA ELKINS, mezzo soprano

Margreta Elkins, whose beautiful mezzo soprano voice and lovely presence have been enjoyed by Covent Garden audiences since 1958, is well-known for her close association with Joan Sutherland. They met for the first time in Melbourne when they were both competing in the Mobil Quest. She recalls with amusement Joan's advice at the time not to permit her impending marriage to interfere with her career. When she saw Joan again, in London, not only had she, too, married but she had a young son. Margreta has appeared with Joan in a number of operas, including the London Handel Society's presentations of *Alcina, Rodelinda,* and *Guilo Cesare; Lucia di Lammermoor*

Margreta Elkins

(in Genoa and London); and in Covent Garden's new production of *I Puritani* in 1964. That year Margreta Elkins also appeared in *Othello* at Covent Garden and Manchester.

As Margaret Geater she grew up in Queensland where she took part in such outdoor activities as golf and horse-back riding that have helped to provide vitality characteristic of so many Australian singers. Both her mother, who came from Inverness in Scotland, and her father, who had been a member of the Canterbury Boys' Choir in England, had good voices. It therefore seemed natural that their daughter should take singing lessons and study piano at boarding school. When she was seventeen she won a Queensland government scholarship to study dramatic art and musical theory. Later, while in Melbourne, she studied privately with the well-known singer, Pauline Bindley, and took part in several important competitions. She reached the finals in the *Sun* Aria Contest in 1952 and won second place in the Mobil Quest in 1955. She also studied at the Sydney Conservatorium with the renowned oratorio singer, Harold Williams.

Before moving to Melbourne she married Harry Elkins, and it was as Margreta Elkins that she appeared in her native Brisbane with the National Opera of Australia in 1953, singing the role of *Carmen*. Ernest Briggs of the Brisbane *Courier Mail* wrote of her performance: " . . . a triumph! In warmth of tone, control of nuance, clarity of diction, ease of deportment, she gave the role a vitality that should make Queenslanders intensely proud of her success. Margreta Elkins' ability to assess the highly contrasted moods ranging from the gaminerie and sensuousness of Carmen in the first act to the subtle gradations of the aftermath of passion in the tense finale indicate that she may develop into a star of International opera". Miss Elkins did, indeed, develop into a star of international opera but she has never considered Carmen a congenial role. In an interview with William Wells, broadcast over Station WRFM, New York, on 28th February, 1965, she said she felt that she was too tall for the part and did not have the temperament for it.

Other roles that she sang during 1954 and 1955, when the National Opera Company toured Australia and New Zealand, were Azucena in *Il Trovatore,* Suzuki in *Madame Butterfly* and Siebel in *Faust*. She mentioned in the interview with Wells that at one point during this period she had sung Azucena every night for two weeks, something that she would not, of course, think of doing today. During this same period she also appeared as soloist at ABC concerts and made a number of recordings.

In 1956 she used the prize-money she had received as a successful participant in the Mobil Quest the year before to finance a trip to London. There she was engaged to appear with the Grand Opera Society of Dublin in the title role of *Carmen* and as Dorabella in *Cosi Fan Tutte*. For the next three seasons she toured England and Scotland with the Carl Rosa Opera Company, singing Maddelena in *Rigoletto,* Rosina in *The Barber of Seville,* Nichlaus in *Tales of Hoffmann* and Ascanio in *Benvenuto Cellini*. The critic of the *Manchester Guardian* wrote in 1958 of her performance in the last mentioned role: "Margreta Elkins in the difficult part of Ascanio, Cellini's apprentice, showed a fine, big voice which is yet cuttingly exact on intonation and wonderfully flexible in all but the very top register. Her singing of the difficult entr'acte aria in Act III was something to remember long after the performance."

It was also in 1958 that Margreta Elkins joined the Royal Opera Company at Covent Garden after a third audition. Her first appearances were made with Astrid Varnay in *Die Walkure* in two Ring Cycles. (Joan Sutherland was a Rhinemaiden and the Forest Bird in these same cycles.) Subsequently she sang The High Priestess in *Aida*, Ulrica in *Un Ballo in Maschera*, Alisa with Sutherland in *Lucia di Lammermoor*, Amneris in *Aida*, Flora in *La Traviata*, Diana in *Iphigenie in Tauride,* and Hippolyta in Benjamin Britten's *Midsummer Night's Dream*. After singing Alisa to Maria Callas'

Lucia when Callas re-recorded the opera in 1959, Margreta Elkins was sent by Covent Garden to study the roles of Amneris and Azucena in Milan. On her return she sang the Ice Queen in the Sadler's Wells production of *Schwanda the Bagpiper.*

In 1961, when she appeared in Covent Garden's production of *Der Rosenkavalier, Opera* magazine's critic wrote:

> The redeeming feature of the rather overplayed initial love scene was the Octavian of Margreta Elkins. She was the most credible Octavian I have seen. Miss Elkins' lanky build well conveyed the boy's youth, making the unbroken voice entirely acceptable. Furthermore, she was good on the ear, showing a true feeling for Strauss' music and singing throughout with great delicacy; occasionally a little more volume would have been welcome. Her acting was up to the same high standard. Study of the role has clearly given her a great insight into this curious character. Particularly moving was the the moment in the third act when it seems as if Sophie will reject Octavian; Miss Elkins' look at the Marschallin at this point conveying a whole wealth of emotion, was masterly.

Later that year she added to her English, Italian and German roles the Russian character, Marina, in Moussorgsky's *Boris Godounov.*

In 1962 she created the role of Helen of Troy in Tippett's new opera *King Priam* which was performed first at the dedication of the new cathedral in Coventry and later at Covent Garden. Writing of the latter occasion the critic of the *Times* said: "Miss Elkins with her creamier, duskier, tonal allure cleverly emphasized the Grecian hedonist amidst the brighter, clearer and more incisive Trojan voices of slaty and knife-edged despair". Later that year, at the same opera house, she sang Flora in *La Traviata.*

In 1965 Margreta Elkins sang in the United States for the first time — again with Joan Sutherland. She appeared as Ruggiero in the American Opera Society's presentation of *Alcina,* in concert form at Carnegie Hall in New York; as Siebel in *Faust,* with the Philadelphia Lyric Opera Company, and with the Connecticut Opera Association in Hartford. She received excellent reviews for all performances. Of her Ruggiero Alan Rich wrote in the New York *Herald Tribune* on 6th January: "Margreta Elkins . . . an Australian contralto, tall and handsome, was easily the most secure stylist of the evening. Her voice was warm and rich, and she worked with ease and breadth of phrasing." Reviewing the March performance of *Faust* in Hartford, he spoke of her as ". . . the most forceful and interesting singer of all".

On the advice of her teacher, Miss Elkins limited the number of her appearances during the 1964-65 opera season because she was in the process of changing her voice from a mezzo to a lyric soprano. During the 1965 Sutherland-Williamson season in Australia she sang in *Lucia di Lammermoor*, *La Traviata*, *Faust*, *Eugene Onegin* and *L'Elisir d'Amore*.

Miss Elkins' recordings include *Guilio Cesare*, *Sonnambula* and *I Puritani* (all with Sutherland), *Die Walkure* with Birgit Nilsson, and *Lucia di Lammermoor* with Callas.

LAURIS ELMS, contralto

Lauris Elms' career at Covent Garden was interrupted in 1959 when she returned to Australia to be with her husband. He had been on leave from Melbourne University and studying at Oxford the year before. Many people in London, however, still remember the unusual quality of her contralto voice. When Richard Bonynge was making plans for the Sutherland-Williamson Opera Season of 1965, he engaged her to sing chief contralto roles in *Eugene Onegin*, *Semiramide*, *La Sonnambula* and *La Traviata*.

Lauris Elms was given a contract at Covent Garden in 1957 after her

Lauris Elms

first audition there and already had considerable previous experience as a singer. She had also the advantage of growing up in a family that had a long musical tradition. Both her grandmothers had been noted for their "musical evenings" and through one of these she was related to Anna Bishop, the wife of the English composer, Sir Henry Bishop, who came to Australia on a concert tour. Miss Elms' mother was an accomplished pianist, and it was her admiration for an uncle who played the violin that prompted her to study this instrument for ten years. Later she studied singing in Melbourne with Mme Wielaert who encouraged her to participate in several competitions which she won. These provided not only money for further training, but the opportunity to appear in broadcasts on commercial radio stations. She also became contralto soloist in the *Village Glee Club* — an ABC programme of folk songs and ballads with a special appeal to listeners in rural areas.

In 1953 she appeared with the Royal Philharmonic Society in a concert with Walter Susskind who was visiting Australia as an ABC Celebrity Artist. At this time she was also singing in operatic productions of the National Theatre Movement, including *The Consul, La Traviata* and *Tales of Hoffmann.* In 1954 she was a finalist in the Melbourne *Sun* Aria contest and was offered a scholarship to study in Paris with Dominique Modesti. Using prize money she had won in various competitions, Lauris Elms was able to go to France to take advantage of this opportunity.

After studying in Paris with M. Modesti for two years, she was placed third in the International Singing Competition in Geneva and joined the Covent Garden Company in 1957. At first she appeared as guest artist as the Fortune Teller in *The Masked Ball* in performances in Cardiff and Manchester and in other provincial cities, but was soon asked by Rafael Kubelik to become a permanent member of the company. At Covent Garden she sang mezzo-soprano roles in *Elektra, The Trojans* and *Tales of Hoffmann;* appeared with three other Australians, Sylvia Fisher, Elsie Morison and Joan Sutherland in Poulenc's *The Carmelites* and played Mrs Sedley in *Peter Grimes* — which she later recorded for Decca under the baton of the composer, Benjamin Britten.

The next year she sang the title role of *Micah, Friend to Samson* in six performances of that oratorio at the Leeds Centenary Festival. One of these occasions was a Command Performance which Queen Elizabeth, Prince Philip and the Princess Royal attended on 10th June, 1958. That summer Lauris Elms went to Israel with two other Covent Garden singers and the conductor, Rafael Kubelik, to appear in nine performances of Beethoven's *Ninth Symphony* arranged as part of the celebration of that country's tenth anniversary. During this period the *Manchester Guardian* referred to her as "a fine artist showing imagination and style", and *Opera* spoke of "an exceptionally good

227

performance," adding: "Her dark mezzo voice contrasted finely with Blanche Thebom's".

Since her return to Australia, Lauris Elms has mainly confined her professional activities to those which do not take her far from home. She has been able, however, to fulfil concert engagements in New Zealand and Australia, appearing as soloist in a variety of works ranging from Mozart arias to Bartok's *Bluebeard's Castle,* Honneger's *Joan of Arc* and de Falla's *Love the Magician.*

NOTES.

Joan Hammond
[1]Rosenthal, H., *Sopranos of Today,* London, John Calder, 1956.

Sylvia Fisher
[1]John Sinclair, Melbourne *Herald.*
[2]*The Times,* 24th January, 1949.
[3]That same month Neville Cardus wrote in the *Sunday Herald:* "I am told that it will not be possible for *Rosenkavalier* to be presented in Manchester because . . . Sylvia Fisher won't be available on that particular date . . . and nobody in all England has been discovered capable of acting as deputy for this lovely Australian singer."
[4]Andrew Porter, *Opera,* March, 1953.
[5]*Financial Times,* 10th December, 1954.
[6]*Music and Musicians,* September, 1954.
[7]Ibid, December, 1955.
[8]Ibid, August, 1962.
[9]Chicago *Sun Times,* 3rd November, 1959.

John Cameron
[1]With Elsie Morison, Joan Sutherland and William Herbert, John Cameron belongs to a small group of carefully selected singers who recorded rare music for the *Lyre Bird Press* which was established in Paris in 1932 by the late Louise Hanson-Dyer, the well-known patron of music from Melbourne. He has also made full recordings of Gilbert & Sullivan operas with Richard Lewis.

Elsie Morison
[1]*The Australian Theatre Year Book,* Melbourne, F. W. Cheshire, 1958.

Donald Smith
[1]*Opera,* May, 1962.
[2]*Music and Musicians,* March, 1964.

Jenifer Eddy
[1]Valerie Collins, a dramatic soprano, won the 1956 Shell Aria and left soon afterwards

for Vienna where she studied at the Academy of Music and at the Vienna State Opera. Since then she has sung in Germany, Holland, France, the United States and Canada, in opera, oratorio, and recitals. In 1964 she became "principal young dramatic soprano" at the Staatsoper in Oldenburg, Germany.

Marie Collier
[1]*Opera,* April, 1961.

Ronald Dowd
[1]That this did not eventuate was due in part to the high costs of production that could not be met without the large government subsidies which subsequent experience in Australia and elsewhere has proved necessary.

Elizabeth Fretwell
[1]Of Charles Mackerras' conducting of the score of *Peter Grimes* the reviewer wrote: "This was operatic conducting on the very highest level and, following his excellent Figaro, confirmed what many of us have long suspected, that we have another British (he is actually Australian) operatic conductor in our midst."

8

Joan Sutherland

ITALIAN AUDIENCES CALL her "La Stupenda"; critics in the English-speaking world refer to her as the "Queen of Bel Canto" and everywhere she sings she is acknowledged to be a "Prima Donna Assoluta". In a sense Joan Sutherland was "to opera born" but her achievement is the result of hard work and years of cultivation of a naturally fine voice.

Her mother was her first teacher and having been herself trained by Burns Walker — a pupil of the great Nellie Melba — knew the importance of not forcing young voices.

Although Mrs Sutherland had given up all thought of an operatic career for herself when she married her tall auburn-haired Scottish suitor, she still sang the famous "vocalizes" that she had learned from Walker — a heritage from Manuel Garcia that his pupil Mme Mathilde Marchesi had passed on to Melba. As a child Joan Sutherland imitated her mother as she practised but she was not permitted to try to reach notes above high C and, as time went on, she centred her ambition on becoming a Wagnerian soprano. This idea was so well fixed in her mind that she included "Elsa's Dream" and "Hall of Song" among her selections for the important competitions in which she took part as a girl. It was not until some years later that her husband, Richard Bonynge, noted that she was reaching E and F in alt without effort as she went about the house singing. Only then was he able to convince her that coloratura roles would not injure her voice. Both he and his wife acknowledge, however, the importance of Mrs Sutherland's early concern and they speak with enthusiasm of her own manner of singing, which left her voice "as fresh at seventy-four as those of many singers one-third her age".

Although her father died when she was only six, Joan Sutherland has happy recollections of the many times he took her and her sister swimming at the beach below the cliffs at Point Piper, near Sydney. It was while returning from one of these trips that he collapsed on the long flight of steps leading up to their home. Not only was this a deep personal blow to the family but it necessitated Joan's preparation to earn her living as quickly as possible. She became a secretary; but neither she nor her mother ever lost sight of the real goal, which was to become a great singer.

She took advantage of every possible opportunity to prepare for the operatic career which was foremost in her mind. She won a scholarship to study with the Sydney teacher, Aida Summers (Dickens) and took part in the City of Sydney Eisteddfod and the Sydney *Sun* Aria Contest. The former provided broadcasting engagements with the ABC and the latter, besides providing prize money, brought with it the distinction of success in the biggest individual singing contest in her native State. In 1950 she won first place in the Vacuum Oil Company's "Mobil Quest" — a nationwide commercial radio programme, in which she had been a finalist the year before when it was instituted. This recognition in 1949 and an offer from a cousin to match the £1000 first prize in the Mobil Quest should she win it the next year, encouraged her to give up her secretarial position and to devote her time to the study of singing.

After a farewell recital in the Sydney Town Hall on 20th April, 1951, Joan Sutherland, accompanied by her mother, set out for London[1] and the Royal College of Music where she was to study with Clive Carey, the well-known English tenor who as a young man had been associated with Melba and Jean de Reszke. Ten years later Carey stated in an interview that "her voice was just as beautiful when she first came to me in 1951 as it is now." She had to sing thirteen different arias in three auditions at Covent Garden, however, before she was finally given a contract with the Royal Opera Company in 1952. This provided for a salary of £10 a week when singing in London and £15 while on tour. She made her debut as the First Lady in *The Magic Flute* on 28th October, 1952, and shortly after appeared in the minor role of Clothilde on the occasion of Maria Callas' London debut in *Norma.*

There followed five years of hard work with the Royal Opera Company during which she sang a variety of roles, among them Eva in *Die Meistersinger,* Helmwige, the Forestbird and Woglinde in the *Ring,* all three soprano roles in *Hoffmann,* Micaela in *Carmen,* the off-stage priestess in *Aida,* the title role, Amelia in the *Masked Ball,* Lady Penelope Rich in Benjamin Britten's *Gloriana,* Agatha in *Der Freitschutz,* Pamina in the *Magic Flute,* and Jenifer in the world premiere of Tippett's *The Midsummer Marriage.*

Meanwhile, in 1954, Joan Sutherland had married Richard Bonynge whom she had known in Australia. He had won the principal pianoforte awards at the City of Sydney Eisteddfod in 1949 — the year she won the *Sun* Aria — but he had gone to London soon after, having obtained both a teacher's and a performer's diploma at the New South Wales State Con-

Joan Sutherland and her husband at home in Switzerland

servatorium of Music. There he had studied with Lindley Evans[2] who, as a young man, had been Melba's accompanist in Australia during the last ten years of her life. Bonynge credits Evans with having encouraged his interest in voices as well as in instruments and with laying the foundation for a knowledge of eighteenth and nineteenth century music which later made it possible for him to select appropriate roles for his wife's voice and to write the embellishments and cadenzas for them.

The year 1957 provided two important opportunities for Joan Sutherland. She had always loved the music of Handel and Mozart and this year she received special recognition for her singing of the works of both composers. She was appearing as Mme Herz in Mozart's *Der Shauspieldirektor* at Glyndebourne when the director of the Vancouver Festival heard her and invited her to sing there the following year in Gunther Rennert's production of *Don Giovanni*. She made her North American debut in July, 1958, in

233

Canada. Irving Kolodin, music critic for the *Saturday Review,* recalling the enthusiasm he had felt for Sutherland's singing on that occasion, wrote: "Donna Annas are assuredly rarities and this singer from Australia via London, qualified." When she appeared in the same role at The Staatsoper in Vienna the following year the *Neue Osterreich* commented: "None of our leading singers can compare with her", and after a performance of *Don Giovanni* at Glyndebourne in 1960 a Milan critic reported that she "excelled Callas".

Sutherland's appearance as Alcina with the Handel Opera Society in 1957 was another event of great importance in her career and the next year she was selected to sing the part of the Israelite Woman in *Samson* with the Covent Garden Opera Company, both at the Leeds Festival and in London. Of this performance William Mann of the *Times* wrote: "It was worth waiting three hours to hear the liquid gold and springing mercury of her voice in 'Let the Bright Seraphim' ". In June, 1959, Joan Sutherland again won acclaim, this time for her singing of *Rodelinda* at the Purcell-Handel Memorial Festival, the first performance of this early Italian opera to be given in England since Handel's day. "Joan Sutherland triumphed in the

Sutherland in Alcina *at La Fenice, Venice*

title role", a critic wrote, "Her beautiful voice has just the right timbre for Handel and her techniques are flawless".

Three months before, on 17th February, 1959, Joan Sutherland had won undisputed recognition as a great prima donna. In 1956 Sir David Webster, the Director of Covent Garden, had suggested that she prepare to sing the title role in a new production of *Lucia di Lammermoor* being planned for presentation at the Royal Opera House after a thirty-year absence. Lucia had been one of Melba's most famous roles but few of her successors had been able to meet the demands of the music. Sutherland was sent to Italy to study with the veteran conductor, Tullio Serafin, and the young producer, Franco Zeffirelli, both of whom had been engaged for the forthcoming London event. Much has been written of Sutherland's triumph on this occasion but its significance is summarized best in an article written in January, 1960, by Evan Senior, then editor of *Music and Musicians:*

> If 1959 is remembered in the history of music for anything, it will be remembered as the year when Britain regained, after many years, a footing on the international opera stage. Not since the heyday of great stars such as Melba and Eva Turner has this happened. It was 17th February, 1959, when the curtain rose on Covent Garden's new production of Donizetti's *Lucia di Lammermoor.* When it fell at the end of the performance everyone in the theatre knew that a British singer had reached the rank of international stardom. For in the cheering audience that night, primed beforehand as to what was expected, were representatives of opera houses from all over Europe and beyond. And within the next few days Joan Sutherland found herself the subject of world headlines and the focal point of offers from all the great international opera houses.

During the next two years Sutherland sang Lucia in Milan, Genoa, Venice, Palermo, Vienna, Cologne and Paris, where she was acclaimed as having "one of the century's great voices". In recognition of these achievements the Queen, in 1961, conferred on her the title of Commander of the Order of the British Empire.

Lucia was the first of a number of revivals of 18th and 19th century operas in which Sutherland was soon to appear. Richard Bonynge had been delving in the manuscripts of neglected operas by Bellini, Donizetti and Rossini to find works that would display his wife's virtuosity in high tessitura roles. In 1960 she sang Donna Elvira in Bellini's opera *I Puritani* when it was produced after a lapse of seventy-five years, first at Glyndebourne, and later at the Edinburgh Festival. Of the Glyndebourne performance *Time* magazine wrote:[3] "Her voice was precise, agile, light-textured and luminous". *The Observer,* London, praised her "extraordinary beauty of tone" and the 235

Lucia, *Melbourne, 1965*
*Photo: News and
Information Bureau*

Daily Mail found in the performance "an almost intolerable poignancy". Howard Taubman of the *New York Times* said: "Her voice has remarkable accuracy, flexibility and colour. There are few coloraturas in any age who have learned to use their voices with such control and assurance. At the full or in pianissimo, in legato passages or in pages of brilliant fioriture she handles herself with comforting smoothness. She brings a sense of style to Bellini's flowing melodies."

Elvira was to become one of Sutherland's most spectacular roles. She sang it the next year in Italy and two years later in the United States. Harold Schonberg reviewing the American Opera Society's performance of this opera, in concert form, at Carnegie Hall on 16th April, 1963, wrote: ". . . naturally the lion's share of attention went to Miss Sutherland. She is today's queen of 'bel canto' style and in an opera like *I Puritani* all of her vocal genius comes surging out." Of a performance the next February by the Boston Opera Society under the stage direction of Sarah Caldwell, the same critic wrote: "Miss Sutherland demonstrated once more that in this literature she is unique among today's sopranos . . . It was an exciting evening . . . Some of the glamour and electricity of a vanished age of prima donnas stalks the house when she is in action." A few months later Frank Granville Barker reviewed a London performance of the same opera. He wrote in the May issue of *Music and Musicians:* "At Covent Garden *I Puritani* was revived for Joan Sutherland . . . who gave her most ravishing and accomplished performance since the *Lucia di Lammermoor* that launched her as an international prima donna. The voice itself, in fact, sounded richer and more powerful than ever before so that she was able to sing with added warmth and dramatic compulsion."

Just a year after the first performance of *Lucia* at Covent Garden, Joan Sutherland made her Italian debut in Venice in Handel's *Alcina* on 19th February, 1960, and was called "La Stupenda" and acclaimed "Prima Donna Assoluta". She chose this same opera for her debut in the United States which was made some months later with the Dallas (Texas) Opera Company. The original sets were brought from Venice and Zeffirelli again acted as producer. Joan Sutherland feels that she benefited greatly from his help in delineating roles; it was he who taught her to run across the stage while singing The Mad Scene in *Lucia,* a feat that has occasioned great admiration and added an air of naturalness to the performance. Maria Callas, noting its difficulty, is reputed to have said: "This I would not do for anyone".

On another February evening, this time in 1961, Joan Sutherland made her New York debut at Carnegie Hall in the American Opera Society's

Joan Sutherland, Dorothy Cole and Luciano Pavarotti in La Sonnambula, *Melbourne, 1965*

concert version of Bellini's opera, *Beatrice di Tenda* which was being presented in that city for the first time in 100 years. Her mother would have liked to attend this performance but remained in London to look after her young grandson, Adam Bonynge. It therefore, came as a great shock to Sutherland to learn of her mother's death shortly before the concert began. But as Evan Senior noted in the review from which we quoted earlier, it was not in Joan Sutherland's nature to exhibit "an opera star temperament"; she sang as she was scheduled to do knowing that this would have been her mother's wish.

Reviewing this performance for the March 1961 issue of *Musical America,* Robert Sabin wrote: "Very few living vocalists could even attempt the fantastically difficult role of *Beatrice di Tenda* with anything but gruesome results. But Miss Sutherland, whether pouring out trumpet tones high above the staff or floating arpeggiated figures like silvery cobwebs in the moonlight, sang with absolutely no sense of effort or vulgar display." Of her singing of the same role in Milan three months later on 10th May, 1961, a special correspondent for the *Times* wrote in an article that appeared next day in London:

> Vincenzo Bellini's *Beatrice di Tenda,* revived last night at La Scala where it has not been heard for more than a century, is an opera for a star; and Miss Joan Sutherland, fresh from her triumph here in *Lucia di Lammermoor* proved that she is a worthy successor to Giuditta Pasta, who created the role of Beatrice when this work was first given in Venice in 1833. Indeed, if we are to believe what some of the critics said then, it may well be that Miss Sutherland with her astonishing vocal reserves, is able to make more of the final scenes than her famous predecessor could. Listeners were quickly able to accept the fact that the opera is another stage in Miss Sutherland's triumphal progress . . . Beatrice dominates her opera by the amount as well as the quality of her music and Miss Sutherland tirelessly shaped the elegant, expressive intricacies of Bellini's melody, never sacrificing musicianship to dramatic effect but creating the necessary effects through expressive phraseology, technical certainty and unfailing vocal control. The audience . . . was properly, traditionally and warmingly vociferous in its enjoyment.

But it is *Lucia* that most often brings Joan Sutherland's name to mind and it was in this role that she made her debuts at La Scala, Milan, and at the Metropolitan Opera House in New York in 1961; the former in May, the latter in November.[4] Audiences were as enthusiastic as ever. It had been expected that at La Scala the factions of reigning prima donnas might not be sympathetic toward a rival from abroad who was appearing for the first time in their citadel but any fears proved unwarranted and the nature of the response was clear by the time the cheering started at the end of the aria, 'Regnava nel silenzio'.

Of the New York debut a suburban newspaper wrote: "Coloratura Joan Sutherland stormed the Metropolitan last night and won one of the greatest ovations in the historic house's seventy-seven-year history for her *Lucia di Lammermoor* . . . Standees had been in line since 7 a.m. to hear the voice from 'the continent down under' that had given the Metropolitan Dame Nellie Melba and Marjorie Lawrence."[5] Harold Schonberg of the *New York Times* reported next morning that the audience "went wild when she finished the first half of the Mad Scene and required five minutes for order to be restored, and then erupted again for twelve minutes after the singing of 'Spargi d'amaro pianto' ". He spoke of her cadenza with the flute as being ". . . as exciting a piece of singing as the lyric stage can show today. Her well articulated trills, the precision of her scales, the security in her upper range and, in addition, the good size of her voice, were a throwback to a style of singing that is supposed to be extinct."

Miss Sutherland admitted in an interview the next day that this acclaim rather frightened her, partly because it made her wonder whether she could

Lucia, *Melbourne, 1965.*

sustain such enthusiasm in later performances. She need not have been anxious, however, because three years and many performances later, when she opened the Metropolitan Opera season on 12th October, 1964, she again won ovations from the audience and praise from the critics. The house had been sold out months before and queues started to form long before tickets went on sale for standing room. One New York newspaper gave this description of the scene:

> In the prematurely chill October weather the standees outside the 'Met' huddled deep in their coats and started their five day vigil for the sale of opening night tickets. As the line lengthened, an observer inquired 'aren't you cold?' A shaggy-haired young man lifted his chin briefly from the pelt of fur that enveloped him from ears to toes. 'For Joan', he declared, 'it's worth it.'[6]

Miss Sutherland's appeal for young people is apparent, too, in a review that appeared in *The* {Greenwich} *Village Voice* on 15th October, 1964. After referring to her singing as being "in the nature of a continued miracle", Leighton Kerner wrote:

> The impact of three years returned, reinforced by a warmth of timbre that has been steadily growing in her voice. Moment by moment and scene by scene the great Australian soprano shattered all apprehension that perhaps the thing was not quite as glorious as memory had pictured it.

Ten days after her debut at the Metropolitan Opera House on 26th November, 1961, Joan Sutherland sang in a concert version of Bellini's *La Sonnambula* presented by the American Opera Society at Carnegie Hall. Of this performance Harold Schonberg wrote in the *New York Times:* "The glory of Miss Sutherland's singing is only partly in the fact that she can throw off high E flats with prodigality and accuracy; that her trill is a real one; and that she is mistress of all kinds of scale and arpeggio work. Her vocal beauty lies just as much in the fact that she is a musician, and can turn a phrase like one. When fireworks are needed, there she is; but when a cantabile line is demanded, she can spin forth a smooth effortless, modulated tone that is as beautiful as anything to be heard today."

Joan Sutherland had first sung the role of the heroine, Amina, when this opera was presented at Covent Garden in the autumn of 1960 and Richard Bonynge considered it one of his wife's best roles. When she appeared in it with the Metropolitan Opera Company during the 1962 and 1963 seasons New York audiences were again most enthusiastic. Louis Biancolli of the *World Telegram* reported: "Her singing of 'Ah, non credea'

A curtain call after Lucia, Melbourne, 1965.

was a moment to remember the rest of one's life . . . from the time a single spotlight suddenly fell on the head and shoulders of the sleep-walking Amina . . . Miss Sutherland walked in the fabled footsteps of Pasta, Malibran and Patti".

Joan Sutherland returned to London in the spring of 1962 and gave several performances in *The Magic Flute, Alcina,* and *La Traviata* at Covent Garden. By this time, however, she was showing the strain of having attempted too much, trying to fit in long recording sessions with performances on stage; her doctors ordered rest. She was able, however, to make several previously scheduled appearances at La Scala in May when Meyerbeer's nineteenth century opera *Les Huguenots* was revived. These performances attracted a great deal of attention from opera goers because the work had not been heard since 1899 when Toscanini had conducted, and because the role of Marguerite de Valois had been made famous by Dame Nellie Melba. Edward Downes of the *New York Times* cabled from Milan: "Miss Sutherland easily carried top honours." An Associated Press dispatch to the *Herald Tribune* reported: "The audience ovation went to Miss Sutherland for her brilliant, flawless singing. Despite a chronic back ailment that is forcing her to curtail 241 her appearances Miss Sutherland followed Meyerbeer's stage directions and sang the second act finale from horseback."

It was this back-ailment that had necessitated the cancellation of a concert tour of Australia, planned for mid-1962. Her doctors forbade any long trips by plane such as the journey to Australia would have required if it were not to upset the rest of her schedule for the year. To provide an opportunity for her countrymen to hear and see Sutherland in some of her principal roles, The Australian Fixed Trusts arranged for the production in Bristol, in October, of a one-hour television programme entitled *The Joan Sutherland Show* which was later seen throughout Australia. Betty Best, a London correspondent, wrote a graphic account of the fifteen hours required for this production and of the characteristic courage with which Miss Sutherland met the ordeal of performing in an armour-like surgical corset which it was then necessary for her to wear at all times. Miss Best commented: "The Sutherland recipe for defeating torture is simple. You face it and laugh at it. You may even be infuriated by it. But you never give in to it."[7]

In December, 1962, Sutherland appeared again at La Scala in another seldom heard opera, Rossini's *Semiramide,* which had not been produced in Milan since 1881.[8] As the music editor of *Time* pointed out, for years after its debut in 1823 this opera "was considered Rossini's crowning triumph" and ". . . shines with bel canto flourishes — and a soprano role that is one of the most difficult in all opera". He noted that Sutherland was the only living soprano who could hope to cope with it and added: "After the performance the La Scala audience was grateful to Rossini and Sutherland . . . giving her twenty-eight curtain calls after the final curtain." Sutherland herself is reported to have said that she loved playing the role of a wicked woman for a change instead of the 'insipid virgins' that were her usual fate.

Desmond Shawe-Taylor, reviewing the Milan performance in the *Sunday Times,* London, on 6th March, 1963, wrote: "As a sheer feat of vocalization Joan Sutherland's Queen of Babylon was prodigious: it ranks among her very highest achievements . . . Roulades, scales, arpeggios were thrown off with accuracy and ease, while over two and a half octaves her tone remained consistently round, pure and lustrous." He added: "The sheer physical pleasure afforded by such singing at a time when it has grown increasingly rare can hardly be exaggerated. In addition Miss Sutherland phrased neatly, looked handsome and comported herself with regal dignity."

The next winter Sutherland appeared in the United States in concert versions of *Semiramide* with the Los Angeles Philharmonic Orchestra and with the American Opera Society at Carnegie Hall. Irving Kolodin, reviewing the latter performance for the *Saturday Review,* referred to "a sunburst of

Lucia, *Melbourne, 1965. Photo:* Sun, *Melbourne.*

a top E, squarely on target, at the climax of 'Bel raggio lusinghier' " and noted that Joan Sutherland's performance was "the cause of joyous transports" for most individuals in the audience. Winthrop Sargent pointed out in the *New Yorker:* "Of course the presence of the unique Joan Sutherland was a distinct advantage since she, of all living sopranos, is probably the only one equipped for the tremendous display of vocal fireworks the title role demands".

While admitting that she loves the music of these unusual old operas and enjoys portraying the demented heroines that have come to be thought of as her speciality, Miss Sutherland is quick to point out that she sings roles in the standard repertoire, too, and that of these Violetta in *La Traviata* is a favourite. She opened the season of the Philadelphia Opera Company in this role on 12th November, 1963. Her singing of "Sempre libera" with embellishments was spoken of as "especially brilliant" and her appearance as "handsome". Richard Bonynge conducted and was given credit for the high quality of the total performance. During the 1964 season at the Metropolitan *La Traviata* alternated with *La Sonnambula* as a vehicle for Miss Sutherland.

Harold Rosenthal, who was one of the first London critics to prophesy a great future for her, would like to see her "at least reconsider Mozart, Weber and Verdi" at the present time. He wrote: "She was, it will be recalled, one of the finest Gildas, a most beautiful-sounding Pamina and Desdemona and possibly one of the best interpreters of Agathe we have heard".

The year 1965 saw the culmination of plans for an Australian opera season. The Sutherland-Williamson International Grand Opera Company was formed and, with the co-operation of the Elizabethan Theatre Trust, presented seven operas during a three months season in Melbourne, Adelaide, Sydney and Brisbane.[9] Sutherland sang three times a week, alternating some of her roles with other prima donnas like Elizabeth Harwood, an immensely popular Lucia.

As soon as the season was announced people began to compare it with Melba's homecoming in 1911. Many asked the question that seems always to come to the minds of Australians when confronted with reports of the success of one of their countrymen: "Is she really as good as they say she is?" All doubts were dispelled, however, by the end of the first performance on 10th July, 1965; applause rang out in Her Majesty's Theatre, Melbourne, and the audience demanded twenty-seven curtain calls. The opera that night was *Lucia* but the same kind of response greeted her appearances in *Semiramide, La Sonnambula, Faust,* and *La Traviata.* The company was made up of distinguished young artists of international repute[10] but everyone wanted to hear Joan Sutherland. As on "Melba nights" during the opera seasons of 1911, 1924, and 1928, houses were packed whenever Sutherland sang but at other times there were empty seats. This was understandable but unfortunate because the whole company had been carefully selected by Richard

Bonynge the year before and all performances were well worth hearing.

It had been hoped that Miss Sutherland would sing the title role in Bellini's *Norma* during the 1964-65 season at the Metropolitan Opera House but she declined to do so saying that she felt that she was not "ready". When reminded of her success in this opera at the Vancouver Festival in 1963 she paid tribute to the contributions that had been made to these five performances by an exceptionally strong supporting cast and by her husband who had been the conductor. A review in *Opera* for December, 1963, states: "The insight that he brought to the music of *Norma* lent strength and confidence to orchestra and singers" and calls attention to "his sensitivity to music of this genre, and to the niceties of its balance and ensemble".

Richard Bonynge's contribution to his wife's development has been so important that Miss Sutherland always speaks of "our career", adding "I think of us as a duo". Talking with the Bonynges one is impressed by the extraordinary dynamism of their relationship which, with their continual striving for perfection, must contribute immeasurably to their great artistic achievement. Asked about his dominant influence she says that they often have heated discussions as to how music should be sung but adds "I usually give in, at last, because I know that Richard is right. He has a knack of drawing things out of the voice that you didn't know were there."

Clemence Dane, in her recent book, *London Has a Garden*,[11] speaks of her enjoyment of Sutherland's performance of Alcina in 1962 when "she sang like a mockingbird on a moonlight night, which is the loveliest sound I know. I got much the same pleasure from listening to her as years ago when, once or twice, I heard Melba sing.

"Perhaps there are two sorts of great singers, the Voices and the Skin-Changers. The Skin-Changers are born impersonators whose voices crown their acting gifts . . . But the Sutherlands and Melbas are VOICES . . . they act with their voices, they be glamour through their voices, they make the audience laugh or shiver by means of their voices. It is a different art. The VOICES are music."

NOTES.

[1]Before going to England she had sung in all the capital cities and many of the   245

country districts of Australia and had appeared under the batons of Eugene Goossens and Henry Krips.

[2]Mr Evans has done much to encourage young talent through the weekly children's programme on the ABC national radio network. He has given assistance in a variety of ways to thousands in his unseen audience.

[3]June 13, 1960.

[4]After the performance Amelita Galli-Curci, then nearly eighty, wrote to a friend, "The press notices did not surprise me at all; with that rich and wholesome equipment she is blessed with! She also has the intelligence and the balance to take it all in her stride." — Article on Galli-Curci by Francis Robinson in *Show Magazine,* New York, April, 1964.

[5]The Elizabeth (N.J.) *Daily Journal,* November 28, 1961.

[6]Feature article by F. M. Eckman, New York *Post,* Sunday, October 18, 1964. Reprinted by permission of New York *Post.* Copyright 1966, New York Post Corporation.

[7]*Australian Women's Weekly,* November 21, 1962.

[8]Melba had sung the role at the Metropolitan Opera House on 12th January, 1894, soon after her debut, and subsequently there and in Chicago and Philadelphia during the next two seasons.

[9]Richard Bonynge was the artistic director and principal conductor.

[10]Besides the Australians Elizabeth Allen, Robert Allman, Margreta Elkins, Lauris Elms, Clifford Grant, and Joy Mammen, casts included Elizabeth Harwood, Monica Sinclair, Morag Beeton, Aberto Remedios, and Joseph Ward of Great Britain; John Alexander, Dorothy Cole, Spiro Malas, Andre Montal, Cornelius Opthof, Joseph Rouleau, and Doris Yarick from the United States and Canada; the Italian-born tenor Luciani Pavarotti; and the New Zealand baritone Ronald Maconaglieu.

[11]P.117. Published by W. W. Norton and Co., New York, 1964.

Appendixes

Bibliography

Index

1. THE MUSICAL BACKGROUND: VISITING OPERA COMPANIES AND SINGERS

By Ronald Campbell

SINCE THE EVENING in 1847 when the versatile Eliza Winstanley of Sydney made her first overseas appearance at the Manchester Theatre Royal, increasing numbers of Australians have been contributing to world music. Eliza did not emphasise her origin with one of the aggressively antipodean professional names assumed by later compatriots like Amy Castles, who narrowly escaped being dubbed "Madame Bendigoniana" in an excess of local patriotism;[1] instead, she chose to perform under her unassuming married name of Mrs O'Flaherty.

Although she was only twenty-eight and her birthplace had yet to celebrate its sixtieth anniversary, she had already put thirteen years of Australian experience behind her. In 1834, when she began her career as a fifteen-year-old prima donna, many Sydneysiders could look back to 26th January, 1788, as the day when they first saw the hitherto inviolate waters of Port Jackson from one of the ships of Captain Phillip's First Fleet.

Until the bugles, drums and fifes of the Royal Marines echoed back from the wooden hills enclosing Sydney Harbour, the only man-made music heard on the Australian continent was the honking of didgeridoos, the menacing bellow of the bull-roarer, the clatter of rhythm sticks and the chanting of Aborigines round their ceremonial fires. Yet children born during the first year of the settlement were still living fifty years later, in the year Mendelssohn died and Eliza Winstanley left her homeland to charm the theatregoers of Britain and America.

Only thirty years later Sydney-born Lucy Chambers, singing in Italy and France, was described as a "creole" by baffled continental journalists[2], and the applause had scarcely subsided before, in 1888, the voice of Nellie Melba delighted the most sophisticated ears in the world. As only a century had passed since Surgeon Worgan of HMS *Sirius* landed Australia's first piano on the marshy shores of Sydney Cove, two moderate lifetimes sufficed to bridge the gap between the chanting of the Port Jackson natives and Melba's debut at Covent Garden.

In her brilliant wake followed a long array of the ambitious, talented or merely hopeful, stretching from Frances Saville to Joan Sutherland and beyond. Regardless of time, distance and expense, the advice of the experienced, the warnings of the disillusioned, and the very real hardships suffered by some of the unlucky, the optimists battled on year after year. Sixty years later no English operatic cast, either at Covent Garden, Sadler's Wells or Glyndebourne, was complete without its quota of top-ranking Australians.[3] No

An early visiting opera company — principal singers of one of George Musgrove's grand opera ventures. Musgrove often worked in partnership with J. C. Williamson

longer a curiosity, the Australian singer had become as integral a part of the musical scene as the Italian of a generation or so before.

Nothing is more remarkable than that a continent so thinly peopled should produce so many notable singers, and that some of the most renowned should have flourished before World War I, when the Australian population was never above four million, more than half of them living remote from the type of civilization of which opera forms a part.

Early bush instruments were often home-made. For violins the materials ranged from kerosene tins and agar boxes to choice woods. Flutes and flageolets were made from bamboo, while dead sheep supplied the bones. Accordions did not become common until about 1870, and banjos came in with "Minstrel Shows" a little later.

Australian distances were enormous, roads bad, communication slow and difficult; unless they were featured in one of the weekly newspapers which formed the main links between the bush and the world, the names of home-grown singers were practically unknown outside the larger towns. If the doings of Melba were more extensively chronicled, it was because she was no ordinary singer, but a figure in the glittering European social panorama and the friend of kings, princes and millionaires. When The Bush read of her, it was with awe and wonder.

But though The Bush might have silenced Orpheus himself, the people of the small towns, with their leavening of professional men and white-collar workers, their churches, lodges and schools, were much better off musically. Church choirs, piano and violin teachers, school concerts and musical evenings may not have produced any notable talent but they developed audiences for the professional musical troupes which travelled the country until motion pictures elbowed the live artist off the road. Australia provides the only example of a thinly-peopled country, remote from European culture, assuming a musical importance out of all proportion to its numbers and development.

One of the earliest of Sydney's musical enthusiasts seems to have been Captain John Piper, the Collector of Customs, who not only included a music room in the mansion he built on the point bearing his name, but had himself rowed about the harbour by a crew of trained musicians. The captain earned a niche in Australian musical history as the first man in the country to maintain a private band.

Bands have seldom been given full credit for their share in the development of Australian music, both vocal and instrumental, but they undoubtedly provided the first public musical entertainment the country knew and helped to blaze the trail leading to La Scala. As the modern brass band did not come into existence until long after the founding of Sydney, early Australian bands would have been the combinations of brass and reed instruments known as "military" bands. Their composition was not standardized; sometimes they were reinforced by flutes, violins and even harps. Frequently they included the now obsolete serpent, described as "terrifying alike to eye and ear". A gigantic wood-wind, vaguely related to the bassoon, the serpent was about eight feet long with a note which, according to Berlioz, "would better have suited the sanguinary rites of the Druidical worship than those of the Catholic religion".

The music dispensed by these primitive combinations consisted mainly of popular or traditional songs, blared out in march time or arranged to suit the dances of the period and with their serpents, basset-horns, hautboys, key-bugles, clarinets, string basses and drums were familiar in Sydney and Hobart from earliest times. Later, the first settlers of Adelaide were enlivened by the band of HMS *Buffalo,* but the original Melburnians were less fortunate. Until long after the foundation of the city in 1834, a mere company of infantry was considered sufficient to protect Melbourne from foreign invasion, and the soldiers were so short of music that on one melancholy occasion a drum and fife had to serve for a military funeral.

250   According to "Garryowen", Australia's first civilian band was established

in Melbourne in 1839, when the township was five years old. It consisted of a dozen more or less regular players equipped with key-bugles, clarinets, flutes, a piccolo, a triangle and a drum. Under Bandmaster George Tickell, a plasterer by trade, this unorthodox outfit first appeared on Christmas Eve, 1839, when the hospitality of the innkeepers made the occasion memorable. Shortly afterward, Melbourne established a band reliable enough to head the procession when the foundation stone of the first court house was laid on 25th July, 1842, a year otherwise musically notable for the birth of Arthur Sullivan.[5]

The growth of Melbourne and the development of its music were so rapid that half a century later Frederick Cowen's orchestra drew audiences of 15,000 to symphony concerts held in an Exhibition Building half a mile from what had been the winding, pot-holed track along which Tickell's band had blared its way. When the great gold rushes began in 1851, the influx of diggers included many musicians. One bandmaster is recorded as having brought his entire band with him, though its original constitution was not mentioned in the annals. This enterprising musician was Samuel Prout of Devonport, who arrived in Victoria in 1851 and established Prout's Ballarat Band, long known not only for its playing but for its brilliant uniform of green and yellow, topped by a plumed helmet.[6]

Among other bands formed during the digging days were the professional combinations usually called "German", which first made their appearance in South Australia during the copper-mining era. Many such bands played in the streets of the larger towns until World War I. Groups of itinerant music makers are also shown in some of S. T. Gill's historic drawings depicting life during the goldrush period. In one Melbourne scene a small band is shown playing outside a horse saleyard in Bourke Street. It must have been a profitable location, as a German band played there regularly until 1914.

Most British civilian bands were originally associated with mines, foundries, factories and industry generally. That to some extent Australia followed the same pattern is shown by the number of fine bands which sprang up on the various mining fields all the way from Kalgoorlie and Boulder City in Western Australia to Mount Lyell in Tasmania, Broken Hill in New South Wales and Charters Towers in North Queensland.

Wherever Welsh migrants were found in any numbers, brass bands flourished, so that the coalfields of Newcastle, Cessnock, Maitland, Kurri Kurri, Kembla and much later, Wonthaggi and Morwell, became famous band centres. Railways, tramways, fire brigades, police forces and other public organizations all possessed bands, as did many lodges and friendly societies. The development of the military and naval forces brought still more bands into the field, the members learning their instruments as part of their training.

Interest is said to have declined after World War II but in the heyday of the brass band Australia could boast innumerable combinations, many of 251

Nellie Stewart   *Lempriere Pringle*

acknowledged merit. Until recent years, a brass band was regarded as essential by most communities. The weekly band concert drew crowds to sports grounds in suburban and country towns, while bands played in retail centres on late shopping nights, printed programmes sometimes being distributed to listeners. Bands entertained spectators during the intervals at all important cricket and football matches.

The bandsmen were all amateurs, as were most of the bandmasters, whose most tangible reward was a permanent job at whatever calling they followed. While working as tradesmen by day, they turned themselves into enthusiastic teachers at night. Through their efforts boys who would never have known the difference between a crotchet and a quaver learned to play and appreciate music otherwise beyond their comprehension.

Band music became so popular that early in the century such big touring combinations as Sousa's and the Besses o'th' Barn visited Australia, giving numerous concerts in all the principal cities. When the Besses o'th' Barn band arrived in Melbourne in 1907 it was escorted through the streets by a massed band of Melbourne players more than a thousand strong. No other type of music could have aroused such a demonstration.

The professional street bands lasted well into the twentieth century, when they were gradually crowded out by the increase of traffic and the din of car horns and pneumatic drills. The last of the German bands, with their reper-

252

toire of Strauss, Lehar and Waldteufel disappeared in 1914, never to return. In the 1920's there were a few optimistic attempts to revive street music, but the days were over when the passer-by could hear "Poet and Peasant" played in a city arcade or at a suburban street corner. The establishment of a Universal Military Training scheme in 1910 produced a spate of regimental bands which broke up when the scheme was abandoned after World War I. Most of the players joined civilian bands, although some joined cinema orchestras and became professional musicians.

Although their function is primarily religious, the work of Salvation Army bands in promoting Australian music cannot be overlooked. From a modest beginning in Adelaide in 1881, many Salvation Army bands have reached a high standard of technical and musical achievement, while innumerable individuals have learned their art in Salvation Army practice rooms, all the better, perhaps, because attendance at rehearsals is usually considered a semi-religious obligation. Salvation Army bands come in all sizes, from the big headquarters bands in the state capitals to the combinations consisting of cornet, baritone and bass drum sometimes found in remote hamlets.

Many authorities consider that the introduction of radio caused the decline of the brass band. Yet, ironically, band music was placed first in most of the polls organized by Australian radio stations to establish popularity ratings in the early days of broadcasting.

When Barnett Levey, merchant and publican, obtained permission in 1829 to organize concerts at the Royal Hotel in Sydney the instrumental portion of the programme was supplied by the band of the West Middlesex Regiment. Levey's enterprises must have been financially rewarding, for in 1832 he rebuilt his concert hall as the Theatre Royal, which two years later became the venue of the first opera presented in Australia, *Clari, the Maid of Milan,* with 15-year-old Eliza Winstanley in the title role.

One of the sixty-odd plays adapted from the French by John Howard Payne, the American actor and dramatist, *Clari* was turned into an opera by Henry Rowley Bishop, whose runaway wife Anna was to figure largely in the musical chronicles of colonial Australia. Included in *Clari* was one of the greatest song-hits of all time, the deathless "Home, Sweet Home", a number probably well known in Sydney by 1834, and later often sung as an encore by Nellie Melba.

Before the enterprising Eliza Winstanley left to try her luck in Britain another chapter of the chronicles of Australian music was being written in Hobart, headquarters of a flourishing whale fishery and chief town of the island then known as Van Diemen's Land.

In 1822, when Gounod and Wagner were small boys and King George IV had just been crowned, this outpost of civilization was invaded by Australia's first important musician, John Phillip Deane, a versatile instru- 253 mentalist who had played in the London Philharmonic Orchestra. Deane spent thirteen years as organist at St David's Church, Hobart. His daughter was a pianist and singer; one son played the violin and another the 'cello. An acquisition to the town, the Deane family arranged concerts in the Argyle Rooms, later called the Argyle Theatre, and was responsible for most of the public entertainment in Hobart until 1835, when William Vincent Wallace arrived.

A twenty-five-year-old Irish prodigy, destined to become Australia's first musical legend, Wallace was born in 1812 in Waterford, where his father was the bandmaster of the 29th Foot. At fourteen, young Wallace was one of the violinists in a Dublin theatre orchestra of which at nineteen he was appointed conductor. He had a growing reputation both as performer and composer when he left Ireland in search of the health which forever eluded him. With him came his wife, who seems to have played little part in his musical career, his brother Spencer and his sister Eliza, an excellent soprano, who subsequently married the basso, John Bushelle, and became known as Madame Wallace-Bushelle. During a brief stay in Hobart, Wallace and his sister gave several recitals before moving on to Sydney, where they were hailed as heralds of a new musical era.

After appearing in Mexico, the United States, South America and India, Wallace returned to Europe, where he met Edward Fitzball, one of the most prolific dramatic authors of the time, who proposed that he compose an opera to a libretto based on the popular French play, *Don Cesar de Bazan.* This happy suggestion resulted in the phenomenally successful *Maritana,* which was first presented at Drury Lane in 1845, remained in high favour until the end of the nineteenth century and is still occasionally performed by amateurs.

Nowhere was *Maritana* better received than in Australia. So many people believed that Wallace composed the opera either in Hobart or Sydney[7] that he was adopted as an Australian composer and it is not impossible that some of the melodies subsequently incorporated in the score of *Maritana* were composed during Wallace's sojourn in Sydney. In any case, he undoubtedly left his mark on Australian music. With his brother and sister, he opened Sydney's first college of music, while in conjunction with the Deane family, who followed him from Hobart, he organized Australia's first oratorio performance, consisting of excerpts from *The Messiah* and *The Creation.*

Probably the most widely travelled composer of his century, he died in France in 1864, the same year as Meyerbeer. His *Maritana, Matilda of Hungary* and *The Amber Witch* were all tuneful and easily staged, while the underwater scenes in *Lurline* anticipated some of the Rhine settings in Wagner's *Rheingold.*

Wallace's sister survived until 1878. Widowed at twenty-one, she travelled to England, where she showed her quality by starring at Drury

Lane.[8] Returning to Sydney she spent the rest of her life singing and teaching. Her son, John Wallace-Bushelle, won local acclaim as a vocalist. The works of Wallace, together with those of Balfe, Benedict and Bishop, proved gold-mines to Australian opera companies of the nineteenth century. The "books" being English, everyone could follow the story while the music presented little difficulty even to the novice.

In 1838 the opening of the famous Royal Victoria Theatre provided Sydney entrepreneurs with a stage and auditorium adequate for opera. Surprisingly large for a town the size of Sydney, it seated 1900 — almost as many as present-day Covent Garden. In 1842, the year Arthur Sullivan opened his eyes on the world, the Royal Victoria housed Australia's first complete presentation of *The Messiah.*

Doubtless everyone concerned benefited from the presence in the colony of Isaac Nathan, an English musician of great experience who had studied under Domenico Corri and achieved distinction for his settings of the Hebrew poems of his friend Lord Byron. Nathan was a man of letters as well as a musician. Among his literary works were the *History and Theory of Music* and his memoirs of Maria Malibran, Caroline Lamb and Byron. For some time he was musical historian and instructor to the Princess Charlotte, but his financial claims on the royal family were rejected after the death of William IV, and he migrated to Sydney. Nathan proved of enormous service to Australian music. The best teacher the country had so far possessed, he did notable work in improving church music and encouraging choral societies. Many of the leading singers of the early colonial times were indebted to him for tuition while his *Don John of Austria,* presented at the Victoria Theatre in 1847, was the first opera actually composed and performed in Australia.[9]

Among Nathan's other activities were his efforts to transcribe the tribal songs of the Aborigines who even in his day were disappearing from New South Wales. In 1864, this friend of Lord Byron who surprisingly became Australia's first opera composer, was killed by a fall from a Sydney horse-tram.[10]

In 1842 while Melbourne and Adelaide were still villages, Jerome Carandini landed in Hobart. Described as a dancer and singer, Carandini was the eldest son of the Marchese Carandini de Sargano. He had been engaged at the Modena Opera House before the political upheavals of the 1840's turned him into a refugee and sent him to faraway Hobart as one of the retinue of Australia's first woman impressario, a Mrs Clarke, who, having tried her luck in Hobart with straight drama, returned from a visit to England with a group of all-round artists.

After making their bow in concerts at the Argyle Rooms, the company began operations in earnest at the Royal Victoria Theatre in a long-forgotten comic opera entitled *John of Paris.* As the Hobart of those far-off days was

Mr and Mrs J. C. Williamson in Struck Oil

enlivened by a considerable rough element, actors needed courage as well as ability. Mrs Clarke's troupe had both. They played in Tasmania for over four years, a remarkable feat when it is remembered that the population of the island was under 25,000 and that, except for an occasional season in Launceston, one hundred miles north, theatrical and musical activity was restricted to one small town. Playing on Mondays and Fridays, they alternated opera and drama, sometimes venturing into ballet or a promenade concert.[11] It would be interesting to hear what a modern prima donna would say were she asked to sing Lucia and play Lady Macbeth in the same week, but Mrs Clarke's leading lady, Theodosia Yates-Stirling, actually performed this feat and was quite equal to dancing a hornpipe and appearing in an Irish farce in addition. The Hobart troupers also made their own costumes, painted scenery and gave lessons to local aspirants to vocal or dramatic renown.

Hard though they must have worked, they found time for romance. In 1843 Carandini — sometimes called "The Marquis" or "The Count" — married seventeen-years-old Marie Burgess, whose father, like Vincent Wallace, had migrated from Britain in quest of health. Shortly after her marriage Marie made her first public appearance in Hobart. In 1845, when the company began to break up, she went to Sydney with her husband, who opened a dancing school while she herself took lessons from Isaac Nathan.

Beginning her operatic career in Auber's *Fra Diavolo,* she developed into one of the most popular and successful Australian contraltos of the time. During the gold rush era she sang in opera with Catherine Hayes, and became a favourite on the Bendigo diggings when she appeared in Heffernan & Crowley's ornate Shamrock Concert Hall, accompanied by piano, violin and flute against a background of clinking glasses from the bar which ran down along one side. On the same bill were Sara Flower, Frank Howson, a Mr Lyell, a Mrs Handcock and the "inimitable" Charles Thatcher whose somewhat scurrilous topical songs provided a strong contrast to excerpts from *Norma, Cenerentola, The Enchantress* and *Lucretia Borgia*.

In the 1860's Madame Carandini took her own concert company, which included her daughter Rosina and the tenor Walter Sherwin, on an extended tour of Australia and New Zealand, India and the United States. Travelling by steamer, waggon and stage coach they were the first musical entertainers to penetrate the far north of Queensland, where they received a great welcome in Cooktown, the port for the Palmer River goldfields. In 1870 when the political climate of Italy had become more favourable, Carandini himself returned to regain his estate and title but died before he could establish his claim. His wife survived him by almost a quarter of a century. Of their eight children, five daughters were accomplished musicians. The eldest, Rosina, who married E. H. Palmer in 1860 was well-known as a concert artist and teacher.

Of the other members of the Hobart company, Frank and John Howson were equally at home as singers, producers and instrumentalists, but the most versatile of Mrs Clarke's players was probably Theodosia Yates-Stirling, a descendant of the Mrs Yates[12] who played opposite David Garrick in eighteenth century London. While still a girl Theodosia became chorus mistress at Drury Lane, but in the 1840's, when the English theatre drifted into one of its periodical declines, she joined Mrs Clarke and sailed for Van Diemen's Land.

Much more than a talented soprano who could act, she was so competent a musician that she was reputed to have scored Donizetti's *Lucia* from memory when the music failed to arrive from England.

While in Hobart, she married the leader of the orchestra, James Guerin, and as Madame Guerin, became one of the early colonial stars. Guerin, however, died about 1855 and his widow, marrying again, became the mother of an even more gifted daughter, Nellie Stewart.

By 1846, the Hobart company having disbanded, the Guerins, the Howsons and the Carandinis went to Sydney where they added greatly to the musical activity of the town. Nothing like their gallant four-year effort has been seen in Australia since. In addition to straight dramas, Shakespearean plays, farces, ballets and concerts, these pioneers presented a long list of operas, many of them for the first time in Australia.

Mrs Clarke's Hobart troupers helped to establish the tradition which in after years sent theatrical and concert artists of all types into the remotest parts of the continent. The hardships these pioneers cheerfully endured in their long treks by land and sea would not be tolerated today, while their rewards would appear beneath contempt by later standards. Not for nothing was the Sydney street corner where old time theatricals gathered known as "Poverty Point".

Although the show-boats of the Mississippi had no Australian counterparts, many troupes of entertainers travelled on the steamers of the Murray, Darling, Lachlan and Murrumbidgee rivers when playing the towns along their banks, while from time to time tent theatres appeared on the road. The wanderings of the early Australian entertainers were not confined to their own country. Australian opera and concert companies became familiar in New Zealand, India, China, Japan and Java. For forty years the Lynch Family of Bellringers rang their chimes from Hobart to Yokohama. Another long-lived family show, the Kennedys, was no less mobile. The break-up of the Hobart company and its migration to Sydney made the Harbour City a lively place musically in the 1840's. Reinforced by the Carandinis, Mesdames Guerin and Wallace-Bushelle and the Howson family, the choir at St Mary's was the finest the town had heard. Most of the artists took pupils and, aided by local talent, appeared in occasional performances of opera so that by mid-century educated Sydney was probably more familiar with the works of Balfe, Benedict, Wallace, Flotow, Bishop, Halevy and Meyerbeer than at any time since.

To the Melbourne musical enthusiast of the same period, the outlook was not so promising. Picking his way along the unpaved tracks which served as streets the most inspired prophet would have found it hard to convince himself that in less than twenty years the settlement, which had originated with a handful of migrants from Tasmania, would be the birthplace of the world's most celebrated Queen of Song. The chief town of what was then called the Port Phillip District of New South Wales, Melbourne had a population of between five and six thousand. With the exception of officials and the military, practically all were dependent on the sheep industry of the interior. Life, even in towns, was still primitive. A few stone and brick buildings showed among the wattle-and-daub cottages which housed the majority, although newcomers were still forced to live in tents. Remnants of a tribe of Aborigines, who had never seen a white man until a few years before, camped along the river Yarra, or hung around the outskirts of the town.

Nevertheless Melbourne possessed a theatre of sorts as early as 1841 — though it was merely a flimsy wooden structure set on piles and appropriately named the Pavilion. In the early period, Melbourne's few professional musicians usually performed in the tap-rooms of inns for what is picturesquely called "throw money". Occasionally an artist of higher class drifted into the settlement and out again.

In 1839 the redoubtable Mrs Clarke of Hobart held a "soiree" in the Lamb Inn and the following year a French couple named Gautrot set up as teachers of piano, violin and voice. They both loomed large in Melbourne's first concert, held at the Caledonian Hotel in February, 1841 to raise funds for a hospital. Opera was well represented in the programme, which opened with the overture to *The Marriage of Figaro* and included arias from Rossini's *Siege of Corinth* and Bellini's *Sonnambula.*

At that time, when it was possible for an artist to arrive in Australia quite unheralded and make ad hoc arrangements for public appearances, a surprising number came to Australia and remained either for a long period or for the rest of their lives. Doubtless the economic and political state of Europe impelled them to make so long and hazardous a journey, but they must also have possessed the spirit of adventure. It was fortunate for Australia that they came. As performers and teachers, these forgotten "professors" as they were usually styled had an enormous influence on Australian music and brought the day nearer when the tide reversed and the native-born began making themselves heard in the concert-halls and opera houses of the world.

The year 1845 brought the memorable George Selth Coppin to Australia. If for nothing else, he would have had a place in stage records as a competent violinist and a popular low comedian and in political annals as a member of the Victorian legislature, but it was as Australia's first real impresario that he attained immortality.

The son of an English provincial actor-manager, Coppin was born in Steyning, Sussex, in 1819 and reared in his father's company, where he learned to sweep out the theatre, trim the lamps, deliver handbills, stick up posters, sell tickets, lead the orchestra and play small parts. At twenty-one, he doubled the roles of fiddler and comedian in the historic old theatre on the Green in Richmond, Surrey. A year or two later, when theatrical prospects in Britain looked grimmer than usual, he tossed a coin to decide whether he would migrate to America or Australia. Australia won and he and his wife Maria set out for Sydney in the 565-ton ship *Templar.*

In Australia, Coppin reversed the entrepreneur's normal experience by losing in commercial ventures all except the last of the several fortunes he made in the theatre. No man had more irons in the fire. He played in Sydney, Melbourne, Adelaide, Geelong, Hobart, and Launceston, built a number of theatres, speculated in hotels, mines and pleasure gardens, sat in the Victorian parliament for years and is credited with introducing camels and English thrushes into the country. When he died in 1906 at the age of eighty-seven, he had seen Melbourne grow from a frontier town into one of the world's great cities.

In 1850, just before the first Australian gold strikes, the Sydney pianist and concert manager Henry Marsh persuaded Sara Flower to come to Australia, though London critics thought her contralto voice far too good for the colonies. "Her Cinderella", said one newspaper, "in the most effervescent of Rossini's compositions . . . her Stella in *The Enchantress* . . . have stamped her as an artist of undoubted merit".[13] Australian newspapers concurred. When she made her Sydney debut on 3rd May, 1850, a local critic announced that pure contralto notes were now to be heard in Sydney for the first time.

She was also among the first artists to visit the goldfields at Sofala and the Turon but whether her enthusiastic listeners actually pelted her with nuggets is questionable. According to legend, almost every stage or concert celebrity visiting the goldfields, from G. V. Brooke to Lola Montez, was bombarded with nuggets of gold, but it is unlikely that such extravagant and dangerous demonstrations were frequent, even at a time when a few brash diggers were recorded as having lit their pipes with banknotes.

For fifteen years, Sara Flower was part of the musical scene, both on the goldfields and in Sydney; she took pupils at her Darlinghurst home and sang in opera whenever she had an opportunity. In 1851 she journeyed to the Moreton Bay settlement, where — since Brisbane lacked a suitable hall — she sang from a hotel billiard table. A few years later, she was singing ballads at the Shamrock Hotel in Bendigo.

Among Sara Flower's pupils were Marie Carandini and Frank Howson's daughter Emma.[14] All three figured on the programme at the opening of the Great Hall of Sydney University in 1859, when Sara Flower's voice was pronounced "beyond praise". Her brief but vivid life was over at forty-five; she died in 1865 a few weeks after the end of the American Civil War.

Proof that the gold discoveries had broken down the artistic isolation of

Howard Vernon as Ko Ko

260

the Australian colonies came in 1854 with the visit of Catherine Hayes, the first internationally recognized singing star to come to the southern continent. The antithesis of Sara Flower, Catherine Hayes was a reserved young Irishwoman who came to Sydney from Honolulu in the course of the longest tour undertaken by a singer up to that time. Born in 1828 in Vincent Wallace's home town of Waterford, she was a protegee of the Bishop of Limerick, who raised a large fund to enable her to study singing in Dublin, where, while still a girl, she was one of Ireland's most popular vocalists.

Charmed by her full clear soprano, both Franz Liszt and Julius Benedict predicted a notable future for her and advised her to study under Manuel Garcia in Paris, where in 1845 she made her operatic debut as Elvira in *I Puritani*. In the same year, she became the youngest prima donna to sing at La Scala, Milan.

Four years later, the "Irish Lind" created a sensation when she appeared at Covent Garden. But her European success was nothing compared with the furore she caused when she toured America under the management of her future husband, Every Bushnelle. From California, where speculators ran up the price of the best seats at her concerts to a thousand dollars, she went to South America, and then to Hawaii, Australia, India, Malaya and Java. Affectionately known as Kate Hayes, she was an immense favourite in Australia, where in addition to making numerous concert appearances, she was the star of the company organized in 1856 by George Coppin to give Melbourne its first opera season. Among the operas in which she sang were *Maritana, The Bohemian Girl, Norma, Sonnambula,* and *The Barber of Seville* and *The Marriage of Figaro*. Her supporting artists included Marie Carandini, Sara Flower, Frank, John and Emma Howson, while the conductor was L. H. Lavenu, who came as her accompanist and, like so many others, remained to spend the rest of his life in Australia. Long-remembered both for her voice and for the unusual charm of her personality, Catherine Hayes died in the London suburb of Sydenham in 1861 at the early age of thirty-three.[15]

With Catherine Hayes the name of Manuel Garcia first shows up in the pattern of Australian music. Although he never set foot in the country, Garcia had a far-reaching influence on the development of the Australian voice. The world's most celebrated teacher of singing, he was born in Zapa, Spain, in 1805. He was the only distinguished musician to become a centenarian and lived to see his method of teaching world-famous. In Australia, its value was attested not only by Catherine Hayes and, later, Ellen Christian, who had it direct from the maestro himself and founded The Garcia School of Music in Sydney, but by Ilma di Murska, Nellie Melba, Frances Alda and many others who studied under Garcia's chief disciple Mathilde Marchesi.

Music ran in Garcia's veins. His father, also Manuel, was a composer who wrote forty operas, a singer who created the role of Count Almaviva in *The* 261

Barber of Seville and an impresario who took the first opera company to America. Manuel the younger spent his boyhood amid the alarms and atrocities of the Napoleonic wars. When the long conflict was over, he accompanied his parents to Naples, Paris and London. In 1825, his father formed a troupe called "The Spanish Family of the Garcias" and took them to America.

A hard taskmaster, the elder Garcia believed in squeezing the last ounce out of an artist so that his son returned from an arduous tour with his voice ruined by overwork. When the troupe disbanded, he turned this experience to account by making a lifelong study of the human voice and working out his system of training. His first pupil was his sister, the legendary Maria Malibran, a contralto with an additional soprano register, who became the most noted woman vocalist of her period. Garcia also taught his scarcely less celebrated younger sister, Pauline Viardot. But the greatest of all his innumerable pupils, amateur or professional, man or woman, was the immortal Jenny Lind, who came to him with her voice so wrecked by overstrain and faulty production that it was feared she might never sing again.

A year of his training worked such magic that the great Swedish soprano was in better voice than ever. The King of Sweden recognised Garcia's services to the national cantatrice by creating him a Chevalier of the Order of Merit.

Garcia's investigation into the mechanism of the human throat resulted in the publication of his "Method of Teaching Singing" which remained a standard work for generations. In 1854 his invention of the laryngyscope made him the first man to see a living human glottis, and gave surgery a new instrument.

The success of Catherine Hayes drew attention to the rich rewards awaiting popular musicians in the land of gold. Close behind her came another celebrated soprano, Anna Bishop, who might have served novelist George du Maurier as an inspiration when he created Trilby, the tone-deaf girl who sang only when under the influence of the mesmeric Svengali. Anna Bishop, however, was not tone-deaf, nor did she need a hypnotist to create her voice, though apparently it had to be liberated before it could attain its greatest beauty. The role of liberator was played by Robert Nicholas Charles Bochsa, Bohemian pianist, composer, conductor and above all harpist.[16] He created a sensation when he eloped with the young wife of Henry Rowley Bishop, director of the Royal Academy of Music.

The daughter of a drawing master, Anna Bishop — born Riviere in 1814 — was a child prodigy at the piano until Bishop discovered that she had a soprano voice of ravishing quality. As a woman concert pianist had little chance of distinction she was readily persuaded to give all her attention to singing. Bishop, who was knighted by Queen Victoria in 1842, had an impressive reputation as composer, conductor and all-round musical authority.

The long catalogue of his works includes eighty operas, ballets, oratorios and cantatas. He committed what was probably his first folly when, as a middle-aged widower, he fell in love with the gifted Anna Riviere who, overwhelmed by the attentions of so distinguished a man, became his second wife at the age of sixteen.

In 1938 he made another blunder when he was instrumental in having Nicholas Bochsa appointed to the staff of the Royal Academy of Music, where Anna fell under his spell.

Ignoring Bishop's protests, Bochsa changed her singing style by turning her into an Italianate dramatic soprano and completed his work of devastation by carrying her off to the Continent. Instead of retribution dogging the guilty pair, years of triumph followed. For several seasons Anna was prima donna and Bochsa chief conductor at the San Carlo Opera House, Naples. In 1847 they went to America, where Anna became the first English artist to sing in Mexico City. When the gold rush inscribed Australia on the entertainment map and the news of Catherine Hayes' financial success spread, they crossed the Pacific, giving their first Sydney concert in the Prince of Wales Theatre at the end of 1855, the year of Sir Henry Bishop's death.

Despite strong opposition from the rival theatre where Lola Montez was exhibiting her allegedly shocking "Spider Dance", the house was packed. With two such celebrated women in town, Sydney gossips must have had a field day. Unfortunately, Bochsa, a sick man when he landed in Australia, died after three performances. Tolerant Sydney gave the dead harpist an impressive farewell, a huge crowd heaping his grave with flowers while an orchestra played a requiem he had composed a week earlier.

Arrangements had already been made for Anna to sing Norma a few days later. Courageously pulling herself together, she gave a fine performance, afterwards remaining in Australia for a considerable time and appearing in a Melbourne opera season organised by Coppin, to whose daughter Polly she stood godmother. Before leaving Australia she erected a striking memorial to Bochsa in the Camperdown (N.S.W.) Cemetery.[17]

The story in South Australia began, much as it did in New South Wales, with the ferrying ashore of the colony's first piano in 1836. In this case the historic instrument belonged to Susannah, wife of the first governor, Captain John Hindmarsh of HMS *Buffalo*. The Hindmarsh piano had a more hazardous passage than Worgan's instrument, as it had to be brought through the surf at Holdfast Bay.

The original settlers of Adelaide were predominantly middle-class people who had migrated under a plan conceived by Edward Gibbon Wakefield and under the auspices of the South Australian Company. Most of the newcomers brought effects of considerable value, so that for a time Adelaide presented the anomalous spectacle of a cultured and well-dressed population trying to

Gladys Moncrieff

maintain the standards of an English county town while living in tents and huts.

The band of HMS *Buffalo* provided Adelaide with its first public music although, like the Hell in Bernard Shaw's *Man and Superman* the town was filled with amateurs. Even the police chief, Captain Alexander Tolmer, did not think it beneath his dignity to play the fiddle at concerts.

Early in the history of the colony an influx of German migrants helped greatly to raise musical standards. Most of them were Lutherans who, suffering religious persecution in their own country, chose South Australia rather than America as a refuge. Later other settlers came from Germany, and in one way or another, most of them enriched the intellectual and musical life of the community.[18]

Somewhere a monument should be raised in honour of that advance guard of civilization, the early music teachers of Australia. Usually underpaid and overworked women who taught the piano, they trained church choirs, played church organs, arranged programmes and acted as accompanists for charity concerts, receiving for this extra-curricular work nothing more tangible than a vote of thanks. As Marie Narelle has recorded, many of them in fringe areas rode or drove long distances to take music to reluctant pupils on farms and selections. Other teachers spent their lives as governesses on remote sheep and cattle stations battling with children whose interests were all outdoors. Few of these outback and small-town teachers were gifted or highly qualified, but they helped to spread music over the land from which sprang the Amy Sherwins and Ada Crossleys of the future. In the city and country alike, some of the finest teachers were found in the convent schools. Many of the nuns were exceptionally gifted, while large convents usually retained the services of the best outside teacher available. As convent schools became established in all but the smallest townships they became oases in the musical deserts of the interior.

By 1860, the second period in Australian history was coming to an end. The gold rush had spent its initial force, and the migrants who now poured into the country knew nothing about the early colonial days. As if to prove that Australia was neither a penal settlement nor an outlying South Sea island, the year 1861 brought the first English cricket team and the first opera company from overseas. The same year saw the birth of Australia's first and greatest ambassador, Helen Porter Mitchell.

It was a momentous year. It witnessed the death of Queen Victoria's husband, Albert the Prince Consort; the inauguration of President Lincoln, the opening of the American Civil War, and the first crossing of the Australian continent. It also saw the arrival in Melbourne of Lyster's Grand Opera Company and the beginning of what has been called the Golden Age of opera in Australia.

Prior to Lyster's advent, Australian opera seasons, like Coppin's 1856 venture, had usually been ad hoc affairs, built around a few visiting singers with a hastily rehearsed chorus and orchestra. The principals provided their own costumes, while the chorus utilized whatever was available — a system which called for considerable ingenuity on the part of the artist whose funds were low. As late as 1888, when the opera company organized by the basso Edward Farley was playing in Dunedin, New Zealand, Farley himself dressed for the part of a Russian grandee in *Fatinitza* by donning a pair of sea-boots and pinning a lady's fur boa to his street overcoat.

Nevertheless, although the managements of the period could not always do it justice, opera was a popular form of entertainment in Australia's mid-Victorian era. In 1860-61 a small company assembled by Signor and Signora Bianchi enjoyed a successful tour, when, with an orchestra numbering only five, they played for sixteen weeks in Adelaide — surely a record for a town of less than 20,000 people, even though many of them were of German origin.

As with every visiting impresario with the exception of Thomas Quinlan, Lyster recruited his chorus and orchestra locally. But there was nothing improvised about his organization. All his principals had been together a long time, while his productions were on a scale which informed contemporary critics asserted could not be bettered outside the great musical centres of the Old World.

William Saurin Lyster was one of the many remarkable Irishmen thrown up by the country which in the nineteenth century produced a chain of celebrities stretching from Moore and Balfe to Shaw and Wilde. He was born in Dublin in 1827 and, though closely related to a score of prelates and other notables, began his career as a typical adventurer by shipping on a whaler at the age of thirteen.[19]

After many other early adventures he turned to the stage and took over a small opera company headed by the tenor Henry Squires and his wife, Lucy   265

Escott. Although no musician himself, Lyster, a born impresario, was passionately fond of opera. Under his control the company became so successful that he eventually brought it to Australia, opening at the Theatre Royal, Melbourne, on 9th March, 1861, in *Lucia di Lammermoor*.

He had an amazing impact on the Australian lyric stage. What he had primarily intended as a tour developed into permanent residence and, with a few short breaks, he remained closely connected with Australia until his death in 1880. During what might be called the two Lyster decades, Australians and New Zealanders had the opportunity of hearing more opera than at any time since. In addition to all the standard works, he introduced every new piece that came out in Europe, so that a list of his productions would read like an operatic encyclopaedia.

In 1872 he gave Australia its first Wagnerian productions — *Tannhäuser* and *Lohengrin* — and wrote off the resultant loss with a smile. He took opera to places anyone less enthusiastic would have considered off the musical map. In 1864 he let Brisbane have its first taste of Verdi, Rossini, Bellini and Meyerbeer — though since there was no theatre he was forced to present concert versions in a hall without costumes or scenery.

A true soldier of fortune, the enterprising Irishman was prepared for anything. One year, while taking his company to Adelaide by sea, storms forced the ship to seek refuge in Warrnambool. Instead of fuming with impatience, Lyster presented *William Tell* in the Mechanics Institute Hall. The bad weather reduced the attendance to vanishing point but a local enthusiast showed his appreciation of Lyster's enterprise by paying for every empty seat in the hall.

Much could be written about the army of artists who marched under Lyster's flag during the two decades he dominated Australian opera. At first his company was almost a family concern, as he and his brother Fred married the two principal contraltos, Georgina Hodson and Rosalie Durand. Fred Lyster not only sang an effective baritone, he also translated the librettos of foreign operas into English.[20]

Soon after establishing himself in Australia, Lyster began to reinforce the ranks of his original company by engaging visiting artists, developing Australian singers and bringing in fresh talent from abroad. Many of his importations remained permanently to enrich the Australian musical soil. His most eminent guest artists were Anna Bishop, who sang with his company in 1868, Ilma di Murska, who came to Australia seven years later and Antoinette Link, who appeared in his Wagnerian productions. The importations included Martin Simonsen and his wife, Fanny, founders of an operatic family which culminated in their grand-daughter, New Zealand born Frances Alda, prima donna of the Metropolitan, New York, for twenty years.

266 At one period it would have been difficult to name any good Australian

singer who had not appeared with a Lyster company, or any first-class conductor who had not been on his payroll. An interesting Australian who starred with one of the Lyster companies was the contralto Lucy Chambers, daughter of a former town clerk of Sydney. Catherine Hayes was so impressed by her voice that she generously offered to sponsor her studies in Italy, but eight years elapsed before she broke down family opposition and went abroad. Sydney training was evidently on sound lines, for she was highly successful on the Continent, making her debut in Florence in 1864.

In 1869 when Lyster was in Europe seeking new principals for Australia, he sought her co-operation, and through her obtained the services of the best operatic combinations ever to appear in this country. During the season, Lucy Chambers made her Australian debut as Maffeo Orsini in *Lucrezia Borgia,* while later in the year she was a leading figure in a music festival at the University of Sydney. Like most Australian singers of her era she fininished her career doing concert and oratorio work and teaching.

Another of Lyster's native-born artists was Howard Vernon, like Lucy Chambers, one of the first Australians to meet with success abroad. His immense Australian prestige, however, was due to a long association with Gilbert & Sullivan operetta, which began in 1881 and lasted until the First World War.

For some years Lyster's leading tenor was Armes Beaumont who, though not an Australian by birth, arrived in Tasmania as a child and became one of the country's musical legends. According to one story, Lyster discovered him at a performance of *The Messiah* in 1868 when, at a moment's notice, he substituted for Henry Squires who was suddenly taken ill. Immensely popular and greatly talented, Beaumont was as much at home in concert and platform work as in every grade of opera, but his career was wrecked by a shooting accident which occurred on Lyster's country property and caused him gradually to go blind. Fortunately, however, he was able to continue teaching until the end of his life.

Another Lyster find was Edward Farley whose splendid bass voice lifted him out of the chorus. Long regarded as the best basso in Australia, Farley was equally effective in oratorio — he was a notable Elijah — but like many other Australian singers of the period, he lacked opportunity and was frequently in financial deep water, from which he vainly tried to extricate himself by the common but reckless expedient of going into management on his own, a step much more easily taken then than now.

One of the most famous of all Lyster's guest artists was the celebrated soprano Ilma di Murska, a student of Mathilde Marchesi. In 1873, after twenty years of sensational success in Europe and the United States, she sailed for Australia with a small concert party. Immensely successful in this country, she was at once engaged to head Lyster's company, giving Sydney and

Melbourne operatic singing which remained the Australian standard for many years. With Ilma di Murska the Australian musical world first became conscious of the name of Marchesi, which was to have a talismanic effect on Australian singing for more than thirty years.

Whatever merits Mathilde Marchesi may have had as a singer in her own right — and she was highly regarded as a mezzo soprano in the 1850's — it was as nothing compared with her talent as a teacher of singers and as the leading apostle of the great Manuel Garcia.

Born Mathilde Graumann in Frankfort-on-Main in 1821, Marchesi studied in Vienna under Otto Nikolai and Mendelssohn, who taught her the classical style. But it was Garcia in Paris who inducted her into the Italian method, filled her with enthusiasm for his system of voice production and laid the foundation of her future career.

After some years of concert work in London, she married the Sicilian baritone Salvatore Marchesi who, like Carandini in Australia, was an aristocratic political exile. Together they sang in opera and concerts and taught the Garcia method in Vienna, Cologne and Paris. Like their celebrated preceptor, they were long lived, Salvatore reaching the age of eighty-six, while his wife survived until her ninety-second year. It was Salvatore who gave Londoners their first Wagnerian opera when he produced *The Flying Dutchman* in 1870, with Santley as the hag-ridden Hollander, Foli as Daland and Ilma di Murska as Senta. As Melba's mentor, Marchesi loomed so large in the thoughts of every ambitious Australian vocalist that, at the turn of the century, nearly every singer who went abroad sought to study with her.

An epoch ended when Lyster died in Melbourne in 1880, leaving Australian music heavily in his debt. Almost every musician who came to the country during the two Lyster decades appeared under his direction at one time or another. As a concert manager, he organised several big Sydney musical festivals and arranged the tours of such artists as the pianist Arabella Goddard and Henry Ketten. When such attractions failed to draw he recouped his losses by offering other forms of entertainment. It was Lyster who brought the illustrious Italian tragedian, Adelaide Ristori, and her entire company, to Australia and who toured the first Japanese acrobats ever seen here. But it was as an impresario that he merited the bronze bust set up to his memory in the Melbourne Public Library. During his regime, grand opera was a popular form of entertainment in Australia, and no man worked harder to make it a permanent feature of Australian life.

He did not always have the field to himself. In 1871 Pompei and Cagli arrived from India with an opera company which had been playing successfully in the East. The newcomers opened auspiciously but soon fell into difficulties from which they were rescued by Lyster, who bought Pompei out. As Lyster & Cagli's Royal Italian Opera Company, the combination flourished. Several

Alberto Zelman

of the principals remained in Australia for years, while the musical director, Alberto Zelman, adopted the country permanently, greatly enriching its artistic life.

The best-known of the many excellent conductors employed by Lyster, Zelman was born in Trieste in 1832, of Italian parents. Having studied under Luigi Ricci, he was appointed Kapellmeister at Trieste Cathedral, later becoming a well-known conductor in Northern Italy. When his operatic wanderings took him to India with an opera company, he remained in Calcutta teaching and conducting until lured to Australia by Pompei & Cagli. On Lyster's death he stayed in Melbourne, being for many years organist at St Ignatius' Church and conductor of the Melbourne Liedertafel and the Deutche Turn Verein. Generations of racegoers knew him as the conductor of the military band at Flemington Racecourse. With another former Lyster conductor, Julius Siede, he organised the musical programmes for the Melbourne International Exhibition of 1888, frequently acting as deputy conductor to Sir Frederick Cowen.

At the turn of the century, the genial Zelman was one of the best-known identities in Melbourne. A quaint and striking figure who might have served as a model for Rembrandt, he was described as "a mass of hair and whiskers topped by a dusty felt hat", but despite his eccentricities he was a thorough musician who composed many orchestral works, violin solos and masses and was much sought-after as a teacher. His chief gift to his adopted country was his elder son Alberto who was born in 1874 and considered by 269 many the finest Australian violinist of his time. A gifted teacher and the founder of the Melbourne String Quartet and the Melbourne Symphony Orchestra, Zelman junior kept Melbourne orchestral music alive during the First World War, when players were so scarce that concerts had to be held on Saturday afternoons to half-filled benches. While on a visit to Europe in 1922, he conducted successfully in Berlin and London but died in 1927 at the early age of fifty-three.

Among the many notable singers who appeared under Lyster's banner was the tenor Pietro Cecchi, who arrived in Australia in 1871 as a member of a quartet headed by the American soprano Agatha States, the other members being the basso Susini and the baritone Orlandini.

Unable to assemble a supporting company or obtain a theatre, the four gave concert versions of a number of operas with the pianist Giorza supplying the place of an orchestra. So fine were the voices that the performances attracted large audiences. Cecchi, who stayed in Australia, settled in Melbourne and made frequent appearances with Lyster's company. When his singing career was over he became an influential teacher, the most celebrated of his pupils being the future Nellie Melba.

After the turmoil of the gold rush non-conformist influences became very strong in some parts of Australia. Many people strongly disapproved of the stage — although they did not all take the high stand of the Tasmanian clergyman who inveighed against *Faust* because of the undue advertisement it gave the devil. No exception could be taken, however, to vocal and instrumental music unaccompanied by the degrading spectacle of playacting. All but the most austere communities welcomed concert parties, especially when billed as "families".

A striking example of a successful concert party was the highly talented team of musicians known to generations of Australians as the "Lynch Family of Bellringers", although bell-ringing was only one of their many musical accomplishments. Taking to the road in 1867, the Lynch family travelled for more than fifty years. Flourishing long after the original members of the troupe had died or retired, they carried music to the least likely places and having neither chorus, scenery nor elaborate stage costumes to transport, they could show a profit where an opera company would have starved. Other well-known combinations were the Kennedy Family, and Marie Carandini's concert company.

The last family concert parties to tour Australia carried their own death warrants with them by supplementing their musical programmes with motion pictures. One such company was the Brescians, brought to Australia in 1903 by T. J. West and Harry Hayward.[21] The party, which consisted of thirteen members of the Martinengo and Hayward families, brought the best films hitherto shown in Australia and New Zealand. They were used to provide half the programme, but proved so popular that it was not long before astute managements realized that theatres could be filled without the aid of live artists. Even then, the concert type of entertainment took a long time to die. Both on the road and in semi-permanent locations in cities, it struggled on until sound films and the depression dealt it the *coup de grace.*

Although New Zealand's record in the operatic field is unimpressive, the Dominion played an important off-stage role in the development of Australian music. Boosted by the gold-rushes of the 1860's, the population of the islands increased rapidly. Instead of concentrating in a few big cities, New Zealanders tended to spread out into a number of prosperous towns in which the habit of theatregoing took hold in a manner unknown in Australian centres of the same size. Quite a number of these towns possessed well-appointed municipal theatres and a public accustomed to paying city prices for worthwhile musical or dramatic attractions so that in its heyday New Zealand offered Australian entrepreneurs a profitable touring ground for everything except the most elaborate shows.

Until films, economic crises, currency restrictions, radio, television and the general chaos caused by wars and depressions wrecked the old-time structure of the Australian theatre, the entrepreneur who had lost on the Melbourne and Sydney swings could always hope to balance his books on the New Zealand roundabouts.

Following the death of Lyster, Martin and Fanny Simonsen went into management. Franco-Italians, they had been associated with Lyster for some years, Fanny as a leading soprano and her husband as violinist, chorus master, producer and general handy-man. With their son Jules and daughters Leonora,[22] Martina and Frances — afterwards Frances Saville — the Simonsens had the nucleus of an opera company. In addition they had Armes Beaumont as principal tenor and several excellent Italian singers from the residue of Lyster's organization.

But though the 1880's were years of great prosperity in Australia, the best days of grand opera were over. Even in Lyster's lifetime French operetta spread to Australia, tickling the ears not only of the groundlings but of the stalls and dress circle with the effervescent tunes of Offenbach, von Suppe, Charles Lecoq, Edmond Audran and Robert Planquette. When these were followed by the elegant and highly respectable Gilbert & Sullivan operas, grand opera as a year-round entertainment began to wane. Nevertheless, the Simonsens persevered for years and won an assured place in Australian musical history.

Another pair of artists who experienced all the ups and downs of the touring operatic life in Australia were the American tenor, Charles Turner and his wife, Annis Montague, a soprano of high quality. Born in Hawaii, before the islands became United States territory, Annis Montague studied and

271

sang in Europe and America for some years before coming to Australia with her husband in 1881.

The pair made their Australian debut at a concert arranged in Sydney by Ellen Christian. Thereafter they kept an opera company on the road until Turner's premature death ten years later. Carrying opera where it had never been presented before, they were playing in Mackay during Melba's brief residence in North Queensland. The future diva took Mrs Turner and her husband driving and had what was probably her first close-up acquaintance with touring professionals.

Prominent in the early 1880's was the Ballarat-born Alice Rees, described in pre-Melba days as one of the few first class singers Australia had produced. Taught by her father, an amateur of local note, she made her Melbourne debut at a concert held for the benefit of Julius Siede. When Rees died, his daughter studied under Lucy Chambers and adopted music as a profession, appearing first in Gilbert & Sullivan opera and then joining a troupe called the Associated Artists, which consisted mainly of stranded or expatriated Italians. According to competent judges, Alice Rees might well have been among Australia's top three singers but in 1886 just as she was attaining her full power, she married

The Theatre Royal, Melbourne, in Lyster's time

Max Vogrich, the Hungarian pianist and composer, and retiring from the stage, spent most of her time in America.

The tempo of the Australian musical stage quickened considerably in the 1880's, largely due to the rise of J. C. Williamson and George Musgrove, entrepreneurs whose vision and ability would have made them outstanding anywhere in the world. The better remembered of the pair is Williamson, who built up so great a reputation that although he died in 1913 there is still box-office magic in his name. An American of mixed Scottish-Irish descent, James Cassius Williamson was born in Pennsylvania in 1845. Stage-struck while still in knickerbockers he made his earliest professional appearances as a schoolboy in Milwaukee. By 1871, when he went to San Francisco, he was a star Broadway comedian.

His subsequent success was partly based on a dialect comedy-drama which he bought in California for a few dollars and rewrote as *Struck Oil,* and partly on his marriage to Margaret Virginia Sullivan, a charming and talented San Francisco actress professionally known as Maggie Moore.[23] In 1874 the pair presented *Struck Oil* in Australia with phenomenal box-office results. Returning four years later from a world tour with the play, Williamson established himself permanently in this country and eventually became the most powerful theatrical magnate in the British dominions. One of his most profitable speculations was the purchase of the Australian and New Zealand rights in the Gilbert & Sullivan operas, which he cast and presented in a manner equal to the D'Oyly Carte productions at the Savoy Theatre, London. Having snatched Gilbert & Sullivan out of the hands of the theatrical pirates who abounded in those days of loose copyright laws, he gave the first authorized production of *The Lass Who Loved a Sailor* on 15th November, 1879, when *H.M.S. Pinafore* was produced at the Theatre Royal, Sydney. Williamson appeared in the role of Sir Joseph Porter with Maggie Moore as Josephine.

For many years afterwards, scarcely an evening passed without a Gilbert & Sullivan production somewhere in Australia or New Zealand, either by one of Williamson's official companies, an amateur operatic society or one of the juvenile troupes which helped the operas rocket to popularity. One of the most famous juvenile performances of *Pinafore* was that given at the Bijou Theatre, Melbourne, in 1880. Among the sixty children in the cast were Flora Graupner, later an adult star of light opera and musical comedy, and Mary Weir, the brilliant young dancer who afterwards became the second Mrs J. C. Williamson. Captain Corcoran was played by the son of the producers, G. B. W. and Mrs Lewis. He created a precedent, seldom followed by full-grown Corcorans, by singing his apostrophe to the moon in Act II to his own accompaniment on the guitar.

Other children's *Pinafore* troupes took the field, but before long, Pollard's Lilliputians — duly authorized by Williamson — had the junior field to them- 273 selves. During the decades which followed they planted the Gilbert & Sullivan banner wherever it could be flown. As so often happened, the public succumbed to the fascination of clever and well-trained child actors playing grown-up parts, and Pollard's Lilliputians was probably the most continuously successful of all Australian touring companies. As well as Gilbert & Sullivan, the Lilliputians presented such standard light operas as *Les Cloches de Corneville, Boccacio, Tambour Major, Olivette* and *La Mascotte,* but as nothing could prevent the artists growing up, the composition of the company changed frequently. On several occasions, operations had to be suspended altogether until reinforcements could be trained. Few organizations did more to familiarize Australians with high-class light music than the juvenile companies, while many fine artists graduated from their ranks.

Until the 1900's there was no such thing as a Gilbert & Sullivan opera company in Australia. The players switched about between grand opera, opera bouffe, musical comedy and the Savoy operas with all the versatility of the time. Specialization and the Gilbert & Sullivan cult lay ahead.

When Henry Bracy became Williamson's chief producer of musical plays, his strong direction, combined with the conducting of Leon Caron and, later, Gustav Slapoffski, helped materially to set the Gilbert & Sullivan opera in the Savoy mould. One of the reasons for the early success of these operas in Australia was the care which Williamson bestowed on the dressing and mounting, which made his productions indistinguishable from those seen in London. The costumes were replicas of the originals, while the scenery was invariably reproduced from the original sets painted by Joseph Harker and Hawes Craven. No liberties were taken with the text, while the "business" remained much as Gilbert had originally devised it.

The year 1885 saw the Australian premiere of the most popular of all the collaborators' works, *The Mikado,* with Nellie Stewart as Yum Yum and Howard Vernon as Ko Ko, the part he was to make so completely his own. The first Australian artist to play in Japan, Vernon introduced some of the authentic gestures of Japanese actors into his role, with the result that although he remained within the Savoy framework his performance was unique. It was witnessed by Mrs Richard D'Oyly Carte, who was so impressed that on returning to London she insisted that George Grossmith, the Savoy Ko Ko, introduce Vernon's "business" into his own interpretation of the part.

Although by 1905 Williamson believed that the Savoy operas were wearing thin, he decided to try another season in each of the capital cities and to carry the operas to towns like Kalgoorlie, Broken Hill, Ballarat, Bendigo and Geelong and to similar centres in New Zealand.[24] The tour, twice round Australia and once through New Zealand, lasted nearly two years and the company broke new ground by presenting *Utopia Limited* for the first time outside Britain.

Since the original *Pinafore*, Australia has seen many notable exponents of the principal roles. Old-time Gilbert & Sullivan enthusiasts asserted that Florence Young's Josephine outshone all rivals; others were equally vehement on behalf of Dolly Castles or Viola Wilson. Gladys Moncrieff, who was to succeed Nellie Stewart as the First Lady of the Australian Theatre, took an important step in her career when she appeared as Casilda in *The Gondoliers* in Sydney in 1914. Born in Bundaberg, Queensland, she began her career in small-time vaudeville, eventually securing a small part in a Sydney production of *A Sunshine Girl*. After her experience in Gilbert & Sullivan she never looked back, scoring heavily in Romberg's *Maytime* just after the first War, and making the hit of her career in the Lonsdale-Fraser Simson musicals *The Maid of the Mountains* and *A Southern Maid*. Informed contemporary opinion was that she was better in the roles than the London original, Josie Collins, but although she made successful appearances in England, she could never divorce herself from her homeland. The long list of her successes includes *The Chocolate Soldier, The Merry Widow, Rio Rita, Ma Mie Rosette, The Street Singer* and *Collitt's Inn* by the Australian composer Varney Monk.

The years between the Wars brought a number of young Australian artists into the Gilbert & Sullivan field, among them Herbert Browne and Marie Bremner who was born in Melbourne and studied at the Albert Street Conservatorium. Although her experience of Gilbert & Sullivan opera was limited to two years with the 1931 company, she was one of the most prominent musical comedy artists of the 1930's, appearing in *Lilac Time, The Desert Song* and *The New Moon*.

As time passed, J. C. Williamson invested in every form of theatrical venture from ballet to motion pictures, but though he made many forays into the field of grand opera he never attempted to emulate Lyster and establish a semi-permanent organization. His first important opera season was in 1893 when, partnered by George Musgrove, he presented an Italian company in *Cavalleria Rusticana* and *I Pagliacci* with Italian Del Torre in the roles of Nedda and Santuzza, which she had created in England. Instead of being played on the same evening, each opera was given separately, supported by the Torquoise Ballet.

The 1890's were years of depression, unpropitious for costly theatrical speculations, but in 1901, Williamson gave Australia its first performance of Verdi's *Otello*, Ponchielli's *La Gioconda* and Puccini's *La Boheme*, Dalia Bassich being Australia's first Mimi. In 1910, again under Williamson's auspices, Australia met Puccini's other famous heroine, Cho Cho San, better known as Madame Butterfly, the part being played on alternate nights by Amy Castles and the French soprano, Bel Sorel. Sung in English, the opera ran for six weeks in Sydney, creating a world record.

With no opposition except from silent films, the Australian theatre and   275 music generally, flourished during the prosperous years leading up to World War I, when grand opera regained much of the popularity it had enjoyed during the old days of Lyster. The year 1911 saw what was so far the biggest event in Australian musical history, the advent of the first Melba-Williamson Grand Opera Company, an enterprise in which diva and entrepreneur shared equally. As Australians had never yet heard Melba, properly supported, in full scale opera, the event caused enormous interest. The season, which opened at Her Majesty's Theatre, Sydney, on 2nd September, 1911, with Melba and McCormack in *La Traviata,* was a triumph, the most brilliant so far recorded, whetting public appetite so much that a big welcome awaited the Quinlan Opera Company which under Williamson auspices arrived in Melbourne in June 1912.

By far the largest company ever to visit Australia, this consisted of almost 200 people, including principals, chorus and an orchestra capable of giving symphony concerts.[25] The impresario behind this vast theatrical enterprise, which travelled with 300 tons of scenery, fifty-six hundredweight of music and 3,500 costumes was Thomas Quinlan, a Dubliner who gave up accountancy to become a professional singer and then embarked in management. Among the many celebrated artists who appeared under his direction were Caruso, Kubelik, Kreisler and Sousa. In 1908 he even persuaded Melba to sing in Ireland and, having learned something about Australia from her, he suggested they join forces and take a company on a global tour.

Quinlan's schemes were too grandiose for the astute diva, instead, he joined Sir Thomas Beecham as business manager and later took over most of his company. Like Beecham, Quinlan believed that opera should be sung in English to English-speaking audiences — a view regarded as revolutionary half a century ago. Beecham spent a fortune trying to convert the English public to his way of thinking, while Quinlan carried the doctrine round the world.

Organized in 1910, the Quinlan Grand Opera Company opened with a successful season at His Majesty's Theatre, London. As Quinlan had rifled the British lyric theatre for artists, his productions, though not glittering social events, were of so high a standard that the enterprise prospered. After touring the big provincial centres, he announced that he intended taking the company to South Africa and Australia.

Considering the vast preliminary expense involved and the difficulty of recouping himself in countries with small populations, many people thought the impresario was out of his mind. Some members of the chorus and orchestra resigned rather than risk being stranded in the wilds of Sydney or the Great Karoo.

Incredible as it might seem to anyone looking back from the days of enormous operatic deficits and government subsidies, the tour was a triumph. South Africa, riding the crest of a golden wave, responded magnificently to the first major opera season ever held in the Union. Many wealthy Johannesburgers attended the opera every evening as a matter of course. Australians were equally enthusiastic. The first night, at Her Majesty's Theatre, Melbourne, on 7th July, 1912, when the now familiar *Tales of Hoffmann* was presented in Australia for the first time, created a furore. The Australian soprano, Lalla Miranda, appeared as the Doll, with Edna Thornton as Guiletta and Enrichette Onelli as Antonia. Other operas which Quinlan presented for the first time in Australia were Wagner's *Tristan and Isolde,* Debussy's *Prodigal Son,* Puccini's *Manon Lescaut* and *Girl of the Golden West.*

Both Quinlan and Williamson were so well satisfied that arrangements were made for another visit the following year. Unfortunately, conditions changed by the time the big combination landed in South Africa in June 1913. The Transvaal was in the grip of an industrial upheaval and opera was a secondary consideration.

Although the South African season was a loss, Quinlan hoped that Australia would balance his accounts. However luck was against him. The company landed in Melbourne in time to strike a smallpox scare which kept the theatres half-empty. Nevertheless, Quinlan had a brilliant company and would have done better had he not overestimated the Australian appetite for Wagner. His star attractions were *The Meistersingers* and the cycle of four operas comprising *The Ring of the Nibelungen.* The public of Melbourne and Sydney yawned at them all, and though Quinlan hastily returned to Verdi and Puccini and gave orchestral concerts in the Sydney Town Hall, his finances were badly shaken. Still another disaster occurred when a general strike in New Zealand forced him to cancel a season in the Dominion and sail direct to Canada. Despite everything, he was willing to try a third venture in 1915, but the outbreak of war wrecked all his plans and the man whom Puccini had once called the "Garibaldi of opera" goes down in history as the only impresario ever to carry a complete company — principals, chorus and orchestra — not once, but twice, around the world.

Williamson died in Paris in 1913, so that the Quinlan company was the last operatic enterprise in which he was concerned. He was then at the apex of his career, as the company he controlled had acquired a virtual monopoly of better-class theatres in Australia and had strong links with South Africa and London. Although never a great actor, in his youth he had been regarded as a competent dialect comedian, while as an entrepreneur he had no superior in Australia and few, if any, elsewhere. Williamson's first wife, Maggie Moore, was the daughter of a Sydney couple who had migrated to San Francisco during the gold rush. That she played several of the soprano leads in Gilbert & Sullivan indicates that she had at least an acceptable voice but her real strength lay in sentimental comedy. Her favorite role was Lizzie Stofel in *Struck Oil,* a part played in America, Australia and England for nearly forty

277

years and on more occasions than she could number. Born in 1851, she died in San Francisco in 1926.

Up to World War I, Australian troupers roamed far and wide. In 1889, the first entrepreneur on the Rand goldfields was the Australian musician Luscombe Searelle, composer of the operetta *Estrella,* played in Sydney a year or two before by the Montague-Turner opera company. Searelle demonstrated Australian enterprise and versatility by transporting an entire theatre as well as an opera company to the embryo city of Johannesburg, moving artists, scenery, costumes and a prefabricated iron building up from the coast by bullock-team and horse coach.

When the outfit reached Johannesburg a few hours sufficed to erect a practicable theatre with a stage, private boxes and even a bar. Almost before the name "Theatre Royal" appeared across the facade, Searelle, who was his own conductor, waved his baton to begin the first Rand performance of *Maritana* with his sister-in-law, nineteen-year-old Amy Fenton, in the name part. In a sense, Australian stage history was being repeated on the Rand, for in 1854 George Coppin had erected a prefabricated iron theatre, the Olympic, in Melbourne, to cope with the gold rush.

Carandini singing in Melbourne. Photo: State Library of Victoria

Among the various partners with whom Williamson was associated, George Musgrove was by far the most notable. He was born in Dublin in 1854, his mother a sister of Georgina Hodson, the wife of W. S. Lyster. Musgrove entered the theatre as box-office manager of one of Lyster's companies, and acquired a passion for grand opera which eventually ruined him. On Lyster's death, he became manager for Emily Soldene, the celebrated opera bouffe artist, who brought the first can-can dancers to Australia, and shocked all the respectable Australians who packed in to see them in *Chilperic* and *Genevieve de Brabant*.

Musgrove made his first big hit by staging *La Fille de Tambour Major* on his own account with Nellie Stewart in the lead. For long periods he was in partnership with Williamson, but his big operatic ventures were undertaken singlehanded. In 1901, having made a large fortune staging *The Belle of New York* in England and Australia, he brought out an excellent opera company under the direction of Gustav Slapoffski, formerly a conductor with the Carl Rosa organization. As Williamson also had an opera company in the field at the same time, Australia celebrated the inauguration of Federation by having more opera than ever before or since. More than 160 performances were given in Sydney alone, although the population of that city was only about half a million.

The season of 1901 was the high point of George Musgrove's career. In the Princess Theatre, Melbourne, which had been built to his specifications, he controlled one of the most beautiful theatres in the world. His opera company which included the Tasmanian baritone, Lempriere Pringle, was phenomenally successful.[26] During the Federation ceremonies Musgrove was appointed director of entertainments in connection with the visit of the Duke and Duchess of York (afterwards King George V and Queen Mary) while later he managed Nellie Melba's first triumphal concert tour of her native country.

In 1907 he brought out a complete German opera company which got away to a magnificent start with the first Australian production of *Die Walkure* but ended in a failure from which his pride, if not his pocket, never really recovered. This was mainly owing to quarrels among the artists whose feuds reached a point where no one, including Musgrove himself, knew what opera would be performed on any particular evening.

Musgrove was a perfectionist in everything. His Shakespearian productions early in the century were long remembered while his attitude to the theatre is exemplified in Williamson's story of how he once watched a Musgrove production of *A Midsummer Night's Dream* being superlatively well played to a half-empty theatre.

"George," he said, "This isn't paying. Why don't you take it off?"

"Because I like it," returned Musgrove.

279

Musgrove died in 1916, fifty-five years after his uncle landed from California.

Closely associated with him was Nellie Stewart, one of the most talented and certainly the most popular Australian players of her time. Nellie Stewart was the daughter of the Theodosia Yates-Stirling of the old Hobart days, who after the death of her first husband, James Guerin, married one Richard Towsey, a young fellow who abandoned gold prospecting to try his luck on the stage as Richard Stewart. Born in 1855, their daughter made her first stage appearance as a child of five with the celebrated Charles and Ellen Kean. While still a young girl, she toured the world with what was practically a family show called Rainbow Revels. Apart from a little time in Melbourne with David Miranda,[27] father of the future prima donnas Lalla and Beatrice, and some lessons in London from Alberto Randegger, she had little formal training in singing but she had unusual talent, shown by her success during the 1880's when she sang the lead in practically every light opera from *Orpheus en Enfer* to *Patience*. In 1888, Australia's Centenary Year, she sang Marguerite in Gounod's *Faust* for twenty-four consecutive performances. Such efforts may have been the reason she lost her singing voice in the middle 1890's, but she made a second reputation as a straight actress, excelling in romantic comedy.[28] She died in 1931, within a few months of Melba.

Among Musgrove's legacies to Australian music was Gustav Slapoffski,[29] who came as musical director of the 1900 company and remained to become the dynamic bald-headed old maestro who died in Melbourne half a century later.

Slapoffski's links with Australia dated back to 1831 when his grandfather, Captain William Hunter, landed in New South Wales as aide-de-camp to Governor Bourke. Years later, the captain returned to England with two Sydney-born daughters, one of whom eventually married an exiled Russian fiddler and became the mother of Gustav Slapoffski.

After studying at the Royal College of Music, the younger Slapoffski became a professional violinist. During the 1870's he was leader of the orchestra at the Opera Comique during the historic seasons of *H.M.S. Pinafore* and *The Sorcerer*. Following a long and varied experience in Britain and America he became one of the conductors of the Carl Rosa company, which played an annual twelve-week season in London and toured the British Isles for the remainder of the year. When he engaged the chorus for the first Musgrove opera season, he found the musical standard of the applicants so deplorable that he invoked the aid of Professor Marshall-Hall, from whose Albert Street Conservatorium he obtained a team of intelligent young singers with fresh brilliant voices. The season, which finished with a sixteen weeks tour of New Zealand, was so successful that when Melba made her first concert tour of Australia she demanded that Slapoffski conduct the orchestra.

At one time both Slapoffski and his wife, a leading soprano with the 1900 company, taught at the New South Wales conservatorium, while for years no Australian Gilbert & Sullivan company was complete without his familiar figure at the conductor's desk. His encyclopedic knowledge of grand opera proved of inestimable value to the National Theatre Movement in its early years. His most spectacular effort was at the Exhibition Oval, Adelaide, when he conducted ten massed bands and a choir of three thousand in the Melba Memorial concert. The old maestro died in 1951 at the age of ninety-three.

Grand opera was not among the arts which flourished in Australia during World War I. In the main, the theatre offered revues, light American musicals and revivals of mature English and continental comic operas which had held the stage for years. In any case, German and Austrian artists marooned here in 1914 were interned, and Italians were looked on askance until their country joined the Allies.

In 1916, the Gonzales company, an Italian organization which had been touring in the East, arrived under the auspices of a new impresario, Sir Benjamin Fuller.

Though scarcely a first-rate organization, the Gonzales company contained a number of fine singers, among them Scamuzzi, a notable baritone, Capelli and Balboni, tenors, and the sopranos Visoni and Gonzales. Some of them remained in Australia after the war finished, but the company, frequently changing its name and composition, did not finish as successfully as it had started. In 1918, when it was under the control of Frank Rigo, one-time stage manager for Melba, it was closed down by the post-war influenza epidemic. Later, it was taken over by Count Ercole Fillipini. When Fillipini died, his wife, a musician in her own right, carried on, thus giving audiences the unusual sight of a woman at the conductor's desk, but the company lacked the social glamour associated with grand opera and eventually faded out. Rigo, however, assured himself of a place in Australian musical history by introducing the Melbourne soprano, Gertrude Johnson, destined in later years to become the founder of, and the driving force behind, the National Theatre Movement.

The highlight of Fuller's career as an operatic impresario was his Melbourne Centenary season in 1934-35, when he brought out an opera-in-English company headed by Florence Austral, Muriel Brunskill, Horace Stevens, Browning Mummery, Frederic Collier, Thea Phillips and Ben Williams. Artistically, the company was an immense success, but its eighteen months tour of Australia and New Zealand was reported to have cost Fuller £30,000.

Although its founder was dead, the firm of J. C. Williamson, now headed by his one-time secretary, Sir George Tallis, lost no time in getting under way with its first post-war opera season. With Amy Castles as prima donna, the Williamson company of 1919 included a number of Australian singers in Nellie Leach, Strella Wilson, Elsa Treweek, Leah Myers, Gertrude Johnson and Fred Collier, together with several members of the Gonzales combination. But for most people, opera in Australia reached its between-wars peak with the two Melba-Williamson seasons, in 1924 and 1928.[30]

In those years, when the war was swiftly fading into the background and the Depression had not yet thrown its shadow, performances were given which dimmed the memories of the fabulous pre-1914 period. After that, whatever followed — the Williamson Imperial Opera Company and even Fuller's big effort — seemed slightly anti-climactic. It is improbable that such seasons as Melba's, Quinlan's, or Musgrove's will ever occur again. World War II saw the eclipse of the great luminaries of opera and concert platform.

The jet age has also seen the fading of the flowers of comic opera who once flourished in the genial climate of Australia. All could act, some superlatively well. Many had voices which, trained and disciplined, would have graced any opera house. The years of Melba and Alda were also the years of Nellie Stewart, Flora Graupner, Dolly and Eileen Castles, Carrie Moore and Florence Young, who, taught by Marchesi, had been told that there was no soprano role in opera to which she might not aspire.

But although the key may have changed, the melody flows on. Eliza Winstanley, standing on the deck of the ship as it staggered around the Horn, was travelling to a greater destiny than she knew. Today, less than a century after her death, the lone voice of the Currency Lass has swelled to a crescendo which rings round the world.

2. QUESTIONS ASKED ARTISTS

1. Did you grow up in a family that had special musical interests?
   If so, what were they?
2. Did you show evidence of an interest in music at an early age?
   If so, in what way?
3. Did any particular person (teacher or other) show an awareness of your talent and encourage you to develop it?
   How?
4. What musical activities did you take part in as a child in school, church, community, eisteddfodau, etc.?
5. What awards did you win that might have helped to further your career?
6. What made possible your going abroad for further study: awards or prizes,

a farewell concert, savings, family "backing"?

7. With whom did you study in Australia and abroad?

8. What have been the principal events in your professional career?

3. COMPETITION RESULTS

I. THE *SUN* ARIA (ROYAL SOUTH STREET COMPETITIONS)[1]

1924	1.	Lawrence Power
	2.	Morva Davies
1925	1.	Pauline Gallagher
1926	1.	Edward Hocking
1927	1.	Arnold Matters
1928	1.	Nance Marley
	2.	Florence Erikson
	3.	Sydney Holmes
1929	1.	May Craven
1930	1.	Norman Menzies
1931	1.	Adele McKay
1932	1.	Emilie Hooke
	2.	Nancy Studley
	3.	Etta Bernard and Jeanne Teychenne
1933	1.	Newstead Rush
	2.	Beatrice Oakley
	3.	Joan Jones and William Laird
1934	1.	Dennis Dowling
	2.	Hinemoa Rosieur
	3.	Alan Coad
1935	1.	Nance Osborne
1936	1.	Sylvia Fisher
1937	1.	Joan Jones
1938	1.	Alfredo Luizzi
	2.	Mavis Webster
	3.	Vera Hickenbotham
1939	1.	Mavis Webster
1940	1.	Joyce Ross
	2.	Frances Forbes

	3.	Vera Hickenbotham
1941	1.	Amelia Scarce
	2.	Kathleen Seabrook
	3.	Frank Lasslett and Peggy Knibb
no contests 1942-1944		
1945	1.	John Lanigan
	2.	Jean Thompson
	3.	Patricia Howard
1946	1.	Maxwell Cohen
	2.	Morris Williams
	3.	Patricia Howard and Robert Simmons
1947	1.	Charles Skase
	2.	Keith Neilson
	3.	Nita Maughan
1948	1.	Mary Miller
	2.	Joan Arnold
	3.	Robert Simmons
1949	1.	Betna Pontin
	2.	Joan Arnold
	3.	Halinka de Tarczynska
1950	1.	David Allen
	Reserve Award. Nina Foley	
1951	1.	Verona Cappadona
	R.A.	Joyce Simmons
1952	1.	Violet Harper
	R.A.	Wilma Martin
1953	1.	Lynette Kierce
	R.A.	Jenifer Eddy and Robert Allman

283

1954	1.	Cavell Armstrong	1960	1.	June Barton
	R.A.	Loris Elms		R.A.	Roslyn Dunbar
1955	1.	Leonard Delany	1961	1.	Janice Hearne
	R.A.	Loris Sutton		R.A.	Patricia Connop
1956	1.	Loris Sutton	1962	1.	Maureen Howard
	R.A.	Brian Hansford		R.A.	Patricia Wooldridge
1957	1.	Brian Hansford	1963	1.	Raymond Myers
	R.A.	June Barton		R.A.	Valerie Pennefather
1958	1.	Robert Bickerstaff	1964	1.	Malvina Major
	R.A.	Diana Munn		R.A.	Imelda Fitzgerald
1959	1.	Tello Siciliano	1965	1.	Kiri Te Kanawa
	R.A.	June Barton		R.A.	Robert Dawe

II. THE *SUN* ARIA (GEELONG)

1925	1.	Arnold Ashworth	1930	1.	Miss F. Erilson
	2	William Cadzon		2.	Norman Menzies
	3.	Olwer Marshall and May Daley		3.	Miss M. Cumming
1926	1.	William A. Bossence	1931	1.	Myra Hardenack
	2.	Maisie Ramsay		2.	Eulalie Moore
	3.	Colin J. Thomson		3.	Harold Murphy
1927	1.	Lorna Miller	1932	1.	Anne Harvey
	2.	May Daley		2.	Charles E. Lomas
	3.	Mrs Florence Pryor		3.	Lola Edwards
1928	1.	Marjorie Lawrence	1933	1.	Ailsa McKenzie
	2.	Alice Wells		2.	John Dudley
	3.	Ernest Wilson		3.	Rene Craig and Mary Lilley
1929	records unavailable				

III. THE *SUN* ARIA (BENDIGO)

1925-1930 not available					Miss I. Turner
1931	1.	Kathleen Carroll	1933	1.	Jeanne Teychenne
	2.	Monica Miller		2.	Charles E. Lomas
	3.	Godfrey Beckwith		3.	W. Howling
1932	1.	Miss M. Butler	1934	1.	Margaret Black
	2.	Nance Osborne		2.	Lena Worland and
	3.	Joan Jones and			Gladys Richards

1935	1.	Freda Northcote	William Laird and
	2.	Molly Hislop	Miss S. Richards
	3.	Miss M. Daniels and	

IV. *SUN* ARIA (CITY OF SYDNEY EISTEDDFOD)[2]

1933	Ruby Zlotkowski	1947	Eleanor Houston
	Norman Barnes	1948	Florence Taylor
1934	Merle Ambler	1949	Joan Sutherland
	Robert Nicholson	1950	June Gough (Bronhill)
1935	Phyllis Thompson	1951	Angelina Arena
	Colin Chapman	1952	Marjorie Conley
1936	Catherine Williams	1953	Tessa Schell
	Arthur Broadhurst	1954	Jean Brunning
1937	no eisteddfod	1955	Heather Begg
1938	Mildred Walker	1956	Russell Cooper
	Neville Beavis	1957	Kevin Mills
1939	Marie Ryan	1958	Heather McMillan
	Raymond Nilsson	1959	Elaine Blight
1940	Nancy Buchanan	1960	Roslyn Dunbar
	Hugh Godfrey	1961	Robert Colman
1941	Edna McClelland	1962	Valerie Morgan
	Allan Ferris	1963	Jan Bartlett
1942-1945	no eisteddfod	1964	Pettine-Ann Croul
1946	Rosina Raisbeck	1965	Serge Baigildin

V. AUSTRALIAN NATIONAL EISTEDDFOD (SHELL ARIA), CANBERRA

1955	1.	Jennifer Eddy		2.	June Barton
	2.	Valerie Collins		3.	Nita Maughan
	3.	Geoffrey Chard	1959	1.	Kevin Stumbles
1956	1.	Valerie Collins		2.	June Barton
	2.	Robert Bickerstaff		3.	Arthur Mee
	3.	Neil Warren-Smith	1960	1.	Yvonne Minton
1957	1.	Gloria McDonnell		2.	Elaine Blight
	2.	Russell Cooper		3.	Roslyn Dunbar
	3.	Kevin Mills	1961	1.	June Barton
1958	1.	Robert Bickerstaff		2.	Patricia Connop

	3.	Waverney Ford	1964	1.	Jan Bartlett
1962	1.	Patricia Woodridge		2.	Marion Miller
	2.	Janice Hearne		3.	Thomas McDonnell
	3.	Robert Haase	1965	1.	Pettine-Anne Croul
1963	1.	Raymond Myers		2.	Waverney Ford
	2.	Barry Purcell		3.	Ian Holston
	3.	Geoffrey Harnett			

VI. COMMONWEALTH A.B.C. VOCAL COMPETITIONS

1950	Elise Longwill, soprano, (W.A.)
1951	Kevin Miller, tenor, (S.A.)
1952	Marjorie Conley, soprano, (N.S.W.)
1953	Lynette Kierce, soprano, (Vic.)
1954	Patricia Wyatt, soprano, (W.A.)
1955	Neil Warren-Smith, bass-baritone, (Vic.)
1956	Russell Cooper, bass-baritone, (N.S.W.)
1957	Patricia Connop, soprano, (W.A.)
1958	Lynette Howieson, soprano, (W.A.)
1959	Gloria McDonnell, soprano, (Vic.)
1960	Nance Grant, soprano, (Vic.)
1961	Ruth Gurner, soprano, (S.A.)
1962	Janice Hearne, soprano, (S.A.)
1963	Althea Bridges, soprano, (N.S.W.)
1964	Elizabeth Tippett, mezzo-soprano, (Vic.)
1965	Janet Lasscock, soprano, (S.A.)

VII. MOBIL QUEST[3]

1949	1.	Ronal Jackson			Marjorie Conley
	2.	Trudy Daunt	1953	1.	Elizabeth Allen
	3.	William Smith		2.	Robert Allman
1950	1.	Joan Sutherland		3.	Raymond McDonald
	2.	David Allen	1954	1.	Ronald Austron
	3.	William Smith		2.	John Shaw
1951	1.	Margaret Nisbett		3.	Raymond McDonald
	2.	Clifford Powell	1955	1.	Marjorie Conley
	3.	June Bronhill		2.	Margreta Elkins
1952	1.	Donald Smith		3.	Heather Begg and
	2.	Eric Mitchelson			Conrad Berensen
	3.	Elizabeth Allen and	1956	1.	Noel Melville

	2. Heather Begg	2.	Robert Bickerstaff
	3. Lance Lloyd	3.	Richard Bromley and
1957	1. Nance Grant		Peter Campbell

VIII. THE DAME NELLIE MELBA BEQUEST SCHOLARSHIP

First Award (1935-6) — Hinemoa Rosieur (N.Z.)
Second Award (1937-9) — Jean Love (Vic.)
Third Award (1940-2) — Sybil Willey (Qld.)
Fourth Award (1943-5) — Elsie Morison (Vic.)
Fifth Award (1946-8) — Sylvia Biddle (Qld.)
Sixth Award (1949-51) — Joyce Simmons (Vic.)
Seventh Award (1952-3) — Jean Munro (Qld.)
Eighth Award (1958-60) — Aldene Splatt (Vic.)
Ninth Award (1962-4) — Elizabeth Tippett (Vic.)
Tenth Award (1965-) — Margot Cory (Vic.)

4. PROGRAMME OF THE ELASSER BENEFIT CONCERT

Programme of the Elasser Benefit Concert held at the Melbourne Town Hall on 17th May, 1884.

Here Melba, appearing as Mrs Armstrong, met for the first time the flautist John Lemmone who later became her manager and accompanist.

MELBOURNE TOWN HALL
Saturday evening, May 17, 1884.

ELSASSER FUND
Under the immediate Patronage and in the Presence of
His Excellency Sir William F. Stawell and Lady Stawell.
His Excellency Sir William Des Voeux (Governor of Fiji) and Lady Des Voeux.

GRAND BENEFIT CONCERT
Supported by the entire musical Profession of Melbourne.

———

— PROGRAMME —
PART I

1. National Anthem

           MR OTTO VOGT

2. ORGAN SOLO

           "Fanfare Militaire"   J. Lemmens
           MR J. R. EDESON

3. SONG

           "Thoughts of Thee"   Blumenthal
           MR GORDON GOOCH

4. SONG

           "Charite"   Pinsuti
           MRS CUTTER

5. SERENADE

           "Goodnight, Beloved"   Balfe
           MR ARMES BEAUMONT

6. PIANOFORTE SOLO

           "Invitation to the Valse"   Weber
           (Arranged by A. Henselt)
           HERR ADOLPH LIEBERMANN
           (First Appearance)

7. DUET for soprano and tenor
           "E il sol dell'anima" . . . "Rigoletto"   Verdi
           SIGNOR and SIGNORA COY

8. CAVATINA

           "Ah fors e lui" . . . "Traviata"   Verdi
           MRS ARMSTRONG (Miss Mitchell)
           (First Appearance)

9. BALLAD

           "Will he Come"   Sullivan
           MISS CHRISTIAN

10. STRING QUARTETTE

           Andante and Allegretto, D minor   Mozart

MESSRS G. WESTON, P. MONTAGUE, E. A. JAGER and S. HART

Interval of Five Minutes

PART II

1. SONG

"The King's Minstrel" Pinsuti
MR S. LAMBLE

2. SONG

"I'm Alone" Benedict
(By request)
MADAME SIMONSEN

3. FLUTE SOLO

"Fantasie de Concert" Briccialdi
MR JOHN LEMMONE
(First Appearance)

4. ARIA

"Roberto, o tu che adoro" Meyerbeer
(Roberto il Diavolo)
MISS A. VANDEPEER
(First Appearance)

5. ORGAN SOLO
(a) Gavotte "Mignon" Thomas
(b) Gavotte "Stephanie" Czibulka
MR DAVID LEE

6. BALLAD

"Sunshine and Shade" Randegger
MR ARMES BEAUMONT

7. SONG

"La Serenata" (Angel's Serenade) G. Braga
MISS FANNY E. SAMUEL
(With Violin Obligato by Mr G. Weston)

8. ORGAN SOLO

"Grand Offertoire in G" Wely
MR T. H. JONES
(First Appearance)

———

Owing to the length of the programme the audience is requested not to insist on encores.

———

CONDUCTORS:

MR JULIUS BUDDEE   SIGNOR ZELMAN   MR T. H. GUENETT   289

MR W. HUNTER   MR OTTO VOGT   MR DAVID LEE
MR AUSTIN TURNER MR JOS SUMMERS MR ALFRED PLUMPTON

———

Balcony and reserved chairs, 5s.; Unreserved, 3s.; Area, 2s.
The Grand Piano has been kindly lent by Messrs Nicholson and Co.
Doors open at 7 o'clock. Concert to commence at 8 o'clock.

Carriages to be ordered at 10.30

JULIUS HERZ, Hon. Sec.

5. MELBA'S LECTURE ON DICTION TO THE STUDENTS OF THE GUILDHALL SCHOOL OF MUSIC, LONDON.

(Reproduced in The Argus, *Melbourne, 27th June, 1911.)*

THE OPINION IS held largely that English is not a musical language, or at least not a language which lends itself felicitously to expression in music. I rather think that, for a time, I held that opinion myself. My maturer judgment and experience tell me that I was wrong, and, although the English language lends itself to expression in music less readily than the Italian, it is, in that respect at least equal to the French, and certainly superior to the German — (cheers) — and that the reason why I held that opinion for a time — and why others hold it still — is that the art of English diction, whatever it may have been in other days, of which we have no direct knowledge, has been during our own time in a very uncultivated condition. It is true that there are exceptional instances to the contrary, and that occasionally we hear our native language spoken in song with distinction and clearness; but it is, alas! equally true that our ears are tortured too frequently by mispronunciations and verbal obscurities, and at times to such an extent that it is difficult to decide in which particular language the singer is delivering his message. (Cheers and laughter).

After all, what are we singers but the silver-voiced messengers of the poet and the musician? That is our call, that is our mission; and it would be well for us to keep it constantly and earnestly in our minds. What we should strive for is to attain as nearly to perfection as possible in the delivery of that message — (cheers) — sacrificing neither the musician for the poet nor the poet for the musician. If we sing a false tone or mispronounce one word we are apt to awaken the critical faculty which, consciously or unconsciously, exists in every audience; to create a spirit of unrest, and destroy the burden of our message. A similar disastrous effect, of course, may be made by a miscalculation of breathing power, an inappropriate facial expression, or by many another unartistic happening on the singer's part. As, however, these reflections would lead us into wider considerations than those we are prepared for today, let us return to the subject of English diction.

I think it will be generally admitted as an ideal that the English language should be sung as it should be spoken, with just sufficient added distinctness, or one might even use the word "exaggeration", to counteract the obscuring effect of the singer's voice and the piano or other musical accompaniment. (Hear, hear). You have observed that I have said "as the English language should be spoken" — (hear, hear) — and I am sure that the thought has occurred to you that the majority of people, singers and non-singers, do not habitually speak the language with justice, distinction and grace. (Cheers). How many persons do you know who could read aloud a verse of poetry, or of fine prose, in a manner to include the qualities mentioned? Not many, I fear. And yet I have a strong feeling that that is what the singer should be able to do before he or she enters seriously into the training of the singing voice. (Cheers). In a word, if verbal diction were early acquired, vocal diction would not be so serious a stumbling block to our singers. (Cheers).

> "She dwelt among the untrodden ways
>   Beside the springs of Dove,
> A maid whom there were none to praise
>   And very few to love."

These words of Wordsworth are very simple, very beautiful, surely very singable; and yet, I suppose, I am not the only person present today who has heard them sadly mutilated in song. (Hear, hear). I have heard the word "Dove" given as "Doive" — (laughter) — the word "whom" as "oom", and the word "love" — a particularly long-suffering word in song, by the way — (laughter) given as "loive". (Laughter). Suppose that a man (I am particularly addressing the lady students at the moment) — suppose that a man, anxious to communicate to you the condition of his sentiments, were to say to you, "I loive you" (laughter) he would surely excite either your ridicule or your distrust. (Laughter). In any case the exhilarating message would be dreadfully discounted by the preposterous delivery. (Laughter). Perhaps, if singers knew that audiences unconsciously made that discount every time the beautiful old Saxon word is mishandled in song, they would make some effort to sing the word as it is spoken.

291

For another example: Would any man, with the possible exception of an Irishman, address you as "darrling", or draw your fugitive attention to the emotions of his "hearrt", as do singers in your concert rooms daily? (Laughter). In speaking "darling" or "heart" your tongue never curls up to touch the "r"; then why should it in song? Consider for a moment the word "garden". Speak it aloud to yourself. It is a simple word of two syllables, in the pronunciation of which the tongue is practically unemployed. It is too simple a word, apparently, for a great many singers — a determined attack must be made on the unoffending "r", and the result is a word of three syllables, which sounds anything but English. (Laughter). The "r" in garden is the third letter in a six-lettered word. It occupies the same position in the word "forest"; but if you will speak the word "forest" to yourself, you will find that your tongue comes into active employment. I think, then, that it logically follows that when you sing "garden" the "r" should be passive, and when you sing "forest" the "r" should be active; and I feel sure that in this, and in all that is implied in the passing examples I have ventured to give you, I shall have the approval of the eminent professors of elocution and singing who add so much lustre and efficiency to this splendid school of music. (Cheers).

If you wish to sing beautifully — and you all do — you must love music, and the nearer you get to music the more you will love it. If you wish to sing your native language beautifully — and you all should — you must love your native language; and the nearer you get to it the more you will love it. (Hear, hear).

Aim high. Let your ambition be ever on tip-toe. (Hear, hear). Fill your minds with Shakespeare's sonnets, Keats' "Ode to a Grecian Urn", Shelley's "Ode to a Skylark", Matthew Arnold's "Forsaken Merman", Swinburne's "Spring Song", "In Atalanta", and many other of the poetic ecstasies with which your beautiful language is so rich. (Hear, hear). Let them become the delightful companions of what might otherwise be sometimes lonely hours; learn to speak them aloud with distinction and understanding, and so enable yourselves to bring to your singing the added glory of a perfect diction. (Loud cheers).

THE MELBA METHOD

(First section of the Introduction to a book of exercises with the same title by Dame Nellie Melba, published by Chappell & Co. Ltd., London and Sydney, 1926.)

IT IS EASY to sing well and very difficult to sing badly! How many students of singing are really prepared to accept that statement? Few, if any. They smile and say: "It may be easy for you, but it is not for me." And they seem to consider that there the matter ends.

But if they only knew it, on their understanding and acceptance of that axiom depends half their success. Let me say the same thing in other words: "In order to sing well, it is necessary to sing easily."

For some unknown reason, practically all teachers and students accept this statement with enthusiasm. But though they accept it, comparatively few achieve it, which is one of the prime reasons why there are never at any one time many singers who can be called great vocalists as well as artists. For, undoubtedly, more than one famous singer has become famous in spite of the way she sang, rather than because of it.

If, as I have said, teachers agree that in order to sing well it is necessary to sing easily, how is it that there are so many methods of teaching singing, each of which contradicts all others and condemns them as utterly bad?

If we look into these conflicting methods, we generally find that they are built up round an idea which has proved helpful in some cases. The reason for this help not being properly understood, the idea is seized upon and acclaimed as a panacea for all ills.

A little thought will reveal the absurdity of this. No single exercise, vowel, or position of mouth or tongue (as the case may be) can cure all difficulties.

The only method that can be helpful must be built up on common-sense and a close observation of Nature's laws. The only way to overcome a difficulty is to find its root cause. And one very general cause of trouble is that so few people have any real idea of what "ease" means. The beginner at any game watches the champion and groans: "It looks so easy". It is easy, or the player would not be a champion.

Or you hear Heifetz play, and every budding violinist despairingly says: "Everything seems easy to him." It is, or he would not play in the entrancing way he does.

Indeed, so little is the necessity for ease understood, that many people feel that they are not getting their money's worth unless the performer seems to be working a little to get his effects, even though that effect may defeat his aim. Therefore we sometimes see a performer, who is not entirely free from the spirit of the showman — if he be a pianist, throw up his hands much higher than is necessary to get weight into his big chords; or, if he be a violinist, sway from side to side and make great play with his bow; or, if a singer, get red in the face, almost to the point of bursting a blood-vessel, over a top note. Then the audience feels someone is really working for their entertainment, and go away exclaiming how wonderful it has been!

What, then, is ease as applied to singing? I take it to mean singing without any unnecessary muscular action. That sounds very simple, but is it? 293

How many of us know when we are making unnecessary movements? Not one in a hundred.

For nearly everyone is self-conscious instead of being conscious of self. The former is fatal to success. The latter is entirely necessary.

What is self-consciousness, and how can it be cured? For it should really be treated as a disease that MUST be cured. So-called self-consciousness arises from a state of divided consciousness, and that state is nearly always caused by fear. As fear is paralysing, there can be no freedom or ease in singing while the mind entertains such a dangerous guest. We fear we may be laughed at if we try to sing as the teacher suggests; we fear we may make unpleasant sounds; we fear we cannot reach a high note or sustain our breath for a long one; and many other things do we fear.

In every case, fear takes our attention away from what we should be doing in order to sing well, and causes us to stiffen muscles that should be free to work, or to be at rest.

Therefore, we must strive to banish fear, and the best way is by being conscious of ourselves.

Consciousness of self means that we keep our minds quiet and free from disturbing influences so that we may concentrate on the particular part of the body that needs to be active at the moment, and thus realise not only what we ought to do, but also what we are doing. When we come to know that certain actions produce certain results, and when we can, at will, perform those actions, uncertainty is removed, and uncertainty is at the root of most of our fears. In singing, as in all else, the precept "Know thyself" is of the utmost importance.

When we know what we wish to do, and how to do it, we find ourselves at the point from which I began, and realise that IT IS easy to sing well.

NOTES.

Appendix One

[1]Other singers who adopted regional names were Dorothy Canberra and Madame Ballara, of Ballarat.
[2]Brewer, F. C., *Drama and Music in N.S.W.*, Sydney, The Govt. Printer, 1892.
[3]For the vicissitudes of Australian singers in England, see "Poverty Point" column, *The Bulletin*, Sydney, from 1899 to 1902.
[4]Manifold, J. S., *Violin, Banjo and Bones*, The Ram's Skull Press, Ferntree Gully.
[5]"Garryowen", *The Chronicles of Early Melbourne* (1835-1852), Melbourne, Fergusson & Mitchell, 1888; Smith, J. (Ed.), *The Cyclopaedia of Victoria*, Melbourne, 1903.
[6]The *Australian Bandsman*, Sydney, 6th October, 1929.

[7]Doubtless Wallace helped to create his own legend. When in Sydney, he claimed to be a professor at the Royal College of Music. No such appointment is listed in the archives. *See* Orchard, *Music in Australia.*

[8]A versatile artist, she sang the title role in *Maritana* in London, and Polly Peacham in *The Beggar's Opera* in Sydney.

[9]His great-grandson, the Australian conductor Charles Mackerras, conducted orchestras in many cities of Europe and Australia before becoming musical director of the Hamburg Opera.

[10]For a more complete account of his life see Mackerras, C., *The Hebrew Melodist,* Sydney, Kurrajong Press, 1963.

[11]Stewart, N., *My Life's Story,* Sydney, 1923.

[12]She is buried at Richmond, Surrey, near the theatre in which George Coppin played.

[13]The *Sun,* Sydney, 25th August, 1958.

[14]Emma Howson subsequently sang in Italy, Malta and England.

[15]The *Times,* London, 12th August, 1861.

[16]Bochsa's astonishing musical gifts impressed Napoleon Bonaparte so greatly that he was sent to the Paris Conservatorium where, according to contemporary accounts, he mastered every instrument in the orchestra. A virtuoso of the harp, he improved the instrument mechanically, composed for it and is regarded as one of the greatest harpists of all time. Among his pupils were Napoleon's two empresses, Josephine and Marie Louise. Although Bochsa's prestige was so great that the fall of Napoleon did not affect it, he eventually fled to England as a result of one of the many scandals associated with his early career. In London he became conductor at Drury Lane, where his showmanship irritated purists as much as it fascinated the public.

[17]When the cemetery was turned into a park, the Bochsa Memorial was preserved in a special enclosure.

[18]van Abbe, D., "The Germans in South Australia", *Australian Letters,* Adelaide, October, 1960.

[19]The *Daily Mirror,* Sydney, 19th November, 1962.

[20]Usually printed as 48-pp pamphlets by Azzipardi, Hildreth & Co., Melbourne, and sold in the theatre. Examples can be seen in the Mitchell Library, Sydney. As the house-lights were not lowered during the performance, the words could be followed, but old-time theatregoers long recalled the disconcerting "flick" which announced that the audience had reached the end of each page.

[21]Both West and Hayward became leading motion picture exhibitors — West in Australia and his former partner in New Zealand. See *Here's to Life!* by Harry Hayward.

[22]Leonora became the mother of Frances Alda.

[23]After her divorce from Williamson, she married the actor, H. R. Roberts.

[24]A member of the company during this period was Vinia de Loitte, the Comtesse de Vilme-Hautemont, one of Sydney's most interesting personalities and the second wife of Howard Vernon.

[25]The principals with his two companies included John Coates, John Harrison, Robert Parker, Robert Radford, Lalla Miranda, Agnes Nicholls, Edna Thornton, Charles Magrath, Gladys Ancrum, Rosina Buckman, Jeanne Brola, Felise Lyne and Maurice D'Oisley. Richard Eckhold and Tiellio Voghera were the leading conductors.

[26]The prima donna was Agnes Janson.

[27]Miranda taught in Nicholson Street, Carlton, but advertised that he would call on pupils.

[28]Nevertheless she was selected to sing the ode "Australia", composed by Charles Kenningham, at the opening of the first Federal Parliament in Melbourne in 1901.

[29]See the *Slapoffski Memoirs,* serialized in the *Sydney Mail* in 1934.

[30]Among the principals during these two seasons were Toti dal Monte, Lina Scavizzi, Dino Borgioli, Apollo Granforte, John Brownlee, Arangi Lombardi, Hina Spani, Rossi Morelli, Elena Danieli and Browning Mummery.

Appendix Three

[1]Up to and including 1949 three place awards were made but details of some early placegetters are not available. From 1950 only a winner and reserve award winner were chosen.

[2]In the years 1933 to 1941 separate winners were chosen in men's and women's sections.

[3]An aria contest except for 1956 when a ballad competition was held.

Bibliography

GENERAL

Alda, F., *Men, Women and Tenors,* Houghten Mifflin & Company, Boston, 1937.

Armstrong, W., *Percy Grainger,* Doubleday, New York, 1950.

Braddon, R., *Joan Sutherland,* Collins, London, 1962.

Brentnall, T., *My Memories,* Robertson & Mullens, Ltd., Melbourne, 1938.

Brewer, F. C., *The Drama and Music in New South Wales,* Sydney, 1892.

Brockway, W., and Weinstein, H., *The World of Opera,* Pantheon Books, New York, 1962.

Brook, D., *Singers of Today,* Rockcliff, London, Revised, Ed. 1958.

Chamier, J. D., *Percy Pitt and Covent Garden,* Arnold, London, 1938.

Colson, P., *Melba,* Grayson, London, 1932.

Damrosch, W. J., *My Musical Life,* Scribner's, New York, 1923.

Dawson, P., *Fifty Years of Song,* Hutchinson & Co., London, 1951.

Duval, J. H., *Svengali's Secrets and Memoirs of the Golden Age,* Robert Speller & Sons, New York, 1958.

Eaton, Q., *Opera Caravan,* Farrar, Straus, & Cudahy, New York, 1957.

Eaton, Q., *The Boston Opera Company, Its History,* Appleton-Century, New York, 1965.

Ewen, D., Ed., *Living Musicians,* The H. W. Wilson Co., New York, 1940.

Foster, R., *Come Listen To My Song,* Collins, London-Sydney, 1949.

Lady Galway, *The Past Revisited,* Harnell Press, London, 1953.

Garden, M., and Biancolli, L., *Mary Garden's Story,* Simon & Schuster, New York, 1951.

Gelatt, R., *The Fabulous Phonograph,* Appleton-Century, New York, 1966.

Gelatt, R., *The Music Makers — Some Outstanding Musical Performances,* Knopf, New York, 1953.

Glackens, I., *Yankee Diva-Lillian Nordica,* Coleridge Press, New York, 1964.

Gollancz, V., *Journey Toward Music,* E. P. Dutton, New York, 1965.

Grant, J., and Searle, G., *The Melbourne Scene 1803-1956,* Melbourne University Press, 1957.

Earl of Harewood, Ed., *Kobbe's Complete Opera Book,* Putnam, London, 1954.

Hunt, H., *Australian Theatre Year Book,* Melbourne, F. W. Cheshire, 1957.

Hurst, P. G., *The Age of Jean de Reszke,* Johnston, London, 1958.

Hutton, G., *Melba,* Great Australians Series, Oxford University Press, Melbourne, 1962.

Klein, H., *The Golden Age of Opera,* Routledge, London, 1933.

Klein, H., *Great Women Singers of My Time,* Routledge, London, 1931.

Kolodin, I., *The Musical Life,* Knopf, New York, 1958.

Kolodin, I., *The Story of the Metropolitan Opera, 1883-1950,* Knopf, New York, 1953.

Krehbiel, H. E., *Chapters of Opera,* Henry Holt & Co., New York, 1911.

Lahee, H. C., *Famous Singers of Today and Yesterday,* L. C. Page Books, Boston, 1898.

Lahee, H. C., *Grand Opera in America,* L. C. Page, Boston, 1902.

Lawrence, M., *Interrupted Melody,* Appleton-Century-Crofts, Inc., New York, 1940.

Lawrence, R., *The World of Opera,* Thomas Nelson & Sons, New York, 1956.

Leiser, C., *Jean de Reszke and Great Days of Opera,* Gerald House, London, 1933.

Lyng, V., *Non Britishers in Australia,* Melbourne University Press, 1935.

Mallfeld, J., *A Handbook of Operatic Premiers, 1731-1962,* Detroit Studies in Music No. 5, Bibliography Hendrichessen, 1963.

McArthur, E., *Flagstad A Personal Memoir,* Knopf, New York, 1965.

Marchesi, B., *Singers Pilgrimage,* G. Richards, London, 1923.

Marchesi, M., *Marchesi and Music,* Harpers, London, 1897.

Melba, N., *Memories and Memoirs,* Thornton Butterworth, Ltd., London, 1925.

Miller, P. L., *The Guide to Long Playing Records (Vocal Music),* Knopf, New York, 1963.

Moresby, E. I., *Australia Makes Music,* Longmans, Green, Melbourne, 1948.

Murphy, A. G., *Melba,* Chatto & Windus, London, 1909.

Nichols, B., *The Sweet and Twenties,* Weidenfeld & Nicolson, London, 1958.

Odell, G. C., *Annals of the New York Stage,* Columbia University Press, New York, Vol. XI, 1879-1882 (Sherwin); Vol. XV, 1891-1894 (Melba).

Orchard, W. A., *The Distant View,* Currawong Publishing Company, Sydney, 1943.

Orchard, W. A., *Music in Australia,* Georgian House Pty. Ltd., Melbourne, 1952.

Parker, D. C., *Percy Grainger — A Study,* G. Schirmer, New York, 1918.

Peltz, M. E., *Introduction to Opera,* 2nd Enlarged Edition 1963, Barnes & Noble, New York (Paper Edition).

Portus, G. V., *Fifty Famous Australians,* Herald & Weekly Times Ltd., Melbourne, c.1940 (Melba).

Reid, C., *Thomas Beecham An Independent Biography,* E. P. Dutton & Co., New York, 1962.

Reid, C. L., *Bel Canto, Principles & Practice,* Coleman-Ross, New York, 1950.

Reid, M. O., *And The Ladies Came to Stay — History of the Presbyterian Ladies' College of Melbourne,* published by the college, Melbourne, 1961.

Rosenthal, H. D., *Two Centuries of Opera at Covent Garden,* Putnam, London, 1958.

Rosenthal, H. D., *Sopranos of Today,* Calder, London, 1956.

Rosenthal, H. D., *Great Singers of Today,* Calder, London, 1966.

Russell, F., *Life of Henrietta Sontag,* Exposition Press, New York, 1964.

Sandborn, P., and Hilb, E., *Metropolitan Book of the Opera,* Simon and Schuster, New York, 1939.

Schichel, R., *The World of Carnegie Hall,* Messner, New York, 1960.

Seligman, V. J., *Puccini Among Friends,* Macmillan, London, 1938.

Selsam, W., (compiler), *Metropolitan Opera Annals,* The H. W. Wilson Company, New York, 1947.

Shaw, B., *London Music (1889-1894),* Constable, London, 1932.

Shaw-Taylor, D., *Covent Garden,* Max Parish, London, 1948.

Sheean, V., *Oscar Hammerstein,* Simon & Schuster, New York, 1956.

Spielvogel, N., *History of Ballarat,* 1935.

Steigman, B. M., *Accent on Talent, New York's High School of Music and Art,* Wayne University Press, Michigan, 1964.

Tate, H., *Australian Musical Possibilities,* E. A. Vidler, Melbourne, 1924.

Taylor, R. L., *The Running Pianist,* Doubleday & Co., Inc., New York, 1950.

Thompson, J., *On Lips of Living Men,* Lansdowne Press Pty. Ltd., Melbourne, 1962.

Thompson, O., *The American Singer,* The Dial Press, New York, 1937.

Todd, R. H., *Looking Back — Some Early Recollections of Australia,* The Smelting Works Pty. Ltd., Sydney, 1938.

Wagner, A., *Prima Donnas and Other Wild Beasts,* Argonaut Books, Larchmont, New York, 1961.

Ward, R., *The Australian Legend,* Oxford University Press, Melbourne, 1958.

Waters, T., *Much Besides Music,* Georgian House Pty. Ltd., Melbourne, 1951.

Wechsberg, J., *Red Plush and Black Velvet,* Little, Brown, Boston, 1961.

Weisstein, U., *The Essence of Opera,* Free Press, New York, 1964.

Withers, W. B., *History of Ballarat,* Privately Printed, 1887.

Wood, Sir Henry J., *My Life of Music,* Gollancz, London, 1938.

MELBA: Feature articles and special reviews

Argus, Melbourne, 24 February, 1931, "A Tribute to Dame Nellie Melba".

Evening Standard, London, 8 July, 1899, "Rambler's Reflections".

Musical America, New York, 10 March, 1931, Haughton, J. A., "A Long Succession of Triumphs".

Musical Courier, New York, June, 1962, "Mapleson Cylinders, Treasures Amid Scratches".

New York Times, 19 December, 1903. Review of Farewell Concert of the Season.

New York Times, 22 October, 1913. Review of concert of operatic arias with New York Symphony Orchestra.

New York Times, 1 March, 1931, Downes, O., "Melba's Art of Song".

Opera, London, February, 1955, Shawe-Taylor, D., "A Gallery of Great Singers".

Pall Mall Gazette, London, 12 February, 1897. Review of a Harrison concert.
Sydney Morning Herald, 24 February, 1931, "A Tribute to Dame Nellie Melba".

DICTIONARIES, ENCYCLOPEDIAS, ETC.

Australian Encyclopedia, Vol. 1-15, Grolier Society 1965, Sydney.
Australian Encyclopedia, Vol. 1 & 2, Angus & Robertson, Ltd., Sydney, 1925.
Brown, J. D. and Strattan, S., *British Musical Biography,* Chadfield & Son Ltd., Derby, England, 1897.
Buffen, F. F., *Music Celebrities,* Chapman Hall, London, 1893.
Duckles, V., *Music References and Research Materials,* Free Press of Glenco, USA, and Collier, London, 1964.
Ewen, D., (Ed.) *Living Musicians,* H. H. Wilson Co., New York, 1940.
Ewen, D., *Encyclopedia of Opera,* A. A. Wyn, New York, 1955.
Grove's Dictionary of Music & Musicians, Macmillan, London, 1954.
Le Grandi, Vol. 1, Biography & Records, Instituti perlq Collaborazione Cultural, Rome, 1964.
Rosenthal, H. and Warrack, J., *Concise Oxford Dictionary of Opera,* Oxford University Press, London, 1964.
Thompson, O., (Ed.) — revised by Sabin, R., *International Cyclopedia of Music and Musicians,* Dodd Mead & Co., New York, 1964.
Ross, A., *Opera Directory,* Sterling Publishers, USA, Calder, London, 1961.
Rous, S. H., *The Victor Book of the Opera,* Victor Talking Machine, Camden, 1919.
Westerman, G., (Rosenthal Ed.) *Opera Guide,* E. P. Dutton, New York, 1965.
Who's Who in Music, Hafner, New York, 1962.

PERIODICALS

Music and Musicians, London.
Opera, London.
Opera News, New York.

MAGAZINE AND NEWSPAPER ARTICLES

"Australian Image", *Texas Quarterly,* Summer, 1962, University of Texas, Austin, Texas.
Barrett, Sir James, "The Life and Work of Marshall-Hall", An Address delivered at the Melbourne University Conservatorium, 1935.
Barrymore, F., "The Great Melba", Sydney, *Women's Weekly and Woman,* 6th, 13th, 20th and 27th May, 1957.
Bishop, J., "Melba Toast", *Australian Book Review,* Vol. 2, No. 1, 1962.
Bonynge, R., "The Birth of Bel Canto", *Opera,* Vol. 17, No. 6, June, 1966.
Brier, P., "Pioneers of Music in Queensland", published by the Musical Association of Queensland, 1962, Mimeo.
Brier, P., "A Short History of Music in Queensland", unpublished manuscript, 1960.

Brownlee, J., "Melba and I", *Saturday Review,* 25th December, 1950.

Campbell, M., "Fritz Hart", *Magazine of the Past and Present Students Assn.* of The Melba Conservatorium, No. 16, 1949.

Cardus, N., "Melba as I Knew Her", *Sydney Morning Herald,* 17th May, 1941.

Cardus, N., "Australian Scene", *The Penguin Music Magazine,* VII, 1948.

Crowe, J. S., "Music in Australia", *The Australian Review,* July, 1939, Vol. 6, No. 31, pp. 30-39.

Elvins, H., "Melba Anniversary", *Australian Musical News,* March, 1932.

Ericson, R., "Melba Disk Honors Soprano Centenary", *New York Times,* Sunday, 27th August, 1961, section 2, Records.

Eyer, R., "Dame Nellie", *New York Tribune Magazine,* 28th May, 1961.

Gelatt, R., "The Prima Donna Was a Peach", *New York Times Book Review,* 17th September, 1961.

Goossens, E., "Music in Australia", *Chesterian,* October, 1949.

Hall, J., "A History of Music in Australia", (a series of articles 1950-1953) in *Canon, The Music Magazine,* Sydney.

Hart, F., "Some Memories of Dame Nellie Melba", *Magazine of the Past and Present Students Association* of The Melba Conservatorium, Christmas Number, 1934.

Horner, J., "A Short History of Music in South Australia", *Australian Letters,* Vol. 2, No. 4, March, 1960.

Horner, J., "Prima Donna Assoluta", *Australian Book Review,* Vol. 2 & 3, January, 1963.

Hurst, P. G., *The Golden Age Recorded,* Oakwood Press (England) 1963. (Articles on Melba and Frances Saville).

Kolodin, I., "A Voice with a Mind of Its Own", *Saturday Review,* New York, 25th November, 1961. (Sutherland.)

Lynch, Kathleen, "Cultural Developments in Queensland", University of Queensland, unpublished thesis, 1960.

Robinson, F., "Galli-Curci, A Memoir of a Beloved and Dazzling Artist", *Show,* April, 1964, Vol. 4, No. 4. (Reference to Joan Sutherland).

Sterling, L., "Development of Australian Music", *Historical Studies, Australia & New Zealand,* Vol. 3, No. 9, 1944-1949.

White, D., "Florence Austral", *The Record Collector,* Vol. XIV, No. 1 & 2. (England).

Index